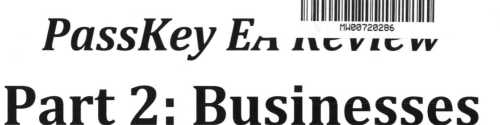

PassKey EA Review

Part 2: Businesses

IRS Enrolled Agent Exam
Study Guide
2015-2016 Edition

Authors:
David V. Sherwood, CPA, EA
Christy Pinheiro, EA, ABA®
Richard Gramkow, EA
Kolleen Wells, EA

PassKey Publications
Ladera Ranch, California

Editor: Cynthia Willett Sherwood, MSJ

This study guide is desig~~ned~~ ~~...~~ **~~...~~~~akers~~ who will take their exams in the 2015-2016** ~~testi~~ ___~~May~~ 1, 2015 to February 29, 2016).

PassKey EA Review, Part 2: Businesses, IRS Enrolled Agent Exam Study Guide 2015-2016 Edition

ISBN: 978-1-935664-37-6

Second Printing. PassKey EA Review
PassKey EA Review® is a U.S. Registered Trademark

All Rights Reserved ©2015 PassKey EA Review DBA PassKey Publications Licensing Inc. Revised and updated every year based on updated IRS EA exam specifications. United States laws and regulations are public domain and not subject to copyright. The editorial arrangement, analysis, and professional commentary are subject to this copyright notice. No portion of this book may be copied, retransmitted, reposted, duplicated, or otherwise used without the express written approval of the publisher. Questions for this study guide have been adapted from previous IRS Special Enrolled Examinations and from current IRS publications. The authors have also drafted new questions.

All the names used in this book are fictitious and any resemblance to real people, companies, or events is purely coincidental.

PassKey Publications, Ladera Ranch, CA
www.PassKeyPublications.com

Table of Contents

New Tax Laws Affecting Businesses in 2014 _____ *8*

Introduction _____ *11*

Ten Steps for the IRS EA Exam _____ *17*

Unit 1: Business Entities and Requirements _____ *21*

Unit 2: Accounting Periods and Methods _____ *44*

Unit 3: Business Income _____ *69*

Unit 4: Business Expenses _____ *82*

Unit 5: Employee Compensation & Fringe Benefits _____ *106*

Unit 6: Business Deductions & Credits _____ *119*

Unit 7: Basis of Business Assets _____ *129*

Unit 8: Depreciation _____ *143*

Unit 9: Disposition of Business Assets _____ *157*

Unit 10: Partnerships in General _____ *176*

Unit 11: Partnership Distributions & Liquidations _____ *195*

Unit 12: C Corporations in General _____ *204*

Unit 13: Corporate Transactions _____ *220*

Unit 14: Corporate Distributions & Liquidations _____ *234*

Unit 15: S Corporations _____ *245*

Unit 16: Farming Businesses _____ *267*

Unit 17: Exempt Organizations _____ *280*

Unit 18: Retirement Plans for Businesses _____ *290*

Unit 19: Trusts and Estates _____ *310*

Answers to Practice Questions _____ *329*

Index _____ *379*

Do you want to test yourself?
Then get the PassKey EA Exam Workbook!

PassKey EA Review Workbook:
Six Complete Enrolled Agent Practice Exams

This workbook features hundreds of Enrolled Agent practice questions, with detailed answers, to accompany the PassKey EA Review study guides.

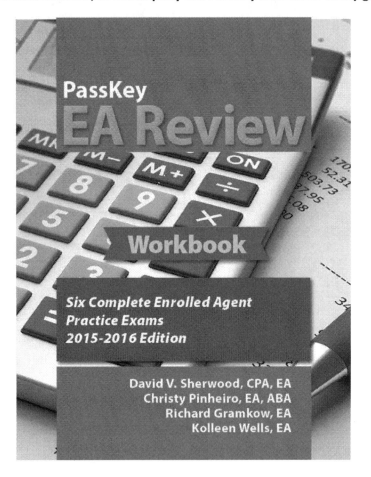

All of the answers are clearly explained in the back of the book.
Test yourself, time yourself, and learn!
Ordering information at www.PasskeyPublications.com

Recent Praise for the PassKey EA Review Series

Love PassKey!
Michelle D. Stroschen
I passed all three parts on my first attempt. I would definitely recommend! Reasonably priced and up-to-date information.

A great EA review book.
William Highfield (Lafayette, Colorado)
I used the Complete book as a study guide and passed all my tests the first time. Don't get the idea the tests were easy, but the book was so well organized and inclusive that the memorization and familiarization processes went very well.

You will pass with PassKey. I did!
Anne Stone (New Jersey)
I never prepared taxes for anyone but myself in the past. I found the material easy to follow and to understand. These were the only materials I used and I actually had fun studying.

Thanks!
Nathaniel Tassler (Monument, Colorado)
Using only your books, I was able to pass all three sections of the EA exam on my first try, in under two months.

Worked like a charm!
Brian Lang (New York, New York)
I passed on my first try.

Great book on the Enrolled Agent exam!
Stanley R. Marquardt
I loved the book. It was everything I was looking for. Great information and easy to read.

Thank you to all the contributors of PassKey Publications.
Ton T. Tran
The PassKey EA Review was the reason I was able to pass the EA exams on the first try.

Highly recommend this book as it allowed me to pass on my first try!

Don McNay

I really liked the EA Review book and give it my highest recommendation. It was easy to read, but had all the information I needed. The practice tests and quizzes were excellent.

Best education and preparation.

Sandra Cromwell

Love the lesson book with the tests at the end of each chapter. Excellent and concise presentation.

Excellent study guide.

Janice Raresheid

I found the content of this book to be well organized and easy to read/comprehend. I feel this book serves as a great tool and reference guide for anyone preparing for the EA exam or anyone who is interested in learning more about taxes.

Five stars.

Pasquale Casella

Great practice book. I used it and passed the exam on my first try.

Very helpful when trying to get your EA.

Betty A. Schulze (Sydney, Ohio)

It has all the information you need to study and has questions at the end of each chapter.

Helped me pass!

Stephen N. Cassin

Excellent review and easy to read. I passed Part 2 on the first try.

EA exam preparation.

William McGee

This guide (Complete) offers clear and concise coverage of all three areas to be assessed on the SEE. It is organized in a straightforward manner to allow a consistent study path for any preparer. This guide and the examples and study questions would benefit any preparer, even those who do not plan to attempt the SEE in this cycle.

Essential Figures for Tax Year 2014
Part Two: Businesses

Here is a quick summary of some of the important tax figures for the current enrolled agent exam cycle (May 1, 2015 to February 29, 2016):

2014 Social Security Taxable Wage Base: $117,000. A combined tax rate of 12.4% applies up to this limit, consisting of employee and employer portions of 6.2% each. The Social Security tax rate for self-employed persons is 12.4%.

2014 Medicare Taxable Wage Base: No limit. A combined tax rate of 2.9% applies, consisting of employee and employer portions of 1.45% each. The Medicare rate for self-employed persons is 2.9%.

Section 179 Expense: $500,000 of qualified expenditures/phase-out at $2 million; up to $250,000 in expense for qualified leasehold improvement, restaurant, and retail improvement property.

Bonus Depreciation: Up to 50% for new assets placed in service in 2014.

Mileage Rates:
- Business miles: 56¢ per mile
- Medical or moving miles: 23.5¢ per mile
- Charitable purposes: 14¢ per mile

Maximum Exclusion for Employer-Provided Transportation Benefits:
- $250 per month for parking benefits
- $250 per month in combined highway vehicle transportation and transit passes

Retirement Plans:
   Limit on Employee Deferral Contributions to Defined Contribution: $17,500 (with additional $5,500 catch-up contributions for participants age 50 or over)
   Limit on Contributions to SIMPLE Plans: $12,000 (with additional $2,500 catch-up contributions for participants age 50 or over)
   Limit on Contributions to Profit-sharing and SEP Plans: $52,000
   Maximum Compensation for Employer Contributions to Profit-sharing Plans: $260,000

Combined Estate and Gift Tax Exclusion: $5.34 million

New Tax Laws Affecting Businesses in 2014

Final Tangible Property Regulations: These regulations, which have been ten years in the making and will affect virtually every business taxpayer, became mandatory for the 2014 tax year. The regulations outline rules for determining whether an expenditure relating to tangible property is a deductible repair or a capital expenditure. The four main regulations involve:

- Capital expenditures
- Acquisition or production of tangible property
- Improvements for tangible property
- Materials and supplies

Form 3115 and Changes in Accounting Methods: In February 2015, Revenue Procedure 2015-20 waived the requirement for certain small business taxpayers to file Form 3115, *Application for Change in Accounting Method*, to comply with the tangible property regulations. In January 2015, the IRS issued two revenue procedures that outline the rules for obtaining consent to change certain methods of accounting for federal income tax purposes. Revenue Procedure 2015-13 provides the procedures for advance (non-automatic) consent. Revenue Procedure 2015-14 provides the procedures for automatic consent, which requires the attachment of Form 3115 to a timely filed tax return for the year in which the change is applicable.

Tax Increase Prevention Act of 2014: On December 19, 2014, Congress passed legislation that retroactively extended for one year more than 50 provisions which had expired at the end of 2013. Provisions related to businesses that were extended for tax year 2014 include the following:

- Section 179 expense deduction of $500,000, with a $2 million cap.
- Expense deduction of $250,000 for qualified leasehold, retail improvements, and restaurant property
- First-year bonus depreciation of 50% for qualified property
- Research and Development Credit
- Work Opportunity Credit
- Energy-efficiency credits for multifamily and residential developers
- Five-year recognition period for S corporation built-in gains tax
- 100% exclusion for gain on qualified small business stock
- Parity for employer-provided mass transit and parking benefits of $250 per month

Affordable Care Act for Employers: Implementation of the employer mandate for health coverage has been delayed until 2015 for large employers and until 2016 for certain small employers. The IRS has released draft instructions on the reporting requirements for new health forms 1094-B and 1095-B. Both forms are voluntary for tax year 2014.

Small Business Health Care Tax Credit: For tax year 2014, the maximum Small Business Health Care Tax Credit increased to 50% of premiums paid for small business employers and 35% of premiums paid for small tax-exempt employers.

Form 1023-EZ: The IRS introduced this new form to simplify applying for tax-exempt status under section 501(c)3. An organization with $50,000 in annual gross receipts or assets of $250,000 or less can use this shortened form.

Section 501(c)4 Regulations Delayed: The IRS received more than 150,000 written comments, the highest number ever in response to a proposed regulation, when it issued proposed rules governing the political activities of section 501(c)4 social welfare organizations. As a result, the IRS announced it would repropose the regulations after taking into account the comments. The regulations are designed to clarify the volume of political activity in which a social welfare organization can engage without jeopardizing its tax-exempt status.

Use of Truncated Taxpayer Identification Numbers: The IRS issued final regulations that allow the use of truncated taxpayer identification numbers (TTINs) on payee statements, such as various Forms 1099, and certain other documents required to be furnished to taxpayers. Social Security numbers, employer identification numbers, and other TINs will have their first five numbers replaced with Xs or asterisks to safeguard against identity theft.

Partnership Start-Up Costs/Organizational Expenses: Final regulations require a new partnership to continue to amortize start-up and organizational expenses using the same amortization period adopted by the terminating partnership.

Research Tax Credit Election Rules: The IRS issued two regulations that revise the rules to make it simpler for businesses to claim the Research Tax Credit.

Introduction

Congratulations on taking the first step toward becoming an enrolled agent, a widely respected professional tax designation. The Internal Revenue Service licenses enrolled agents, known as EAs, after candidates pass a competency exam testing their knowledge of federal tax law. As an enrolled agent, you will have the same representation rights as a CPA, with the ability to represent taxpayers in IRS audits and appeals—an EA's rights are unlimited before all levels and offices of the IRS.

The PassKey study guide series is designed to help you study for the EA exam, which is formally called the *IRS Special Enrollment Examination* or *"SEE."* This guide is designed for the 2015 to 2016 testing season, which begins May 1, 2015 and closes February 29, 2016. Those who take the EA exam during this time period will be tested on tax law applicable to tax returns for the 2014 calendar year.

Exam Basics

The EA exam consists of three parts, which candidates may schedule separately and take in any order they wish. The computerized exam covers all aspects of federal tax law, with Part 1 testing the taxation of individuals; Part 2 testing the taxation of businesses; and Part 3 testing representation, practice, and procedures.

Each part of the EA exam features 100 multiple choice questions, with no written answers required. The exam may include some experimental questions that are not scored. You will not know which of the questions count toward your score and which do not.

Computerized EA Exam Format
Part 1: Individual Taxation-100 questions
Part 2: Business Taxation-100 questions
Part 3: Representation, Practice, & Procedures-100 questions

You will have 3.5 hours to complete each part of the exam. The actual seat time is four hours, which allows time for a pre-exam tutorial and a post-exam survey. An on-screen timer counts down the amount of time you have to finish.

The testing company Prometric exclusively administers the EA exam at thousands of testing centers across the United States and in certain other countries. You can find valuable information and register online at *www.prometric.com/SEE.*

Testing Center Procedures

The testing center is designed to be a secure environment. The following are procedures you will need to follow on test day:

1. Check in about a half-hour before your appointment time, and bring a current government-issued ID with a photo and signature. If you do not have a valid ID, you will be turned away and will have to pay for a new exam appointment.
2. You will be given a locker for your wallet, phone, and other personal items. The EA exam is a closed-book test, so you are not allowed to bring any notes or reference materials into the testing room. You may bring your own soft earplugs, but the center also supplies sound-blocking headphones.
3. No food, water, or other beverages are allowed in the testing room.
4. You will be given scratch paper and a pencil to use, which will be collected after the exam.
5. You will be able to use an onscreen calculator during the exam, or Prometric will provide you with a handheld calculator. You cannot bring your own.
6. Before entering the testing room, you will be scanned with a metal detector wand.
7. You will need to sign in and out every time you leave the testing room. Bathroom breaks are permitted, but the test timer will continue to count down.
8. You are not allowed to talk or communicate with other test-takers in the exam room. Prometric continuously monitors the testing via video, physical walk-throughs, and an observation window.

Important Note: Violation of any of these procedures may result in the disqualification of your exam. In cases of cheating, the IRS says candidates are subject to consequences that include civil and criminal penalties.

Exam-takers who require special accommodations under the Americans with Disabilities Act (ADA) must contact Prometric at 888-226-9406 to obtain an accommodation request form. The test is given in English; a language barrier is not considered a disability.

Exam Content

Each May, using questions based on the prior calendar year's tax law, the IRS introduces multiple new versions of each part of the EA exam. If you fail a particular part of the exam and need to retake it, do not expect to see the identical questions the next time.

Prometric's website includes broad content outlines for each exam part. When you study, make sure you are familiar with the items listed, which are covered in detail in your PassKey guides. The IRS no longer releases test questions and answers from prior exams, although questions from 1999 to 2005 are still available on the IRS website for review. Be aware that tax law changes every year, so be familiar with recent updates and do not rely too heavily on these earlier questions and answers.

Your PassKey study guides present an overview of all the major areas of federal taxation that enrolled agents typically encounter in their practices and are likely to appear on the exam. Although our guides are designed to be comprehensive, we suggest you also review IRS publications and try to learn as much as you can about tax law in general so you are well-equipped to take the exam.

In addition to this study guide, we highly recommend that all exam candidates read:

- **Publication 17, *Your Federal Income Tax*** (for Part 1 of the exam), and
- **Circular 230, *Regulations Governing the Practice of Attorneys, Certified Public Accountants, Enrolled Agents, Enrolled Actuaries, and Appraisers before the Internal Revenue Service*** (for Part 3 of the exam).

You may download these publications for free from the IRS website.

Note: Some exam candidates take *Part 3: Representation, Practice, and Procedures* first rather than taking the tests in order, since the material in Part 3 is considered less complex. However, test-takers should know that several questions pertaining to taxation of *Individuals* (Part 1) and *Businesses* (Part 2) are often included on the Part 3 exam.

Exam Strategy

Each multiple choice question has four answer choices. There are several different question formats, and examples of each format are featured in your PassKey study guides.

Format One-Direct Question
Which of the following entities are required to file Form 709, *United States Gift Tax Return*?
A. An individual
B. An estate or trust
C. A corporation
D. All of the above
Format Two-Incomplete Sentence
Supplemental wages do not include payments for:
A. Accumulated sick leave
B. Nondeductible moving expenses
C. Vacation pay
D. Travel reimbursements paid at the federal government per diem rate

> **Format Three-All of the Following Except**
>
> There are five tests which must be met for you to claim an exemption for a dependent. Which of the following is not a requirement?
>
> A. Citizen or Resident Test
>
> B. Member of Household or Relationship Test
>
> C. Disability Test
>
> D. Joint Return Test

There may also be a limited number of questions that have four choices, with three incorrect statements or facts and only one with a correct statement or fact, which you would select as the right answer.

During the exam, you should read each question thoroughly to understand exactly what is being asked. Be particularly careful when the question uses language such as "not" or "except."

If you are unsure of an answer, you may mark it for review and return to it later. Try to eliminate clearly wrong answers from the four possible choices to narrow your odds of selecting the right answer. But be sure to answer every question, even if you have to guess, because all answers left incomplete will be marked as incorrect. Each question is weighted equally.

With 3.5 hours allotted for each part of the exam, you have slightly more than two minutes per question. Try to answer the questions you are sure about quickly, so you can devote more time to those that include calculations or that you are unsure about. Remember the clock does not stop for bathroom breaks, so allocate your time wisely.

To familiarize yourself with the computerized testing format, you may take a tutorial on the Prometric website. However, the tutorial only illustrates what the test screens look like; it does not allow you to revisit questions you have left open or marked for review, as you can do during the actual exam.

Scoring

The EA exam is not graded upon a curve, and the IRS does not reveal either a percentage of correct answers needed to pass or a predetermined pass rate. Each question on the exam is worth one point. The IRS determines scaled scores by calculating the number of questions answered correctly from the total number of questions in the exam and converting to a scale that ranges from 40 to 130. The IRS has set the scaled passing score at 105, which corresponds to the minimum level of knowledge deemed acceptable for EAs.

After you finish your exam and submit your answers, you will exit the testing room, and a Prometric staff member will print results showing whether you passed or failed. Test results are automatically shared with the IRS, so you do not need to submit them yourself.

If you pass, your printed results will show a passing designation but not your actual score. The printout also will not indicate which specific questions you answered correctly or incorrectly.

If you fail, you will receive a scaled score, so you will be able to see how close you are to the minimum score of 105. You will also receive the following diagnostic information to help you know which subject areas to concentrate on when studying to retake the exam:

- *Level 1: Area of weakness where additional study is necessary. It is important for you to focus on this domain as you prepare to take the test again. You may want to consider taking a course or participating actively in a study group on this topic.*
- *Level 2: May need additional study.*
- *Level 3: Clearly demonstrated an understanding of subject area.*

These diagnostic indicators correspond to various sections of each part of the exam.

If necessary, you may take each part of the exam up to four times during the testing window between May 1 and February 29. You will need to re-register with Prometric and pay fees each new time you take an exam part.

You may carry over passing scores for individual parts of the exam up to two years from the date you took them.

Pass Rates

The yearly pass rates for the SEE vary by exam. In the prior year testing period, the highest pass rate was for Part 3, with a nearly 90% success rate. Just over 80% of test-takers passed Part 1. The pass rate for Part 2 was much lower, averaging about 60%. Prometric notes that it can be misleading to compare pass rates for the various exams because the same individuals do not take each one. The number of candidates who take Part 1 is nearly double the number of candidates taking either Part 2 or Part 3.

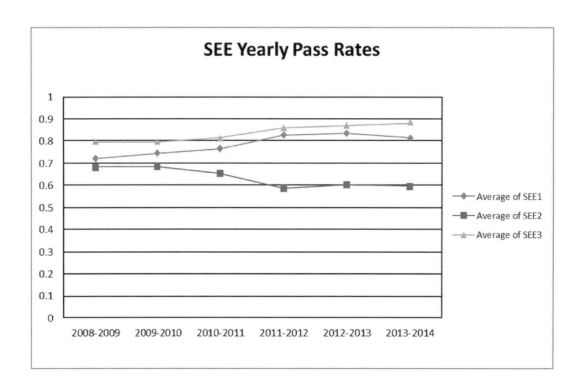

Applying for Enrollment

Once you have passed all three parts of the EA exam, you can apply to become an enrolled agent. The process includes an IRS review of your tax compliance history. Failure to timely file or pay personal income taxes can be grounds for denial of enrollment. The IRS's Return Preparer Office will review the circumstances of each case and make determinations on an individual basis. You may not practice as an EA until the IRS approves your application and issues you an enrollment card, a process that takes up to 60 days.

Successfully passing the EA exam can launch you into a fulfilling and lucrative new career. The exam requires intense preparation and diligence, but with the help of PassKey's comprehensive *EA Review*, you will have the tools you need to learn how to become an enrolled agent.

We wish you much success.

Ten Steps for the IRS EA Exam

STEP 1: Learn

Learn more about the enrolled agent designation and explore the career opportunities that await you after passing your EA exam. In addition to preparing income tax returns for clients, EAs can represent individuals and businesses before the IRS, just as attorneys and CPAs do. A college degree or professional tax background is not required to take the EA exam. Many people who use the PassKey study guides have no prior experience preparing tax returns, but go on to rewarding new professional careers.

STEP 2: Gather Information

Gather more information before you launch into your studies. The IRS publishes basic information about becoming an EA on its website at www.irs.gov/Tax-Professionals/Enrolled-Agents. You will also find valuable information about the exam itself on the Prometric testing website at www.prometric.com/see. Be sure to download the *Candidate Information Bulletin*, which takes you step-by-step through the registration and testing process.

STEP 3: Obtain a PTIN

PTIN stands for *Preparer Tax Identification Number*. Before you can register for your EA exam, you must obtain a PTIN from the IRS. The PTIN sign-up system can be found at www.irs.gov/ptin. You will need to create an account, provide personal information, and pay a required fee. The fee for 2015 is $64.25.

Since tax return information is used to authenticate your identity, you should use a previous year's individual tax return if you're applying for a PTIN and you filed your tax return in the past eight weeks.

It generally takes about 15 minutes to sign up online and receive your PTIN. Candidates who choose to use the paper Form W-12, *IRS Paid Preparer Tax Identification Number (PTIN) Application and Renewal*, will have to wait about four to six weeks to have their PTINs processed.

Foreign-based candidates without a Social Security number are also required to have a PTIN in order to register to take the exam; they will need to submit additional paperwork with their Form W-12.

STEP 4: Register with Prometric

Once you have your PTIN, you may register for your exam on the Prometric website by creating an account to set up your user ID and password. You must also complete Form 2587, *Application for Special Enrollment Examination*.

STEP 5: Schedule Your Test

After creating an account, you can complete the registration process by clicking on "Scheduling." Your exam appointment must be scheduled within one year from the date of registration. You can choose a test site, time, and date that are convenient for you. Prometric has test centers in most major metropolitan areas of the United States, as well as in many other countries.

You may schedule as little as two days in advance—space permitting—through the website or by calling 800-306-3926 Monday through Friday. Be aware that the website and the phone line show different inventories of available times and dates, so you may want to check both for your preferred testing dates.

The testing fee is nonrefundable. During the 2014 to 2015 testing period, the fee for each exam part was $109.

Once you've scheduled, you'll receive a confirmation number. Keep it for your records because you'll need it to reschedule, cancel, or change your appointment.

STEP 6: Adopt a Study Plan

Focus on one exam part at a time, and adopt a study plan that covers each unit of your PassKey guides. You'll need to develop your own individualized study program. The period of time you'll need to prepare for each exam is truly unique to you, based on how much prior tax preparation experience you have and your current level of tax knowledge; how well you understand and retain the information you read; and how much time you have to study for each test.

For those without prior tax experience, a good rule of thumb is to study at least 60 hours for each of the three exam sections. *Part 2: Businesses* may require additional study preparation, as evidenced by the lower pass rates. But one thing is true for all candidates: for each of the tests, start studying well in advance of your scheduled exam date.

STEP 7: Get Plenty of Rest, Exercise, and Good Nutrition

Get plenty of rest, exercise, and good nutrition prior to the EA exam. You'll want to be at your best on exam day.

STEP 8: Test Day

Be sure to arrive early at the test site. Prometric advises to arrive at least 30 minutes before your scheduled exam time. If you miss your appointment and are not allowed to take the test, you'll forfeit your fee and have to pay for a new appointment.

Remember to bring a government-issued ID with your name, photo, and signature. Your first and last name must exactly match the first and last name you used to register for the exam.

STEP 9: During the Exam

This is when your hard work finally pays off. Focus and don't worry if you don't know the answer to every question, but make sure you use your time well. Give your best answer to every question. All questions left blank will be marked as wrong.

STEP 10: Congratulations. You Passed!

After celebrating your success, you need to apply for your EA designation. The quickest way is by filling out Form 23, *Application for Enrollment to Practice Before the Internal Revenue Service*, on the IRS website. You may also pay online. Once your application is approved, you'll be issued an enrollment card, and you'll be official—a brand new enrolled agent!

Unit 1: Business Entities and Requirements

> **More Reading:**
> Publication 583, *Starting a Business and Keeping Records*
> Publication 1635, *Understanding Your EIN*
> Publication 334, *Tax Guide for Small Business*
> Publication 1779, *Independent Contractor or Employee*
> Publication 505, *Tax Withholding and Estimated Tax*

Overview of EA Exam Part 2: Businesses

For Part 2 of the enrolled agent exam, you will be expected to know a broad range of information about tax provisions that affect various types of businesses. You will need to understand the different types of businesses, including sole proprietorships, partnerships, corporations, and farming businesses, as well as trusts and estates, retirement plans, and tax-exempt organizations, and the special tax laws that apply to each.

Specifically, Part 2 of the exam is broken down into the following sections and corresponding percentages of questions: *Businesses* (Business entities; partnerships; corporations in general; forming a corporation; S corporations), 45%; *Business Financial Information* (business income; business expenses, deductions, and credits; business assets; analysis of financial records; advising the business taxpayer), 40%; *Specialized Returns and Taxpayers* (trust and estate income tax; exempt organizations; retirement plans; farmers), 15%.[1]

We start with an overview of the different types of business entities. Each has its own drawbacks, risks, and benefits. We briefly review each type below and will examine the more complex entities in greater depth in later units.

Sole Proprietorship

A sole proprietorship is not a separate legal entity; it is an unincorporated business that is generally owned and controlled by one person. It may be a single-person business or it may have many employees, but there is only one owner who accepts all the risk and liability of the business. It is the simplest business type and also the easiest to start. An estimated 70% of businesses in the United States are sole proprietorships.

---

[1]Prometric specifications for tests administered during the prior year exam cycle.

A sole proprietorship cannot be passed on to a new owner as the same business entity because, by definition, a sole proprietorship is owned and operated by a single, specific individual. If a business operated as a sole proprietorship is sold, it must be operated by the new owner as either a different sole proprietorship or as a different type of business entity.

A taxpayer does not have to conduct full-time business activities to be considered self-employed. Operating a part-time business in addition to having a regular job or business may also be self-employment, and may therefore constitute a sole proprietorship. An activity qualifies as a business if its primary purpose is for profit and if the taxpayer is involved in the activity with continuity and regularity. A hobby, which is not conducted for profit, does not qualify as a business.

Sole proprietors often receive Forms 1099-MISC from their customers showing income they were paid. The amounts reported on Forms 1099-MISC, along with any other business income, are reported and taxed on the taxpayer's personal income tax return. Income and expenses from the sole proprietorship are reported on Schedule C, *Profit or Loss from Business,* of Form 1040.

		$		Form 1099-MISC	
		3 Other Income	4 Federal income tax withheld		Copy B For Recipient
		$	$		
PAYER'S federal identification number	RECIPIENT'S identification number	5 Fishing boat proceeds	6 Medical and health care payments		
		$	$		
RECIPIENT'S name		7 Nonemployee compensation	8 Substitute payments in lieu of dividends or interest		This is important tax information and is being furnished to the Internal Revenue Service. If you are required to file a return, a negligence
		$	$		
Street address (including apt. no.)		9 Payer made direct sales of $5,000 or more of consumer	10 Crop insurance proceeds		

A taxpayer may use the simplified Schedule C-EZ if he:
- Had business expenses of $5,000 or less
- Did not claim any depreciation expense
- Used the cash method of accounting
- Did not have inventory at any time during the year
- Did not have a net loss from the business and had no prior year passive activity losses
- Was the sole proprietor for only one business
- Had no employees during the year
- Did not deduct expenses for business use of his home and had no depreciation or amortization to report for the year

A self-employed individual with net earnings of $400 or more from self-employment is required to pay self-employment tax by filing Schedule SE, *Self-Employment Tax*, with his Form 1040.

> **Example:** Darlene works as an independent contractor for Conway Company. Conway sends Darlene a Form 1099-MISC that shows she received $25,000 for contract work in 2014. She also received payments of $7,000 from several individuals for contract work she completed on their homes. Although she did not receive Forms 1099-MISC for the $7,000, Darlene must include the payments as self-employment income, along with the $25,000 from Conway, on her Schedule C.

Married Couple Businesses

Often, a small business is operated by a husband and wife without incorporating or creating a formal partnership agreement. The business is usually considered a partnership, whether or not there is a formal partnership agreement.

If both spouses materially participate as the only members of a jointly owned and operated business, the business may be treated as a *qualified joint venture*. This allows them to avoid the complexity of filing a partnership return, but still allows each spouse to take credit for self-employment earnings from the business for Social Security purposes. Items of business income, gain, loss, deduction, and credit are split between the spouses in accordance with their respective interests in the business. The spouses then file separate Schedules C and separate Schedules SE. This option is available only to married taxpayers who file joint tax returns.

A qualified joint venture is available only to businesses owned and operated by spouses as co-owners and not in the name of a state law entity; husband and wife owners of a limited liability company or a limited partnership do not qualify.

> **Note:** Federal tax law makes many references to laws specific to a "husband and wife." These laws now apply to same-sex spouses who were legally married in a state that recognizes same-sex marriage.

Partnerships

A partnership is a relationship that exists between two or more persons who join together to carry on a trade or business. Each person contributes money, property, labor, or skill and expects to share in the profits and losses of the business.

A partnership must file an annual information return to report the income, deductions, gains, and losses from its operations, but the partnership itself generally does not pay income tax. Instead, any profits or losses "pass through" to its partners, who are then responsible for reporting their respective shares of the partnership's income or loss on their individual returns.

> **Example:** James and Madeline are father and daughter who operate Hunnicutt Consulting. Each is active in the business, and each has an equal share in partnership interests and profits. The partnership must file Form 1065 to report its income and loss for the year. The partnership must also issue a Schedule K-1 to each partner. In 2014, Hunnicutt had $80,000 of income. Since they share profits and losses equally, James and Madeline will each report $40,000 of self-employment partnership income on their individual tax returns. Partnership income is reported on page 2 of Schedule E, *Supplemental Income and Loss (From rental real estate, royalties, partnerships, S corporations, estates, trusts, REMICs, etc.)*

A partnership must always have at least one *general partner* whose actions legally bind the business and who is legally responsible for a partnership's debts and liabilities.

A limited partnership is a partnership that has at least one limited partner in addition to its general partner(s). A limited partnership allows an investor to own an interest in a business without assuming personal liability or risk beyond the amount of his investment. A *limited partner* has no obligation to contribute additional capital to the partnership, and therefore does not have an economic risk of loss for partnership liabilities.

A partnership can look very different depending on how it is structured; it can be anything from a small business run by a married couple to a complex business organization with hundreds of general partners and limited partners as investors. A partnership can have an unlimited number of partners.

An unincorporated organization with two or more owners is generally classified as a partnership for federal tax purposes if its members carry on a business and divide its profits. However, a joint undertaking merely to share expenses is not a partnership. For example, co-ownership of rental property is not considered a formal partnership unless the co-owners provide substantial services to the tenants.

> **Example:** Anderson and Sal are cousins who own a rental property together. Each owns a 50% interest in the rental. Anderson takes care of any repairs, and Sal collects and divides the rent. They do not have any other business with each other. The co-ownership of the rental property is not considered a partnership for tax purposes. Instead, they would divide the income and expenses based on their ownership percentages, and each would report his respective share on Schedule E on his individual return.

A partnership's annual tax return is filed on Form 1065, *U.S. Return of Partnership Income.* Partners are not employees of the business, and they should not be issued Forms W-2. Instead, the partnership must furnish a copy of Schedule K-1 to each of its partners, showing the income and losses allocated to him. A partnership return must show the name and address of each partner and the partner's share of taxable income. The return must be signed by a general partner. A limited partner may not sign the return or represent a partnership before the IRS.

A **Limited Liability Partnership (LLP)** is an entity that is formed under state law by filing articles of organization as an LLP and is generally used for specific professional services, such as those offered by a law firm. Typically, an LLP allows each partner to actively participate in management affairs but still provides limited liability protection to each partner. A partner in an LLP generally would not be liable for the debt or malpractice of other partners and would only be at risk for his interest in the partnership's assets.[2]

> **Example:** Leigh and Martin are CPAs in California who decide to go into business with each other. They form an LLP by registering their business with California's secretary of state. Once they complete their registration, they open an office and begin accepting accounting clients. For tax purposes, their business will be taxed as a partnership, and they will be required to file a Form 1065 every year. In a limited liability partnership, the partners enjoy some protection against personal legal liability.

C Corporations

When forming a corporation, prospective shareholders provide money, property, or both in exchange for the issuance of the corporation's capital stock. A corporation is considered an entity separate from its shareholders and must elect a board of directors who are responsible for oversight of the company. A corporation conducts business, realizes net income or loss, and distributes profits to shareholders.

Most major companies are organized as C corporations. A C corporation may have an unlimited number of shareholders and may be either foreign or domestic. A C corporation must file annual income tax returns on Form 1120, *U.S. Corporation Income Tax Return,* to report its net income and losses, and pay tax on its income. Its after-tax profits may also be taxable income to its shareholders when distributed as dividends, resulting in double taxation.

The corporation does not receive a tax deduction when it distributes dividends to shareholders, and shareholders cannot deduct any losses of the corporation. A corporation generally takes the same deductions as a sole proprietorship to figure its taxable income, but is also allowed certain special deductions.

---

[2] The laws regarding LLPs and LLCs vary greatly from state-to-state. Information is generally available online through a state's secretary of state's office or the governor's office.

S Corporations

An S corporation is a distinct form of entity organized under applicable state law. For federal income tax purposes, an S corporation is generally not subject to tax; instead its income, losses, deductions, and credits are passed through to its shareholders in a manner similar to a partnership. However, the S corporation itself may be responsible for tax on certain built-in gains and passive investment income.

An S corporation is required to file an annual income tax return to report its income or loss using Form 1120S, *U.S. Tax Return for an S Corporation.* It also reports each shareholder's applicable share of income or losses on Schedules K-1. The shareholders report the pass-through income or loss on their individual tax returns. As a result, the shareholders of S corporations are generally able to avoid double federal taxation on their corporate income.

S corporations must meet the following requirements:

- Be a domestic corporation.
- Have only allowable shareholders (partnerships, corporations, and nonresident aliens are not eligible).
- Have no more than 100 shareholders.
- Have only one class of stock (voting and nonvoting stock are not considered to be separate classes of stock, as long as they have identical rights to distribution and liquidation proceeds).
- Not be an ineligible type of corporation (certain financial institutions, insurance companies, and domestic international sales corporations are not eligible for S corporation status).

Limited Liability Companies (LLC)

A limited liability company (LLC) is another type of corporation that may be formed under state law. Depending upon whether it has a single member (owner) or multiple members, it will be treated for federal tax purposes either as a part of the owner's individual tax return (a "disregarded entity," as described further below) or as a partnership, unless it elects to be treated as a corporation. Most LLCs are taxed as partnerships. Thus, like the owners of S corporations and partnerships, the members of an LLC can avoid double taxation. An LLC can provide the liability protection of a corporation with the tax benefits of a partnership. Unlike a partnership, none of the members of an LLC are personally liable for its debts. If a limited liability company (LLC) is treated as a partnership for tax purposes, it must file Form 1065 annually and one of its owners must sign the return.

Personal Service Corporations (PSC)

The IRS classifies a business as a personal service corporation (PSC) if its principal activity during the prior tax year is performing personal services. Personal services include any activity performed in the fields of accounting, actuarial science, architecture, consulting, engineering, health (including veterinary services), law, and the performing arts. The majority of a PSC's stock is typically owned by employees, retired employees, or their estates.

> **Note:** Unlike other corporations, personal service corporations are always taxed at a flat rate of 35%. The PSC tax rate applies only to C corporations. If the taxpayer makes an S election and has his income directly taxed as distributions, the 35% tax rate does not apply.

Farmers and Fishermen

Farming businesses are primarily engaged in crop production, animal production, or forestry and logging. They may include stock, dairy, poultry, fish, fruit, and tree farms, as well as plantations, ranches, timber farms, and orchards. It is the nature of the activity and not the entity type that determines whether a business qualifies as a farming business.

Congress has enacted many tax laws specific to farming that provide special tax treatment and reflect the highly unpredictable nature of the business. For example, farmers have a different schedule for paying estimated taxes; they may postpone gain or income in certain cases that other businesses cannot; they can deduct a higher percentage of mileage expenses than other businesses; and they are given special tax considerations when disaster strikes.

Farming and fishing businesses operating as sole proprietorships report income and loss on Schedule F, *Profit or Loss from Farming*, of Form 1040. A farmer is typically self-employed if he operates his own farm or rents farmland from others to engage in the business of farming. Self-employed farmers and fishermen must also complete Schedule SE to determine self-employment taxes due.

A farming business may also be organized as a partnership or a corporation.

Tax-Exempt Organizations (Nonprofit Entities)

The Internal Revenue Code (IRC)[3] outlines the requirements for tax-exempt organizations. They must be organized and operated exclusively for charitable, educational, or

---

[3] The Internal Revenue Code is the basis of federal tax law. It is enacted by Congress in Title 26 of the United States Code.

religious purposes, and none of their earnings may be used to benefit any private shareholder or individual.

Nonprofit organizations may be created as corporations, trusts, or unincorporated associations, but never as partnerships or sole proprietorships. Most organizations must request tax-exempt status by filing Form 1023, *Application for Recognition of Exemption.* However, churches, including synagogues, temples, and mosques, are treated as tax-exempt by default and do not have to apply for exemption.

An exempt organization must annually file Form 990, *Return of Organization Exempt from Income Tax,* to report its income and losses. Form 990 is usually an informational return only, but a nonprofit organization may be taxed on activities outside the scope of its tax-exempt status.

Entity Classification Election Rules

Certain business entities may choose how they will be classified for tax purposes by filing Form 8832, *Entity Classification Election.*

An LLC with a single owner is classified as an entity "disregarded," or as being separate, from its owner for income tax purposes, unless the owner files Form 8832 and chooses to be taxed as a corporation. Thus, a single-owner LLC owned by an individual is treated in a manner similar to a sole proprietorship and the owner is subject to the tax on net earnings from self-employment. Similarly, a single-owner LLC owned by a corporation or a partnership is included in the owner's tax return as if it were a division of the corporation or partnership.

A domestic LLC with at least two members is considered a partnership by default, unless it files Form 8832 and elects to be treated as a corporation.

An election to change an LLC's classification cannot take effect more than 75 days prior to the date the election is filed; nor can it take effect later than 12 months after the date the election is filed. Once a business entity makes an election to change its classification, it generally cannot change the election again within five years (60 months). The 60-month limitation does not apply if the previous election was made by a newly formed eligible entity and was effective on the date of formation.

> **Example:** Kelly and Ned are married and own their own business, an LLC, which they elect to classify as a partnership for tax purposes. A few months later, they decide to change the classification and be taxed as a corporation, so they file Form 8832. At this point, if Kelly and Ned change their minds again and want their business to be classified as a partnership, they would have to wait at least 60 months (five years).

Employer Identification Number (EIN)

An employer identification number is used for reporting purposes. Unlike Social Security numbers that are assigned to individuals, EINs are assigned to business entities.

A business must apply for an EIN if any of the following apply:

- The business pays employees
- The business operates as a corporation, exempt organization, trust, estate, or partnership
- The business files any of these tax returns:
    - Employment
    - Excise
    - Alcohol, Tobacco, and Firearms
- The business withholds taxes paid to a nonresident alien
- The business establishes a pension, profit sharing, or retirement plan

If a sole proprietor has no employees, he is not required to obtain an EIN. However, an EIN can be requested by a sole proprietor who simply wishes to protect his Social Security number for privacy reasons. This way, a sole proprietor can provide his EIN rather than his SSN to companies that need to issue him a Form 1099-MISC for independent contractor payments.

If a sole proprietor decides to form a business entity such as a partnership or corporation, he will be required to request an EIN for each separate entity. A new EIN is required for any of the following changes:

- When a sole proprietor or partnership decides to incorporate
- When a sole proprietor takes on a partner and becomes a partnership
- When a partnership becomes a sole proprietorship (for example, when one partner dies)
- When a sole proprietor files for bankruptcy under Chapter 7 or Chapter 11
- When a taxpayer terminates one partnership and begins another partnership
- When a business establishes a pension, profit sharing, or retirement plan

New EIN Not Required: A business does not need to apply for a new EIN in any of the following instances:

- To change the name of a business
- To change the location or add locations (stores, plants, enterprises, or branches of the same entity)
- If a sole proprietor operates multiple businesses (including stores, plants, enterprises, or branches of the same entity)

Further, a single-member limited liability company (LLC) classified as a disregarded entity may use the owner's SSN or EIN and does not need a separate EIN, unless the business is required to file employment or excise tax returns.

Taxpayers can apply for an EIN online or manually file Form SS-4, *Application for Employer Identification Number.*

Recordkeeping for Businesses

Adequate records help a taxpayer to monitor business operations, verify his income and expenses, and support expenses on his tax return. Except in a few cases, the law does not require a business to keep any specific kind of records or to use a particular recordkeeping system, so long as the system clearly shows a business's income and expenses.

The taxpayer's recordkeeping system should include a summary of business transactions, which is usually made in the taxpayer's books, such as accounting journals and ledgers. The books must show the business's gross income, as well as its deductions and credits. Additional documents must be kept to support these entries. These include sales slips, paid bills, invoices, receipts, deposit slips, canceled checks, credit card charge slips, cash register tapes, Forms 1099-MISC, invoices, mileage logs, and cell phone records.

Electronic records are acceptable so long as they provide a complete and accurate record of data that is accessible to the IRS in a legible format. They are subject to the same controls and retention guidelines as those used for the taxpayer's original hard copy books and records.

Taxpayers must keep records as long as they are needed for the administration of any provision of the Internal Revenue Code. Usually this means the business must keep records long enough to support income and deductions until the statute of limitations for a related tax return has expired.

> **Definition:** A **statute of limitation** is a time period to review, analyze, and review tax-related issues. The Internal Revenue Code requires that the IRS assess, refund, credit, and collect taxes within specific time limits known as the statute of limitations. When they expire, the IRS can no longer assess additional tax, allow a claim for refund by the taxpayer, or take collection action.

Generally, a taxpayer must keep records for at least three years from when a tax return was due or was filed, whichever is later. If a business has employees, it must keep all employment tax records for at least four years.

Taxpayers must keep records relating to property until the statute of limitations expires for the year in which the property is sold or otherwise disposed of. These records are needed to figure any depreciation, amortization, or depletion deductions, and to figure basis for computing gain or loss. A taxpayer may need to keep records relating to the basis of property even longer since they may be important in determining the basis of replacement property.

Business funds should be kept separate from personal funds. The IRS is more likely to audit a business and deny deductions and losses if there is no clear separation between business and personal expenses. A separate bank account for business-related transactions is advisable, with business-related bills paid from it rather than from a personal account.

Financial Statements

Financial statements are the formal records of a business's financial activities. There are many types of financial statements, but the two most common ones used for tax reporting purposes are the income statement and the balance sheet.

Income Statement: The income statement is also called the profit and loss statement. It indicates the business's revenue, expenses, and net income or loss during a period, such as a month, quarter, or fiscal or calendar year.

Balance Sheet: The balance sheet is a summary of a business's assets, liabilities, and equity on a specific date, such as at the end of its fiscal year. A balance sheet provides a snapshot of the business's financial condition. Balance sheet accounts are carried forward from year to year, unlike income statement accounts, which are closed out at year-end and only reflect business operations within a specified period.

Business Reporting Requirements

Businesses are subject to a number of reporting requirements, including the following:

Form 8300: When a business receives a cash payment of more than $10,000 from one transaction or from two or more related transactions, it must file Form 8300, *Report of Cash*

Payments Over $10,000 Received in a Trade or Business, by the fifteenth day after the date of the cash transaction. By January 31 of the year following the reportable transaction, it must also provide to each person whose name is required to be included in Form 8300 a written statement that shows the aggregate amount of reportable cash transactions the business reported to the IRS for that person. These requirements are intended to assist in efforts to combat money laundering.

Form W-2: A business must complete and file with the Social Security Administration Forms W-2, *Wage and Tax Statement,* showing the wages paid and taxes withheld for the year for each employee. A copy of the W-2 must be given to each current and former employee who received taxable wages or salaries during the year by no later than January 31 of the following year. Employers filing 250 or more Forms W-2 must file electronically unless granted a waiver by the IRS.

Form W-9: A taxpayer uses this form to provide his correct taxpayer identification number (TIN) to any individual or entity who is required to file an information return with the IRS.

Form 1099: A business must report nonemployee compensation paid during the year to certain independent contractors by providing a Form 1099-MISC by January 31 of the following year. Copies of the 1099s must be sent to the IRS by February 28, or by March 31 if the business files them electronically. Specifically, the amounts that businesses are required to report on Forms 1099 include:

- Commissions, fees, and other compensation paid to a single individual when the total amount is $600 or more during the year
- Interest, rents, annuities, and income items paid to a single individual when the total amount is $600 or more

Payments to corporations are generally exempt from Form 1099 reporting requirements. Forms 1099-MISC should only be used for payments that are made in the course of a trade or business. Personal payments are not reportable.

Example: Brett hires a painter to paint his home. The job costs $2,500. Brett is not required to report the payment to the painter because it is for his personal residence. Since it was a personal payment, Brett cannot deduct the cost on his tax return. However, the painter is still required to report the income on his personal return. The following year, Brett calls the same painter to paint the interior of his business office, which he owns. The job costs $1,000. Since the cost is a business expense, Brett is required to issue a Form 1099-MISC to the contractor.

Form W-4: When a business hires an employee, it must have the employee complete a Form W-4, *Employee's Withholding Allowance Certificate.*

Form W-4 tells the employer the employee's marital status, the number of withholding allowances the employee is claiming, and any additional amount to use when deducting federal income tax from the employee's pay.

If an employee fails to complete a Form W-4, the employer must withhold federal income taxes from his wages as if he were single and claiming no withholding allowances.

Employment Taxes and Self-Employment Tax

An employer uses information from the employee's Form W-4, as well as the IRS withholding tables, to calculate how much to withhold from each wage payment. The employer must also withhold the employee's share of Social Security and Medicare taxes from wages, and pay the corresponding employer's share of each tax.

Employers must report federal income taxes withheld and employment taxes on Form 941, *Employer's Quarterly Federal Tax Return*, or Form 944, *Employer's Annual Federal Tax Return*. Businesses must also make federal tax deposits of income and employment taxes electronically, generally by using the Electronic Federal Tax Payment System (EFTPS).

In 2014, only the first $117,000 of an individual's employee compensation and/or net earnings from self-employment is subject to the Social Security tax. There is no cap on the Medicare tax.

Social Security and Medicare Taxes	
Social Security tax rate	**2014**
Employer's portion	6.2%
Employee's portion	6.2%
Total for self-employed taxpayer	12.4%
Maximum earnings subject to Social Security taxes	$117,000

Medicare Tax Rate	**2014**
Employer's portion	1.45%
Employee's portion	1.45%
Total for self-employed individual	2.9%
Maximum earnings subject to Medicare taxes	No limit

An additional Medicare tax of 0.9% applies to an individual taxpayer's earned income that exceeds the following thresholds:

Filing Status	Threshold Amount
MFJ	$250,000
MFS	$125,000
Single, HOH, or QW	$200,000

A taxpayer's earned income (including wages, taxable fringe benefits, bonuses, tips, commissions, and self-employment income) that is subject to Medicare tax is also subject to the additional Medicare tax to the extent it exceeds the applicable threshold amount for his filing status. An employer is required to withhold the additional Medicare tax if an employee is paid more than $200,000, regardless of an employee's filing status or whether the employee has wages paid by another employer. There is no employer share of the additional Medicare tax. A taxpayer may be subject to the additional Medicare tax even if amounts are not withheld from his wages.

Self-employed Taxpayers: Self-employed taxpayers can deduct half of their SE tax in figuring their adjusted gross income. Self-employed taxpayers cannot deduct one-half of the 0.9% additional Medicare tax.

An individual general partner in a partnership is considered to be self-employed, and his income is subject to self-employment tax, just like a sole proprietor's. Income reported by the partnership to limited partners is considered passive activity income (and is generally not subject to self-employment tax).

Note: If a business does not have a Social Security number or taxpayer identification number for a payee such as an independent contractor, it must withhold federal income taxes at a 28% rate. U.S. source income received by a foreign person (a nonresident alien) is subject to withholding rate of 30%.

Trust Fund Recovery Penalty (TFRP)

Trust fund taxes refer to amounts withheld from employees' wages (Social Security, Medicare, and income tax) by employers and held in trust until they are remitted to the Treasury. If a business does not deposit its trust fund taxes in a timely manner, the IRS may assess a trust fund recovery penalty (TFRP). The amount of the penalty is equal to the unpaid balance of the trust fund taxes.

The TFRP may be assessed against any person who:

- is **responsible** for collecting or paying withheld income and employment taxes, or for paying collected excise taxes, and
- **willfully fails** to collect or pay them.

Once the IRS asserts the penalty, it can take collection action against the personal assets of anyone who is deemed a "responsible person." It is not only the executives of businesses or the top finance and accounting personnel who may be held responsible for the TFRP. A responsible person may also include a person who signs checks for the company or who otherwise has authority to spend business funds, such as a bookkeeper. For the IRS to determine that an individual willfully failed to pay the required taxes, the responsible person:

- Must have, or should have, been aware of the outstanding taxes, and
- Intentionally disregarded the law or been plainly indifferent to its requirements (no evil intent or bad motive is required).

Using available funds to pay other creditors when the business fails to pay employment taxes is an indication of willfulness.

Example: Greta ran her own accounting business and also processed the payroll for her local church. The church had four employees. Greta prepared and signed the payroll tax returns and all the checks and then gave them to the pastor to mail. The pastor did not mail the payroll tax reports or remit the payments to the IRS; instead, he used the money to purchase a new church organ. Greta knew the pastor was misusing the funds, but did not report the information to authorities. The IRS assessed the TFRP against the pastor, the church, and Greta. Even though Greta was just the bookkeeper, she knew that the pastor was improperly handling the payroll tax funds and she did nothing about it, so the IRS can assess the TFRP against Greta.

Federal Unemployment (FUTA) Tax

A business reports and pays FUTA tax separately from federal income tax, and Social Security and Medicare taxes. FUTA tax is paid only by the employer. The standard FUTA tax rate is 6% on the first $7,000 of each employee's wages. However, the employer may receive a credit of 5.4% when it files Form 940, *Employer's Annual Federal Unemployment (FUTA) Tax Return*, resulting in a net FUTA tax rate of 0.6%.

Employee and Worker Classification

Because businesses are responsible for withholding and/or paying income, employment, and FUTA taxes and reporting payments to independent contractors, they must accurately determine whether a person they pay is an independent contractor or an employee. A business is generally not required to withhold or pay taxes in connection with payments to independent contractors. However, it must understand the relationship that exists with each person it pays to perform services. A person performing services for a business may be:

- An independent contractor
- An employee
- A statutory employee
- A statutory nonemployee

The IRS evaluates three primary characteristics to determine the relationship between a business and workers it pays for services:

- **Behavioral Control:** Covers whether the business has a right to direct or control how the work is done.
- **Financial Control:** Covers whether the business has a right to direct or control the financial and business aspects of the worker's job. Factors include how the worker is paid, whether expenses are reimbursed, and whether tools and supplies are provided.
- **Type of Relationship:** Relates to how the worker and the business owner perceive their relationship, such as whether there are written contracts or employee-type benefits, such as vacation pay or a retirement plan.

Whether a person is classified as an employee or an independent contractor depends on the facts and circumstances of each individual case.

Example: Rich, an electrician, submits a job estimate to a housing complex for electrical work at $16 per hour for 400 hours. He is to receive $1,280 every two weeks for the next ten weeks. Rich will receive $6,400, regardless of whether he works more or less than 400 hours to complete the work. He also performs electrical installations under contracts with other companies that he obtains through ads placed on Craigslist. Rich would likely be classified as an independent contractor.

Example: Donna is a salesperson employed full-time by an auto dealership. She is on duty in the showroom on certain assigned days and times. She uses lists of prospective customers that belong to the dealership. She develops leads and reports results to the sales manager. Because of her experience, she requires minimal assistance in closing and financing sales. She is paid a commission and is eligible for bonuses offered by the dealership. The business also pays the cost of her health and group-term life insurance. Donna is classified as an employee of the dealership.

If the determination of whether a worker is an employee or independent contractor is still unclear after weighing the various facts and circumstances of an individual case, Form SS-8,

Determination of Worker Status for Purposes of Federal Employment Taxes and Income Tax Withholding, can be filed with the IRS. The form may be filed by either the business or the worker. The IRS will review the case to officially determine the worker's status.

Employers who misclassify workers as independent contractors rather than employees may face substantial tax penalties for failing to pay employment taxes and failing to file payroll tax forms.

An independent contractor is considered self-employed and pays self-employment tax if net earnings are $400 or more. He reports income on Schedule C. There is generally no tax withholding on income received as a self-employed individual, as long as he has provided his tax identification number to the payer. However, an independent contractor may be required to make quarterly estimated tax payments.

Statutory Employees: Some workers are classified as statutory employees. They are issued Forms W-2 by their employers, but statutory employees report their wages, income, and allowable expenses on Schedule C, just like self-employed taxpayers. The difference is that statutory employees are not required to pay self-employment tax, because their employers must treat them as employees for Social Security tax purposes. Examples of statutory employees include:

- Full-time life insurance salespeople
- Traveling salespeople
- Certain commissioned truck drivers
- Directors (members of boards) of corporations
- Officers of nonprofit organizations
- Certain home workers who perform work on materials or goods furnished by the employer

If a person is a statutory employee, "statutory employee" in box 13 of Form W-2 should be checked.

Statutory Nonemployees: There are two main categories of statutory nonemployees: direct sellers and licensed real estate agents. They are treated as self-employed for federal tax purposes, including income and employment taxes, if:

- Payments for their services are directly related to sales, rather than to the number of hours worked, and
- Services are performed under a written contract providing that they will not be treated as employees for federal tax purposes.

Compensation for a statutory nonemployee is reported on Form 1099-MISC. The taxpayer then reports the income on Schedule C.

> **Example:** Adele works as a full-time real estate agent for G&G Realtors. She visits G&G's offices at least once a day to check her mail and her messages. She manages dozens of listings and splits her real estate commissions with G&G. She does not work for any other real estate company. Adele is classified as a statutory nonemployee. G&G issues Adele a Form 1099-MISC for commissions, and she files Schedule C to report her income and expenses.

Employing Family Members

The tax requirements for a business that employs family members may differ from those applicable to other employees. The rules vary depending on the family relationship and the type of business entity.

Child working for a parent: If the parent's business is one of three types (a corporation, an estate, or a partnership in which only one of the child's parents is a partner), payments for the child's services are subject to all federal taxes, including income, unemployment, Social Security, and Medicare.

If the parent's business is a sole proprietorship or a partnership in which each partner is the child's parent, payments for the child's services are subject to income tax withholding regardless of age. If the child is under 18, payments are not subject to Social Security and Medicare taxes. If the child is under 21, payments are not subject to FUTA tax.

> **Example:** Bradford and Cherie are married partners in a restaurant that they own and operate. Their daughter, Lexie, age 15, works as a hostess at the restaurant on the weekends. Her parents pay her $10 an hour. Bradford and Cherie must withhold income tax on Lexie's earnings. However, because of her age, her income is not subject to Social Security, Medicare, and unemployment taxes.

Parent working for a child: Payments are subject to income, Social Security, and Medicare taxes, but not FUTA tax, regardless of the business entity type.

Spouse employed by a spouse: Payments are generally subject to income, Social Security, and Medicare taxes, but not FUTA tax. However, FUTA tax is applicable if the spouse works for a corporation or a partnership in which the employing spouse is a partner.

Business Entities Snapshot

Character	Sole Proprietorship	C Corporation	S Corporation	Partnership
Formation	No state filing required.	State filing required.	State filing required.	No state filing required.
Existence	Automatically dissolved upon death.	Perpetual life.	Perpetual life.	Varies from state to state.
Liability	Sole proprietor has unlimited liability because the sole proprietorship is not a separate legal entity.	Shareholders are not responsible for the debts of the corporation.	Shareholders are typically not responsible for the debts of the corporation.	General partners are liable for the debts of the partnership.
Operational Requirements	None.	Board of directors, annual meetings, and annual reporting required.	Board of directors, annual meetings, and annual reporting required.	No formal requirements.
Management	Sole proprietor has full control of management and operations.	Management reports to the directors, who are elected by the shareholders.	Management reports to the directors, who are elected by the shareholders.	Partners may have an oral or written operating agreement.
Taxation	Not a separate taxable entity. Sole proprietor pays all taxes on his/her individual return.	Taxed at the entity level. Dividends paid to owners are also taxable income for them.	Generally no tax at the entity level. Income/loss is passed through to shareholders.	Generally, no tax at the entity level. Income/loss is passed through to partners.
Pass Through?	Yes.	No.	Yes.	Yes.
Double Taxation	No.	Yes.	No.	No.
Transferability of Interest	No.	Yes.	Yes.	Varies.

Unit 1: Study Questions

(Please test yourself and check the correct answers at the back of the study guide.)

1. A domestic LLC with at least two members that does not file Form 8832 is automatically classified as _____ for federal income tax purposes.

A. An S corporation.
B. A partnership.
C. A qualified joint venture.
D. A personal service corporation.

2. Don and Selma are married and run a small pet grooming business together. They want to treat their business as a qualified joint venture. Which of the following statements is correct?

A. They may choose to report their qualified joint venture as a sole proprietorship on two separate Schedules C, so long as they file jointly.
B. They may choose to report their qualified joint venture as a sole proprietorship on two separate Schedules C, so long as they file separate tax returns (MFS).
C. They must file a partnership tax return for their business activity.
D. They may file a single Schedule C, listing Don as the sole proprietor one year and Selma as the sole proprietor the next year.

3. In which of the following instances is a partnership not required to obtain a new EIN?

A. The partners decide to incorporate.
B. The partnership is taken over by one of the partners and is subsequently operated as a sole proprietorship.
C. The general partner ends the old partnership and begins a new one.
D. The partnership adds other business locations.

4. Which of the following is considered a drawback of the C corporation entity?

A. It may have many different shareholders.
B. It may have investors who are nonresident aliens.
C. Profits are subject to double taxation: once at the corporate level and again at the shareholder level when distributed as dividends.
D. It is run by a board of directors.

5. A sole proprietor may not be required to file Schedule SE if his net earnings for 2014 were:

A. Less than $400.
B. $400 or more.
C. Less than $5,000 but more than $400.
D. More than $5,000.

6. Mandy and her friend, Tammy, work together, making beaded necklaces and selling them at craft shows. They run their business jointly and attempt to make a profit, but they do not have any type of formal business agreement. They share with each other the profits or losses of the business. They received $24,900 in 2014 from selling necklaces, and they had $1,900 of expenses. Where and how is the correct way for Mandy and Tammy to report their income?

A. Split the income and report the profits as other income on each taxpayer's individual Form 1040.
B. Each must report her own income and expenses on separate Schedule Cs.
C. Mandy and Tammy should calculate income and subtract expenses, and each should report the net amount as "other income" on her individual Form 1040.
D. Mandy and Tammy are working as a partnership and should report their income on Form 1065.

7. Julian is self-employed and has a small business selling used DVDs. The gross income from his business is $20,000 and his business expenses total $9,500. Which schedule must Julian complete to report his business income and expenses?

A. Schedule F.
B. Schedule C.
C. Schedule D.
D. Schedule A.

8. All of the statements are correct about the following business entities except:

A. S and C corporations may have an unlimited number of shareholders.
B. An LLC typically provides the liability protection of a corporation but the tax benefits of a partnership.
C. "Pass through" entities include LLCs, LLPs, S corporations, and partnerships.
D. A sole proprietorship bears all the liabilities and risks of a business.

9. A sole proprietor would be required to obtain a new EIN in which of the following instances?

A. If he is required to file excise tax returns.
B. If he changes the name of his business.
C. If he changes location.
D. If he operates multiple locations.

10. A personal service corporation (that is a C corporation) is always taxed at a_____ rate.

A. 15%.
B. 28%.
C. 35%.
D. 39.6%.

11. Federal law requires businesses to provide a Form 1099-MISC for each independent contractor paid at least _____ for services during a year.

A. $400.
B. $500.
C. $600.
D. $1,000.

12. Dan is a full-time life insurance salesman and a statutory employee. He receives a Form W-2 for his earnings. How should he report his income?

A. On Form 1040 as regular wage income.
B. On Schedule C, not subject to self-employment tax.
C. On Schedule C, subject to self-employment tax.
D. On Schedule K-1.

13. The IRS evaluates all of the following characteristics to assess the relationship between a business and its workers except:

A. Type of relationship.
B. Financial control.
C. Income level.
D. Behavioral control.

14. Caden, age 16, works behind the counter of a juice bar owned by his mother, a sole proprietor. Which of the following taxes, if any, should be withheld from his paycheck?

A. Income tax.
B. Income tax, Social Security and Medicare taxes.
C. Income tax, Social Security and Medicare taxes, and FUTA tax.
D. None of the above.

15. When a business receives a cash payment of more than $10,000 from a single transaction, it is required to file:

A. Form 1099-MISC.
B. Form W-2.
C. Form 8300.
D. Form 941.

16. Which of the following organizations does not require an EIN?

A. An estate.
B. A C corporation.
C. Nonprofit organizations.
D. A sole proprietorship with no employees.

17. A business that fails to pay required payroll taxes may be subject to:

A. A penalty for underpayment of estimated tax.
B. The trust fund recovery penalty.
C. A penalty for substantial valuation misstatement.
D. A penalty for gross understatement of income.

Unit 2: Accounting Periods and Methods

> **More Reading:**
> Publication 334, *Tax Guide for Small Business*
> Publication 538, *Accounting Periods and Methods*

Tax Year

The tax year is an annual accounting period for reporting income and expenses. Individuals generally file their tax returns on a calendar-year basis. Certain businesses have the option to file their tax returns on either a calendar-year or a fiscal-year basis.

Calendar Tax Year: Twelve consecutive months beginning January 1 and ending December 31.

Fiscal Tax Year: Generally twelve consecutive months ending on the last day of any month except December. However, one variation of a fiscal year end does not fall on the same date each year. A 52/53-week tax year is a fiscal tax year that varies from 52 to 53 weeks but does not necessarily end on the last day of the month. For example, some businesses choose to end their fiscal year on a particular day of the week, such as the last Friday in June or the Saturday that falls closest to January 31.

> **Example:** Paula works for the state of California. The state's budget follows a fiscal year that runs from July 1, 2014 through June 30, 2015. This is a 12-month period not ending in December. Most federal and state government organizations operate on a fiscal-year basis, as do some corporations.

Short Tax Year: A tax year of less than 12 months. A short tax year may result in the first or last year of an entity's existence, or when an entity changes its accounting period (for example, from a fiscal year to a calendar year, or vice versa). Even if a business is not in existence for a full year, the requirements for filing the return and paying any tax liability are generally the same as if a full 12-month tax year had ended on the last day of the short tax year.

> **Example:** Eduardo and Jared started a business partnership in 2012. Eduardo died on November 1, 2014; therefore, the partnership is no longer in existence. Jared decides to continue the business as a sole proprietor. He must request a new employer identification number since his business structure has changed. The partnership is dissolved, and a final partnership tax return must be filed for the short tax year from January 1, 2014 to November 1, 2014.

> **Example:** Jillian formed the Rare Books Corporation on February 1, 2014. She immediately started having financial troubles and dissolved her corporation on October 31, 2014. Jillian must file a corporate return for a short tax year covering the nine-month period that Rare Books was in existence.

A business adopts a tax year when it files its first income tax return. Any business may adopt the calendar year as its tax year. A new C corporation may generally elect to use a fiscal year instead. However, the IRS may require use of the calendar year in the following instances:

- The business keeps no books.
- There is no annual accounting period.
- The present tax year does not qualify as a fiscal year.
- The Internal Revenue Code or income tax regulations require use of a calendar year.

Form 1128, *Application to Adopt, Change, or Retain a Tax Year*, is used to request a change in the tax year.

If a business files its first tax return using the calendar tax year and later changes its business structure (such as moving from a sole proprietorship to a partnership), the business must continue to use the calendar year unless it receives IRS approval or is otherwise forced to change in order to comply with the IRC.

A taxpayer's death marks the end of his final tax year as an individual taxpayer and the following day is the beginning of the first tax year for his estate. The executor or personal representative of the estate is responsible for filing the individual's final income tax return (Form 1040), income tax returns for the estate (Form 1041), and possibly an estate tax return (Form 706).

> **Example:** Desmond is an unmarried physician. He dies on July 1, 2014 and his son, Raleigh, is named the executor of his estate. Raleigh is responsible for filing Desmond's final individual tax return (Form 1040). The final Form 1040 covers the period from January 1 through July 1. In addition, he must file income tax returns for the estate for the period that begins on July 2 and ends when the estate's assets have been distributed. Raleigh must request an EIN for his father's estate, which is considered a separate entity for tax purposes. Desmond's assets are valued at approximately $15 million on the date of his death. Therefore, in addition to the income tax returns, an estate tax return must be filed.

The executor chooses the estate's tax period when he files its first income tax return. Generally, the estate's first tax year is any period of 12 months or less that ends on the last day of a month. If the executor selects the last day of any month other than December, the estate has adopted a fiscal tax year. The due date for Form 1041 is the fifteenth day of the fourth month following the end of the entity's tax year.

Required Tax Year

Partnerships, S corporations, and PSCs generally must use a required tax year. An entity does not have to use a required tax year if it receives permission from the IRS to use another permitted tax year or if it files an election under section 444 (as described further below). Unless it can establish a business purpose for using a fiscal year, an S corporation or PSC must generally use a calendar year.

A partnership, an S corporation, or a PSC can file Form 1128, *Application to Adopt, Change, or Retain a Tax Year* to support its business purpose for using a fiscal year. For example, a seasonal business (such as a ski resort) may elect a fiscal year based on a genuine business purpose. It is not considered a legitimate business purpose to elect a particular fiscal tax year so that partners or shareholders may defer income recognition.

Unless it can establish a business purpose for a different tax year, a partnership's required tax year must generally conform to its partners' tax years. If one or more partners with the same tax year owns a majority (more than 50%) interest in the partnership's capital and profits, the tax year of those partners is the required tax year for the partnership.

Example: Haley Partnership has two partners, both of which are C corporations. Corporation A owns a 30% partnership interest in Haley and operates on a calendar year. Corporation B owns the remaining 70% of the partnership interest and operates on a fiscal year ending February 28.

Partners	Partnership Interest	Tax Year
Corporation A	30%	Calendar year (Dec 31)
Corporation B	70%	Feb. 28 (fiscal year-end)

Since Corporation B owns a majority interest in Haley Partnership, the partnership must file on the same tax year as Corporation B.

If there is no majority interest tax year, the partnership must use the tax year of all of the principal partners (those who have an interest of 5% or more in the partnership's capital and profits). If there is no majority interest tax year and the principal partners do not have the same tax year, the partnership must use the tax year that would result in the least aggregate deferral of income to its partners.

Example: Andrew and Bella each have a 50% interest in the Chef Supplies Partnership. Andrew uses the calendar year and Bella uses a fiscal year ending November 30. Chef Supplies must adopt a fiscal year ending November 30 because this results in the least aggregate deferral of income to the partners, as shown in the following table.

With Year End 12/31:

	Year End	Interest	Months of Deferral	Interest × Deferral
Andrew	31-Dec.	50%	0	0
Bella	30-Nov.	50%	11	5.5
Total Deferral				**5.5**

With Year End 11/30:

	Year End	Interest	Months of Deferral	Interest × Deferral
Andrew	31-Dec.	50%	1	0.5
Bella	30-Nov.	50%	0	0
Total Deferral				**0.5**

Section 444 Election

A partnership, an S corporation, or a PSC can request to use a tax year other than its required tax year by filing Form 8716, *Election to Have a Tax Year Other Than a Required Tax Year*. This is known as a section 444 election and it does not apply to any business that establishes a genuine business purpose for using a different tax year.

A partnership or an S corporation that makes this election must make certain required payments based upon the value of the tax deferral the owners receive by using a tax year different from the required tax year. A PSC that makes the election must make certain distributions to its owner-employees by December 31 of each applicable year. A business can request a section 444 election if it meets all of the following requirements:

- It is not a member of a tiered structure.
- It has not previously had a section 444 election in effect.
- It elects a year that meets the deferral period requirement.

The deferral period depends on whether the entity is using the election to retain its tax year or to adopt or change its tax year. If it intends to retain its tax year, it may only do so if the deferral period is three months or less. The deferral period is the number of months between the beginning of the retained year and the end of the first required tax year.

If the entity is requesting adoption or a change to a tax year other than the required tax year, the deferral period is the number of months from the end of the new tax year to the end of the required tax year. Generally, the IRS will allow a section 444 election only if the deferral period is less than the shorter of:

- Three months, or
- The deferral period of the tax year being changed.

Example: Davidson Partnership, a newly formed partnership owned by two calendar-year partners, begins operations on December 1, 2014. Davidson wants to make a section 444 election to adopt a September 30 tax year. Davidson's deferral period for the tax year beginning December 1, 2014 is three months, the number of months between September 30 and December 31.

The section 444 election remains in effect until it is terminated. If the election is terminated, another section 444 election cannot be made for any tax year. The election also ends automatically when any of the following occurs:

- The entity changes to its required tax year.
- The entity liquidates.
- The entity becomes a member of a tiered structure.
- The IRS determines that the entity willfully failed to comply with the required payments or distributions.
- The entity is an S corporation and the S election is terminated. However, if the S corporation immediately becomes a PSC, it can continue the prior section 444 election.
- A PSC ceases to be a PSC. Again, however, if a PSC becomes an S corporation, it can continue the prior election.

Filing Due Dates for Entities

Most individuals and partnerships use the calendar year, and the normal due date for filing their income tax returns is April 15 of the following year. For those on a fiscal year, returns are due on the fifteenth day of the fourth month following the end of the year. For these and other entities' returns, if the due date falls on a Saturday, Sunday, or legal holiday, it is delayed until the next business day.

If a corporation uses the calendar year, its tax returns are due on March 15 of the following year. If the corporation is on a fiscal year, the tax return is due on the fifteenth day of the third month following the end of the tax year.

Example: A calendar-year C corporation dissolved on July 22, 2014 and ceased all operations. Its final return is due by October 15, 2014 (the fifteenth day of the third month following the close of its short tax year). The return will cover the period from January 1, 2014 through July 22, 2014.

Nonprofit entities using the calendar year must file their information returns by May 15. For nonprofit entities using a fiscal year, returns are due on the fifteenth day of the fifth month following the end of the year.

Entities and individuals may request extensions of time to file their federal income tax returns. An extension does not grant the entity additional time to pay the tax due. The tax due must be paid by the filing deadline, or the entity will be subject to interest and penalties on the amount of unpaid tax.

Study Note: For Part 2 of the EA exam, you must memorize filing deadlines for partnerships, C corporations, and the other entities covered in this study guide.

Accounting Methods

An accounting method is a set of rules used to determine when and how income and expenses are reported. No single accounting method is required of all taxpayers. However, the taxpayer must use a system that reflects income and expenses, and it must be used consistently from year to year.

Businesses generally report taxable income under one of the following accounting methods:

- Cash method
- Accrual method
- Special methods of accounting for certain items of income and expenses
- Hybrid method using elements of the methods above

The special methods include, for example, those related to accounting for long-term contracts, farming operations, and installment sales. Different rules apply to each accounting method.

Note: The most common accounting method is the **cash method**, which is used by most individuals and many small businesses. The **accrual method** is used by most large corporations and is a more accurate method of recognizing income and expenses, because it reflects when taxable income is actually earned.

A business owner may use different accounting methods if he has two separate and distinct businesses. Two businesses will not be considered separate and distinct unless a separate set of books and records is maintained for each business.

> **Example:** Blake is a self-employed enrolled agent. He prepares tax returns from January through April every year. He is also a motivational speaker who is booked for many paid engagements. He reports his tax preparation business using the accrual method and his speaking business using the cash method. He keeps separate books and records for each business. Blake may use different accounting methods because he has two separate and distinct businesses with separate sets of records.

Cash Method

The cash method of accounting is the simplest method to use, but the IRS restricts its use to businesses of certain types and sizes. The following businesses are required to use the accrual method rather than the cash method:

- A corporation (other than an S corporation) with average annual gross receipts exceeding $5 million
- A partnership with a corporate partner (other than an S corporation) and average annual gross receipts exceeding $5 million
- Any business that carries, produces, or sells inventory, unless the business has average annual gross receipts of $1 million or less
- Any tax shelter, regardless of its size
- Any corporation with long-term contracts

An entity (other than a tax shelter) with gross receipts that do not exceed the applicable threshold described above can use the cash method. Average annual gross receipts are determined by adding the gross receipts for the current tax year and the two preceding tax years and dividing the total by three.

Gross receipts for a short tax year are annualized. An entity that fails to meet the applicable gross receipts test for any tax year is prohibited from using the cash method and must change to the accrual method, effective for the tax year in which the entity fails to meet the test.

> **Example:** Cameron and William Davis form the Davis and Davis Architectural Corporation, a C corporation, in 2014 and its annualized gross receipts for the year are $4.2 million. The corporation may use the cash method because it has gross receipts under $5 million and does not have any inventory.

Example: Green Bay Corporation produces inventory and its gross receipts are $200,000 for 2012, $800,000 for 2013, and $1,100,000 for 2014. The company's average annual gross receipts are therefore $700,000 ([$200,000 + $800,000 + $1,100,000] ÷ 3 = $700,000). Green Bay Corporation may continue to use the cash method.

Example: Crape Company makes golf car parts. The company carries inventory throughout the year. Crape's gross receipts have never exceeded $900,000. Therefore, even though it carries inventory, Crape may continue to use the cash method because its average annual gross receipts are less than $1 million.

A business that produces, purchases, or sells inventory and has average annual gross receipts in excess of $1 million is generally required to use the accrual method.[4]

Exceptions to the Rules Outlined Above: The following entities may use the cash method of accounting:

- A qualified family farming corporation with gross receipts of $25 million or less
- A qualified personal service corporation
- Artists, authors, and photographers who sell works that they have created

Study note: You should memorize the basic rules of which entities can and cannot use the cash method and the accrual method for the EA exam.

Under the cash method, a taxpayer generally deducts expenses when they are paid, based upon the presumption that the expenses relate to the current tax year and that they would not be deductible if paid in advance. This means that a business generally cannot attempt to lower its taxable income by paying expenses applicable to future years. The taxpayer would instead capitalize costs paid in advance and deduct them in the years to which they apply.

However, there is an exception called the 12-month rule under which the cash-basis taxpayer is not required to capitalize amounts paid for periods that do not extend beyond the earlier of the following:

- 12 months after the benefit begins, or
- The end of the tax year after the tax year in which payment is made.

---

[4] There is a limited exception for "qualifying small business taxpayers" with average annual gross receipts between $1 million and $10 million that may be exempt from this requirement and be allowed to use the cash method. To be eligible, a qualifying small business taxpayer's principal activity cannot be in certain industries, including manufacturing, wholesale trade, or retail trade. Its principal activity must involve the provision of services, which may include providing property (inventory) related to those services, or the fabrication or modification of personal property. For example, a business with gross receipts of $1 million whose primary business is bicycle repair but that also has a very limited inventory of bicycles for customers to use during the repair (like a "loaner bike") period might qualify for this exception.

Example: Sherry is a sole proprietor and pays $3,000 in 2014 for an insurance policy that is effective for three years (36 months), beginning on July 1, 2014. This payment does not qualify for the 12-month rule. Therefore, only $500 (6/36 × $3,000) is deductible in 2013, $1,000 (12/36 × $3,000) is deductible in 2015, $1,000 (12/36 × $3,000) is deductible in 2016, and the remaining $500 is deductible in 2017 when the policy expires.

Example: Garrison Partnership is a calendar-year business. It pays $15,000 on July 1, 2014 for a business liability policy that is effective for one year beginning on that date. The 12-month rule applies, and the full $15,000 is deductible in 2014.

Example: Mikayla is a sole proprietor who rents retail space for her eyebrow threading business. She pays two years of rent in advance in order to receive a substantial discount from her landlord. She cannot use the 12-month rule because the benefit from her advance payment exceeds the 12-month time period. She must recognize the rent expense over the two-year period.

Constructive Receipt of Income: Under the cash method, taxpayers report income when it is actually or "constructively" received during the tax year. Income is constructively received when the amount is credited to the taxpayer's account or made available without restriction so that the taxpayer or his agent has access to the funds. The taxpayer does not need to have physical possession of the payment.

Example: Patel Brothers Partnership operates on the cash method. Interest income is credited to Patel's bank account in December 2014, but the partners do not withdraw it until January 2015. The partnership must include the interest income in its gross income for 2014, not 2015. The partnership had ownership and control of the income in 2014, so it is taxable in the year received.

Income is not considered to be constructively received if control or use of it is restricted.

Example: Better Jail Bonds LLP is a cash-basis partnership that bills a customer on December 10, 2014. The customer sends the company a check postdated to January 2, 2015. The check is received on December 31, 2014 but cannot be deposited until 2015 because it was postdated. Better Jail Bonds would include this income in gross income for 2015, since constructive receipt did not occur until then.

Accrual Method

Under the accrual method of accounting, a business generally records income when a sale occurs or income is earned, regardless of when the business gets paid. Income is generally reported when one or more of the following occurs:

- Payment is received (subject to certain exceptions for advance payments as described in Unit 3, *Business Income*).
- The taxpayer earns the income.
- The income is due to the taxpayer.
- Title has passed.

A business that uses the accrual method must also report costs when they are incurred, either as expenses or as capitalized assets. It does not matter when the business actually pays for the expenses.

The accrual method gives a more accurate assessment of a business's financial situation than the cash method. Income earned in each period is more accurately matched against the expenses for that period, so a business gets a better picture of net profit or loss.

> **Example:** Ali's Computer Inc. is a calendar-year, accrual-basis corporation. The business sold a computer on December 28, 2014 for $2,500. Ali billed the customer in the first week of January 2015, but did not receive payment until February 2015. Ali must include the $2,500 in his 2014 income, the year the company actually earned the income, even though the related billing and payment did not occur until the next year.

Hybrid Accounting Method

Businesses may also use a hybrid accounting method that is a combination of the cash, accrual, and perhaps other special methods, so long as the hybrid method clearly reflects income and is used consistently. However, the following restrictions apply:

- If inventory is necessary to account for income, the business must use the accrual method for purchases and sales. The cash method can be used for other income and expense items.
- If an entity uses the cash method for reporting income, it must use the cash method for reporting expenses.
- If an entity uses the accrual method for reporting expenses, it must use the accrual method for reporting income.

Changing Accounting Methods

When a business files its first tax return, it may choose any permitted accounting method. Subsequent changes, either in the overall accounting method or the treatment of a material item, generally require that the taxpayer obtain IRS approval. Prior approval is needed for:

- Changes from cash to accrual or vice versa, unless the change is required by tax law
- Changes in the method used to value inventory, such as switching from LIFO to FIFO (see discussion of these methods below)
- Changes in the method of depreciation or amortization

The taxpayer must file Form 3115, *Application for Change in Accounting Method*, to request a change in either an overall accounting method or the accounting treatment for an individual item.

Note: With the implementation of the final tangible property repair regulations for tax year 2014, many business taxpayers will need to file Form 3115 and request an accounting method change to comply with the new rules.[5] The IRS issued two revenue procedures in January 2015 to update the procedures of how to change an accounting method for federal income tax purposes. Specifically, the regulations detail ways to obtain advance (non-automatic) consent and automatic consent for an accounting change.[6]

However, IRS consent is not required for the following:

- Making an adjustment in the useful life of a depreciable or amortizable asset (but a taxpayer cannot change the recovery period for MACRS or ACRS property)
- Correcting a math error or an error in figuring tax liability
- A change in accounting method when the change is required by tax law, such as when a business's average gross receipts exceed $5 million

Example: Gary is a general partner in Ultimate Consumer Goods and discovers an error in the useful life of a depreciable asset. The asset should have been depreciated over 15 years rather than five. Ultimate Consumer Goods does not have to ask the IRS for permission to correct the depreciation error.

---

[5] The regulations are covered in Unit 7, *Basis of Business Property.*

[6] In February 2015, the IRS released an additional revenue procedure to clarify and simplify the Form 3115 filing requirements for small business taxpayers. For tax year 2014, businesses with assets totaling less than $10 million or average annual gross receipts totaling $10 million or less are permitted to make certain tangible property changes without filing Form 3115.

Inventory Accounting

A business that produces or sells products must track its inventory in order to correctly calculate income. Businesses often make a full physical inventory count at the end of each tax year, as well as at other reasonable intervals. The recorded inventory balances are then adjusted to agree with the actual counts.

Physical inventory counts may identify irregularities such as theft, as well as damaged goods and obsolete products.

> **Example:** Wrightwood Grocery Store takes a physical inventory once a month. During the physical inventory, store employees are required to record any damaged goods such as dented cans and ripped packaging. When the physical inventory is completed, the manager does a reconciliation to her records. She adjusts the books to reflect adjustments for shrinkage and damaged merchandise.

A taxpayer's inventory should include all of the following, if applicable:

- Merchandise or stock in trade
- Raw materials
- Work in process
- Finished products
- Supplies that physically become a part of items for sale (labels, packaging, etc.)
  A taxpayer's inventory may include:
- Purchased merchandise if title has passed to the taxpayer, even if the merchandise is still in transit or the business does not have physical possession of it for another reason
- Goods under contract for sale that have not yet been segregated and applied to the contract
- Goods out on consignment
- Goods held for sale in display rooms or booths located away from the taxpayer's place of business
  The following merchandise is not included in inventory:
- Goods the business has sold, if legal title (ownership) has passed to the buyer
- Goods consigned to the taxpayer
- Goods ordered for future delivery if the business does not yet have title

> **Not Included in Inventory:** Land, buildings, and equipment used in a business are not included in the calculation of inventory.

Shipping Terms and Transfer of Ownership

Certain shipping terms dictate when a taxpayer must take an item out of its inventory and recognize income from a sale. The terms indicate the point at which title (ownership) of goods transfers from seller to buyer. The three most common terms are:

1. **FOB Destination:** Title passes to the buyer at the point of destination (when the goods arrive at the buyer's location).
2. **FOB Shipping Point:** Title passes to the buyer at the point of shipment (when the goods leave the seller's premises). FOB shipping point is also called "FOB origin."
3. **C.O.D.** ("cash on delivery" or "collect on delivery"): Payment is made upon delivery and title passes at that time. For a business that sells by mail on a C.O.D basis, the merchandise is generally included in the seller's closing inventory until the buyer pays for it.

Example: Weiss Fine Furniture is a calendar-year, accrual-basis corporation that manufactures custom household furniture. It does not accrue income until the furniture has been delivered and accepted by the buyer. In 2014, the company receives an order for furniture to be custom manufactured for a total price of $20,000. Weiss ships the furniture FOB destination to the customer on December 26, 2014, but it is not delivered and accepted by the customer until January 3, 2015. Weiss will bill its customer for the $20,000 contract price and recognize the income from this sale in 2015, because the furniture had not been accepted and the title had not passed to the buyer until 2015. In this case, the method of shipping is important, because it determines in which year the business will recognize the income.

Inventory Methods

The value of a business's inventory is a major factor in figuring taxable income. Several common methods are used to assign costs to the items in inventory. They include the specific identification method, the average cost method, FIFO, and LIFO.

Specific Identification Method

This method is used when it is possible to identify and match the actual cost to specific items in inventory. It is most useful with an inventory that includes a limited number of highly specific and high-dollar items, such as custom goods or rare items like artwork or gemstones. The business simply accounts for each individual item as it is sold.

Example: The Classic Custom Autos dealership sells rare collectible cars. Each car is tracked individually by its vehicle identification number and its actual cost. When a car is sold, the cost is taken out of inventory. This is an example of specific identification inventory valuation.

Average Cost Method

This method is commonly used when a business has quantities of items that are largely interchangeable rather than individually unique. It allows the business to calculate an average cost per unit without tracking the individual units as they are purchased, manufactured, or sold. The formula for figuring average cost is:

Average Unit Cost = (Total Cost of Units Purchased or Manufactured)/ (Total Quantity of Units)

Aggregate Inventory Cost = (Average Unit Cost) × (Units in Current Inventory)

Example: Anna owns a pet store. She purchases five dog leashes at $10 apiece. The following week, the price of the leashes goes up, and she purchases five more leashes at $20 apiece. Anna then sells five leashes the following week. The weighted average cost of Anna's inventory is calculated as follows:

Total cost of leashes:
(Five leashes at $10 each) = $50
(Five leashes at $20 each) = $100
Total number of units = 10 leashes
Weighted average = $150 / 10 = $15

The average cost per leash for the 10 leashes Anna has purchased is $15. If she applies this average cost to the five leashes unsold at the end of the week, the calculated cost of the leashes on hand would be $75 ($15 × 5 leashes).

FIFO (First-in, First-out)

The first-in, first-out (FIFO) method is a variation of the average cost method in which it is assumed that inventory items are sold in the order they are acquired or produced, with the oldest goods sold first and the newest goods sold last. This assumption would mirror the actual flow of inventory items in certain businesses, such as rotating stock in a grocery store.

The actual quantities in inventory at the end of the tax year are assigned costs based upon the cost of items of the same type that the business most recently purchased or produced. The formula for figuring inventory based on the FIFO method is as follows:

Unit Cost Per Item = (Cost/Quantity) for the most recent lot of the item that was purchased or produced

Aggregate Inventory Cost = (Unit Cost Per Item × Quantity) for each item

In an economy with rising prices (inflation), the use of FIFO will typically assign a higher value to ending inventory than other methods and thus result in reporting lower cost of sales and higher taxable income.

Example: Rabbata Electronics, a cash-basis, calendar-year taxpayer, sells car audio equipment. Beginning inventory on January 1 included 300 car stereos with cost per unit of $20. On January 10 the business purchased 600 stereos at $20.10; on January 16 it purchased 400 stereos at $20.20; and on January 25 it purchased 500 stereos at $20.30. In January the business sold 1,200 car stereos. Under FIFO it is assumed that the oldest merchandise is sold first. Rabbata Electronics had a beginning inventory of 300 stereos. Those units are assumed to have been sold first, followed by the units purchased on January 10 and January 16. Thus, the cost assigned to the units on hand at the end of January is determined as follows:

Beginning inventory	**300**
January 10 purchases	600
January 16 purchases	400
January 25 purchases	500
Total units available	1,800
Units sold	(1,200)
Units in inventory at end of January	**600**

Composition based upon FIFO assumption:

January 25 purchases		500 @ $20.30 = 10,150
Unsold portion of January 16 purchases	100 @ $20.20 = 2,020
Total inventory at end of January	600	$12,170

LIFO (Last-in, First-out)

The last-in, first-out (LIFO) method assumes that the newest inventory purchased or produced is sold first, and the oldest inventory is sold last. Since the prices of goods, labor, and materials generally rise over time, this method will typically result in assigning a lower aggregate value to inventory on hand, higher amounts being recorded as the cost of sales, and lower taxable income. As a result, use of the LIFO method is subject to highly complex rules governing its calculation and close scrutiny by the IRS. The formula for figuring inventory using the LIFO method is as follows:

Unit Cost Per Item = (Cost/Quantity) for the oldest lot of the item that was purchased or produced
Aggregate Inventory Cost = (Unit Cost Per Item × Quantity) for each item

Example: Using the same background information for Rabbata Electronics outlined above but using a LIFO assumption rather than FIFO, the 300 units on hand at January 1 are assumed to have a LIFO cost per unit of only $10 because Rabbata has been in business for 20 years and the unit costs of its purchases have approximately doubled during that period due to inflation. Therefore, the cost assigned to the units on hand at the end of January is determined as follows:

Beginning inventory	**300**
January 10 purchases	600
January 16 purchases	400
January 25 purchases	500
Total units available	1,800
Units sold	(1,200)
Units in inventory at end of January	**600**

Composition based upon LIFO assumption:

Beginning inventory	300 @ 10.00 =	3,000
Unsold portion of January 10 purchases	300 @ 20.10 =	6,030
Total inventory at end of January	**600**	**$9,030**

In comparison to the earlier FIFO example, the aggregate cost assigned to ending inventory using LIFO would be lower. Since the income generated by Rabbata in January from selling 1,200 units would be the same using either inventory method, its taxable income would be higher using FIFO instead of LIFO.

Unless a business has used the LIFO method from its inception, it must obtain permission from the IRS to change to LIFO from another method of inventory valuation. Permission is requested by filing Form 970, *Application to Use LIFO Inventory Method.*

Differences between FIFO and LIFO

Economic Climate	FIFO	LIFO
Periods of rising prices (Inflation)	(+) Higher value of inventory	(-) Lower value of inventory
	(-) Lower cost of goods sold	(+) Higher cost of goods sold
Periods of falling prices (Deflation)	(-) Lower value of inventory	(-) Higher value of inventory
	(+) Higher cost of goods sold	(+) Lower cost of goods sold

Other Inventory Valuation Methods

In addition to the inventory accounting methods already described, the following methods, or conventions, are commonly used to assign value to inventory: cost, lower of cost or market, and retail.

Cost Method: All direct and indirect costs are included.

- For merchandise on hand at the beginning of the tax year, cost means the ending inventory price of the goods.

- For merchandise purchased during the year, cost means the invoice price minus appropriate discounts, plus transportation or other charges incurred in acquiring the goods. It may also include other costs that must be capitalized under the uniform capitalization rules (discussed later in the unit).

- For merchandise produced during the year, cost means all direct and indirect costs, including those that have to be capitalized under the uniform capitalization rules.

A trade discount is sometimes given for volume or quantity purchases. The cost of the actual value of inventory must be reduced by trade discounts.

Lower of Cost or Market Method: This method may be used for inventory, such as fashion clothing, that tends to lose value quickly. The market value of each item on hand is compared with its cost and the lower of the two is used as its inventory value. Market value is typically based upon the normal selling price at the date the inventory is being valued.

If inventory is offered for sale below market in the normal course of business, inventory can be valued at the lower price, less the direct cost of disposition. This method may also be used for items that cannot be sold at normal prices or are unusable because of damage, imperfections, changes of style, odd or broken lots, or other similar causes.

In these cases, items should be valued at their actual selling price minus the direct cost of disposition, even if another method is used to value the rest of the entity's inventory. However, the lower of cost or market method cannot be used in conjunction with the LIFO method.

The lower of cost or market method applies to the following:

- Goods purchased and on hand
- The basic elements of cost (direct materials, direct labor, and certain indirect costs) of goods being manufactured and finished goods on hand

Example: Graham makes motorcycle accessories at his factory. Under the lower of cost or market method, the following items would be valued at $600 in closing inventory.

Inventory Item	Cost	Market	Lower
Leather jacket	$300	$500	$300
Motorcycle helmets	$200	$100	$100
Leather motorcycle chaps	$450	$200	$200
Total	**$950**	**$800**	**$600**

Graham must value each item in the inventory separately. He cannot value the entire inventory at cost ($950) and at market ($800) and then use the lower of the two figures.

Retail Method: Under the retail method the total retail selling price of goods on hand at the end of the tax year in each department or for each class of goods is reduced to approximate cost by using an average markup expressed as a percentage of the total retail selling price. For example, if a store marks up its merchandise by 35%, that percentage would be used as a basis for estimating the cost of its current inventory.

Cost of Goods Sold (COGS)

The methods described above to determine the value of a business's ending inventory allow calculation of cost of goods sold (COGS), which is deducted from a business's gross receipts to determine its gross profit. The following expenses related to inventory sold are included in COGS:

- The cost of products or raw materials, including freight
- Storage
- Labor costs[7]
- Factory overhead

---

[7] In a manufacturing business, labor costs allocable to the cost of goods sold include both the direct and indirect labor used in fabricating the raw material into a finished, saleable product. Other labor costs not associated with the manufacturing process, such as selling or administrative expenses, are not included in the COGS equation.

Example: In calculating COGS, American Custom Shoes includes the cost of leather and thread in the shoes it manufactures, as well as wages for the workers who produce the shoes. COGS is recorded as an expense as the company sells its goods.

The equation for cost of goods sold is as follows:
Beginning Inventory +
Inventory Purchases and Production Costs -
Ending Inventory =
Cost of Goods Sold

Example: Doggie Delights Inc. is an accrual-basis corporation that manufactures custom dog sweaters. The value of sweater inventory was $2,500 at December 31, and is $3,500 at January 31. In January, Doggie Delights has $20,000 of sales. In the same month, the corporation also has a number of expenses, including wages for the sweater designers ($5,000) and the cost of raw materials such as yarn, appliqué, and rhinestones ($3,000). The wages and the cost of the raw materials are directly related to the production of the inventory (the sweaters) and are included in the cost of goods sold calculation. Other costs not directly related to the manufacture of the sweaters, which might include items like a receptionist's salary ($1,500), telephone charges ($130), and advertising ($1,200) are also expensed, but are not part of COGS. The income statement for January would look like this:

Gross income from sales:	$20,000
COGS: ($2,500 + $5,000 + $3,000 - $3,500)	(7,000)
Gross profit	13,000
Other expenses: ($1,500 + $130 + $1,200)	(2,830)
Income for January	**$10,170**

When a business incurs a casualty or theft loss of inventory, it increases the cost of goods sold by properly reporting beginning and ending inventories. Alternatively, the business can record the loss separately as a casualty or theft loss. If the entity chooses to report a casualty loss, it must adjust opening inventory to eliminate the loss items and avoid counting the loss twice.

Uniform Capitalization Rules (UNICAP)

The uniform capitalization rules (commonly referred to as UNICAP) provide detailed guidance regarding the direct costs and certain indirect costs related to the production of goods or the purchase of merchandise for resale that businesses must capitalize as part of the cost of inventory. These costs cannot be deducted when incurred. They must be capitalized and deducted later when the inventory is used or sold.

Example: MTG Studios produces movies for Hollywood. Film production is subject to the UNICAP rules, so MTG must capitalize all of its costs, including set design, costumes, special effects, film editing, and salaries for actors and production workers. When a film is finally completed and distributed, MTG Studios is allowed to deduct the production costs as COGS.

Example: Creative Costumes manufactures Halloween costumes. During August, Creative Costumes purchases raw materials to produce costumes for the upcoming holiday. All the materials and shipping costs associated with the inventory must be capitalized rather than expensed. As the costumes are sold, Creative Costumes expenses the costs associated with the inventory as cost of goods sold. At the end of each month, Creative Costumes does a physical inventory count and adjusts COGS for any damaged or stolen inventory.

Businesses subject to the uniform capitalization rules include the following:

- Retailers or wholesalers that purchase merchandise for resale,
- Manufacturers that produce real or tangible property for sale; and
- Taxpayers who construct assets for their own trade or business.

However, the uniform capitalization rules do not apply to the following:

- Resellers of personal property with average annual gross receipts of $10 million or less for the three prior tax years.
- Personal or nonbusiness property (such as a hobby that produces occasional income).
- Research and experimental expenditures.
- Intangible drilling and development costs of oil and gas or geothermal wells.
- Property produced under a long-term contract.
- Timber raised, harvested, or grown, and the underlying land.
- Qualified creative expenses incurred as self-employed writers, photographers, or artists that are otherwise deductible on their tax returns.
- Loan originations.
- Property provided to customers in connection with providing services. It must be de minimis and not be included in inventory in the hands of the service provider.
- The costs of certain producers who use a simplified production method and whose total indirect costs are $200,000 or less.

Unit 2: Study Questions

1. Which of the following date ranges would be considered a fiscal tax year?

A. January 1, 2014 to December 31, 2014.
B. February 15, 2014 to February 15, 2015.
C. July 1, 2014 to June 30, 2015.
D. May 1, 2014 to May 31, 2015.

2. All of the following costs must be included in inventory except:

A. Cost of shipping raw materials to the business's factory.
B. Cost of shipping finished product orders to customers.
C. Raw materials.
D. Direct labor costs.

3. Which of the following changes in accounting method does not require prior approval from the IRS?

A. A change from FIFO to LIFO inventory valuation.
B. A change from the cash method to the accrual method.
C. A change in the overall method of figuring depreciation.
D. A correction of a math error in depreciating an asset.

4. Which of the following entities can use the cash method of accounting?

A. A family farming corporation with average gross receipts of $22 million.
B. A C corporation with average gross receipts of $50 million.
C. A tax shelter with average gross receipts of $50,000.
D. A corporation with long-term contracts and average gross receipts of $900,000.

5. Which would generally not be considered the end of an acceptable tax year?

A. January 31.
B. April 15.
C. December 31.
D. The last Friday in February.

6. Which of the following entities cannot use the cash method of accounting?

A. A partnership that produces inventory for sale to customers and has $1.2 million of average annual gross receipts.
B. A C corporation without inventory that has $4.5 million of average annual gross receipts.
C. A qualified family farming corporation with $24 million of average annual gross receipts.
D. A sole proprietor with inventory and $500,000 of average annual gross receipts.

7. Under the lower of cost or market method of valuing inventory, what is the value of the inventory as a whole, based on the table below?

Item	Cost	Market
Shirts	$200	$500
Shoes	$300	$200
Shorts	$225	$150
Total	**$725**	**$850**

A. $725.
B. $850.
C. $750.
D. $550.

8. Helen is the owner of Banner Custom Sofas, a calendar-year, accrual-basis S corporation. She sells five sofas to Sonny's Interior Design on December 21, 2014 and bills Sonny's for $2,500 on that date. Sonny's pays the invoice on January 15, 2015. Banner would include this income in:

A. 2014.
B. 2015.
C. 2016.
D. None of the above.

9. Vargas Cellular Corporation was organized on April 1, 2014. It elected the calendar year as its tax year. When is the first tax return due for Vargas Cellular for this short tax year?

A. April 15, 2014.
B. April 15, 2015.
C. March 15, 2015.
D. May 15, 2015.

10. Which of the following activities would make a taxpayer subject to the uniform capitalization rules?

A. An individual taxpayer who produces items as a hobby and occasionally sells them at a profit.
B. A taxpayer who produces property for sale to wholesale retailers.
C. A taxpayer who acquires land and holds it for investment.
D. A freelance artist who carries an inventory of artwork valued at $1.2 million.

11. Ray operates a retail clothing store using the accrual method and reports income on Schedule C, *Net Profit or Loss from Business.* He also runs a lawn care service that he operates only in the summer months. Which of the following statements is correct?

A. The lawn care business is required to use the accrual method of accounting because Ray has already elected this method for his other business, and all businesses operated by one individual must use the same method of accounting.
B. The lawn care business may use either the cash or accrual method, so long as both businesses have separate and distinct records.
C. Ray may keep one set of records for the two businesses and use different methods of accounting for them.
D. Ray must combine the income for both businesses and keep one set of record books for both.

12. Ben owns a jewelry store. All of the following transactions are examples of constructive receipt of income in 2014 except:

A. Ben receives a check payment on December 31, 2014, but does not deposit the check in the bank until January 2, 2015.
B. Ben receives a direct deposit of funds to his bank account on December 15, 2014, but does not withdraw any of the funds until March 2015.
C. Ben receives a signed IOU from a delinquent account in November 2014. He receives payment on this account on January 10, 2015.
D. An escrow agent receives a payment on Ben's behalf that is restricted for his use. It is an advance payment for a custom ring, but he cannot access any of the funds until the ring is delivered and inspected. On December 28, 2014, the ring is delivered and the restriction is lifted. Ben picks up the cash on January 9, 2015.

13. Chris is the owner-shareholder of Dress Down Fridays, a calendar-year S corporation. He manufactures clothing items for resale to the general public and also sells them to wholesale distributors. Chris is trying to figure out his inventory calculations in order to file his 2014 tax return. Which of the following items should be included in his year-end inventory?

A. 2,000 t-shirts out on consignment to a retailer.
B. The machinery used to manufacture the clothing.
C. An order of fabric that was in transit from a supplier, FOB destination (the title had not yet passed to Chris).
D. 1,000 shirts that were shipped COD to a retailer and had arrived there December 31.

14. Which of the following types of property are not exempt from the uniform capitalization rules?

A. Qualified expenses of a writer, photographer, or performing artist.
B. Timber and the underlying land.
C. Services provided to customers.
D. Audio recordings produced by a corporation.

15. Thomas is a cash-basis sole proprietor who reports income and loss on Schedule C. He purchases a bulk order of watches for his mail order business. The watches cost $5,000, and the related shipping cost is $350. What is the correct treatment of the shipping cost he paid for delivery of the watches?

A. Thomas may elect to deduct the $350 shipping cost on his tax return as an expense.
B. Shipping cost paid on the watches must be added to the basis of the inventory.
C. Thomas cannot deduct the shipping cost and cannot capitalize it.
D. Thomas may elect to deduct the shipping cost as an itemized deduction on Schedule A.

16. A business must adopt its first tax year by:

A. The due date (including extensions) for filing a return.
B. The due date (not including extensions) for filing a return.
C. The date the EIN is established.
D. The first time the business pays estimated payments.

17. All of the following practices are acceptable methods of accounting for inventory except:

A. The taxpayer includes in inventory only the direct costs associated with manufacturing the goods.
B. The taxpayer has a theft loss of inventory when a disgruntled employee steals substantial amounts of merchandise. The taxpayer chooses to increase his cost of goods sold to account for the stolen items and properly reports his beginning and ending inventory.
C. The taxpayer values his inventory using the lower-of-cost or market method, applying the method to each item in his inventory.
D. The taxpayer has two businesses, and he keeps a separate set of books for each business. He chooses to use LIFO for the first business and FIFO for the second one.

18. All of the following activities are exempt from the uniform capitalization rules except:

A. Resellers of personal property with average annual gross receipts of $25 million.
B. Intangible drilling and development costs of oil and gas or geothermal wells.
C. Research and experimental expenditures.
D. Property produced under a long-term contract.

19. Soft Pillows Partnership, a bedding manufacturer, had the following expenses during the tax year:

Beginning inventory	$80,000
Ending inventory	52,500
Raw materials purchased	12,000
Manufacturing costs	80,000
Freight-in costs	550
Freight-out to customers	750

Calculate Soft Pillow's cost of goods sold (COGS) for the year:

A. $67,050.
B. $120,050.
C. $120,800.
D. $670,800.

Unit 3: Business Income

More Reading:
Publication 525, *Taxable and Nontaxable Income*
Publication 334, *Tax Guide for Small Business*
Publication 925, *Passive Activity and At-Risk Rules*

Gross income reportable by a business for tax purposes includes all types of income received, unless specifically exempt from taxation, in the form of money, property, or services. Sources of income for a business include the following:

- Income received for services
- Income received for manufacturing or selling merchandise
- Gains from the sale of business or investment property
- Income from the discharge of indebtedness (debt cancellation income)
- Income from an interest in an estate or trust
- Portfolio income from investments
- Fair market value of property or services received through bartering
- Rental activities and royalties

In addition to earning income that is exempt from tax, businesses may engage in transactions for which taxation of income is deferred to a later date. An example is a section 1031 exchange, which allows for deferral of income on the exchange of business or investment property.

In this unit, we review the details of various types and treatments of business income.

Advance Payment for Services

An advance payment for services to be performed in a later tax year is generally taxable in the year it is received, even by an accrual-based taxpayer. However, if there is an agreement that the service will be completed by the end of the next tax year, recognition of the income can be delayed until the next year. The taxpayer cannot postpone the recognition of income beyond the next year.

Service Agreement: If a taxpayer receives an advance payment for a service agreement on property he sells, leases, builds, installs, or constructs, he can postpone reporting income, but only if he offers the property without a service agreement in the normal course of business. Postponement is not allowed if:

- The taxpayer will perform any part of the service after the end of the tax year immediately following the year he receives the advance payment.

- The taxpayer will perform any part of the service at any unspecified future date that may be after the end of the tax year immediately following the year he receives the advance payment.

Example: Ross is an accrual-based, calendar-year taxpayer who owns a television repair business. In 2014, he receives payments for one-year contracts that specify he will repair or replace certain TV components that break. Ross includes each payment evenly in gross income over a one-year period as it is earned.
Example: The Best Service Tennis Club is a calendar-year, accrual-based taxpayer that holds tennis clinics for new players. On November 1, the club receives payment for a one-year contract for 24 one-hour clinics beginning on that date. The club gives six clinics in 2014. The club must include one-fourth (6/24) of the payment in income for 2014 and three-fourths (18/24) of the payment in 2015, even if the club does not give all of the clinics by the end of 2015.

Guarantee or Warranty: Generally, an accrual-basis taxpayer cannot postpone reporting income received under a guarantee or warranty contract.

Advance Payment for Sales

Special rules apply to including income from advance payments on agreements for the future sale of goods to customers, such as gift certificates or cards that can be redeemed later for goods. The advance payment is generally included in income in the year it is received, even by a taxpayer reporting under the accrual method.

However, there is an alternative method in which the advance payment can be included in gross receipts under the method of accounting the taxpayer uses for tax purposes or the method of accounting used for financial reporting, whichever is earlier.

Example: Tangerine Specialty Foods uses the accrual method of accounting for tax and financial reporting purposes and accounts for the sale of goods when it ships the goods. A customer purchases a $100 gift card from Tangerine's website on December 28, 2014 using a credit card. Tangerine ships the gift card to the customer on January 3, 2015. Under the alternative method of reporting income for advance payment of sales, Tangerine may recognize the $100 of gross receipts in either 2014 (the tax year in which it received the payment) or 2015 (the tax year in which it shipped the gift card.)

Passive Activity Limits

Certain types of business activities are considered passive activities and are subject to passive activity limits on the deductibility of losses. The rules apply to individuals, estates, trusts (other than grantor trusts), personal service corporations, and closely held corporations. They also apply to owners of grantor trusts, partnerships, and S corporations. Before applying the passive activity limits, a taxpayer must determine the effects of at-risk limits,[8] which apply to individuals (including partners and S corporation shareholders), estates, trusts, and certain closely held corporations.

There are two kinds of passive activities:

- Trade or business activities in which the taxpayer does not materially participate during the year. The taxpayer materially participates in an activity if he is involved in the operations of the activity on a regular, continuous, and substantial basis.
- Rental activities, even if the taxpayer does materially participate, except for real estate professionals.

Study Note: There are additional exceptions related to limits on deductibility of passive losses from rental activities. These exceptions are more relevant to individual taxpayers and are generally tested on Part 1 of the EA exam.

The determination of whether a taxpayer materially participated is based upon satisfaction of at least one of several tests, including whether the taxpayer's participation in the activity:

1. Was for more than 500 hours.
2. Was substantially all the participation in the activity of all individuals for the tax year, including the participation of individuals who did not own any interest in the activity.
3. Was for more than 100 hours during the tax year, which was at least as much as any other individual for the year.
4. Included any five of the ten immediately preceding tax years.
5. Included a personal service activity in which he materially participated for any three preceding tax years.

If a taxpayer owned an activity as a limited partner, he is generally not treated as materially participating in the activity. However, he may be treated as materially participating if he met test (1), (4), or (5) above. Further, he would not be treated as a limited partner if he were also a general partner in the partnership at all times during the partnership's tax year.

---

[8] At-risk limits are explained in detail in later units pertaining to the specific types of entities that may be affected.

A taxpayer's participation in an activity includes his spouse's participation.

A closely held corporation or a personal service corporation is treated as materially participating in an activity only if one or more shareholders who own more than 50% of the corporation materially participate in the activity.

Passive Activity Loss Limitations: Losses from passive activities that exceed the income from passive activities in a given year are generally disallowed. The taxpayer uses Form 8582, *Passive Activity Loss Limitations,* to summarize income and losses from passive activities and compute deductible losses, and Form 8582-CR, *Passive Activity Credit Limitations*, to summarize the credits from passive activities and compute the amount of passive activity credit allowed.

Disallowed passive losses are carried forward to the next taxable year. A similar rule applies to credits from passive activities. Generally, the taxpayer can deduct in full any previously disallowed passive activity losses in the year he disposes of his entire interest in the activity. Form 8582-CR may also be used to make an election to increase the basis of credit property upon disposal.

Example: Marjorie owns a 25% interest in a partnership that runs a hair salon and a 10% interest in an S corporation that runs a yoga studio. She has no involvement in the day-to-day operation of either business; therefore, her interest in each business is considered a passive activity. In 2014, the hair salon partnership has an ordinary loss of $40,000, of which $10,000 is allocated to Marjorie because of her 25% ownership. The yoga studio business has ordinary income of $75,000, of which $7,500 is allocated to Marjorie because of her 10% ownership. As Marjorie's losses from passive activities for the year exceed her income from passive activities by $2,500 ($10,000 of loss minus $7,500 of income), deduction of the excess loss is disallowed. Marjorie may carry forward the $2,500 excess loss to the next year.

Definition: Ordinary income is income that is subject to regular tax rates, as opposed to capital gain income that is generally subject to more favorable tax rates.

A former passive activity is an activity that was a passive activity in an earlier tax year, but is not a passive activity in the current tax year. A prior year's disallowed loss from the activity can be deducted up to the amount of current year income from the activity.

Passive activity income does not include:

- Portfolio income, such as interest, dividends, annuities, and royalties not derived in the ordinary course of a trade or business, or gain or loss from the disposition of property that produces these types of income or that is held for investment.
- Personal service income. This includes salaries, wages, commissions, self-employment income from trade or business activities in which the taxpayer materially participated,

deferred compensation, taxable Social Security and other retirement benefits, and payments from partnerships to partners for personal services.

- Any income from intangible property, such as a patent, copyright, or literary, musical, or artistic composition, if the taxpayer's personal efforts significantly contributed to the creation of the property.
- State, local, and foreign income tax refunds.
- Income from a covenant not to compete.
- Alaska Permanent Fund dividends.
- Cancellation of debt income, if at the time the debt is discharged, the debt is not allocated to passive activities.

Note: Although many of the items listed above seem passive in nature, they are by definition excluded from treatment as passive activities.

Grouping Business Activities

A taxpayer can treat one or more trade or business or rental activities as a single activity if the activities form an appropriate economic unit for measuring gain or loss under the passive activity rules. If two activities are grouped into one larger activity, a taxpayer needs only to show material participation in the activity as a whole. If the two activities are separate, he must show material participation in each one.

Generally, when activities are grouped into appropriate economic units, they may not be regrouped in a later tax year. However, if any of the activities resulting from a grouping is not an appropriate economic unit and one of the primary purposes of the grouping is to avoid the passive activity rules, the IRS may regroup the activities.

Example: Malcolm owns a bagel shop and a movie theater at a shopping mall in Cincinnati and a bagel shop and a movie theater in Milwaukee. There may be more than one reasonable method for grouping Malcolm's activities, including the following: 1) the movie theaters and the bagel shops into one activity; 2) a separate movie theater activity and a separate bagel shop activity; 3) a Cincinnati activity and a Milwaukee activity; or 4) four separate activities.

Example: Roberta is a partner in Forever Young LLC, which sells skin care products to drug stores. She is also a partner in Verona Trucking. Forever Young LLC and Verona Trucking are under common control. Verona's main business is transporting goods for Forever Young, and it is the only trucking business Roberta is involved in. Roberta groups Forever Young's wholesale activity and Verona's trucking activity as a single activity.

In general, a rental activity cannot be grouped with a trade or business activity. However, they can be grouped together if the activities form an appropriate economic unit and:

- The rental activity is insubstantial in relation to the trade or business activity,
- The trade or business activity is insubstantial in relation to the rental activity, or
- Each owner of the trade or business activity has the same ownership interest in the rental activity, in which case the part of the rental activity that involves the rental of items of property for use in the trade or business activity may be grouped with the trade or business activity.

Example: Miles and Shira are married and file jointly. Miles is the only shareholder of Eco-Clean Dry Cleaners, an S corporation. Shira is the only shareholder of Fontana Properties, an S corporation that owns a commercial office building, part of which is rented to Eco-Clean. Fontana Properties' rental business and Eco-Clean's dry cleaning business are not insubstantial in relation to each other. Since Miles and Shira file a joint return, they are treated as one taxpayer for purposes of the passive activity rules. The same owner (Miles and Shira) owns both businesses, with the same ownership interest (100% in each). Miles and Shira may conclude that Fontana Properties' rental activity and Eco-Drycleaner's dry cleaning store form an appropriate economic unit and group them as a single business activity.

Rental Income

A business may have income from rental activity for any amounts received or accrued as payment for the use of property. Rental income may also include advance payments and deposits from renters.

Rental income earned by a sole proprietor, and related expenses, are generally reported on the following forms:

- Schedule C, *Profit or Loss from Business*: Used for professional real estate dealers and by owners of hotels, boarding houses, or apartment buildings who provide services for tenants or guests. The services must be substantial and not simply those normally provided with the rental of rooms for occupancy only, such as maid service.
- Schedule E, *Supplemental Income and Loss (from rental real estate, royalties, partnerships, S corporations, estates, trusts, REMICs, etc.)*: Used by taxpayers who are not professional real estate dealers or do not provide substantial services.

Generally, rental income earned by an individual taxpayer is not subject to employment taxes, unless the taxpayer is a professional real estate dealer. A taxpayer qualifies as a real estate dealer if he is primarily engaged in the business of selling real estate to customers.

Rental income reported on Schedule C, including rent received by a real estate dealer from real estate held primarily for sale to customers, is subject to self-employment tax. Income reported on Schedule E typically is not subject to SE tax.

> **Example:** Joe owns two residential rental properties. He manages them and collects rents. He also has a full-time job as a restaurant manager. He is not a real estate dealer. Joe must report his rental income and losses on Schedule E. His rental income is not subject to self-employment tax.

Lease cancellation payments received from a tenant are reported as income in the year received. Advance rental payments received under a lease must be recognized in the year received, regardless of which accounting method is used.

However, a security deposit is not considered income upon initial receipt, if the deposit is refundable to the tenant at the end of the lease. If the taxpayer keeps the security deposit because the tenant did not live up to the terms of the lease or because he damaged property, the deposit amount is recognized as income in the year it is forfeited by the tenant.

A taxpayer in the business of renting personal property, such as equipment, vehicles, or formal wear, includes the rental income on Schedule C. Advance payments for renting personal property must be reported in the year received.

> **Definition: Personal property** is not the same as "personal-use" property that a taxpayer uses for personal purposes. In its most general definition, personal property includes any tangible asset other than real estate. The distinguishing factor between personal property and real property is that personal property is movable, while real property, such as land or buildings, generally remains in one location.

Investment Income

A business may earn interest or dividend income from investments or from lending money to others. A common example is when a C corporation owns stock in another corporation.

For most sole proprietors, dividend income is considered nonbusiness income and is reported directly on Form 1040. However, dividends are treated as business income by professional stockbrokers and securities dealers.

Bartering Income

Bartering occurs when a taxpayer exchanges goods or services without exchanging money. An example of bartering is a plumber doing repair work for a dentist in exchange for dental services. The fair market value of goods and services received in a barter exchange must be included in income by each party in the year received. If the parties agree in advance on the fair market value of goods and services exchanged, it may be used, absent conflicting evidence.

> **Example:** Ethan is a self-employed social media marketer. He and Bryce, a house painter, are members of a barter club where members contact each another directly and bargain. In return for Ethan's marketing services, Bryce paints Ethan's office. Ethan must report the exchange as income on Schedule C. Bryce must also include in his income the fair market value of the services Ethan provided.

> **Definition:** The IRS defines **fair market value** (FMV) as the price at which a property would change hands between a buyer and a seller when both have reasonable knowledge of all the necessary facts and neither is being forced to buy or sell.

Income from Canceled Debt

If a business-related debt is canceled or forgiven, other than as a gift or bequest, the business generally includes in income the amount of the cancellation of debt (COD). However, a cash-basis business is not required to realize income from a canceled debt to the extent that the payment of the debt would have led to a business deduction.

> **Example:** Barbells Partnership is a cash-basis business. The company arranges computer repair services on credit but later has trouble paying its debts. The computer repair company forgives the repair bill. The partnership is not required to recognize the canceled debt as income because payment of the repair bill would have been deductible as a business expense anyway.

In the example above, the canceled debt of an accrual-basis business would be considered income, because a deduction for the repair expense already would have been recorded.

If a taxpayer owes a debt to a seller for property he bought and the seller reduces the amount owed, the taxpayer generally does not have income from the reduction. If the taxpayer is bankrupt or insolvent, the amount of the COD may be excluded from taxable income. If the taxpayer is not bankrupt or insolvent, the amount of the reduction is treated as a purchase price adjustment, and the buyer's basis in the property is reduced.[9]

Additional exclusions may apply to the discharge of qualified farm indebtedness and qualified real property business indebtedness. Taxpayers who use these exclusions are required to reduce specified tax attributes, including loss and credit carryforwards and the bases of assets, by corresponding amounts.

Business-Related Court Awards and Damages

Court awards and settlements that grant compensation for physical injuries or illness are generally excluded from taxation. Most other types of court awards and settlements are taxable income, such as:

- Damages for:
    - Patent or copyright infringement,
    - Breach of contract, or
    - Interference with business operations.
- Compensation for lost profits.
- Interest earned on any type of court award.
- Punitive damages related to business income or business activity.[10]

Amounts Not Considered Business Income

Just as with individual taxpayers, certain types of business-related income and property transfers are not taxable or reportable. Others may be partially taxable, and in some instances the recognition of income is delayed until a later date. Examples include:

- Issuances of stock, including the sale of Treasury stock
- Most business loans (which create debt, not income)
- State and local taxes that are collected in connection with sales or the provision of services and remitted to state or local governments
- Like-kind exchanges of property
- Gain from an involuntary conversion, if the gain is reinvested properly

---

[9]An explanation of basis and how it is calculated can be found in Unit 7.

[10]Punitive damages may be awarded in addition to compensatory damages for actual monetary losses. Punitive damages are subject to income tax but are not subject to self-employment tax.

Unit 3: Study Questions

1. Which of the following is not passive activity income?

A. Income from a trade or business in which a taxpayer does not materially participate.
B. Interest income.
C. Rental income, if the taxpayer is a real estate professional.
D. Both B and C.

2. When is a business not required to realize income from a canceled debt?

A. Canceled debt is always taxable to a business.
B. A business does not have to recognize canceled debt income to the extent that the payment of the debt would have led to a business deduction.
C. Canceled debt is never taxable income to a business.
D. Canceled debt is taxable income for a sole proprietorship or partnership, but not for a C corporation or an S corporation.

3. The Mickelson Tool Corporation rents large tools and machinery for use in construction projects. The company always charges a refundable security deposit and a nonrefundable cleaning deposit when someone rents a machine. Mickelson Tool received the following amounts in 2014:
- Rental income: $50,000
- Security deposits: $4,050
- Cleaning deposits: $1,500

What amount should be included in the corporation's gross income?

A. $50,000.
B. $51,500.
C. $54,050.
D. $55,550.

4. Which of the following would not be considered income for tax purposes?

A. Interest earned on a court award.
B. Damages received in a lawsuit or as settlement for personal physical injuries.
C. Barter income from consulting services.
D. Legal damages awarded for copyright infringement.

5. Camille, a calendar-year, accrual-based taxpayer, owns a studio that teaches ballroom dancing. On October 1, 2014, she receives payment for a one-year contract for 96 one-hour lessons beginning on that date. She gives eight lessons in 2014 and the rest in 2015. How and when must she recognize this payment as income?

A. All income must be recognized in 2014.
B. All income may be deferred until 2015 since that is when most of the lessons are given.
C. 8/96 of the income must be recognized in 2014 and the rest, 88/96, in 2015.
D. All of the income can be split equally between 2014 and 2015.

6. Assume the same facts as in the previous question, except the payment is for a two-year contract for 96 lessons. Camille gives eight lessons in 2014; 48 lessons in 2015; and 40 lessons in 2016. How and when must she recognize this payment as income?

A. All of the income must be recognized in 2014.
B. 8/96 of the income must be recognized in 2014; 48/96 in 2015; and 40/96 in 2016.
C. 8/96 of the income must be recognized in 2014 and 88/96 in 2015.
D. All of the income can be deferred and split equally between 2015 and 2016.

7. Which of the following statements is not correct about grouping passive activities?

A. If two activities are grouped into one larger activity, the taxpayer will need only to show material participation in the activity as a whole.
B. A taxpayer may group two or more trade or business activities if they comprise an appropriate economic unit.
C. The IRS may challenge the grouping of passive activities.
D. A rental activity cannot be grouped with a trade or business activity.

8. Harley is a real estate professional who owns two duplexes and an office building, all of which he rents to tenants. He works on his rental activity full-time. How should Harley report his rental income?

A. On Schedule E.
B. On Schedule C.
C. On Schedule D.
D. Harley's rental income is not taxable because he is a real estate professional.

9. Losses from passive activities are generally deductible only up to the amount of _____ from passive activities in a given year.

A. Other losses.
B. Debt basis.
C. Capital gains.
D. Income.

10. When are advance rental payments taxable?

A. In the year they are received.
B. In the period in which they are accrued.
C. They are not taxable.
D. They are taxable when the checks are cashed.

11. Sean has an ownership stake in several businesses. He does not materially participate in any of them. In 2014, he had the following results from these activities:
- Appliance repair store: $20,000 loss
- Ice cream parlor: $31,000 income
- Cupcake store: $17,500 loss

What is the tax treatment of Sean's ownership of these businesses?

A. Taxable income of $31,000 and deductible losses of $37,500 in 2014.
B. Deductible loss of $6,500 in 2014.
C. No taxable income in 2014; carryover of passive activity loss of $6,500 to 2015.
D. Taxable income of $31,000 in 2014; carryover of passive activity loss of $37,500 to 2015.

12. Allen's Exotic Pets, a cash-basis taxpayer, purchases $1,000 worth of legal services on credit in 2014. His business is struggling, and he is unable to pay the bill. The law firm forgives the bill in 2015. What is the correct statement about how Allen's Exotic Pets should handle the canceled debt?

A. The company must recognize the canceled debt income in 2014.
B. The company must recognize the canceled debt income in 2015.
C. The company must recognize half the canceled debt income in 2014 and half in 2015.
D. The company does not have to recognize the canceled debt income because payment of the legal services bill would have been deductible as a business expense.

13. What is personal property?

A. Personal assets of a taxpayer.
B. Real property owned by a business taxpayer.
C. Assets that are moveable and tangible.
D. Real property owned by a nonbusiness taxpayer.

14. Which of the following is business income?

A. Like-kind exchanges of property.
B. Business loans.
C. The sale of Treasury stock.
D. A barter exchange of services between two sole proprietors.

15. A taxpayer can treat one or more trade, business, or rental activities as a single activity:

A. To avoid the passive activity loss rules.
B. By making an election each year to determine whether or not to group the activities into appropriate economic units.
C. If he does not materially participate in any of the activities.
D. If the activities form an appropriate economic unit for measuring gain or loss under the passive activity rules.

Unit 4: Business Expenses

More Reading:
Publication 535, *Business Expenses*
Publication 538, *Accounting Periods and Methods*
Publication 587, *Business Use of Your Home*
Publication 463, *Travel, Entertainment, Gift, and Car Expenses*

Business expenses are the costs of carrying on a trade or business, and are usually deductible if the business operates to make a profit. However, some costs must be capitalized and depreciated or amortized. Expenses related to employee compensation and fringe benefits are discussed in Unit 5. This unit addresses general concepts and other types of business expenses.

As described in Unit 2, a cash-basis business generally claims deductible business expenses in the period they are paid.

Expenses Under the Accrual Method

Under the accrual method of accounting, a taxpayer generally deducts or capitalizes business expenses when both of the following apply:

- All events have occurred that fix the fact of liability, and the liability can be determined with reasonable accuracy.
- Economic performance has occurred: the property or services are provided or the property is used.

Example: Tessa is an accrual-based, calendar-year taxpayer. She orders office supplies in December 2014 and receives them later in the month. She does not pay the bill for the supplies until January 2015. She can deduct the expense in 2014 because all events have occurred to fix the liability, the amount of the liability can be determined, and economic performance occurred in 2014.

Exception for Recurring Items: Expenses for certain recurring items may be treated as incurred during the tax year even though economic performance has not occurred. In the above example, office supplies may qualify as a recurring item. If so, the taxpayer can deduct them in 2014, even if the supplies are not delivered until 2015 when economic performance occurs. The exception for recurring items applies if all of the following requirements are met:

- The all-events test described above has been met.
- Economic performance occurs by the earlier of the following dates:
    - $8\frac{1}{2}$ months after the close of the year, or

- o   The date the taxpayer files a timely return, including extensions, for the year.
- The item is recurring in nature and the taxpayer consistently treats similar items as incurred in the tax year in which the all-events test is met.
- And either:
  - o   The item is not material, or
  - o   Accruing the item in the year in which the all-events test is met results in a better match against income than accruing the item in the year of economic performance.

A new expense or an expense that is not incurred every year can be treated as recurring if the taxpayer reasonably expects to incur it regularly in the future.

The exception does not apply to workers' compensation or tort liabilities.

Deductible Business Expenses: To be deductible, a business expense must be both *ordinary* and *necessary*. An ordinary expense is one that is common and accepted in the taxpayer's industry. A necessary expense is one that is helpful and appropriate for the particular trade or business. However, an expense does not have to be indispensable to be considered necessary.

Example #1: Louisa is an enrolled agent who sends newsletters to clients with year-end tax-saving tips. The newsletters are a marketing tool for her business and would be considered ordinary and necessary. She can deduct the printing and mailing costs as a business expense.
Example #2: Louisa renovates her home office and spends $8,000 on silk designer curtains for the windows. As she does not meet with clients in her home office, an expenditure of this size would likely not be considered reasonable, and therefore would not be deductible as a business expense.

In addition to being ordinary and necessary, the following rules apply to business expenses:

- Some costs must be capitalized rather than deducted. As described in Unit 2, certain costs that would otherwise be currently deductible are allocated to the cost of producing inventory or holding it for resale. If a cost is included in inventory, it may later be deductible as a component of cost of goods sold. Other costs must be capitalized and either amortized ratably to expense or added to the basis of an asset and recovered when the asset is disposed.
- Personal, family, and living expenses generally cannot be deducted as business expenses.

Business Organizational and Start-up Costs

The costs associated with starting a business generally must be treated as capital expenditures and may not be deducted currently or amortized, subject to the exceptions described below.

The following costs related to a new business may be deductible as current expenses in 2014:

- $5,000 to organize a corporation or partnership, and
- $5,000 of start-up costs.

However, if organizational costs incurred or start-up costs incurred exceed $50,000, there is a dollar-for-dollar reduction until the current deduction for either item is eliminated. Organizational costs or start-up costs that are not currently deductible may be amortized ratably over 180 months (15 years) on Form 4562, *Depreciation and Amortization*. The amortization period starts with the month the taxpayer begins operating the business.

Example: Bronco Corporation has start-up expenses of $51,000 in 2014. Bronco is $1,000 over the $50,000 threshold so it must reduce its deduction for start-up expenses by the amount that it is over the threshold. Bronco can deduct $4,000 of its start-up expenses ($5,000 allowable deduction minus the excess $1,000). The remaining amount of start-up expenses, $47,000 ($51,000 - $4,000 allowable deduction), must be amortized over 180 months.

Example: Clean Water Inc. opened for business on November 1, 2014. Prior to opening, the company incurred $21,200 of start-up expenses for advertising and manager training. Since Clean Water had less than $50,000 of start-up costs, the company can deduct the full $5,000 on its 2014 tax return, and can also claim $180 of amortization [($21,200 - $5,000)/180 = $90 per month × 2 (two months, November and December)].

Organizational Costs: Qualifying organizational costs must be:

- For the creation of a business
- Chargeable to a capital account
- For a partnership, incurred by the due date of the tax return (excluding extensions) for the year business begins
- For a corporation, incurred before the end of the first tax year in which the corporation is in business

Examples of qualifying organizational costs include:

- The cost of temporary directors
- The cost of organizational meetings
- Filing fees for partnerships

- State incorporation fees for corporations
- Legal and accounting fees for setting up the business

Start-up Costs: Business start-up costs are incurred before a business actually begins operations, and include any amounts paid or incurred for:

- Creating an active trade or business; or
- Investigating the creation or acquisition of an active trade or business.

Start-up costs may include:

- An analysis or survey of potential markets
- Advertisements for the opening of a business
- Salaries and wages for employees who are being trained and their instructors
- Travel and other necessary costs for securing prospective distributors, suppliers, or customers
- Salaries and fees for executives and consultants, or for similar professional services

---

Example: Moonlight Corporation received its corporate charter on September 12, 2014. During the remainder of 2014, the company paid $15,500 for Internet and television advertising; $2,000 for training of employees; and $4,000 of consultant fees. Moonlight opened for business on January 8, 2015. The company can elect to deduct $5,000 as start-up costs in the 2014 tax year. It can then amortize the remaining $16,500 beginning in January 2015.

Start-up costs do not include deductible interest, taxes, or research and experimental costs.

If a taxpayer completely disposes of a business before the end of the amortization period, he can deduct the remaining unamortized start-up costs. However, the business can deduct these deferred start-up costs only to the extent they qualify as a loss.

If an individual attempts to go into business and is unsuccessful, the costs incurred may fall into two categories:

- Costs incurred before making a decision to purchase or start a specific business, which are considered personal and thus nondeductible
- Costs incurred in an attempt to purchase or start a specific business, which are capital costs that may be claimed as a capital loss.

The cost of assets acquired in connection with an unsuccessful attempt to go into business must be capitalized and cannot be deducted or recovered until the assets are disposed. If a corporation incurs costs related to an unsuccessful attempt to acquire or start a new business, it can deduct all of its investigatory costs as a business loss.

Taxes

Businesses generally can deduct taxes in the year paid, regardless of which method of accounting the business uses. Under the accrual method, a business can deduct a tax before it pays it, if it meets the exception for recurring items discussed earlier in this unit. Further, an accrual-basis taxpayer may ratably accrue real estate taxes.

Real Estate Taxes: In order for real estate taxes to be deductible, the taxing authority must calculate the tax based on the assessed value of the real estate. If a property is sold, the deductible portion of the real estate taxes must be allocated between the buyer and the seller according to the number of days in the property tax year that each owned the property. The seller is treated as paying the taxes up to but not including the date of sale. The buyer is treated as paying the taxes beginning with the date of sale.

Businesses cannot deduct taxes charged for local benefits and improvements that tend to increase the value of property. These include assessments for streets, sidewalks, water mains, sewer lines, and public parking facilities. A business must instead increase the basis of its property by the amount of the assessment.

However, a business can deduct taxes for local benefits such as maintenance, repairs, or interest charges related to capital improvements.

Example: Lawrence owns a business office on Grand Street. In 2014, the city charges an assessment of $4,000 to each business on Grand Street to improve the sidewalks. Lawrence cannot deduct this assessment as a current business expense. Instead, he must increase the basis of his property by the amount of the assessment.

Example: Waterfront City converts a downtown area into an enclosed pedestrian mall. The city assesses the full cost of construction, financed with 10-year bonds, against the affected properties. The city pays the principal and interest with the annual payments made by the property owners. The assessments for construction costs are not deductible as taxes or as business expenses but are depreciable capital expenses. The part of each payment used to pay the interest on the bonds is deductible as taxes.

Personal Property Taxes: Taxes imposed by a state or local government on personal property used in a taxpayer's trade or business are deductible.

Income Taxes: Federal income taxes are never deductible. However, corporations and partnerships can deduct state and local income and franchise taxes. A self-employed individual who reports income on Schedule C can deduct state and local income taxes as an itemized deduction on Schedule A.

> **Example:** Reiner Company is a calendar-year C corporation incorporated in Utah. Utah imposes a 5% state tax on Reiner's corporate earnings. In 2014, Reiner pays $12,000 of state income tax to Utah. This state tax would be deductible as a business expense on the corporation's federal tax return.

Sales Taxes: Sales taxes collected by a business in connection with the sale of goods or services to its customers are remitted to the taxing authorities, and are excluded from the business's gross receipts and its deductible expenses. When a business pays sales tax in connection with the purchase of goods or services, the tax is considered a component of the cost of the item purchased. Thus, if the item is depreciable property, the sales tax is added to its depreciable basis. If the item is merchandise for resale or to be used in the production of inventory, the tax is capitalized as a component of inventory. If the tax is related to a currently deductible business expense, it is likewise considered part of that expense.

Excise Taxes: Excise taxes that are ordinary and necessary expenses of carrying on a trade or business are deductible. Excise taxes are taxes paid when purchases are made on a specific item, such as gasoline, or activity, such as highway usage by trucks. When paid in connection with the purchase of a specific item an excise tax is considered part of the cost of that item. Therefore, it may be deductible currently or as the item is used, or be subject to capitalization, such as when the item is used in manufacturing inventory. Under the Affordable Care Act, indoor tanning salons are subject to a 10% excise tax, which is a deductible business expense.

Business Bad Debts

Most business bad debts are a result of credit sales of goods or services to customers for which payment has not been received. These are recorded in a business's books as either accounts receivable or notes receivable. If, after a reasonable period of time, a business has tried to collect the amount due but is unable to do so, the uncollectible part becomes a business bad debt.

A debt becomes uncollectible or worthless when there is no longer any chance the amount owed will be paid. A business does not have to wait for the debt to be due or to obtain a court judgment to show the debt is uncollectible.

A business bad debt is a loss from the worthlessness of a debt that was either:
- Created or acquired in a taxpayer's trade or business, or
- Closely related to the trade or business when it became partly or totally worthless.

To be considered closely related to a taxpayer's trade or business, the primary motive for incurring the debt must be business related.

A taxpayer can claim a business bad debt deduction only if the amount owed was previously included in his gross income. Thus, unlike an accrual-basis taxpayer, a cash-basis business typically would not record accounts receivable for credit sales, and would be less likely to have deductible business bad debts.

If a business loans money to a client, supplier, employee, or distributor for a business reason and the balance due later becomes worthless, the business can deduct the balance as a bad debt. However, the loan must have a genuine business purpose in order for this treatment to qualify.

Example: Carol is an accrual-based taxpayer who owns an eyeglass manufacturing company. One of her salesmen, Dawson, loses all his samples and asks Carol for a loan to replace them. Carol loans Dawson $3,000 to replace his eyeglass samples and sample bags. Dawson later quits his job without repaying the debt. Carol has a business-related bad debt that she can deduct as a business expense.

If a taxpayer receives property in partial settlement of a debt, the debt should be reduced by the property's FMV, which becomes the taxpayer's basis in the property. The remaining unpaid balance of the debt can be deducted as a bad debt when and if it becomes worthless.

An entity may later recover a debt that was previously written off as worthless. If a business recovers a bad debt that was deducted in a prior year, the recovered portion must be included as income in the current year tax return. There is no need to amend the prior year tax return on which the bad debt deduction was claimed.

Insurance Expenses

The following types of business-related insurance premiums are deductible:
- Property and casualty insurance (that covers fire, storm, theft, accident, or similar losses)
- Business interruption insurance (that reimburses a business if it is temporarily shut down due to a fire or similar disaster)
- Credit insurance that covers losses from business bad debts
- Liability insurance
- Malpractice insurance
- Contributions to a state unemployment insurance fund (deductible as taxes)

- Vehicle insurance that covers vehicles used in a business (not deductible if a business uses the standard mileage rate to figure vehicle expenses)
- Group-term life insurance for employees
- Group accident, health, long-term care, and workers' compensation insurance for employees

> **Note:** If a partnership pays accident, health, or workers' compensation insurance premiums for its partners, it generally can deduct them as guaranteed payments to the partners. If an S corporation pays accident, health, or workers' compensation insurance premiums for its more-than-2% shareholder-employees, it generally can deduct them and must also include them in the shareholders' wages subject to federal income tax withholding.

As described in Unit 2, if a cash-basis business pays insurance premiums in advance, it may rely upon a 12-month rule and deduct amounts paid that do not extend beyond the earlier of the following: (1) 12 months after the benefit begins, or (2) the end of the tax year after the tax year in which payment is made.

Self-Employed Health Insurance Deduction

A self-employed individual may be able to deduct premiums paid for medical and dental insurance and qualified long-term care insurance for himself, his spouse, and his dependents.

To qualify, a taxpayer must have a net profit reported on his Schedule C (Form 1040), Schedule C-EZ, or Schedule F; be a partner with net earnings from self-employment reported on Schedule K-1; or be a more-than-2% shareholder in an S corporation who had premiums paid or reimbursed by the corporation and reported to him as wages on Form W-2. He cannot take the deduction for any month he was eligible to participate in any employer-subsidized health plan (including one that his spouse was eligible for), even if he or his spouse did not actually participate in the plan.

Interest Expense

A business can deduct interest paid or accrued during the tax year on debts related to a trade or business for which it is legally liable. It does not matter what type of property secures the loan.

A business deducts business-related interest as follows:

- **Cash Method:** A business can deduct interest paid during the tax year. It cannot deduct a promissory note given in payment of interest because it is a promise to pay and not an actual payment.
- **Accrual Method:** A business can deduct interest that has accrued during the tax year.

A taxpayer cannot accelerate a tax deduction by paying interest in advance of when it is due. If a business uses the accrual method, it cannot deduct interest owed to a related person who uses the cash method until payment is made and the interest is includable in the gross income of that person.

If the proceeds of a loan are used for more than one purpose, the related interest must be allocated based upon the use of the proceeds, among the following:

- Personal interest
- Investment interest
- Portfolio interest
- Interest related to a trade or business

Interest charged on income tax assessed on an individual's income tax returns is not a business deduction, even if the tax is related to income from a trade or business. This interest should be treated as a business deduction only in figuring a net operating loss deduction. Penalties on underpaid deficiencies and underpaid estimated tax are not interest and are not deductible.

Rent Expense

A business can deduct expenses for renting property, including real estate, machinery, and other items used to conduct business. However, the cost of acquiring a lease is not considered rent and must be amortized over the term of the lease.

Generally, rent paid in a trade or business is deductible in the year paid or accrued. However, if a taxpayer pays rent in advance, he can deduct only the amount that applies to his use of the rented property during the tax year. The rest of the payment can be deducted only over the period to which it applies.

If a taxpayer has both business and personal use of rented property, he may only deduct the amount actually used for business. To compute the business percentage, the taxpayer must compare the portion of the property used for business to the entire property. The resulting percentage is used to figure the business portion of the rent expense.

Example: Ainsley rents a business office to use both as a personal studio for painting and as a site to run her tutoring business. Her total rental payments for the year are $11,000. The office is 1,000 square feet; she uses 800 square feet for the tutoring business and the remaining 200 square feet for her art studio. Therefore, she uses the office 80% for her business and 20% for personal purposes. The deductible portion of the rent expense is $8,800 (80% × $11,000).

Home Office Deduction

A self-employed taxpayer may be able to deduct certain expenses related to part of his home if the space is used regularly and exclusively for business and it is:

- The taxpayer's principal place of business, and/or
- The place used to meet with patients, clients, or customers in the normal course of business; or
- A separate structure not attached to the home that is used in connection with the business.

A taxpayer can use any reasonable method to calculate the percentage of the home that is used for business. Typically, the square footage of the home used for business is divided by the home's total square footage. Because of the exclusive use rule, a taxpayer is not allowed to deduct business expenses for any part of the home that is used for both personal and business purposes.

A self-employed taxpayer must complete Form 8829, *Expenses for Business Use of Your Home,* and then transfer the total to his Schedule C (Form 1040).

Simplified Home Office Deduction: A taxpayer may also choose to compute his home office deduction using a simplified calculation formula: a deduction of $5 per square foot is allowed for the space in the home that is used for business, up to a maximum allowable square footage of 300 square feet (for a maximum deduction of $1,500.)

Example: Rick is a self-employed insurance broker with a home office he uses exclusively for business. The office measures 15 × 15, or 225 square feet. Rick deducts $1,125 ($5 × 225) using the simplified option.

Under this option, a taxpayer can claim the full amount of allowable mortgage interest, real estate taxes, and casualty losses on his home as itemized deductions on Schedule A. These deductions do not need to be allocated between personal and business use, as is required under the regular method. The simplified option does not include a deduction for depreciation.

Each year, a taxpayer may use either the simplified method or the regular method to calculate the home office deduction. If he chooses the regular method after having used the simplified method in an earlier year, depreciation is calculated using an optional depreciation table for the property.

Employee Use: The home office deduction is also available for an employee who uses part of his home for business. However, there are two additional tests that must be met:

- The business use must be for the convenience of the employer, and
- The employee must not rent any part of his home to his employer and use the rental portion to perform services as an employee for that employer.

Business Travel, Meals, and Entertainment

To be deductible for tax purposes, business expenses for travel, meals, and entertainment must be incurred while carrying on a genuine business activity. Generally, the taxpayer must be able to prove that entertainment expenses, including meals, are directly related to the conduct of business. Adequate records must be retained to support these expenses, including receipts, bills, or canceled checks. An exception is made for expenses other than lodging that cost less than $75.

Travel costs with a business purpose are generally 100% deductible. However, if the travel includes an element of personal travel, the personal portion of the expense may not be deductible. In some instances, the personal portion may be incremental costs related to a spouse's travel. In other cases, a business must determine the nondeductible portion of an expense by multiplying it by a fraction. The numerator of the fraction is the number of personal days during the travel period and the denominator is the total number of days spent traveling.

Example: Paul flies to New Orleans on business and takes his wife with him so she can vacation there. Paul pays $190 for each airline ticket and $200 for a double hotel room. The cost of a single hotel room is $150. Paul can deduct the cost of his plane ticket and $150 for the hotel room. His wife's expenses are not deductible as a business expense.

Only 50% of the cost is deductible for business meals or entertainment incurred while:

- Traveling away from home (whether eating alone or with others) on business
- Entertaining customers at a restaurant or other location
- Attending a business convention or reception, business meeting, or business luncheon
- Obtaining deductible educational expenses, such as meals during a continuing education seminar

Taxpayers are considered "traveling away from home" if their duties require them to be away from home substantially longer than an ordinary day's work and they need to sleep or rest to meet the demands of their work.

The following related expenses are also subject to the 50% limit:

- Taxes and tips on a business meal or entertainment activity
- Cost of a room in which the business holds a dinner or cocktail party

The cost of transportation to a business meal or a business-related entertainment activity is not subject to the 50% limit.

Example: Karen is a business owner who takes a client to lunch. The total restaurant bill is $88. She also pays cab fare of $10 to get to the restaurant. Karen's deductible expense is $54:

Deductible meal expense	$88 × 50% = $44
Deductible travel expense	$10
Total deductible expense	**$54**

Exceptions to the 50% Limit: The following meals are 100% deductible by the employer:

- Meals that are included in employees' wages as taxable compensation
- Meals that qualify as a de minimis fringe benefit, such as occasional coffee and doughnuts
- Meals that are made available to the general public as part of a promotional activity, such as a real estate broker who provides dinner to potential investors at a sales presentation
- Meals furnished to employees when the employer operates a restaurant or catering service
- Meals furnished to employees as part of a teambuilding activity
- Meals that are required by federal law to be furnished to crew members of certain commercial vessels
- Meals furnished on an oil or gas platform or drilling rig located offshore or in Alaska

Special Department of Transportation Rules: There is also an exception for certain individuals subject to the U.S. Department of Transportation (DOT) "hours of service" limits who are traveling away from their tax home. A business is allowed to deduct 80% of employees' meal costs when DOT hours of service limits apply to the following:

- Certain air transportation workers such as pilots, crew, and mechanics regulated by the Federal Aviation Administration
- Interstate truck operators and bus drivers regulated by the Department of Transportation
- Certain railroad employees such as engineers and conductors regulated by the Federal Railroad Administration
- Certain merchant mariners regulated by the Coast Guard

Per Diem Rates for Business Travel: To ease recordkeeping requirements, a business may use a federal per diem rate as an alternative to keeping track of employees' actual expenses during business travel away from home.

Per diem is a daily allowance paid by a business to its employees for lodging, meals, and incidental expenses incurred when traveling. The allowance is in lieu of paying actual travel expenses. There is a per diem rate for combined lodging and meal costs, and a per diem rate for meal costs alone. An employer may use either per diem method for reimbursing employee travel expenses. A self-employed person can only use a per diem rate for meal costs. Per diem payments not in excess of the federal rate are not included in an employee's taxable wages, if an employee submits an expense report to the employer.

The applicable per diem rates vary based on whether the travel is domestic and foreign, and also by location. For example, the per diem rate in large cities like Los Angeles and New York is higher than for smaller cities. The IRS publishes the per diem rates every year in Publication 1542, *Per Diem Rates.*

Deductible Entertainment Expenses: A business is allowed to deduct 50% of business-related entertainment expenses that are incurred for entertaining a client, customer, or employee, as long as either the directly-related test or the associated test described below is met. It is not necessary to prove that the entertainment actually resulted in business income or another business benefit. The IRS looks at whether there is a "clear business setting" associated with the entertainment and whether there are "substantial distractions" at the location that prevent business from being conducted.

Deductible Entertainment Expenses	
General rule	Expenses to entertain a client, customer, or employee are deductible.
Definitions	Entertainment includes any activity generally considered to provide entertainment, amusement, or recreation, and includes meals provided to a customer or client.
Tests	**Directly-related test**
	• Entertainment takes place in a clear business setting, or
	• The main purpose is the active conduct of business, and
	• The taxpayer engages in business during the entertainment, and
	• The taxpayer has more than a general expectation of getting income or some other specific business benefit.
	Associated test
	• Entertainment is associated with the taxpayer's business, and
	• Entertainment occurs directly before or after a substantial business discussion.

A taxpayer cannot deduct entertainment expenses that are "lavish or extravagant" under the circumstances. A taxpayer also cannot claim the cost of a meal as an entertainment expense if he is claiming the meal as a travel expense.

If a taxpayer takes a client to a special event, he cannot deduct more than 50% of the face value of the ticket, regardless of the amount paid.

Example: Following a day of business meetings, Erik wants to take his two best clients to a basketball game, but the tickets are sold out. So Erik pays a scalper $390 for three tickets. The face value of each ticket is $52. Erik may only use the face value of the tickets as a basis for his deduction, and he also must apply the 50% limit. Therefore, his deductible entertainment expense is $78, figured as follows:

Cost of three event tickets (face value of $52 × 3):	$156
Apply the 50% limit ($156 × 50%):	$78

Transportation Expenses: Ordinarily, expenses related to use of a vehicle for business can be deducted as transportation expenses. To claim a deduction for business use of a car or truck, business-related costs must have been incurred for one or more of the following:

- Traveling from one work location to another within the taxpayer's tax home area. (Generally, the tax home is the entire city or general area where the taxpayer's main place of business is located, regardless of where he actually lives.)[11]
- Visiting customers.
- Attending a business meeting away from the regular workplace.
- Traveling from home to a temporary workplace. A temporary workplace can be either within or outside the taxpayer's tax home area.

Self-employed individuals, including partners in a partnership, may choose to use either the standard mileage rate or actual car expenses in order to figure the deduction for vehicle expenses. C corporations generally cannot use the standard mileage rate. However, businesses, including C corporations, may reimburse an employee under an accountable plan for business-related use of his car using the standard mileage rate. Any amounts reimbursed in excess of the standard mileage rate are reportable on the employee's Form W-2 as wages.

Whether using the standard mileage rate or claiming actual expenses, a taxpayer must keep records that identify the vehicle and provide evidence of ownership or a lease. Further, he should maintain a daily log showing miles traveled, destination, and business purpose to

---

[11] Costs related to travel between an individual's home and regular place of work are commuting expenses and not deductible as business expenses.

support the total business miles claimed or the business use percentage to be applied to allocate actual expenses.

Actual vehicle expenses include the costs of the following items:

- Depreciation
- Lease payments
- Registration
- Garage rent
- Repairs and maintenance
- Gas, oil, and tires
- Insurance, parking fees, and tolls

If business use of the vehicle is less than 100%, expenses must be allocated between business and personal use, and only the business use portion is deductible.

Example: Brandon uses a delivery van in his landscaping business. He has no other car, so the van is used for his personal transportation on the weekends. Brandon chooses to deduct actual costs, rather than using the standard mileage rate. Based on his records, Brandon's total vehicle expenses in 2014 are $6,252, which includes the cost of diesel fuel, oil changes, tire replacement, and repairs. Brandon uses the vehicle 75% for business, so his allowable auto expense deduction using the actual expense method is $4,689 ($6,252 × 75%).

For 2014, the standard mileage rate for business use of a vehicle is 56 cents per mile. A taxpayer who elects to use the standard rate cannot deduct actual expenses of operating a vehicle, such as gas, oil, and insurance. However, business-related parking fees and tolls may be deducted in addition to the standard mileage rate.

A taxpayer filing Schedule C or Schedule F can deduct interest on a loan relating to the purchase of the automobile. However, an employee cannot deduct the interest on a loan relating to an automobile purchase.

A business is prohibited from using the standard mileage rate if it:

- Operates five or more cars at the same time
- Claimed a depreciation deduction using any method other than straight-line, including MACRS
- Claimed a section 179 deduction on the car
- Claimed the special depreciation allowance on the car
- Claimed actual car expenses for a car that was leased

Recordkeeping for Travel, Entertainment, & Gift Expenses				
Expense	**Amount**	**Date**	**Description**	**Business Purpose**
Travel	Record of each expense for travel, lodging, and meals.	Dates for each trip and number of days spent on business.	Destination (name of city, town, etc.)	Business purpose for the expense.
Entertainment	Cost of each separate expense.	Date of entertainment.	Location of place of entertainment.	Business purpose for the expense.
Gifts	Cost of the gift.	Date of the gift.	Description of the gift.	Business relationship.
Transportation	Cost of each separate expense.	Date of the expense.	The business destination.	Business purpose for the expense.

Business Gifts

A business can deduct business-related gifts to clients and customers. The deductible amount is limited to $25 for amounts given to any person during the year. If a taxpayer and a spouse both give gifts, they are treated as one taxpayer for this limit, even if they have separate businesses. A gift to the spouse of a business customer or client is generally considered an indirect gift to the customer or client.

The $25 limit for business gifts does not include incidental costs such as packaging, insurance, and mailing costs, or the cost of engraving jewelry, which may be deducted separately. Related costs are considered incidental only if they do not add substantial value to a gift.

Example: Hawaii Fruit Corporation gives a large fruit and nut basket to its best customer, Dominic's Produce Company. The fruit basket costs $57, and the shipping and mailing of the basket costs $17. Hawaii Fruit Corporation can deduct $25 for the basket and $17 for the cost of mailing, for a total deduction of $42.

Example: Corinne sells greeting cards to a boutique. She gives three candy boxes to each of the store's owners to thank them for their patronage. Corinne pays $80 for each package, or $240 total. She can deduct $75 ($25 limit × 3) for the packages.

Exceptions: The following items are considered promotional and not subject to the $25 gift limit:

- An item with the business name clearly imprinted on it that costs $4 or less (examples include imprinted pens, desk sets, and plastic bags)
- Signs, display racks, or other promotional materials to be used on the business premises of the recipient

A business may also deduct gifts to employees. Noncash gifts of nominal value that are distributed to employees to promote goodwill may be excluded from taxable compensation. Gifts of greater value and of cash or cash-equivalent items such as gift cards are considered compensation.

> **Example:** Roggan Corporation gives each of its 75 employees a $25 turkey during the holidays. The company can deduct the cost of the turkeys ($1,875 = $25 × 75). The gift is not taxable to the employee, and the fair market value of the gift is not included in the employee's wages.

Charitable Contributions

Among business entities, only C corporations are permitted to deduct charitable contributions on their income tax returns. The deduction is limited to 10% of taxable income, and is explained further in Unit 13, *Corporate Transactions.*

Self-employed taxpayers cannot deduct charitable contributions as business expenses, but can claim deductions on Schedule A if they itemize deductions. Contributions made by partnerships and S corporations are reported on their respective returns as separately stated items, and may be deductible by their partners and shareholders.

Miscellaneous Business Expenses

Additional expenses that may be deductible by a business include the following:

- Advertising
- Credit card convenience fees
- Certain franchise or trademark fees
- Education and training for employees
- Internet-related expenses, such as domain registration fees
- Interview expense allowances for job candidates
- Outplacement services provided to employees
- Legal and accounting fees directly related to operating the business

- Tax preparation fees for business returns
- License and regulatory fees paid annually to state or local governments
- Penalties paid for late performance or nonperformance of a contract
- Repairs to business property, including the cost of labor and supplies
- Subscriptions and memberships to trade magazines and professional organizations
- Supplies and materials used during year
- Utilities, including heat, lights, power, telephone service, and water and sewage

Deducted or Capitalized Costs

There are certain costs that businesses may choose to either deduct currently or capitalize as an addition to the basis of a related asset. There are specific rules about the circumstances in which each type of item may be deducted, or if capitalized, how its cost may be recovered through depreciation or amortization. Examples of costs that are generally capital in nature, but which a business may elect to deduct currently include research and experimental costs; certain intangible drilling costs; and circulation costs for publishers of newspapers and magazines.

Nondeductible Expenses

The following expenses are not allowed as business deductions:
- Political contributions, including indirect contributions such as advertising in a convention program of a political party
- Lobbying expenses
- Dues for country clubs, golf and athletic clubs, and hotel and airline clubs, even if the club is used for business activity
- Penalties and fines paid to any governmental agency for breaking the law, such as parking tickets or fines for violating local zoning codes
- Legal and professional fees for work of a personal nature

Unit 4: Study Questions

1. Tom operates a computer service/repair business as a sole proprietorship. He drives a sedan when he visits clients, and each of his four technicians drives a van to make their repair visits. Which of the following methods can Tom use to claim deductions for the cost of these vehicles?

A. He can use the standard mileage rate for the sedan, but must use actual expenses for the vans.
B. He must use actual expenses for all of the vehicles.
C. He must use the standard mileage rate for the sedan, but can use actual expenses for the vans.
D. He can choose to use either method.

2. Alexa is a self-employed accountant who reports income and loss on Schedule C. She goes to a continuing education seminar out-of-state and incurs the following expenses:

Seminar	$400
Train ticket	35
Restaurant meal expense	26
Taxi fare to the restaurant	10

What is her deductible expense for this event?

A. $400.
B. $435.
C. $458.
D. $465.

3. In 2014, Helton Partnership, a cash-basis partnership, borrowed $50,000 to purchase machinery. Interest of $2,500 on the loan was due in December 2014. Rather than pay the interest, the partnership refinanced the loan and the interest due into a new loan of $53,800 on December 31, 2014: the original loan amount plus the interest due and an additional $1,300 in loan origination fees. The first payment on the new loan was due January 29, 2015. How much interest is deductible in 2014?

A. $0.
B. $2,500.
C. $2,800.
D. $3,800.

4. Norman is an interstate truck driver subject to the Department of Transportation rules for hours of service. During 2014, he incurs $3,064 in meal expenses while on the job. What is his deductible expense for business meals?

A. $1,532.
B. $2,298.
C. $2,451.
D. $3,064.

5. Kimberly is a sole proprietor and files a Schedule C. How should she report the $2,000 of charitable contributions she made on behalf of her business in 2014?

A. The contributions may be deducted on Schedule A as an itemized deduction.
B. The contributions may be deducted on Schedule C as a business deduction.
C. The contributions may not be deducted.
D. Up to 10% of the taxpayer's charitable contributions may be deducted on Schedule C. The remaining amount must be carried over to the next taxable year.

6. Which of the following is not required in order to meet the directly-related test for entertainment expenses to be deductible?

A. Business was engaged in during the entertainment event.
B. The main purpose of the entertainment was the conduct of business.
C. There was more than just the general expectation of business benefit.
D. The entertainment resulted in profit for the business.

7. Brady owns Super Sweets Company. He gives the following business gifts to a customer:
- Glass display for Super Sweets: $500
- Coffee and tea gift basket: $50
- 20 pens imprinted with the Super Sweets name and logo: $35
- Postage for the gift basket: $20

How much can Brady deduct on his tax return?

A. $25.
B. $525.
C. $580.
D. $605.

8. Delia, a self-employed real estate agent, traveled to a business convention by train and incurred the following expenses:

- Train ticket: $100
- Meals: $80
- Hotel room: $90
- Computer game: $50

How much is deductible as a current business expense?

A. $190.
B. $230.
C. $280.
D. $320.

9. Mountain Suppliers made a business loan to Sugarhill Corporation, a supplier, in the amount of $10,000. After paying $2,000, Sugarhill Corporation defaults, and the debt becomes worthless. How much may Mountain Suppliers deduct as a business bad debt?

A. $0.
B. $2,000.
C. $8,000.
D. $10,000.

10. Marion operates a shoe repair shop in a building she owns. In 2014, she had the following income and expenses:

- Repairs to shop floor: $1,000
- Property tax on business assets: $2,000
- Assessment for sidewalks: $5,800
- Utilities for her store: $1,800

What is the tax treatment of the above expenditures?

A. Deduct repairs, property tax, and utilities as business expenses. The assessment must be added to the basis of the property and depreciated.
B. All of the above expenses are deductible.
C. The property tax must be deducted on Schedule A, and the rest of the expenses may be deducted as business expenses on Schedule C.
D. Only the utilities and repairs may be deducted.

11. Luxe Chocolate Corporation is a cash-basis, calendar-year business. On October 1, 2014, Luxe Chocolate pays $3,600 for a business insurance policy covering three years. The policy coverage begins October 1, 2014 and ends September 30, 2017. How does Luxe Chocolate treat the expense for its insurance policy?

A. The entire $3,600 may be deducted in 2014.
B. 2014 deduction $1,200; 2015 deduction $1,200; 2016 deduction $1,200.
C. 2015: deduction $1,500; 2016 deduction $1,200; 2017 deduction $900.
D. 2014: deduction $300; 2015 deduction $1,200; 2016 deduction $1,200; 2017 deduction $900.

12. Bob owns Jackpot Pawn Shop. He makes a business loan to a client in the amount of $5,000. Bob also loans his brother $1,000 so he can buy a car. His brother, Keith, used to work sporadically at the shop as an employee. Both of the loans are now uncollectible. How much can Bob deduct as a business bad debt expense?

A. $1,000.
B. $4,000.
C. $5,000.
D. $6,000.

13. Lily owns a dress shop. In 2011, she correctly deducted a $10,000 business bad debt after a fabric supplier defaulted on a loan. In 2014, the fabric supplier wishes to do business with Lily again and repays $9,000 of the loan. How must Lily report this payment?

A. She must amend her 2011 tax return to correct the previously reported bad debt deduction.
B. She must reflect this recovery of $9,000 as income in 2014.
C. She can deduct a loss of $1,000 on her 2014 tax return.
D. She is not required to report the $9,000 loan repayment.

14. Maddie rents a small storage unit for her business on February 1, 2014. She is given a discount if she pays the full amount of the lease upfront, which is $1,620 for a three-year lease. What is the amount of Maddie's 2014 deductible expense for leasing the storage unit?

A. $495.
B. $540.
C. $560.
D. $1,620.

15. Mike borrowed $100,000 to purchase a machine for his business. The machine cost $90,000. The rest of the money went into Mike's business account, and he purchased a jet ski with the money later in the year. However, the entire loan was secured by his business assets. Which of the following statements is correct?

A. Mike cannot purchase personal items with a business loan; therefore, none of the interest is deductible.
B. All of the interest is deductible, because it is secured by his business assets.
C. Only the amount of interest allocable to purchase of the business machine is deductible.
D. None of the answers is correct.

16. Garrett operates his printing business out of rented office space. He uses a truck to deliver completed jobs to customers. Which of the following statements is not correct?

A. Garrett can deduct the cost of round-trip transportation between customers and his print shop.
B. Garrett can deduct traveling costs between his home and the print shop.
C. Garrett can deduct the cost of mileage to deliver completed jobs to the post office for mailing.
D. Garrett can deduct the costs to travel to his customers who are disabled and cannot come to his shop.

17. The Castellano Partnership paid the following penalties in 2014. Which are deductible?

A. A penalty paid to the county for violating construction regulations.
B. A penalty imposed by the IRS for late filing of a Form 1065 partnership return.
C. A penalty paid to the city for violating its sign ordinance.
D. A penalty for late performance of a contract.

18. Only-a-Dollar is a retail store in Dallas. It pays a combined 8.25% sales tax to local and state taxing authorities when a customer purchases its merchandise. How should Only-a-Dollar treat this sales tax expense?

A. Include the amount in its gross receipts and its deductible expenses.
B. Add the amount to the depreciable basis of property of the items sold.
C. Capitalize the cost as a component of inventory of the items sold.
D. Exclude from its gross receipts and deductible expenses the sales taxes it collects and remits them to local and state taxing authorities.

19. Which of the following costs qualify as business start-up costs?

A. State and local taxes.
B. Research and experimental costs.
C. A survey of potential markets.
D. Both B and C.

20. Devina is divorced and a sole proprietor who owns a public relations business. She has a nine-year-old son she claims as a dependent. In 2014, she paid $7,400 of premiums for medical and dental health insurance for herself and her son. She reported a net profit of $23,000 on her Schedule C. Which of the following statements is correct?

A. Health premiums are no longer deductible under the Affordable Care Act.
B. She can deduct 50% of the premiums in 2014.
C. She can deduct 100% of the premiums in 2014.
D. She cannot deduct the premiums because she reported a net profit on Schedule C.

21. A business incurs qualifying start-up and organizational costs during 2014. The business can elect to:

A. Deduct $5,000 for its start-up costs, but then cannot deduct its organizational costs.
B. Deduct $5,000 for its organizational costs, but then cannot deduct its start-up costs.
C. Deduct $5,000 for its start-up costs and $5,000 for its organizational costs.
D. Deduct the full amount of its start-up and organizational costs.

Unit 5: Employee Compensation & Fringe Benefits

More Reading:
Publication 535, *Business Expenses*
Publication 15-A, *Employer's Tax Guide*
Publication 15-B, *Employer's Tax Guide to Fringe Benefits*

Employee Compensation

An employer can deduct the compensation it provides its employees if all of the following tests are met:

- The payments must be ordinary and necessary expenses directly related to the trade or business.
- The amounts must be reasonable. Reasonable pay is the amount that like businesses would normally pay for the same or similar services. If the IRS determines pay is excessive, it can disallow deduction of the excess amount.
- There must be proof that services were actually performed (unless the compensation qualifies as supplemental wages, such as maternity leave, sick pay, or vacation pay).
- The expenses must have been paid or incurred during the tax year.

Supplemental wages refers to compensation paid in addition to an employee's regular salary or wages. Supplemental wages also may include the following:

- Bonuses
- Commissions
- Overtime pay
- Severance pay
- Taxable awards
- Prizes
- Back pay
- Retroactive pay increases
- Payments for nondeductible moving expenses

Supplemental wages are taxable to the employee just like regular wages and deductible as a wage expense by the employer.

Example: Doug is a salesman for a department store. In 2014, he earns wages of $20,000; commissions of $12,000; overtime of $5,000; and an end-of-the-year bonus of $1,000. All are taxable compensation to Doug and deductible by his employer.

Transfers of property to an employee can also be considered compensation. The fair market value of the property on the date of transfer is deductible by the business and taxable to the employee. The business would recognize a gain or loss on the transfer equal to the difference between the fair market value and its basis in the property.

In addition to deducting compensation payments to employees, a business can deduct amounts paid to independent contractors, such as those described in Unit 1.

Employment Taxes: A business's deduction for compensation paid to employees is not reduced by the Social Security, Medicare, and income taxes it is required to withhold from them. Further, a business can deduct the amounts paid as the employer's share of Social Security and Medicare taxes, as well as state and federal unemployment and disability fund taxes.

Example: A partnership pays its secretary $18,000 a year. After withholding various taxes, the employee receives $14,500. The business also pays an additional $1,500 of employment taxes on the secretary's wages. The full $18,000 can be deducted as wages. The business can also deduct the $1,500 additional paid as taxes.

A self-employed individual can deduct one-half of his self-employment tax as a business expense in figuring adjusted gross income. This deduction only affects income tax. It does not affect net earnings from self-employment or self-employment tax.

Fringe Benefits

A fringe benefit is a form of additional compensation that may be provided by a business to those who perform services, such as employees and independent contractors.

Study Note: For Part 1 of the EA exam, you must understand fringe benefits from the employee's perspective. For Part 2, you must know how these benefits are treated from the employer's perspective.

A business must include in a recipient's taxable compensation the amount by which the value of a fringe benefit is more than the sum of the following amounts:

- Any amount the law excludes from taxation
- Any amount the recipient paid for the benefit

If the recipient of a taxable fringe benefit is an employee, the benefit is subject to employment taxes and must be reported on Form W-2. If the recipient of a taxable fringe benefit is not an employee, the benefit is not subject to employment taxes, but it may have to be reported on Form 1099-MISC for independent contractors or Schedule K-1 for partners.

Generally, nontaxable benefits are not subject to income tax withholding, Social Security and Medicare taxes, or unemployment (FUTA) tax. However, there are exceptions for certain items. For example, an S corporation shareholder with ownership of more than 2% is not considered an employee for purposes of excluding certain fringe benefits, such as accident and health benefits, and this benefit is therefore subject to income tax withholding. Further, exclusion of an otherwise nontaxable benefit may be disallowed if there is discrimination in favor of highly compensated employees (as described below).

Cafeteria Plans

A cafeteria plan, including a flexible spending arrangement, is a written plan that provides employees an opportunity to choose between receiving at least one taxable benefit, such as cash, and one qualified (nontaxable) benefit. Employees may generally contribute a portion of their salaries on a pretax basis to pay for a portion of the qualified benefits. Having a salary reduction option is typically deemed sufficient to satisfy the requirement to provide a taxable option, even though the amounts are withheld on a pretax basis.

The plan may make benefits available to employees, their spouses, and their dependents. Qualified benefits may include:

- Accident and health benefits (but not Archer medical savings accounts or long-term care insurance)
- Adoption assistance
- Dependent care assistance
- Group-term life insurance
- Health savings accounts (HSAs)
- Flexible spending arrangements (FSAs)

A cafeteria plan cannot include certain other types of fringe benefits, which may nevertheless be deductible by the employer and nontaxable to the employee. Some of these additional items are addressed later in this unit under the heading "Other Types of Employee Fringe Benefits."

Highly Compensated/Key Employees: If a cafeteria plan favors either highly compensated employees (HCEs) or key employees as to eligibility to participate, contributions, or benefits, the employer must include in their taxable income the value of taxable benefits they could have selected. This is intended to discourage employers from offering tax-free benefits to their owners or highly compensated executives, while ignoring lower-paid employees.

A **highly compensated employee** is any of the following:

- An officer,
- A shareholder who owns more than 5% of the voting power or value of all classes of the employer's stock,
- An employee who is highly compensated based on the facts and circumstances, or
- A spouse or dependent of a person described above.

A **key employee** is defined as follows for 2014:

- An officer with annual pay of more than $170,000, or
- An employee who is either a 5% owner of the business or a 1% owner of the business whose annual pay was more than $150,000.

A plan is considered to have favored key employees if more than 25% of all the nontaxable benefits are given to key employees.

Accident and Health Benefits: Nontaxable accident or health benefits may include the following:

- Contributions to the cost of accident or health insurance, including long-term care insurance
- Contributions to a separate trust or fund that directly or through insurance provides accident or health benefits
- Contributions to Archer MSAs or health savings accounts

Adoption Assistance: An adoption assistance program provides payments or reimbursements for qualifying expenses related to adopting a child, with up to $13,190 excludable in 2014.

Dependent Care Assistance: An annual exclusion of up to $5,000 ($2,500 if MFS) may apply to benefits received by an employee under a dependent care assistance program that provides for a qualifying person's care and allows the employee to work. The exclusion cannot exceed the smaller of the earned income of either the employee or the employee's spouse.

Note: Like the other cafeteria plan benefits described above, a dependent care assistance program cannot favor HCEs. However, for a dependent care assistance program, the definition of an HCE differs from the general guidelines above. In this case, and for most of the other types of fringe benefits described in this unit, an HCE is an employee who (1) was a 5% owner at any time during the year or the preceding year, or (2) received more than $115,000 of pay for the preceding year, unless he was not also in the top 20% of employees when ranked by pay in the preceding year.

Group-term Life Insurance Coverage: An employer can exclude the cost of up to $50,000 of group-term life insurance from the taxable wages of an insured employee. The value of insurance coverage that exceeds $50,000 is a taxable benefit and must be included in the employee's wages, after reduction for any amount the employee paid toward the insurance.

Health Savings Accounts: An HSA is an account owned by a company's employee or former employee. Any contributions an employer makes become the employee's property and cannot be withdrawn by the employer. Contributions to the account are used to pay current or future medical expenses of the account owner, his spouse, and any qualified dependent. The medical expenses must not be reimbursable by insurance or other sources.

A qualified individual must be covered by a high deductible health plan with a deductible in 2014 of at least $1,250 for self-only coverage or $2,500 for family coverage. Annual out-of-pocket expenses to the beneficiary are limited to $6,350 for self-only coverage and $12,700 for family coverage. There are no income restrictions on an individual's eligibility to contribute to an HSA; nor is there a requirement the account owner have earned income to contribute. In 2014, an employer can contribute up to $3,300 for self-only coverage or $6,550 for family coverage to a qualified individual's HSA. The contribution limits are increased by $1,000 for qualified individuals who are age 55 or older at any time during the year. No contributions can be made to an individual's HSA after he becomes enrolled in Medicare Part A or Part B.

An employer's contribution amount to an employee's HSA must be comparable for all employees who have comparable coverage during the same period, or there will be an excise tax equal to 35% of the amount the employer contributed to all employees' HSAs. However, an employer is allowed to make larger HSA contributions for a non-highly compensated employee than for a highly compensated employee.

Flexible Spending Arrangements: An FSA is a form of cafeteria plan benefit that reimburses employees for expenses incurred for certain qualified benefits, such as child care or health benefits. The employee must substantiate his expenses, and the distributions from the FSA to the employee are tax-free. An FSA generally cannot provide a cumulative benefit to the employee beyond the plan year. However, an employer may choose to allow an employee a grace period of up to two-and-a-half months from the end of the plan year to use his balance or to carry over up to $500 of unused funds per account. A cafeteria plan may not allow an employee to request salary reduction contributions to a health FSA in excess of $2,500.

Working Condition Benefits

This exclusion from wages applies to property and services an employer provides so that the employee can perform his job. If an employer provides an employee with a product or service and the cost of it would have been allowable as a business or depreciation deduction if he paid it himself, it would be deductible to the employer and excludable from an employee's income.

> **Example:** Gordy works as an accountant. His employer provides him with a subscription to an accounting trade journal. The subscription's cost is not included in Gordy's income because he would have been able to deduct it as a business deduction had he paid for it himself.

A common working condition benefit is an employee's use of a company car for business purposes. An employer who provides a car for an employee can exclude the amount that would be allowed as a deductible business expense if the employee paid for its use.

Alternatively, an employer may include the entire annual lease value of a car in the employee's wages and the employee can then claim any deductible business expense for the car as an itemized deduction on his personal income tax return.

A qualified nonpersonal-use vehicle is one that an employee is unlikely to use more than minimally for personal purposes because of its design. Examples include fire trucks, police cars, hearses, school buses, cement mixers, and tractors.

> **Note:** Any vehicle designed to carry cargo of over 14,000 pounds is automatically qualified as a nonpersonal-use vehicle. Pickup trucks and vans of 14,000 pounds or less are also considered qualified nonpersonal vehicles if they have been specially modified for business purposes and are likely to be used only minimally for personal purposes. Modifications include being marked with permanent decals or painted with advertising logos and being fitted with certain equipment specific to the business. An example of this would be a modified utility van used by an electrician. Even if the van does not meet the 14,000 pound requirement, if the van has been modified specifically to carry tools and equipment, then it may be considered a nonpersonal-use vehicle.

An employer-provided cell phone is another common working condition benefit. There must be a substantial business reason to provide the employee a cell phone; it cannot simply be used to boost an employee's morale, to attract a prospective worker, or as a means of providing additional compensation to an employee.

> **Example:** Evelyn is an advertising executive who frequently visits clients at their locations. She uses her employer-paid cell phone to keep in touch with clients and her own firm while she is out of her office. If Evelyn did not have a legitimate business reason for the phone, its value would be added to her wages and her firm could not deduct it as a business expense.

Accountable Plans

A business can reimburse employees for business-related expenses. There are two types of reimbursement plans:

- **Accountable Plans**: Amounts paid under an accountable plan are deductible by the employer but they are not taxable wages and are not subject to income tax withholding or payment of Social Security, Medicare, and FUTA taxes.
- **Nonaccountable Plans**: Amounts paid under a nonaccountable plan are taxable to employees as wages and are subject to all employment taxes and withholding. Generally, there are no substantiation requirements for a nonaccountable plan.

For expenses to qualify under an accountable plan, the employee must follow strict guidelines in order to have the expenses reimbursed. An accountable plan requires employees to:

- Have incurred the expenses while performing services as employees.
- Adequately account for the expenses, including travel, meals, and entertainment, within a reasonable period of time.
- Provide documentary evidence of travel, mileage, and other employee business expenses.
- Return any excess reimbursement or allowance to the employer within a reasonable period of time, if paid in advance. A cash advance must be reasonably calculated to equal the anticipated expense, and the employer must make the advance within a reasonable period of time.

Example: Dana is a cosmetics saleswoman for Sunshine Cosmetics. She takes two potential clients out to dinner and pays for the meal. She keeps track of her business mileage on a spreadsheet. The following week, she submits her receipts and the spreadsheet to Sunshine Cosmetics for reimbursement. Dana's employer reimburses her for the out-of-pocket expenses she incurred. This arrangement is considered an accountable plan. The reimbursement is not taxable to Dana and is deductible by the employer as a regular business expense (subject to the 50% limitation on deductibility of meal costs).

Example: Maggie is a loan agent who goes to various locations to sign mortgage paperwork. In April, Maggie's employer gives her a $1,000 advance to cover her flight, hotel, and transportation on a business trip to Alaska. Maggie spends $940 on her travel expenses during the trip. When she returns, she submits her receipts to substantiate the expenses. She also pays back the excess advance to her employer. She has met the requirements of an accountable plan, and the advanced funds are not included in her taxable wages.

Other Types of Employee Fringe Benefits

Employee Achievement Awards: Employers may generally exclude from an employee's wages the value of awards given for length of service or safety achievement. An employer's deduction and the tax-free amount for each employee are limited each year to the following:

- $400 for awards that are not qualified plan awards.
- $1,600 for all awards, whether or not they are qualified plan awards

Qualified plan awards are employee achievement awards under a written plan that does not discriminate in favor of highly compensated employees.

Example: Rowell Company awards a set of golf clubs to an employee as a nonqualified plan employee achievement award. The fair market value of the golf clubs is $750. The amount included in taxable wages to the employee is $350 ($750 - $400). Rowell Company can deduct $400 as a business expense.

The exclusion for employee awards does not apply to awards of cash, gift cards, or other intangible property such as vacations or tickets to sporting events.

Athletic Facilities: The value of an employee's use of a health club or athletic facilities may be excluded from wages, but only if the facility is on premises that the employer owns or leases. If the employer pays for a gym membership or a fitness program provided to the employee at an off-site location, the value is included in the employee's compensation.

De Minimis (Minimal) Benefits: An employer may exclude the value of a de minimis benefit provided to an employee from the employee's wages. This is something an employer provides that has so little value that accounting for it would be impractical, such as coffee and doughnuts in the break room. Cash and cash equivalent items, such as gift cards or the use of a credit or debit card, are not excludable as de minimis benefits, except for occasional meal money or transportation fare.

Educational Assistance: An educational assistance program is a separate written plan that allows an employer to provide educational assistance to employees for the cost of tuition, fees, books, supplies, and equipment. The payments may be for either undergraduate or graduate-level courses, and do not have to be work-related.

Up to $5,250 of assistance may be excluded per year per employee. If an employer does not have an educational assistance plan or pays more than $5,250, the excess is taxed as wages to the employee unless the benefits are working condition benefits that the employee would be able to deduct as a business expense if he paid for them himself.

Tuition Reduction: An educational organization can exclude the value of a qualified undergraduate tuition reduction it provides to an employee, his or her spouse, or a dependent child. Graduate education only qualifies if it is for the education of a graduate student who performs teaching or research activities for the educational organization.

Employee Discounts: Employers can exclude from wages the price reductions they give to employees on services or property they offer to customers in the normal course of business, up to the following limits:

- For a discount on services, 20% of the price charged nonemployee customers for the service.
- For a discount on merchandise or property, the company's gross profit percentage multiplied by the price nonemployee customers pay.

Employee Stock Options: A corporation may grant stock options to its employees, as compensation for past service and an incentive for retention, that allow them to purchase the company's stock at a later date. If an employee receives stock options, he may have income when the options are granted, when he exercises them (to buy the company's stock), or when he sells or otherwise disposes of the options or the stock. The nature, timing, and amount of the employee's taxable income and the employer's deduction for compensation expense depend on whether the options are considered to be statutory or nonstatutory options. There are two types of statutory stock options:

- Incentive stock options (ISOs), which allow employees to purchase stock at a pre-established price (exercise price) that may be below the market price on the date of exercise.
- Options granted under employee stock purchase plans (ESPPs).

The tax advantage of a statutory stock option for the employee is that income is not reported when the option is granted or when it is exercised. However, the employer corporation cannot take a deduction for compensation expense. The employee does report income when he ultimately sells the stock. If he satisfies certain holding period requirements, the income is treated as capital gain. If not, it is treated as ordinary income, and the employer is entitled to a compensation deduction at that time.

Nonstatutory or nonqualified stock options (NSOs) also allow employees to purchase stock at a pre-established exercise price. The employee must recognize compensation income, either at the date of grant or on the exercise date, and the employer is entitled to a corresponding compensation expense deduction at the same time.

Meals and Lodging: An employer may exclude from taxable wages the value of meals and lodging it provides to employees if they are provided:

- On the employer's business premises, and
- For the employer's convenience.

For lodging, there is an additional rule: it must be required as a condition of employment. Lodging can be provided for the taxpayer, the spouse, and the taxpayer's dependents, and still not be taxable. The exclusion from taxation does not apply if the employee can choose to receive additional pay instead of lodging.

Situations in which meals may be provided to employees for the convenience of the employer on the employer's business premises include the following:

- Workers such as police officers, firefighters, and other emergency personnel need to be on call for emergencies during the meal period
- The nature of the business requires short meal periods
- Eating facilities are not available in areas near the workplace
- Meals are furnished to all employees on a regular basis, as long as meals are furnished to more than half of the employees for the convenience of the employer
- Meals are furnished immediately after working hours because the employee's duties prevented him from obtaining a meal during working hours

Example: An employer has pizza delivered to the office at a group meeting because the business requires the meeting be kept short, and there are no alternative restaurants in the immediate area.

Meals provided to restaurant employees during, or immediately before or after work hours are also considered furnished for the employer's convenience. Meals provided to employees for the convenience of the employer are not subject to the normal 50% deductibility limit; they are 100% deductible by the employer.

Moving Expense Reimbursements: An employer can generally exclude qualifying moving expense payments or reimbursements from an employee's taxable wages if they are paid under an accountable plan for expenses that would otherwise have been deductible by the employee if he had paid or incurred them without reimbursement. Deductible moving expenses include only the reasonable expenses of:

- Moving household goods and personal effects from the employee's former home to the new home, and
- Traveling, including lodging, from the former home to the new home.

Expenses for meals are not included, and the move must meet both the distance test and the time test. The distance test is met if the new job location is at least 50 miles farther from the employee's old home than the old job location was. The time test is met if the employee works at least 39 weeks during the first 12 months after arriving in the general area of the new job location.

No-Additional-Cost Services: An employer can exclude from an employee's taxable income the value of a service provided to the employee if it does not create substantial additional cost for the business. Typically, no-additional-cost services are excess capacity services, such as airline, bus, or train tickets; hotel rooms; or telephone services provided free or at a reduced price to employees working in those lines of business.

Transportation: Employers can provide transportation benefits to their employees up to certain amounts without having to include the benefit in the employee's taxable income. Qualified transportation benefits include transit passes, qualified parking, rides in a commuter highway vehicle between the employee's home and workplace, and qualified bicycle commuting reimbursements.

In 2014, employees can exclude:

- $250 per month in combined commuter highway vehicle transportation and transit passes, and
- $250 per month in parking benefits.
- $20 per month for expenses incurred when commuting to work by bicycle

Employees can receive transit passes and benefits for parking during the same month; they are not mutually exclusive.

If an employer allows an employee to use a company vehicle for commuting or other personal use, the value of the vehicle's use is taxable to the employee.

Affordable Care Act for Employers

The Affordable Care Act provisions mandating that certain employers provide health insurance for fulltime workers are not in effect for tax year 2014. Implementation of the *employer shared responsibility provisions* was delayed until 2015 for some employers and until 2016 for others, depending on the number of full-time employees.

Under Internal Revenue Code section 6056, applicable large employers must file information returns with the IRS and provide statements to their full-time employees about the health insurance coverage offered. These requirements are optional for 2014 and returns filed voluntarily will have no impact on the tax liability of the employer.

> **Study Note:** Since the employer mandate is not in effect for tax year 2014, it will not be tested in the EA exam for *Part 2: Businesses.* However, the mandate for individuals to obtain health insurance coverage went into effect in 2014, and is likely to be tested on this year's Part 1 exam. The provisions affecting individuals in 2014 are covered in PassKey's EA Review for *Part 1: Individuals.*

Unit 5: Study Questions

1. For cafeteria plans, a "key" employee in 2014 is defined as all of the following except:

A. An officer with annual pay of more than $170,000.
B. A 1% owner of the business with annual pay of more than $150,000.
C. A 3% owner of the business.
D. Both A and B.

2. All of the following are fringe benefits that may be excluded from an employee's pay except:

A. Dependent care assistance of up to $5,000 a year.
B. A cell phone given to an employee for excellent job performance.
C. Moving expense reimbursements.
D. Adoption assistance.

3. The Pancake House provides the following benefits to its employees. Which of these is fully taxable to the employee?

A. Qualified group term life insurance of $50,000.
B. Educational assistance of up to $5,250.
C. A membership at the local athletic club with a value up to $1,200.
D. Free transit passes, up to $250 per month.

4. Heart-Wise Ambulance Services provides meals and lodging for ten paramedics at the workplace as a condition of employment because they are not allowed to leave the premises when they are on a shift. The employees eat and sleep for free. Which of the following statements is correct?

A. All the costs of meals and lodging can be excluded from the employees' wages and deducted as an expense by the employer.
B. The meals and lodging are not taxable to the employee, but the employer can deduct only 50% of the meal expense.
C. The meals and lodging are taxable to the employees and deductible by the employer. The employee may then deduct the costs as employee business expenses.
D. The meals and lodging can be deducted by both the employees and the employer as business expenses.

5. All of the following are excludable from an employee's wages and deductible by the employer except:

A. An outstanding employee achievement award valued at $300.
B. Occasional snacks provided by the employer in the employee break room.
C. Employer-provided vehicles that employees may also use for personal purposes.
D. Meals furnished during work hours for the convenience of the employer.

6. Evermore Inc. reimburses employees for their business travel and transportation expenses. Which of the following is taxable to the employee?

A. Travel reimbursements made under an accountable plan.
B. Travel reimbursements made under a nonaccountable plan.
C. Parking passes at a cost of $250 per month.
D. A qualified bicycle commuting reimbursement.

7. Renee is a full-time employee of Right Angles Engineering, which offers its employees reimbursement through an education assistance program. In 2014, she takes graduate accounting courses and has $5,900 of tuition expenses and $300 of expenses for required books. Right Angles reimburses Renee for all the expenses. How should this reimbursement be treated?

A. All of the amounts are excluded from Renee's income, and the amounts are deductible by Right Angles as a qualified fringe benefit.
B. The first $5,250 of the educational expenses is excluded from Renee's wages as a qualified fringe benefit, and the remaining amount is taxable as wage income to her.
C. Only $5,900 (the tuition costs) of the educational expenses are excluded from the Renee's wages as a qualified fringe benefit, and the remaining amount is taxable as wage income to her. The cost of the books is not a qualified educational expense.
D. All of the reimbursement is taxable as wages to Renee because graduate courses do not qualify for reimbursement under a fringe benefit plan.

8. Which of the following benefits must be included in an employee's income?

A. Child care reimbursed under a qualified flexible spending plan.
B. Employee discounts on products.
C. A holiday gift of a $50 gas card.
D. A holiday gift of a $25 canned ham.

Unit 6: Business Deductions & Credits

More Reading:
Instructions for Form 3800, *General Business Credit*
Publication 334, *Tax Guide for Small Business*
Publication 536, *Net Operating Losses for Individuals, Estates, and Trusts*
Instructions for Form 8903, *Domestic Productions Activities Deduction*
Instructions for Form 4626, *Alternative Minimum Tax-Corporations*

In addition to the deductions already covered, businesses can reduce their taxable income through various business credits and the domestic production activities deduction. We start with a look at the net operating loss, which can allow a business with losses for the year to recover past tax payments or reduce future tax payments.

Net Operating Losses (NOLs)

A net operating loss (NOL) occurs when a business has tax deductions that exceed its income, resulting in negative taxable income for a tax year. C corporations NOLs are discussed in Unit 13. Partnerships and S corporations generally cannot use NOLs, but their partners and shareholders may be able to use their individual shares.

For an individual, estate, or trust to have an NOL, the loss must be caused by deductions from:

- A trade or business that result in an overall loss
- Work as an employee
- Casualty or theft losses (personal or business-related)
- Losses from rental property
- Moving expenses
- A farming business

Depending upon whether it had taxable income in prior years, a business may choose to carry back an NOL to offset prior year taxable income or to carry forward the NOL to offset taxable income in future years.

> **Example:** Harrison is a sole proprietor who owns a flooring business. In 2014, his business has a net operating loss of $13,000. In 2013, Harrison's business had taxable income of $10,000 and in 2012 it had taxable income of $25,000. Harrison may carry back $10,000 to 2012 and $3,000 to 2013.

The default election is to carry back an NOL for up to two years. Any remaining NOL can be carried forward for up to 20 years.

119

> **Note:** A net operating loss that is not used in the carryback and carryforward periods is lost and cannot be deducted in any other tax year.

A business may also elect not to carry back an NOL and only carry it forward. If a taxpayer fails to file a return on time and does not make the proper election, he is forced to carry back the NOL.

There are certain instances in which a business qualifies for a longer NOL carryback period. The following are exceptions to the two-year carryback rule:

- Farmers are eligible for a five-year carryback period for farming losses.
- "Qualified small businesses"[12] may carry back a loss three years if the loss is due to a federally declared disaster.
- Net operating losses due to a casualty or theft may be carried back three years.
- Product liability losses have a ten-year carryback period. An example would be when a business sells an item that is later subject to a recall and lawsuits.

To claim a refund from an NOL, an individual taxpayer may choose to amend a prior year tax return or may use Form 1045, *Application for Tentative Refund*, to apply for a quick tax refund resulting from the carryback of an NOL.

If the taxpayer is self-employed, the net operating loss does not change the amount of self-employment tax to any of the years it is carried forward or back to. Also, if a business or individual owes interest and penalties in a prior year, the NOL carryback will not abate them.

> **Example:** Gregory operates a farming business and files his return on Schedule F. In 2014, he has a net operating loss of $35,000. He had income of $25,000 in the prior year, so he elects to carry back his NOL in order to receive a refund of the income tax he paid. Gregory also owed self-employment taxes in 2013, and the NOL will not reduce this tax. The NOL only reduces the income tax liability. As a farmer, Gregory would be able to carry back the NOL up to five years.

The following items are not allowed when figuring an NOL:

- Any deduction for personal exemptions
- Capital losses in excess of capital gains
- The exclusion of gain from the sale of qualified small business stock
- Nonbusiness deductions in excess of nonbusiness income (hobby losses)
- A net operating loss from another year (a carryback or a carryforward)
- The domestic production activities deduction (DPAD)
- A self-employed taxpayer's contribution to a retirement plan

---

[12] A "qualified small business" for purposes of this rule is a sole proprietorship or a partnership that has average annual gross receipts of $5 million or less during the three-year period ending with the tax year of the NOL.

Income from other sources may eliminate or reduce a net operating loss for the year. For example, if a taxpayer has income from wages, as well as a net operating loss from a small business, the wage income and the NOL will offset taxable income.

> **Example:** Jim runs an auto detailing business as a sole proprietor. In 2014, he had an $8,000 NOL from his Schedule C business. Jim files jointly with his wife, Elaine. She has $23,000 of taxable income from wages. On their jointly filed return, Jim's net operating loss is absorbed by Elaine's $23,000 of wages, making their joint AGI $15,000 ($23,000 - $8,000 NOL).

Business Credits

A variety of tax credits are available for businesses. Credits are generally more valuable than deductions because they are subtracted directly from a business's tax liability. However, most tax credits are available in limited situations, applying only to certain industries or to very specific activities.

General Business Credit

Many business credits fall under the umbrella of the general business credit (GBC). The GBC is not a single credit but is instead a combination of individual credits. Each business credit is claimed on a separate form; the credits are then reported in aggregate on Form 3800, *General Business Credit.*

The GBC is a nonrefundable credit that is subtracted directly from tax, reducing an entity's tax liability dollar for dollar. Generally, credits cannot be claimed to the extent that they would reduce a business's tax bill below its tentative minimum tax. Further, the GBC may not offset any of a business's employment tax liabilities.

If a business is unable to use its entire GBC in the year it was earned, it can generally be carried back to the prior year and forward for up to 20 years. A business's GBC consists of its carryforward of business credits from prior years plus the total of its current year business credits.

> **Study Note:** In addition to eligibility for and deduction of the general business credit as a whole, Prometric's exam specifications reference the Investment Credit and the Disabled Access Credit, suggesting they are the most likely to be tested on the EA exam.

The following are some of the more widely-used general business credits.

Investment Credit (Form 3468): The Investment Credit is the sum of the following five credits: Rehabilitation and Energy Credits, and the Advanced Coal, Advanced Energy, and Gasification projects.

- **Rehabilitation Credit:** This credit is available for businesses that rehabilitate pre-1936 buildings (10%) or certified historic structures (20%) of qualified expenditures.
- **Energy Credit:** This credit is available for businesses that use solar energy to generate electricity or that use geothermal deposits to power their equipment. The credit is between 10% and 30% for qualified fuel cell and other solar energy property.
- **Advanced Coal, Gasification, and Advanced Energy Project Credits:** These credits are designed to reduce greenhouse emissions by retrofitting existing technology to make it cleaner or spurring investment in alternative energy.

The Investment Credit allows businesses to take a deduction for a percentage of certain investment costs from their tax liability in addition to the normal allowances for depreciation. In general, a business cannot claim the Investment Credit for property that is:

- Used mainly outside the United States;
- Used by a governmental unit or foreign person or entity;
- Used by a tax-exempt organization;
- Used for lodging or in the furnishing of lodging; or
- Any property that has already been expensed under section 179 (accelerated depreciation).

Disabled Access Credit (Form 8826): This is a nonrefundable tax credit for an eligible small business that incurs expenses to provide access to persons who have disabilities. The expenses must be incurred for the business to comply with the Americans with Disabilities Act. The amount of the Disabled Access Credit is 50% of qualified expenses, with a maximum credit per year of $5,000. To be eligible, a business must have had gross receipts of $1 million or less or had no more than 30 full-time employees during the preceding tax year.

Example: Helene owns a small roadside café that was built many years ago. To comply with ADA regulations, she retrofitted the café's restroom to allow wheelchair access. Qualified expenses totaled $12,000. Helene can claim the full $5,000 of the credit (50% of a maximum of $10,000 of qualified expenses.)

Work Opportunity Tax Credit (Form 5884): The WOTC provides a credit for hiring qualified veterans and members of certain targeted employee groups through 2014. The amount of the credit varies depending on the targeted group that an employee belongs to (for example, a veteran who receives food stamps or an ex-felon) and the period of unemployment before the employee is hired.

Credit for Small Employer Pension Plan Start-up Costs (Form 8881): Employers can claim a tax credit equal to 50% of the cost to set up and administer the plan, up to a maximum of $500 per year, for each of the first three years of the plan.

Credit for Employer Social Security and Medicare Taxes Paid on Certain Employee Tips (Form 8846): This credit is generally equal to the employer's portion of Social Security and Medicare taxes paid on tips received by employees of restaurants and other food service establishments where tipping is customary. An employer must meet both of the following requirements to qualify for the credit:

- Have employees who received tips from customers for serving food or beverages, and
- Have paid employer Social Security and Medicare taxes on these tips.

The credit does not apply to other tipped employees, such as hairdressers or bellhops.

Credit for Employer Differential Wage Payments (Form 8932): This credit provides certain small businesses with an incentive to continue to pay wages to an employee performing services on active duty in the uniformed services of the United States for a period of more than 30 days.

Credit for Employer-Provided Childcare Facilities and Services (Form 8882): This credit applies to the qualified expenses a business incurs for employee childcare, childcare resources, and childcare referral services. The credit is up to 25% of the cost of the childcare facility plus 10% of resource and referral costs. A business is limited to a credit of $150,000 per tax year.

Credit for Increasing Research Activities (Form 6765): Also known as the research and development credit, this provides a credit for expenses related to qualified research intended for use in developing new or improved technology that would be used in a taxpayer's business.

Small Business Health Care Tax Credit (Form 8941)

The Credit for Small Employer Health Insurance Premiums is a refundable credit that was expanded for 2014 as part of the Affordable Care Act. It is no longer grouped as part of the General Business Credit.

The credit is increased to a maximum of 50% of the cost of health insurance premiums paid for employees by small business employers and a maximum of 35% of premiums paid by small tax-exempt employers. The credit is specifically targeted toward employers with low and moderate income workers and phases out as average annual wages increase. To be eligible for the credit an employer:

- Must pay premiums on behalf of employees enrolled in a qualified health plan offered through a Small Business Health Options Program (SHOP) Marketplace, or qualify for an exception to this requirement.
- Have fewer than 25 full-time equivalent employees for the tax year.
- Pay average annual wages to employees of less than $51,000 for 2014.

> **Example:** Patrick is the owner of a small watch repair business. He has twelve full-time equivalent employees, and pays $50,000 a year toward their health care premiums for coverage purchased through the SHOP marketplace. Based on the average wages of his employees, Patrick qualifies for a 15% credit, so he can claim a credit of $7,500.

The credit can be claimed for a maximum of two consecutive years.

An employer must reduce its health insurance premium expense deduction by the amount of the credit. Because the credit is refundable, even if an employer has no taxable income, the business may be eligible to receive the credit as a refund.

Domestic Production Activities Deduction

The domestic production activities deduction (known as the DPAD, authorized by IRC section 199) is designed to stimulate domestic manufacturing and farming. The DPAD is calculated on Form 8903, *Domestic Production Activities Deduction*. Individual taxpayers, including partners or shareholders in pass-through entities and beneficiaries of trusts and estates, claim the DPAD deduction as an adjustment to income on Form 1040. C corporations claim the deduction on Form 1120.

The DPAD is equal to 9% of the lesser of:

- Qualified production activities income (QPAI), or
- Adjusted gross income for an individual, estate, or trust (or taxable income for all other taxpayers) determined without regard to the DPAD.

However, the deduction is also limited to 50% of Form W-2 wages paid to employees for the year. Payments made to independent contractors and reported on Form 1099-MISC are not wages and do not qualify for purposes of the DPAD.

The following activities are qualified production activities eligible for claiming the DPAD:

- Manufacturing goods in the United States
- Selling, leasing, or licensing items that have been manufactured in the United States
- Selling, leasing, or licensing motion pictures that have been produced in the United States (except for pornography)
- Construction of real property in the United States
- Engineering and architectural services relating to a U.S.-based construction project
- Software development in the United States
- The production of water, natural gas, and electricity in the United States
- The growth and processing of agricultural products and timber

QPAI is the excess of domestic production gross receipts (DPGR) over the sum of:

- Cost of goods sold allocable to DPGR, and
- Other expenses, losses, and deductions (other than the DPAD) properly allocable to DPGR.

A business's gross receipts must be allocated between DPGR and non-DPGR, and its cost of goods sold must then be allocated to each. One of several methods must then be used to allocate other expenses, losses, and deductions. The use of certain of these methods is limited to small businesses that meet specified parameters.

Example: Brent Wise Corporation manufactures building components that it sells wholesale to building contractors. All of Brent Wise's manufacturing activity is in the U.S., and therefore qualifies for the DPAD. In 2014, Brent Wise had QPAI of $650,000 from its manufacturing activity and taxable income (without regard to the DPAD) of $800,000. It paid $225,000 in W-2 wages to its employees. Brent Wise's DPAD deduction would therefore be the lesser of:

- 9% of the $650,000 of QPAI, or
- 50% of the $225,000 of wages.

Thus, Brent Wise's DPAD would be $58,500 (.09 × $650,000).

Example: Raiser Ranch Inc. is a meat processor that has various slaughtering plant locations in the United States as well as two locations in Brazil. Although this type of production activity is qualified for the DPAD, only the U.S. production qualifies for the DPAD. Raiser Ranch must allocate its gross receipts between the factory production in the United States and Brazil to calculate DPGR and non-DPGR.

Gross receipts from the following are not considered DPGR and therefore not eligible for the DPAD:

- Construction services that are cosmetic in nature, such as drywall and painting.
- Leasing or licensing items to a related party.
- Selling food or beverages prepared at restaurants or dining establishments.
- The transmission or distribution of electricity, natural gas, or water (although the production of electricity, natural gas, or potable water in the United States is a qualified activity).
- Any advertising, product placement, customer service businesses, and other telecommunications services.
- Most service type businesses.

Unit 6: Study Questions

1. Lorelei is a sole proprietor who designs and sells custom jewelry direct to customers. She has three full-time employees whose wages average $16,000 in 2014. She paid the health insurance premiums for her employees who are enrolled in coverage through the SHOP marketplace. Which of the following statements is correct?

A. She does not qualify for the Small Business Health Care Tax Credit.
B. She may qualify for a credit of up to 50% of the premiums she paid for her employees.
C. She may qualify for a credit of up to 35% of the premiums she paid for her employees.
D. She may qualify for the Small Business Health Care Tax Credit for up to three years.

2. Which of the following does not qualify for the domestic production activities deduction?

A. Manufacturing goods in the United States.
B. Construction of buildings in the United States.
C. Selling food or beverages prepared at restaurants in the United States.
D. Software development in the United States.

3. Stacy owns the Peach Pit Cannery. In 2014, she renovated her cannery to comply with the Americans with Disabilities Act. The Peach Pit Cannery had gross receipts of $750,000 and spent $15,000 on disabled access upgrades. What is Stacy's current year Disabled Access Credit?

A. $2,500.
B. $5,000.
C. $7,500.
D. $15,000.

4. Bennett Corporation could not use all of its general business credits in 2014. What is the carryover period for the GBC?

A. The GBC may be carried back two years and carried forward five years.
B. The GBC may be carried back five years and carried forward 10 years.
C. The unused GBC cannot be carried over to another tax year.
D. The GBC may be carried back one year and carried forward for 20 years.

5. The Work Opportunity Tax Credit provides a credit for businesses that:

A. Provide job training for out-of-work veterans and other individuals in targeted groups.
B. Give severance to laid-off workers.
C. Invest in federal empowerment zones.
D. Hire unemployed veterans and other individuals in targeted groups.

6. Bettina owns her own photography business, and she has an NOL in the current year. She elects to carry back her losses. How long may she carry back and carry forward her NOL?

A. Back five years, forward 20 years.
B. Back two years, forward 20 years.
C. Back three years, forward 25 years.
D. Back two years, forward five years.

7. Which of the following is not part of the Investment Credit in 2014?

A. Gasification Project Credit.
B. Hydroelectric Power Credit.
C. Rehabilitation Credit.
D. Energy Credit.

8. Which event would create an NOL?

A. Selling a personal-use car for a loss.
B. Selling a primary residence for a loss.
C. Casualty loss from a fire at a business location.
D. Loss from the sale of corporate stock.

9. All of the following statements are correct regarding the DPAD except:

A. The DPAD cannot be more than 25% of the wages a business pays its employees.
B. Businesses with both domestic and foreign business activity must use only their domestic income in calculating the DPAD.
C. The DPAD can be as much as 9% of a company's taxable income.
D. The DPAD is authorized by section 199 of the Internal Revenue Code.

10. Which of the following items is allowed when figuring a net operating loss?

A. Capital losses in excess of capital gains.
B. A net operating loss from another year (a carryback or a carryforward).
C. The domestic production activities deduction.
D. The loss from the theft of business property.

11. The Disabled Access Credit conforms with applicable standards of the:

A. Architectural Standards Act.
B. U.S. Department of Labor.
C. Americans with Disabilities Act.
D. National Organization on Disability.

12. Angela is a sole proprietor who owns a candle-making shop. Angela's net business income is $300,000 for the year. Angela has three full-time employees. She paid her three employees a total of $118,000 of wages during the year. Based on this information, what is Angela's DPAD deduction for the year?

A. She is not eligible for the DPAD because she is a sole proprietor.
B. $150,000
C. $59,000
D. $27,000.

13. Alistair is a sole proprietor who files his return on Schedule C. He had the following profit and losses:
- 2011: Net profit $7,000
- 2012: Net profit $9,000
- 2013: Net profit $6,000
- 2014: Net operating loss $24,000

How should Alistair treat his net operating loss?

A. NOL carryback of $7,000 to 2011; NOL carryback of $9,000 to 2012; NOL carryback of $6,000 to 2013; NOL carryforward of $2,000.
B. NOL carryback of $9,000 to 2012; NOL carryback of $6,000 to 2013; NOL carryforward of $9,000.
C. NOL carryback of $24,000 to 2013.
D. NOL carryforward of $24,000.

Unit 7: Basis of Business Assets

> **More Reading:**
> Publication 551, *Basis of Assets*
> Publication 547, *Casualties, Disasters, and Thefts*

A business asset is any type of property used in the conduct of a trade or business: land, buildings, machinery, furniture, trucks, patents, and franchise rights are examples. Some assets are tangible, and others are intangible. Taxpayers generally must capitalize the cost of business assets, rather than deduct them in the year the cost is incurred.

In order to compute gain or loss on the sale or other disposition of an asset, a business must be able to determine its basis.

Definition: Basis is the amount of a taxpayer's investment in an asset or property for tax purposes. Understanding how to calculate basis in various contexts, including for business entities such as corporations and partnerships, is critical to an individual's success in passing *Part 2: Businesses* of the EA Exam.

The basis of property is also used to determine tax deductions for depreciation, amortization, depletion, and casualty losses. If a business cannot determine the basis of an asset, the IRS will deem it to be zero.

The basis of property is usually its cost: the amount a business pays for the asset. An asset's cost basis also may include amounts paid for the following items:

- Sales tax on the purchase
- Freight to obtain the property
- Installation and testing costs
- Excise taxes
- Legal and accounting fees to obtain property
- Revenue stamps
- Recording fees
- Real estate taxes (if assumed by the buyer)
- Settlement costs for the purchase of real estate
- The assumption of any liabilities on the property

Example: Naomi pays $4,000 for a new commercial dryer for her laundromat. Naomi also pays $500 for shipping and sales tax. The installation cost for the dryer is $250. These costs are added to the purchase price, resulting in a basis of $4,750.

If a business produces real or tangible personal property for use in a trade or business, it may be subject to the uniform capitalization rules described in Unit 2.

> **Note:** Certain events that occur during the period of ownership may increase or decrease basis, resulting in an *adjusted basis*. For example, the basis of property is *increased* by the cost of improvements that add to the value of the property. The basis of property is *decreased* by depreciation deductions, insurance reimbursements for casualty and theft losses, and certain other items such as rebates.

Basis of Real Property

Real property, often called real estate, includes land and anything built on or attached to it. When a taxpayer buys real property, certain fees and other expenses become part of the cost basis in the property.

Settlement Costs: Certain settlement fees and closing costs related to buying a property are added to its basis. These include abstract fees; charges for installing utility services; legal fees, including title search and preparation of the sales contract and deed; recording fees; surveys; transfer taxes; owner's title insurance; and any amounts the seller owes that the taxpayer agrees to pay, such as charges for improvements or repairs and sales commissions.

However, the following settlement fees and closing costs cannot be included in the basis of a property:

- Casualty insurance premiums
- Rent or utility costs related to occupancy of the property before closing
- Any charges for acquiring a loan, such as mortgage insurance premiums, loan assumption fees, cost of a credit report, fees for appraisal reports, fees for refinancing a mortgage, and points. Points are prepaid interest on a loan and are generally deducted as interest over the life of the loan.

Real Estate Taxes: If a taxpayer pays real estate taxes on property he buys that the seller owed, those taxes are added to the basis and cannot be deducted currently.

Assumption of Mortgage: If a taxpayer buys property with an existing mortgage, the basis includes the amount paid in cash for the property plus the amount of the mortgage assumed.

Example: The Oceanside Partnership purchases a commercial building for $200,000 of cash and assumes a mortgage on the building of $800,000. The partnership also pays $5,500 of legal fees to a real estate attorney to handle the purchase. Oceanside's basis in the building is $1,005,500 ($200,000 + $800,000 + $5,500).

Constructing Assets: If a taxpayer builds property or has assets built, the costs of construction are included in the basis. In addition to the cost of land, these may include labor and materials; architect's fees; building permit charges; payments to contractors; rental equipment; inspections; employee wages paid for the construction work; and the cost of building supplies and materials used in the construction. The value of an owner's labor (if a sole proprietor rather than an employee-owner of a corporation) or any other labor for which payment is not made is not included in the basis.

Demolition Costs: Demolition costs increase an asset's basis because they are necessary to prepare the property for use. As such, costs incurred to demolish a building are added to the basis of the land on which the building was located. The costs of clearing land for construction also must be added to the basis of the land.

Example: Tony buys a lot with a badly damaged building on it for $25,000. He demolishes the building and prepares the land for a new structure. The demolition costs $13,000. Tony's adjusted basis in the land is $38,000 ($25,000 + $13,000).

Rehabilitation Costs: Rehabilitation costs increase basis. However, any rehabilitation credits allowed for the expenses must be subtracted.

Repair vs. Improvement Rules

Improvements increase the value of a property or asset. A taxpayer is generally required to capitalize the cost of improvements, thus increasing the property's basis, and claim depreciation deductions over a period of years. Examples of improvements include the installation of new electric wiring, adding a new roof or central air conditioning, or renovation of a kitchen.

In contrast, a repair keeps a property in operating condition but does not add to its value or substantially prolong its life. Examples include repainting a property or replacing broken windows. Unlike improvements, the costs of repairs can be deducted currently.

Example: Douglas repairs a leaky toilet in a rental duplex. The cost of the repair may be deducted as a current expense. The following year, Douglas replaces the entire plumbing system in the duplex with new pipes and bathroom fixtures. This is an improvement that increases the value of the property. Douglas must capitalize the cost of the new plumbing, increasing the property's basis, and depreciate the cost of this improvement over its useful life.

After ten years of various temporary or proposed regulations, the IRS's final tangible property regulations took effect on January 1, 2014.[13] The regulations are hundreds of pages long, extremely complex, and are expected to affect virtually every business taxpayer.[14] The regulations establish the rules governing the capitalization and expensing of physical assets that a taxpayer purchases, repairs, maintains, improves, or disposes.

Study Note: Given the complexity of the rules and their specificity to various types of property and how it is used, it is unlikely an EA test-taker would be expected to be familiar with the details of the repair regulations. Many experienced tax professionals are still interpreting the key changes and how they apply to their business clients. For the EA exam, it should be sufficient to have a basic grasp of the underlying concepts of expensing repairs as current deductions vs. capitalization through depreciation deductions. In this unit, we look at how improvements are categorized and at the safe harbors that the regulations carve out for expensing property. In Unit 8, we discuss concepts of depreciation and amortization.

Under the new regulations, an improvement is classified as a cost involving:

- The **betterment** of a unit of property (UOP),
- The **restoration** of a UOP, or
- The **adaptation** of a UOP to a new or different use.

The regulations divide a building into nine different structural components called "building systems," such as those for plumbing, heating and air conditioning, and electrical, each of which may be a UOP, in addition to the building itself. Under the new, narrower definition of an improvement, costs must be evaluated for a specific building system, and not just for the building as a whole.

For example, the cost to refurbish an elevator may "better" the elevator but would not be significant to the building as a whole, so under the prior rules the cost could have been deducted as a repair. Under the new rules, the cost may be significant to the elevator system as a unit of property and therefore must be capitalized.

---

[13] Treasury Department 9636, *Guidance Regarding Deduction and Capitalization of Expenditures Related to Tangible Property*, October 21, 2013.

[14] The rules may require businesses to make internal changes to accounting practices and procedures for financial and tax accounting purposes. As described in Unit 2, many taxpayers will be required to file Form 3115, *Request for an Accounting Method Change,* to comply with the regulations.

Example: Curtis buys an apartment building in 2011 for $750,000. In 2014 he spends $12,000 to fix wiring in the electrical system. Under the old rules, the $12,000 cost likely would be considered a repair because it is relatively small compared to the overall cost of the building. Under the new rules, the electrical system is a separate structural component or building system. This means that the $12,000 must be compared with the cost of the electrical system alone, not the cost of the whole building. The cost is more significant in this context and thus is more likely to be deemed an improvement.

As the example illustrates, in some instances the regulations make it more difficult to classify costs as repairs and deduct them currently and thus more likely the costs will need to be capitalized. However, the regulations include several safe harbor rules that allow expensing in specific instances:

1. **De Minimis Expensing Safe Harbor #1:** This permits a business to deduct amounts expensed on its financial statements that do not exceed $5,000 per invoice or per item. The rule applies as long as the business has a written capitalization policy or procedure that provides for expensing items that cost less than specified amounts or have an economic useful life of 12 months or less.

2. **De Minimis Expensing Safe Harbor #2:** If the business does not have qualifying financial statements, it may be permitted to deduct items that cost up to $500 per invoice or per item.

3. **Small Taxpayer Safe Harbor for Real Property:** Taxpayers with gross receipts of $10 million or less can expense as repairs, rather than capitalize as improvements, amounts up to the lesser of $10,000 or 2% of the unadjusted basis of a building property, as long as the unadjusted basis is $1 million or less. This is an election the taxpayer must make on his tax return. Once made, the election is irrevocable.

4. **Routine Maintenance Safe Harbor:** This allows for deduction of routine maintenance costs that are required more than once within a ten-year period for buildings, or more than once within the applicable class life period for non-building properties.

Materials and Supplies: In addition to the safe harbor rules listed, materials and supplies (that are not inventory) may be deducted in the year the item is used or consumed in the business. "Material and supplies" are:

- Any unit of property that cost $200 or less.
- Any unit of property that has a useful life of 12 months or less.
- Spare parts acquired to maintain or repair a unit of property.

Example #1: In 2014, Rhonda purchases 50 scanners that cost $199 each for use by employees in her business. Each scanner is a separate unit of property. In 2014, 35 scanners are used and the remaining 15 scanners are stored. The 35 scanners are deductible in 2014, and the remaining 15 will be deductible in the year they are used.

Example #2: Rhonda pays $500 for a box of 10 toner cartridges to use as needed for printers in her business. The toner cartridges represent 10 units of property for $50 each; therefore, each cartridge is deductible as materials and supplies when used. Rhonda does not have qualifying financial statements. However, she makes the de minimis safe harbor election, so she deducts the full $500 in the year of purchase.

Example #3: Rhonda purchases a mold to create widgets for her business. The mold costs $6,000, but it is expected to be useful for only 12 months. Even though the mold is expensive, it is deductible when consumed in her business.

Other Changes to Basis of Business Property

Among the items that increase the basis of property are the following:

- The cost of extending service lines to the property
- Impact fees
- Legal fees, such as the costs of defending and perfecting title
- Zoning costs

Government assessments for items such as paving roads and sidewalks increase the value of a property, and therefore must be added to the property's basis. A business cannot deduct assessments as taxes, but can deduct charges for maintenance, repairs, or interest charges related to the improvements.

A business must decrease the basis of property by amounts that represent a recovery of the business's cost of the property. For example, rebates and casualty losses are among the items that decrease an asset's basis.

Example: Kristin buys a copier that costs $1,200 to use in her business. She sends in a rebate receipt and receives a $50 rebate from the manufacturer. The correct way to account for this rebate is to reduce the basis of the asset to $1,150 ($1,200 - $50).

Items that reduce the basis of property also include the following:

- Deductions for amortization, depreciation, section 179, and depletion (covered in Unit 8, *Depreciation of Business Assets)*
- Nontaxable corporate distributions
- Exclusion of subsidies for energy conservation measures

- Residential energy credits, vehicle credits, and the Investment Credit
- Certain canceled debt excluded from income
- Amounts received for easements

Casualty and Theft Losses

Deductible casualty and theft losses and related insurance reimbursements reduce the basis of property. A casualty is defined as the damage, destruction, or loss of property resulting from an identifiable event that is sudden, unexpected, or unusual.

Deductible losses related to business and income-producing property (such as rental property) are reported on Form 4684, *Casualties and Thefts*, and are deductible without regard to whether they exceed the $100 and 10% of AGI thresholds that apply for personal-use property.

Example: A fire at Ramon's home destroys his couch and coffee table, which are personal-use property, for a loss of $5,000. This loss must be reduced by $100, and Ramon can deduct the portion that exceeds 10% of his AGI. The same fire also damages a business asset, a laptop computer that he had brought home that day in order to catch up on his work. The computer is destroyed, resulting in a business casualty loss of $3,000 that is fully deductible.

A casualty loss is not deductible if the damage or destruction is caused by progressive deterioration due to normal wear and tear from weather conditions or insect damage.

If an entity has business property that is stolen or destroyed, the deductible loss is figured as follows:

The taxpayer's adjusted basis in the property
MINUS
Any salvage value
MINUS
Any insurance or other reimbursement received

Theft may involve taking money or property by the following means: blackmail, burglary, embezzlement, extortion, kidnapping for ransom, larceny, and robbery. The taking of property must be illegal under the state law where it happened, and it must have been done with criminal intent.

Example: Jeff owns a sports shop that sells memorabilia. Two years ago, Jeff purchased a signed Mike Trout baseball jersey for display for $150. The jersey was stolen in 2014. The FMV of the jersey was $1,000 just before it was stolen, and insurance did not cover the loss. Jeff's deductible theft loss is $150, equal to his basis in the jersey.

Casualty losses are generally deductible only in the tax year during which the casualty occurred, even if a business does not repair or replace the damaged property until a later year. Theft losses can be deducted only in the year the business discovers the property was stolen.

Insurance Reimbursements: If a business has insurance coverage for property that is lost or damaged, it must file a claim for reimbursement or it will not be able to deduct the loss. The portion of the loss that is not reimbursable by insurance, such as a deductible, is not subject to this rule.

Example: Howard and Gayle are partners and have a gourmet food truck that is used for business purposes. Howard has an accident that causes $2,350 in damage to the truck. He and Gayle pay the repair bill out-of-pocket so their business insurance costs will not increase. The insurance policy has a $500 deductible. Because the insurance would not cover the first $500 of the loss, this amount is their deductible casualty loss. The amount of their loss in excess of $500 is not deductible because they did not file an insurance claim.

A business that has a casualty or theft loss must decrease its adjusted basis in the property by any insurance or other reimbursement it receives and by any deductible loss.

A business increases its basis in the property by the amounts spent, whether with proceeds of an insurance reimbursement or otherwise, on repairs that restore the property to, or beyond, its pre-casualty condition.

Basis of Securities

The basis of stocks, bonds, and other securities is the purchase price plus any costs of purchase, such as commissions and recording or transfer fees. A taxpayer must keep track of the basis per share of all stock purchases and sales.

Example: In 2014, Yuen Corporation purchases 2,000 shares of Catalyst Corporation stock. The cost of the stock is $24,000, and Yuen Corporation pays a broker's fee of $550 on the purchase and transfer. Therefore, the basis of the stock is $24,550 ($24,000 + $550).

Events that occur after the purchase of the stock can require adjustments to the basis per share of stock. The original basis per share can be changed by events such as stock dividends, stock splits, and DRIP (dividend reinvestment plan) activity.

- Stock dividends involve the issuance of additional shares to current shareholders. The shareholder's total basis is unchanged but is spread over more shares, which decreases the basis per share.

- A stock split is similar to a stock dividend. For example, a two-for-one stock split increases the number of outstanding shares two-fold and decreases the value and the basis per share by half.

As with a stock dividend, the total basis remains the same after a stock split. For example, if a taxpayer has 100 shares with a cost of $50 per share, his basis is $5,000. Assuming a two-for-one stock split, the taxpayer now has 200 shares with a basis per share of $25, which still equals a total basis of $5,000.

Example: In 2014, Zollinger Partnership purchases 100 shares of Better Electronics for $11,000. There is an additional $200 in broker's commissions, so the original basis per share is $112 ([$11,000 + $200] ÷ 100). Later in 2014, Zollinger receives 40 additional shares of Better Electronics' stock as a nontaxable stock dividend. The $11,200 basis must now be spread over 140 shares (100 original shares plus the 40-share stock dividend). The adjusted stock basis is $80 per share ([$11,200 ÷ 140).

Basis Other Than Cost

In certain cases, the adjusted basis of an asset is determined from something other than cost. For example:

Property Received for Services: If a taxpayer receives property for his services, he must include the property's FMV in income. The amount included in income is the taxpayer's basis in the property. If the services were performed for a price agreed on beforehand, this price may be used as the fair market value of the property, as long as there is no evidence to the contrary.

When property is transferred in lieu of wages, the employer is entitled to deduct the property's fair market value at the time of the transfer and the same amount is taxable compensation for the employee. A gain or loss is realized if there is a difference between the fair market value and the adjusted basis of the property.

Bargain Purchases: A bargain purchase is a purchase of an item for less than its fair market value. If, as compensation for services, a taxpayer buys goods or other property at less than the FMV, the difference between the purchase price and the property's FMV must be included in his income. His basis in the property is its fair market value (the purchase price plus the amount included in income.)

Unit 7: Study Questions

1. Reggie purchases 25 printers for use in his business. The printers cost $90 each for a total of $2,250. What is the correct statement about how he should treat this purchase?

A. He must capitalize the total expense of $2,250.
B. He can deduct $90 for the current year.
C. He can choose to expense some of the printers and capitalize others to maximize profit.
D. He can deduct the cost of each printer in the year it is used or consumed in the business.

2. Jade purchases a warehouse for her business, but it is in such bad condition that she decides to demolish it and build a new one. The demolition costs $15,600. How must Jade report this cost on her tax return?

A. The cost for the demolition is added to the basis of the land where the original demolished structure was located.
B. The demolition may be deducted on her tax return on Schedule E.
C. The demolition cost may be deducted on her tax return on Schedule C.
D. The demolition cost must be amortized over 180 months.

3. What item would not be included in an asset's basis?

A. Sales tax.
B. Installation charges.
C. Recording fees.
D. Interest paid on a loan to purchase the asset.

4. Ian buys a building. He makes a $15,000 down payment in cash. He also assumes a mortgage of $180,000 on it and pays $1,000 of title fees and $2,000 of points. What is Ian's basis in the building?

A. $15,000.
B. $195,000.
C. $196,000.
D. $198,000.

5. Alex is having financial difficulties, so he sells his office building to Cheryl, a real estate investor, who plans to use it as a business rental property. Alex was liable for $5,000 in delinquent real estate taxes on the property, which Cheryl agrees to pay. How should Cheryl treat this transaction?

A. Cheryl cannot deduct these taxes as a current expense; she must add the amount to the basis of the property.
B. Cheryl can deduct these taxes as a current expense on her Schedule A.
C. Cheryl can deduct these taxes as a current expense on her Schedule E.
D. Cheryl can deduct these taxes as a current expense on her Schedule C.

6. All of the following items decrease the basis of property except:

A. Casualty or theft loss deductions and insurance reimbursements.
B. The cost of defending a title.
C. Depreciation.
D. Amortization.

7. Anya purchases a die-cut machine for her business that costs $8,000. It has a useful life of less than a year. Under the tangible property regulations, she:

A. Must capitalize the cost of the machine.
B. Can deduct the expense during the current tax year.
C. Can deduct the expense during the next tax year.
D. Must file Form 3115 for the current tax year before she is able to deduct any business expenses.

8. Irina owns a yarn store. In 2014, she has a loss of $14,000 of business inventory due to water damage from a storm. The loss is completely covered by insurance. However, Irina will not be reimbursed by her insurance company until 2015. How should she treat this loss?

A. She should claim the entire loss as a casualty loss in 2014 and then claim the income from the insurance company reimbursement in 2015.
B. She must reduce the amount of her inventory loss in 2014. For 2015, she must include the insurance reimbursement as income.
C. She does not need to report this loss on her 2014 tax return, since she knows she will receive a reimbursement within a short period of time.
D. She must reduce her cost of goods sold in 2014 to reflect the loss and then claim the reimbursement as income in 2015.

9. How does a stock split affect the basis of securities?

A. There is no effect.
B. It increases the basis of stock.
C. It decreases the basis of stock.
D. It decreases the basis of a share of stock but does not affect the total basis of the stock.

10. Under the tangible property regulations, what are the categories for determining what constitutes an "improvement" to property rather than a repair?

A. Betterment, restoration, or adaptation.
B. Prolonging life and creating value.
C. Renovation, amelioration, or restoration.
D. Enhancement and repair.

11. Franco purchases 50 shares of Canine Country stock for $3,500. He pays a broker's fee of $100. He later receives 40 additional shares of Canine Country stock as a stock dividend. The following year, the company declares a two-for-one stock split. Calculate the total basis of Franco's Canine Country stock and his per share basis:

A. Stock basis: $3,500; per share basis: $38.88.
B. Stock basis: $3,500; per share basis: $19.44.
C. Stock basis: $3,600; per share basis: $20.
D. Stock basis: $3,600; per share basis: $40.

12. Priscilla's Pastries, a sole proprietorship, bought a building for $250,000 of cash in March 2014. Priscilla paid the title company $13,000 in settlement fees to purchase the property. She also assumed an existing mortgage of $35,000 on the property. Legal fees of $9,500 were incurred in a title dispute with the former owner in April 2014. The title was finally transferred to Priscilla in May 2014. Property taxes in the amount of $2,600 were incurred on the property after ownership was transferred. What is Priscilla's basis in the building in December 2014?

A. $250,000.
B. $285,000.
C. $307,500.
D. $310,100.

13. A taxpayer does not have qualifying financial statements. Under the de minimis expensing safe harbor rule, he can deduct items that cost up to _____ per invoice or item.

A. $200.
B. $500.
C. $5,000.
D. $10,000.

14. Arrowhead Model Builders is constructing a custom home. Calculate the basis of the property from the following information:

Land purchase price	$125,000
Construction loan	40,000
Points on construction loan	3,000
Tear-down of existing home	20,000
Clearing of brush	10,000
Construction workers' wages	50,000
Construction materials	300,000

A. $227,000.
B. $505,000.
C. $548,000.
D. $545,000.

15. A hailstorm damages a van owned by Marjorie, a sole proprietor who offers mobile chiropractic services. The van's basis is $25,000, and her insurance company reimburses her $4,000 for the hail damage. Marjorie decides to replace the cracked windshield at a cost of $500 and pockets the rest of the insurance money. What is the adjusted basis of her van?

A. $21,500.
B. $28,500.
C. $29,000.
D. $19,500.

16. Chan Delivery Services is having cash-flow difficulties, so it transfers a pickup truck to Bonnie, an employee, in lieu of wages. The company owes Bonnie $7,000 of wages. At the time of the transfer, the truck had a fair market value of $7,000 and an adjusted basis to Chan Delivery of $5,500. How should the company report this transaction?

A. Wage expense of $7,000.
B. Wage expense of $5,500.
C. Wage expense of $2,500.
D. Wage expense of $7,000 and gain on sale of $1,500.

17. In 2014 Vaughn Partnership provides legal services to Andrews Cellular. Andrews Cellular then becomes insolvent. In lieu of payment, Vaughn Partnership accepts a set of gold coins with a fair market value of $5,000 and an electric scooter with a fair market value of $2,000 and an adjusted basis of $1,000. What amount of income must Vaughn Partnership report for this transaction?

A. $7,000.
B. $6,000.
C. $8,000.
D. $5,000.

Unit 8: Depreciation

More Reading:
Publication 946, *How to Depreciate Property*

As discussed in Unit 7, the costs of business assets and improvements generally must be capitalized. They are not currently deductible, unless they qualify for the section 179 deduction or certain specified safe harbor exceptions. Instead, these costs may be recognized as depreciation or amortization expense over lives assigned to individual assets.

Example: Better Produce, Inc. is a canning company that processes fruits and vegetables. In 2014, an older canning machine ceases to function properly. Better Produce has the option to purchase a new machine for $500,000, or completely rebuild its old machine, which will extend its useful life for another five years. Better Produce chooses to rebuild the machine at a cost of $125,000. The $125,000 cost must be capitalized and depreciated over its useful life, which in this case is five years.

Definition: Depreciation is an annual allowance for the wear and tear, deterioration, or obsolescence of an asset. Tax depreciation is based on the original, historical cost of the asset and is not indexed for inflation.

The cost of land and certain land improvements cannot be depreciated. Most other types of tangible property, such as buildings, machinery, vehicles, furniture, and equipment, are depreciable. Likewise, certain intangible property, such as patents, copyrights, and computer software, is amortizable.

In order to be depreciated or amortized, an asset must meet all the following requirements:

- The taxpayer generally must own the property. However, taxpayers may depreciate capital improvements for property they lease (for example, a fence that is built on property that the business leases from another party).
- The taxpayer must use the property in business or in an income-producing activity. If a taxpayer uses the property for both business and personal use, he can only deduct an amount of depreciation based on the business-use percentage.
- The property must have a determinable useful life of more than one year.

The property ceases to be depreciable when the business has fully recovered its cost or when it sells or retires the property from service, whichever happens first.

Depreciation Rules: In order to properly depreciate an asset, a taxpayer must determine the following:

- The depreciable basis of the property
- The depreciation method for the property
- The class life (which is representative of the asset's useful life)
- Whether the asset is listed property
- Whether the taxpayer elects to expense any portion of the asset
- Whether the taxpayer qualifies for any bonus first year depreciation

Nondepreciable Assets: The following assets are not depreciable:

- Property with a useful life of one year or less
- Property placed in service and disposed of in the same year
- Equipment that is used to build capital improvements
- Section 197 intangibles such as copyrights and patents, which must be amortized, not depreciated.

Example: Natalie is a self-employed accountant who must purchase new payroll software every year. She cannot depreciate the software but may instead deduct its cost as a business expense since the item has a useful life of only one year.

Reporting Depreciation: A taxpayer must use Form 4562, *Depreciation and Amortization* to:

- Claim deductions for depreciation and amortization;
- Make an election under section 179 to currently expense certain depreciable property; and
- Provide information on the business/investment use of automobiles and other listed property.

Depreciation begins when a taxpayer places property in service in a trade or business or for the production of income.

Example: Donald buys a machine for his business that is delivered on December 20, 2014. However, the machine is not installed and operational until January 12, 2015. It is not considered placed in service until 2015, and the first depreciation expense deduction can be claimed in 2015. If the machine had been ready and available for use when it was delivered, it would have been considered placed in service in 2014 even if it were not actually used until 2015.

> **Example:** On June 23, Sue bought a house to use as residential rental property. She made several repairs and had it ready for rent in September. At that time, she began to advertise the home for rent in the local newspaper. Sue did not find a tenant until November 10. She can begin to depreciate the rental property in September and start taking other rental expenses because the property is considered placed in service when it is ready and available for rent.

Salvage Value: An asset cannot be depreciated below its salvage (or scrap) value. Salvage value is the asset's estimated FMV at the end of its useful life. Salvage value is affected both by how a business uses the property and how long it uses it.

If it is the business's policy to dispose of property that is still in good operating condition, the salvage value may be relatively large. If the business's policy is to use property until it is no longer usable, its salvage value may be zero.

> **Example:** Cooper Trucking purchases a new delivery truck in 2014 for $125,000. The MACRS class life of the truck is five years. At the end of five years, Cooper Trucking estimates it will sell the used delivery truck at auction for $30,000, so it uses this amount as salvage value. The basis of the truck is $125,000, but the basis for depreciation is $95,000 ($125,000 - $30,000), since the business expects to recover $30,000 at the end of the asset's useful life.

Depreciation Methods

Once a business chooses a depreciation method for an asset, the business must generally use the same method for the life of the asset.

Straight-Line Depreciation: This is the simplest method. To use the straight-line method, a business must first determine the asset's basis, salvage value, and estimated useful life. If the asset has a salvage value, it is subtracted from the basis. The balance is the total depreciation expense deduction the business can take over the useful life of the property. If an asset originally cost $200, has an estimated salvage value of zero, and a five-year recovery period, the straight-line depreciation allowance would be $40 ($200 ÷ 5) each year for five years.

> **Straight-line Depreciation = (Cost minus Salvage Value) ÷ Useful Life**

A business may switch to the straight-line method at any time during the useful life of the property without IRS consent. However, after a business changes to straight-line, it cannot change back to any other method for a period of ten years without written permission from the IRS.

Example: On April 1, 2014, the Redstone Corporation purchases a computer system for $40,000. The system has a five-year life. There is no salvage value. Depreciation is calculated as follows:

Depreciation for 2014 = ($40,000 ÷ 5 years) × (9 months ÷ 12) = $6,000.
Depreciation for 2015 = ($40,000 ÷ 5 years) × (12 ÷ 12) = $8,000.

The Double-Declining Balance Method: This method uses a flat percentage depreciation rate over the life of the asset. For example, if five years is the asset's life, the double-declining balance method has a depreciation rate of [2 ÷ 5], or twice the straight-line depreciation rate. Instead of spreading the cost of the asset evenly over its life, this method expenses the asset by applying a constant rate to the declining balance of the asset, which results in declining depreciation expense each successive period.

The logic for the double-declining balance method is that there should be a greater deduction in the earlier years when the asset is more productive.

Example: For an asset that originally cost $200 and has a five-year life, double-declining balance depreciation is $80 = ([2 ÷ 5]× $200) in the first year; $48 = ([2 ÷ 5]×[$200 - $80]) in the second year; $28.80 = ([2 ÷ 5]×[$200 - $80 - $48]) in the third year; and so on.

Modified Accelerated Cost Recovery System (MACRS)

The modified accelerated cost recovery system (MACRS) is the depreciation method generally used for most tangible property.

Under MACRS, depreciable assets are divided into nine separate classes that dictate the number of years over which their cost will be recovered. Each MACRS class has a schedule that specifies the percentage of the asset's cost that is depreciated each year. For example, computers are depreciated over five years, and office furniture is depreciated over seven years.

Real property is depreciated using the straight-line method, with an equal amount of expense each year. Nonresidential real property, such as office buildings, shopping malls, and factories, is depreciated over a 39-year recovery period. Residential buildings, such as apartment complexes and residential rentals, are depreciated over a 27.5-year period.

The depreciation calculations allocate deductions of the asset's cost over a recovery period roughly consistent with the asset's estimated useful economic life.

MACRS Class Life Table

Property Class	Asset Type
3-year property	Certain tractor units; race horses over two years old; qualified rent-to-own property.
5-year property	Computers; office machinery; automobiles, taxis, buses, and trucks; breeding cattle and dairy cattle; appliances, carpets, and furniture used in residential retail activity; certain geothermal, solar, and wind property.
7-year property	Office furniture and fixtures; agricultural machinery and equipment; any other property that does not have a designated class life.
10-year property	Vessels and water transportation equipment; trees or vines bearing fruit or nuts; single purpose agricultural or horticultural structures.
15-year property	Improvements to land such as fences, roads, and bridges; municipal wastewater treatment plants; qualified restaurant and retail improvement property; qualified leasehold improvement property.
20-year property	Certain municipal sewers; farm buildings (other than single purpose agricultural or horticultural structures).
25-year property	Certain municipal sewers; water utility property.
27.5-year property	Residential rental property, if more than 80% of its gross rental income is from dwelling units.
39-year property	Section 1250 nonresidential real property, such as office buildings, stores, and warehouses.

Section 179 Deduction

The section 179 deduction is a special allowance that allows a business to elect to take a full deduction for the cost of new or used property in the first year it is placed in service, rather than depreciating it over its useful life. To qualify for the section 179 deduction, the property must meet all the following requirements:

- It must be eligible property.
- It must be acquired for business use (and used more than 50% for business in the year placed in service).
- It must have been acquired by purchase.
- It must not have been purchased from a related party, including a spouse, ancestors, or lineal descendants.

Eligible property generally includes the following:

- Tangible personal property, such as machinery and equipment
- Property contained in or attached to a building (other than structural components), such as refrigerators, grocery store counters, office equipment, printing presses, testing equipment, and signs
- Gasoline storage tanks and pumps at retail service stations
- Livestock, including horses, cattle, hogs, sheep, goats, and mink and other furbearing animals
- Off-the-shelf computer software
- Single purpose agricultural or horticultural property
- Storage facilities
- Qualified real property (as described below)

The section 179 deduction may not exceed taxable business income for the year, calculated without regard to the section 179 deduction itself and certain other items. However, an amount disallowed due to this limitation may be carried over for an unlimited number of years.

The deduction can be elected for individual qualifying assets, up to a maximum of $500,000 for 2014. However, to the extent the cost of qualifying section 179 property placed in service by the taxpayer exceeds $2 million, the maximum is reduced on a dollar-for-dollar basis, and eliminated if the total cost of qualifying property is at least $2.5 million.

> **Example:** In 2014, Ashby Corporation purchases refurbished manufacturing equipment for $2.1 million. The cost of the equipment is $100,000 more than the $2 million limit, so Ashby Corporation must reduce its section 179 deduction to $400,000 ($500,000 - $100,000). The remaining cost basis of $1.7 million ($2.1 million - $400,000 deducted under section 179) can be recovered using regular depreciation methods.

For partnerships, the section 179 limits described above apply to both the partnership and to each individual partner. The partnership determines its deduction subject to these limits, and then allocates the deduction among the partners. The partner considers the amounts allocated based upon his interest in the partnership and from any other sources in relation to the same limits.

Qualified Real Property: Businesses generally cannot deduct the costs of real property under section 179. However, a special provision for 2014 allows businesses to use up to $250,000 of the $500,000 limit described above for costs of qualified real property (QRP).

This provision applies only to the following:

- Qualified leasehold improvement property
- Qualified restaurant property (such as renovation of a restaurant building)

- Qualified retail improvement property (such as an interior upgrade of a retail clothing store)

Example: Armando owns an Italian restaurant. In 2014, he renovates the interior by upgrading the booths and remodeling the kitchen at a cost of $260,000. He also purchases a computer for use in his business at a cost of $5,000. Therefore, Armando has the following qualifying expenses for the section 179 deduction:

Computer:	$5,000
Qualified real property:	$260,000
Total asset purchases in 2014: $265,000	

Since the limit for expensing QRP under section 179 is $250,000, Armando may only expense $250,000 of the renovation costs. However, he may still take the section 179 deduction for the full cost of the computer, since the limit for other qualifying property is $500,000. Armando's allowable section 179 deduction is therefore limited to $255,000 ($5,000 computer + $250,000 of QRP). The excess amount of $10,000 may be depreciated over the useful life applicable for this type of real property.

Trade-in Property: If a business buys qualifying property with cash and a trade-in, its depreciable basis for purposes of the section 179 deduction includes only the cash portion of the purchase price.

Example: Fleet Feet, a retail athletic shoe store, traded two wood displays with a total adjusted basis of $680 for a new glass display that cost $1,320. Fleet Feet received an $800 trade-in allowance for the old displays and paid an additional $520 of cash for the new glass display. The shop also traded a used van with an adjusted basis of $4,500 for a new van costing $9,000. Fleet Feet received a $4,800 trade-in allowance on the used van and paid $4,200 of cash for the new van. Only the portion of the new property's basis paid with cash qualifies for the section 179 deduction. Therefore, Fleet Feet's qualifying costs for the section 179 deduction are $4,720 ($520 + $4,200).

Bonus Depreciation

If the cost of business property cannot immediately be deducted as a section 179 expense, a business may elect to take bonus depreciation for certain types of new property. This provision allows a business to write off 50% of certain property costs in the first year, with the remaining cost depreciated over the asset's useful life. Applicable section 179 deductions are generally used first, followed by bonus depreciation, unless the business has an insufficient level of taxable income.

Example: Murray purchases a machine for his business that costs $600,000. He claims $500,000 of the cost as a section 179 deduction. For the additional amount of $100,000, he claims 50% bonus depreciation. The remaining $50,000 cost of the machine must be depreciated over its useful life.

The bonus depreciation allowance generally applies to tangible personal property with a recovery period of 20 years or less, as well as to certain buildings and leasehold improvements, office equipment, and purchased computer software.

Note: The property must be new and in original use condition (unlike the requirement for section 179 deductions, which are allowed for both new and used property.) Bonus depreciation is also not subject to the same $2 million phase-out as the section 179 deduction.

Listed Property

Definition: Listed property is a specific class of depreciable property that is subject to special tax rules because it is often used for both business and personal purposes.

The IRS includes the following as listed property:

- Any passenger vehicle weighing under 6,000 pounds and any other property used for transportation
- Property used for entertainment, recreation, or amusement such as photographic or video-recording equipment
- Certain computers and related peripheral equipment. Computer equipment used exclusively at a business location (including a qualified home office) is not considered listed property.

If an item is used for both business and personal purposes, deductions for depreciation and section 179 are limited to the percentage of business use. Further, if business use is not more than 50%, section 179 deductions and bonus depreciation allowances are not allowed, and depreciation must be calculated using the straight-line method.

Example: In 2014, Eleanor buys and places in service a new computer that costs $4,000. She uses the computer 80% for her business and 20% for personal purposes. She can deduct $3,200 under section 179 for the business portion of the cost (80% × $4,000).

The IRS no longer categorizes cellular telephones as listed property.

Heavy Sports Utility Vehicle Exception: A taxpayer cannot elect to expense under section 179 more than $25,000 of the cost of any heavy sport utility vehicle (SUV) and certain other vehicles placed in service during the tax year. This rule applies to vehicles weighing between 6,000 and 14,000 pounds. Ambulances, hearses, taxis, transport vans, clearly marked emergency vehicles, and other qualified nonpersonal use vehicles are not listed property and are excluded from the $25,000 limit.

Section 280F Depreciation Limits: For certain other passenger vehicles weighing less than 6,000 pounds and used more than 50% for business purposes, the total depreciation deduction is also limited, as outlined under section 280F. The IRS releases guidance each year indicating the depreciation limits for each category of vehicles, adjusted for inflation. In 2014, the limits apply to any passenger automobiles (other than trucks or vans) that cost over $15,800 and trucks and vans that qualify as passenger automobiles that cost over $17,300.

Amortization

Amortization is used to deduct the cost or basis of an intangible asset over its estimated life. With the exception of off-the-shelf computer software, intangible assets generally are not eligible for section 179 deductions. The basis of an intangible asset is usually the cost to buy or create it.

Definition: Intangible property is property that has value, but it cannot be seen or touched.

Examples of intangible assets include goodwill, patents, copyrights, trademarks, trade names, franchises, and favorable relationships with customers or suppliers that are carried over from an acquired business.

A taxpayer may amortize certain start-up costs for purchasing an active trade or business. These include only the investigative costs that help the taxpayer decide whether to purchase the business. Costs incurred in an attempt to purchase a specific business are capital costs that cannot be amortized.

Certain intangible assets, including the preceding examples, are designated as section 197 intangibles and must be amortized over a 15-year period (180 months). Another example is the cost of a covenant not to compete executed in connection with the acquisition of a trade or business. As a section 197 intangible asset, this cost would be amortized over 15 years, even though the covenant agreement may be in place for a shorter period.

Example: Heather is a podiatrist. Another podiatrist is retiring, so she is purchasing his business for $1 million. The practice has $750,000 of tangible assets, including medical equipment and office furnishings. The remainder of the purchase price ($250,000) is attributed to goodwill, which Heather must amortize over 15 years. Her goodwill deduction is $16,667 a year ($250,000 ÷ 15).

Depletion

Depletion is similar in concept to depreciation, and is the method of cost recovery for mining and agricultural activities. Depletion refers to the exhaustion of a natural resource as a result of production, such as by mining, quarrying, or cutting (of timber). Mineral property, timber, and natural gas are all examples of natural resources that are subject to the deduction for depletion. There are two ways of figuring depletion:

- Cost depletion
- Percentage depletion

Some businesses employ cost depletion at the outset of operations when a large number of units of the deposit are extracted and sold, and then convert to percentage depletion later when percentage depletion yields a more sizable deduction.

Cost Depletion: This method allocates the cost of a natural resource over the total anticipated volume to yield cost depletion per unit (expressed in tons, barrels, etc.) A depletion deduction is then allowed each year based on the units exploited.

After a business determines the property's basis, estimates the total recoverable units, and knows the number of units sold during the tax year, it can calculate the cost depletion deduction as follows:

Divide the property's basis for depletion by estimated total recoverable units =
Rate per unit
Multiply the rate per unit by actual units sold =
Cost depletion deduction
Example: In 2014, Brian buys a timber farm, and he estimates the timber can produce 300,000 units when cut. At the time of purchase, the adjusted basis of the timber is $24,000. Brian cuts and sells 27,000 units. Brian's depletion rate for each unit is $.08 ($24,000 ÷ 300,000). His deduction for depletion in 2014 is $2,160 (27,000 × $.08).

Percentage Depletion: Under this method, a flat percentage of gross income from the property is taken as the depletion deduction. Percentage depletion may not be used for timber and its use for oil and gas properties is subject to strict limits.

To figure percentage depletion, the business multiplies a certain percentage, specified for each mineral, by gross income from the property during the year. The percentage depletion deduction generally cannot be more than 50% (100% for oil and gas property) of taxable income from the property, calculated before the depletion deduction and the domestic production activities deduction (DPAD).

Unit 8: Study Questions

1. Bonus depreciation is taken:

A. After a section 179 deduction is taken.
B. Before a section 179 deduction is taken.
C. Before section 179 and regular MACRS deductions are taken.
D. After section 179 and regular MACRS deductions are taken.

2. The Friendship Spirit Partnership bought the Andrews Brothers Partnership. Goodwill and a covenant not to compete associated with the purchase were valued at $100,000. What is the number of years over which these intangible assets can be amortized?

A. Five years.
B. Ten years.
C. 15 years.
D. 25 years.

3. Which of the following would not qualify for a depletion deduction?

A. Oil well.
B. Timber.
C. Diamond mine.
D. Gasoline refinery.

4. Levi owns a convenience store. He purchases two computers from his grandfather and places both in service in 2014 as part of a bona fide business transaction. The computers cost $750 each. Which of the following statements is correct?

A. Levi can claim a section 179 deduction for the computers.
B. Levi can claim regular MACRS depreciation on the computers.
C. Levi is not allowed to depreciate the computers since they were purchased from a related party. But he can claim a section 179 deduction for them.
D. Levi can claim either section 179 or bonus depreciation on the computers.

5. Which of the following types of business property qualifies for the section 179 deduction?

A. A delivery truck.
B. A business building.
C. A residential rental property.
D. A patent.

6. Mary purchases a new computer for $1,100. She uses the property 75% for her business and 25% for personal purposes. What is Mary's section 179 deduction?

A. $0.
B. $275.
C. $825.
D. $1,100.

7. Lou is a sole proprietor who buys a cellular phone for $720 in 2014. Based on his phone records, Lou uses the cell phone 45% for business use and 55% for personal use. What is Lou's section 179 deduction for 2014?

A. $0.
B. $324.
C. $396.
D. $720.

8. Kerman Corporation is a calendar-year, cash-basis corporation that specializes in constructing office buildings. Kerman bought a truck on December 1, 2014 that had to be modified for use in the business. The truck is 100% business-use. Kerman accepted delivery of the modified truck on January 10, 2015. The truck was first used for its intended purpose on January 23, 2015. As of what date can Kerman start depreciating the truck?

A. December 1, 2014.
B. January 10, 2015.
C. January 23, 2015.
D. Never.

9. Which of the following property is a business not able to depreciate?

A. Property placed in service and disposed of in the same year.
B. Fruit trees.
C. Machinery.
D. Buildings.

10. Which of the following vehicles is considered listed property for tax purposes?

A. An ambulance.
B. A passenger automobile weighing 6,000 pounds or less.
C. A taxi.
D. A marked police car.

11. In 2014, Vanner Corporation placed in service section 179 property with a total cost of $2,025,000. The corporation's taxable income in 2014 was $600,000. What is Vanner's allowable section 179 deduction for 2014?

A. $0.
B. $475,000.
C. $500,000.
D. $600,000.

12. TJ buys and places in service professional video-recording equipment. He pays $15,000 of cash and receives a $3,000 trade-in allowance for used video equipment. Both the old and the new video-recording equipment were used 90% for business and 10% for personal purposes. His allowable section 179 deduction is:

A. $16,200.
B. $13,500.
C. $12,600.
D. $15,000.

13. The maximum section 179 expense a business can elect to deduct for qualified real property placed in service in 2014 is:

A. $179,000.
B. $250,000.
C. $500,000.
D. $2 million.

14. Lucy and Jessica are equal partners in a restaurant. In 2014, they purchase a new $30,000 pizza oven for the restaurant and want to take the section 179 deduction for the full cost of the oven. The partnership's ordinary income before the section 179 deduction is $25,000. There were no other qualifying section 179 purchases during the year. What is the amount of section 179 deduction that Lucy can deduct on her individual tax return?

A. $0.
B. $6,000.
C. $12,500.
D. $15,000.

15. Using MACRS, what is the recovery period for depreciating a commercial office building?

A. 20 years.
B. 25 years.
C. 27.5 years.
D. 39 years.

Unit 9: Disposition of Business Assets

More Reading:
Publication 544, *Sales and Other Dispositions of Assets*

There are many different ways that a business can dispose of an asset. A business may recognize a gain or loss for tax purposes if it:

- Sells an asset for cash
- Exchanges property for other property
- Receives payment by a tenant for the cancellation of a lease (treated as if it were a sale of the property)
- Receives property to satisfy a debt
- Abandons property
- Loses property or has it damaged as a result of casualty or theft (and if it receives a related insurance reimbursement for such a loss)

A taxpayer may fully depreciate an asset until its adjusted basis is zero, but continue to use the asset thereafter. If an asset is sold or otherwise disposed of, its adjusted basis is compared to any amounts received to determine whether there is a gain or loss.

The treatment of gains or losses reportable for tax purposes is dependent upon whether they are classified as capital gains and losses or as ordinary income (and whether the capital gains and losses are long-term or short-term). For individual taxpayers, capital gains may be subject to more favorable capital gains tax rates. To properly report the disposition of an asset, a taxpayer must determine whether it is a capital asset, a noncapital asset, or a section 1231 asset.

Gains and losses on dispositions of business assets are generally reported on Form 4797, *Sales of Business Property*.

Capital Assets: Capital assets include personal-use assets; collectibles; and investment property such as stocks, bonds, and other securities (unless held by a professional securities dealer).

Example: Jim owns 15 mechanical toy banks, which he collects as a hobby. He is not a professional dealer. Jim's mechanical banks are considered capital assets.

A gain from the disposition of personal-use property is a capital gain, but a loss is generally not deductible, except for certain casualty losses.

Noncapital Assets: Assets used in a trade or business or as rental property are noncapital assets, including the following:

- Inventory or any similar property held for sale to customers

- Depreciable property used in a business, even if it is fully depreciated
- Real property used in a trade or business, such as a commercial building or a residential rental
- Self-produced copyrights, transcripts, manuscripts, drawings, photographs, or artistic compositions
- Accounts receivable or notes receivable acquired by a business
- Stocks and bonds held by professional securities dealers
- Business supplies
- Commodities and derivative financial instruments

> **Example:** In February 2013, Ines purchases a black-and-white copy machine for use in her business. In March 2014, she decides she needs a color copier instead. Ines sells the used black-and-white copier for $3,000. The copier is a depreciable business asset, so it is treated as a noncapital asset.

Section 1231 Assets: Section 1231 assets include certain business (noncapital) assets that have been held for more than one year, as well as certain business and investment property disposed of in involuntary conversions.

The tax code gives special treatment to transactions involving disposition of section 1231 assets. If the taxpayer has a net loss from all section 1231 transactions, the loss is treated as ordinary loss. If the section 1231 transactions result in a net gain, the gain is generally treated as capital gain (except for depreciation recapture, which is taxed as ordinary income, as discussed below).

> **Example:** Philip owns an antique vase that he purchased at auction two years ago. He also owns a residential rental property that he purchased three years ago and two vehicles. One is a pizza delivery van he bought five years ago and uses exclusively in his restaurant business. The second is his personal-use SUV that he uses for commuting and everyday errands. Phillip's assets are categorized as follows:
>   1. Antique vase: A capital asset, because it is a collectible
>   2. Residential rental property: Section 1231 (rental property held over one year)
>   3. Pizza delivery van: Section 1231 (business property held over one year)
>   4. SUV: A capital asset, because it is a personal-use vehicle

Gain or loss on the following transactions is subject to section 1231 treatment:

1. **Sale or exchange of cattle and horses:** They must be used for draft, breeding, dairy, or sporting purposes and held for 24 months or longer.

2. **Sale or exchange of other livestock:** Other livestock includes hogs, mules, sheep, goats, donkeys, and other fur-bearing animals. They must be used for draft, breeding, dairy, or sporting purposes and held for 12 months or longer.
3. **Sale or exchange of depreciable (or amortizable) property:** Business property that is held for more than one year. Examples include machinery and trucks, as well as amortizable section 197 intangibles such as patents or copyrights.
4. **Sale or exchange of business real estate:** The property must be used in a business activity and held for more than one year. Examples include barns and office buildings.
5. **Sale or exchange of unharvested crops:** The crops and land must be sold, exchanged, or involuntarily converted at the same time and to the same person, and the land must have been held longer than one year. Growing crops sold with a leasehold on the land, even if sold to the same person in a single transaction, are not included.

Example: Six years ago, Mezuel, Inc. purchased a computer for $10,000. The company sells the used computer this year for $700. Mezuel had depreciated the computer down to its salvage value, which was estimated at $1,000. The company has a loss of $300 on the sale of the computer ($1,000 salvage value minus $700 sale price). The computer is a section 1231 asset and the loss is an ordinary loss.

The sale, exchange, or involuntary conversion of inventory is not a section 1231 transaction, even if the inventory has been held for more than one year.

Example: Harwell Company manufactures shipping containers. Harwell has owned land and a building that houses its manufacturing operations for 15 years. The land and the building are therefore section 1231 assets, because they are used in a business and have been held for more than one year. Harwell also has unsold shipping containers in inventory. Inventory is not a section 1231 asset.

The sale of a copyright, literary, musical, or artistic composition is not a section 1231 transaction if a taxpayer's personal efforts created the property, or if it was received as a gift from a previous owner whose personal efforts created it. The sale of such property results in ordinary income.

Example: Debbie is a self-employed writer who reports her income on Schedule C. She writes and publishes a popular crockpot cookbook. A few years later, Debbie sells the copyright of her manuscript to a publisher. This is not a section 1231 transaction, because the copyright was self-created, and it must be reported as ordinary income.

Depreciation Recapture

Depreciation recapture may be required when a business sells previously depreciated or amortized property at a gain. All or a portion of the gain attributable to depreciation (that would otherwise be treated as capital gain) may need to be recaptured as ordinary income. The balance of the gain in excess of the recaptured depreciation is treated as capital gain.

Example: Mort runs a dairy farm as a calendar-year sole proprietorship. In February 2012, Mort buys a tractor (five-year property) that costs $10,000. MACRS depreciation deductions for the tractor are $1,500 in 2012 and $2,550 in 2013 (based upon MACRS table A-14 for 150% declining balance depreciation using a half-year convention). Mort sells the tractor in May 2014 for $7,000. The MACRS deduction in 2014 is $893 (½ of $1,785). The gain on the sale of the tractor that must be treated as ordinary income is figured as follows:

Original purchase price	$10,000
MACRS depreciation deductions ($1,500 + $2,550 + $893)	(4,943)
Adjusted basis	5,057
Amount received in the sale	7,000
Gain realized ($7,000 - $5,057)	**$1,943**

The realized gain is less than the amount of depreciation subject to recapture, so the entire amount is treated as ordinary income.

In determining depreciable recapture for property sold at a gain, there is a critical distinction between two types of property: section 1245 and section 1250. For section 1245 property, any gain attributable to previous depreciation deductions is taxed as ordinary income. For section 1250 property, the depreciation recapture is limited to the portion of previously deducted depreciation in excess of deductions that would have been taken if computed using the straight-line method.

Section 1245 property includes:

1. Personal (tangible or intangible) property, or
2. Other tangible property (not including buildings) that is depreciable and that is:
   a. Used as an integral part of certain specified activities (manufacturing, production, extraction, or furnishing transportation, communications, electrical energy, gas, water, or sewage disposal services), or
   b. A facility used for the bulk storage of fungible commodities.

> **Definition:** A **fungible good or asset** is one that is essentially interchangeable with other goods or assets of the same type, such as a specific grade of a particular commodity. Examples of highly fungible commodities are crude oil and wheat.

A grain silo is considered section 1245 property rather than section 1250 property, even if it is attached permanently to the land. Storage structures for oil and gas and other minerals are considered section 1245 property.

> **Example:** Several years ago, Crystal purchased a used binding machine for $1,000 for her business. She has claimed $400 of depreciation on the machine. In 2014, Crystal sells the machine for $1,100. Her gain is as follows:
>
> | | |
> |---|---|
> | Sale price of the machine: | $1,100 |
> | Minus adjusted basis ($1,000 - $400): | 600 |
> | **Crystal's gain on the sale of the machine:** | **$500** |
>
> A portion of the gain is ordinary income ($400 of depreciation recapture for section 1245 property), and the remainder of $100 is long-term capital gain.

Section 1250 property generally consists of buildings (including their structural components), most other permanent structures, and land improvements of general use and purpose.

Examples of section 1250 property include residential rental property, factory buildings, and office buildings. Since buildings are generally depreciated using the straight-line method, taxpayers usually receive more favorable treatment of depreciation recapture for section 1250 property.

> **Example:** Maeve has owned an apartment building for almost 20 years. She originally purchased the building for $2.5 million. After taking straight-line depreciation deductions, her adjusted basis in 2014 is $800,000 and she sells the property for $4.5 million. Her gain is as follows:
>
> | | |
> |---|---|
> | Sale price | $4,500,000 |
> | Minus adjusted basis | 800,000 |
> | **Gain on sale** | **$3,700,000** |
>
> Because the building is section 1250 property and Maeve has only taken straight-line depreciation, there is no depreciation recapture, and the entire amount of the gain is treated as long-term capital gain. Had the building been depreciated using an accelerated method, as was more common prior to the adoption of the current MACRS system, a portion of the prior year depreciation deductions might have been subject to recapture.

Installment Sales

An installment sale involves a disposition of property in which the seller receives at least a portion of the sales proceeds during a year subsequent to the year of the sale. The resulting gain is typically reported using the installment method. If a business elects out of using the installment method, it must report the entire gain in the year of the sale, even if it does not receive the remaining proceeds until later years.

Each payment received on an installment sale transaction may include the following components:
- Return of the seller's adjusted basis in the property
- Gain on the sale
- Interest income (attributable to financing the sale over a period of time)

The taxpayer must calculate a gross profit percentage, representing the ratio of the gain on the sale (numerator) to the total proceeds to be paid less any interest income (denominator). The denominator will also equal the total of the gain and the return of the seller's adjusted basis in the property. Each year, including the year of sale, the total payments received less the portion attributable to interest is multiplied by the gross profit percentage to determine the portion of the gain that must be recognized.

Note: A taxpayer's gain, or gross profit, is the amount by which the selling price exceeds the adjusted basis in the property sold. The gross profit percentage is generally calculated by dividing the gross profit from the sale by the selling price. You may be required to understand how to calculate gross profit percentage for both Parts 1 and 2 of the EA exam.
Example: A business sells a machine for a price of $6,000, with a gross profit of $1,500, and it will receive payments totaling $6,000 plus interest over four years. The gross profit percentage is 25% ($1,500 ÷ $6,000). After subtracting the applicable interest portion from each payment, the business will apply the gross profit percentage to each installment, including any down payment, and report the resulting amount as installment sale income for each tax year in which it receives payments. The remainder of each payment is the tax-free return of the machine's adjusted basis.

The gain is reported on Form 6252, *Installment Sale Income.*

If the arrangement is modified at a later date or the full amount of the sale price is not paid, the resulting gross profit on the sale may also change.

Example: In 2014, the Greenbelt Partnership sells land under an installment sale. The land has a basis of $40,000, and the sale price is $100,000. Therefore, the gross profit is $60,000. Greenbelt receives a $20,000 down payment and the buyer's note for $80,000. The note provides for four annual payments of $20,000 each, plus 8% interest, beginning in 2015. Greenbelt's gross profit percentage is 60%. Greenbelt will report capital gain of $12,000 for each payment of $20,000 received. Assume that in 2016, Greenbelt and the buyer agree to reduce the purchase price to $85,000, and the remaining payments during 2016, 2017, and 2018 are each reduced to $15,000. The new gross profit percentage is 46.67% for the remaining payments. Greenbelt will report capital gain of $7,000 (46.67% of $15,000) for each of the $15,000 installments paid in 2016, 2017, and 2018.

In certain circumstances, a business may be treated as having received a payment, even though it has not received cash. For example, the receipt of property or the assumption of a mortgage by the buyer may be treated as a payment. If the buyer assumes or pays off a mortgage or other debt on the property sold, the calculation of gross profit percentage is affected.

The mortgage assumption is subtracted before calculating the gross profit percentage, except to the extent that it exceeds the adjusted basis of the property for installment sale purposes. In contrast, if the property is sold to a buyer who holds a mortgage on it and the mortgage is canceled rather than assumed, the cancellation is treated as a payment received in the year of the sale and is not subtracted in calculating the gross profit percentage.

If a business reports the sale of property under the installment method, any applicable depreciation recapture under section 1245 or 1250 is taxable as ordinary income in the year of sale, even if no payments are received in that year. If the gain is more than the depreciation recapture amount, the remainder of the gain would be recognized using the installment method rules. An installment sale generally does not apply to:

- The sale of inventory, even if the business receives a payment after the year of sale
- Dealer sales of real or personal property in the normal course of business
- A sale that results in a loss
- The sale of stock or securities traded on an established market

Installment sales to related persons are generally allowed. However, if a taxpayer sells property to a related person who then sells or disposes of the property within two years of the original sale, the taxpayer will lose the benefit of installment sale reporting.

> **Example:** Resort Properties Corporation sells a motel to a 50% owner of the corporation, Better Lodging Company. The sale price is $2 million, and Resort Properties realizes a profit on the sale of $250,000. Better Lodging agrees to pay in five installments of $400,000. Eighteen months later, Better Lodging sells the motel to another company. Resort Properties must report the entire profit of $250,000 on the sale, even though it has not received all of the installment payments. The installment sale method is disallowed on the related party sale, because the property was disposed of before the end of the two-year holding period.

Like-Kind Exchanges (Section 1031)

A section 1031 "like-kind" exchange occurs when a business or individual exchanges business or investment property for similar property. If an exchange qualifies under section 1031, the taxpayer does not pay tax currently on a resulting gain and cannot deduct a loss until the acquired property is later sold or otherwise disposed of. To qualify for nonrecognition treatment, an exchange must meet all of the following conditions:

- The property must be held for investment or for productive use in a business.
- The property must not be "held primarily for sale" (such as inventory).
- There must be an actual exchange of two or more assets or properties. (The exchange of cash for property is treated as a sale, not as an exchange.)

The simplest form of 1031 exchange is a simultaneous swap of one property for another. Alternatively, it may be arranged as a deferred exchange, in which the disposition of one property and the later acquisition of a replacement property are mutually dependent parts of an integrated transaction. In contrast, simply selling a property and using the proceeds to purchase another similar property is a taxable transaction.

In a deferred exchange, the property to be received must be identified in writing (or actually received) within 45 days after the date of transfer of the property given up. Further, the replacement property in a deferred exchange must be received by the earlier of:

- The 180th day after the date on which the property given up was transferred, or
- The due date, including extensions, of the tax return for the year in which the transfer of that property occurs.

A qualified intermediary must be used to facilitate a deferred exchange. This is an independent party who acquires the relinquished property and transfers it to a buyer. The intermediary holds the sales proceeds to prevent the taxpayer from having actual or constructive receipt of the funds. The intermediary then acquires the replacement property and transfers it to the taxpayer to complete the exchange within the allowable time limits.

Example: A corporation purchases a medical office building for $300,000. After four years, the fair market value of the property is $350,000. If the corporation were to sell the property, it would recognize a gain of $50,000. If the corporation instead arranges a like-kind exchange and either receives a similar property in exchange or invests the proceeds from the exchange of the building in a similar property, the taxable gain could be deferred.

Example: Otis owns a piece of land in Louisiana he wants to exchange, and he arranges a 1031 exchange transaction. When the land sale closes, his escrow company holds the proceeds. Within 45 days Otis identifies an apartment building he wants to buy in Arkansas and negotiates a contract to buy the building. Within the required 180 days, the escrow company releases the funds he needs to close the purchase, and the exchange transaction is complete. The escrow company is considered a qualified intermediary, and Otis has successfully postponed recognition of any gain related to disposition of the original property.

Qualifying Exchanges: To qualify under section 1031, an exchange must involve like-kind property, such as the trade of real property for real property or personal property for personal property.

An exchange of real property generally qualifies more easily as like-kind, regardless of how each property is used or whether each property is improved or unimproved. For instance, the exchange of a building for farmland would qualify, as would the exchange of an apartment building for an office building. In contrast, the exchange of factory machinery for a factory building is not a qualifying exchange.

An exchange of personal property must involve items that are at least similar enough to both be categorized within one of several asset classes established by the IRS. For example, the exchange of a panel truck for a pickup truck may qualify as a trade of like-kind property, but the exchange of a pickup truck for a semi-truck likely would not.

The exchange of equipment or business assets that are used within the United States for similar items used outside the United States would not be considered an exchange of qualifying like-kind property.

All of the following can be exchanged as like-kind property:

- Condos, land, apartment buildings, duplexes, commercial buildings, residential rentals, and retail buildings
- A single business property exchanged for two or more properties and vice versa
- Water rights, mineral rights, oil and gas interests, copyrights, trademarks, and other intangible assets (but not partnership interests or securities)
- Livestock (but not livestock of different sexes)

165

Exchanges involving the following types of property do not qualify for section 1031 exchange treatment:

- Inventory, or any property purchased for resale
- Stocks, bonds, notes, or other securities
- Real property within the United States and real property outside the United States
- Exchanges of shares of corporate stock in different companies
- Exchanges of partnership interests or LLC membership interests
- A personal residence, or personal-use property, such as a personal car
- Land under development for resale
- Corporation common stock

Definition: Boot is a term used to describe cash or other property that is included in an exchange to compensate for a difference in the values of the like-kind properties traded.

Boot: A taxpayer who receives boot in a section 1031 exchange may have to recognize a taxable gain to the extent of the cash and the FMV of unlike property received.

Example: Stephen and Tricia decide they will exchange rental properties. Stephen's rental property is more valuable, so Tricia agrees to exchange her rental property and an additional $10,000 of cash. Therefore, Stephen must recognize $10,000 of any gain he realizes on the transaction, even if section 1031 tax deferral otherwise applies.

The taxable gain cannot exceed the amount of gain that would have been recognized if the property had been sold in a taxable transaction. The amount considered boot would be reduced by qualified costs paid in connection with the transaction.

Example: Andrew's relinquished rental property has an FMV of $60,000 and an adjusted basis of $30,000. His replacement property has an FMV of $50,000, and he also receives $10,000 of cash as part of the exchange. Andrew, therefore, has a realized gain of $30,000 on the exchange, but his taxable gain is only $10,000, equal to the cash (boot) received in the exchange. The rest of his gain is deferred until he disposes of the new property at a later date.

When an exchange involves property that is subject to a liability, assumption of the liability is treated as if it were a transfer of cash and thus considered boot by the party who is relieved of the liability. If each property in an exchange is transferred subject to a liability, a taxpayer is treated as having received boot only if he is relieved of a greater liability than the liability he assumes. This is called "debt reduction" boot, and it occurs most often when a taxpayer is acquiring a less expensive or less valuable property.

Although a taxpayer may have to recognize gain on a partially taxable like-kind exchange, he would never recognize a loss. However, a loss on a like-kind exchange would affect the taxpayer's basis in the property received, and the tax treatment when it is ultimately sold or disposed.

If a taxpayer receives boot in connection with an exchange and recognizes gain, the basis of the property received is equal to the basis of the property given up plus the amount of gain recognized.

Basis of Property Received in a Like-Kind Exchange: The basis of the property received is generally the adjusted basis of the property transferred.

Example: Judy has a rental house with an adjusted basis of $70,000. In 2014, she trades the rental house for an empty lot with an FMV of $150,000. Judy's basis in the lot is $70,000, equal to the adjusted basis of the property she exchanged.

If a taxpayer trades property and also pays money as part of the exchange, the basis of the property received is the basis of the property given up, increased by any additional money paid.

Example: Peyton pays $43,000 cash for a new diesel truck for her business. She receives a trade-in allowance of $13,600 on her old truck, which she had paid $50,000 for two years ago. She has taken depreciation deductions of $39,500 on the old vehicle. She has a $3,100 gain on the exchange ($13,600 trade-in allowance minus her $10,500 adjusted basis for the old truck) but recognition of the gain is postponed under the rules for like-kind exchanges. Her basis in the new truck is $53,500, the total of the cash paid ($43,000) and her adjusted basis of $10,500 in the old truck.

Example: Jorge trades a plot of land (adjusted basis $30,000) for a different plot of land in another town (FMV $70,500). He pays an additional $4,000 of cash. Jorge's basis in the new land is $34,000: his $30,000 basis in the old land plus the $4,000 cash.

Related Party Transactions: Like-kind exchanges are allowed between related parties, including family members. However, if either party disposes of the property within two years after a 1031 exchange, the exchange is usually disqualified from nonrecognition treatment; any gain or loss that was deferred in the original transaction must be recognized in the year the disposition occurs. The two-year holding period rule may not apply:

- If one of the parties involved in the exchange dies
- If the property is subsequently converted in an involuntary exchange (such as a fire or a flood)
- If it can be established to the satisfaction of the IRS that the exchange and subsequent disposition were not done mainly for tax avoidance purposes

Example: Tim and Harry are brothers. Tim owns a residential rental property and Harry owns a tract of land. In 2014, they exchange the properties. Since they are related parties, each must hold the property he acquired for at least two years or the exchange may be disallowed and treated as a sale. In early 2014, Harry dies. In this case, the 1031 exchange is still valid, because the holding period rule does not apply if one of the parties in a related exchange dies before the two-year period expires.

For purposes of this rule, a related person includes:

- A close family member (siblings, spouses, ancestors, and lineal descendants).
- An entity (corporation or partnership) in which the taxpayer owns either directly or indirectly more than a 50% interest. This includes ownership by a spouse or a close family member.
- Two entities in which the same taxpayer owns directly or indirectly more than 50% of each.
- An executor and a beneficiary of an estate.
- A trust for which the taxpayer is the fiduciary and the related party is a beneficiary either of that same trust or a related trust or a fiduciary of a related trust.

The IRS gives close scrutiny to exchanges between related parties because they can be used by taxpayers to evade taxes on gains.

Reporting: A taxpayer who transfers property in a like-kind exchange must file Form 8824, *Like-Kind Exchanges*, with his tax return for the year of the exchange. If the exchange involves a related party, the form must also be filed for each of the following two years.

Involuntary Conversions (Section 1033)

An involuntary conversion occurs when a taxpayer's property is lost, damaged, or destroyed, for which the taxpayer may receive an award, insurance reimbursement, or some other type of payment, as a result of:

- Theft;
- Disaster;
- Condemnation; or threat of condemnation.

A taxpayer typically reports a gain or deducts a loss in the year the gain or loss is realized. However, under section 1033, a taxpayer can defer reporting gain on an involuntary conversion if he receives proceeds from insurance or another source and invests in property similar to the converted property. The gain on the involuntary conversion is then deferred until a taxable sale or exchange of the replacement property occurs at a later date.

> **Example:** A hurricane destroys Denise's residential rental property that has an adjusted basis of $50,000. Denise receives insurance reimbursement for $100,000, the fair market value of the property. Denise buys a replacement rental property six months later for $100,000. Her gain on the involuntary conversion is $50,000 ($100,000 insurance settlement minus her $50,000 basis). However, Denise does not have to recognize any taxable gain because she reinvested all the insurance proceeds in another, similar property.

Replacement Period: The replacement period for an involuntary conversion generally ends two years after the end of the first tax year in which any part of the gain on the condemnation is realized.

A three-year replacement period is allowed for real property that is held for investment, such as office buildings or residential rentals. The replacement period is four years for livestock that is involuntarily converted because of weather-related conditions. If the property is subject to an involuntary conversion in certain federally declared disaster areas, the replacement period can be up to five years.

The replacement property must be purchased before the end of the tax year in which the replacement deadline applies. If the involuntary conversion property is not replaced within the allowed time period, an amended tax return would have to be filed for the year the involuntary conversion occurred, reporting a taxable transaction.

Usually, the taxpayer's basis in the new property will be its cost, reduced by any gain realized on the old property that was not recognized. However, the basis may be increased by any gain the taxpayer recognizes on the involuntary conversion and decreased by the following:

- Any loss the taxpayer recognizes on the involuntary conversion
- Any reimbursement he receives and does not reinvest in similar property

> **Example:** Cody is a general contractor whose business truck is destroyed in an accident. It had been partially depreciated, and its adjusted basis was $40,000. The insurance company sends a check for $55,000 to replace the truck. Two months later, Cody uses all the insurance money to purchase a replacement truck, paying an additional $2,000 out-of-pocket to purchase the new vehicle. The basis in the new truck is $42,000 ($40,000 basis of the old truck + $2,000 additional out-of-pocket cost). This does not have to reported as a taxable transaction because it is a qualified involuntary conversion of business property.

Unit 9: Study Questions

1. The Drake Partnership owned a $20,000 business machine that had been depreciated by $12,000, so the partnership's adjusted basis in it was $8,000. In 2014, the partnership sold the machine for $25,000. What is the nature of the tax treatment resulting from the sale?

A. Capital gain of $17,000.
B. Ordinary income of $12,000 and capital gain of $5,000.
C. Ordinary income of $17,000.
D. Capital gain of $12,000 and ordinary income of $5,000.

2. Which of the following dispositions of depreciable property can trigger depreciation recapture?

A. Installment sale.
B. Gift.
C. Transfer at death.
D. Section 1031 exchange where no money or unlike property is received.

3. Caraway Carwash paid $200,000 for business equipment in January 2014. Caraway sells the equipment for $180,000 in October 2014. Caraway had not taken any depreciation on the equipment. How will this transaction be reported?

A. Caraway has a section 1231 loss of $20,000 on the sale of the equipment. This is treated as an ordinary loss.
B. Caraway has a section 1231 loss of $20,000 on the sale of the equipment. This is treated as a capital loss.
C. This is an installment sale, with a loss of $20,000 that is treated as an ordinary loss.
D. Caraway has an ordinary loss.

4. Which of the following is not section 1245 property?

A. Computer.
B. Office building.
C. Display shelving.
D. Grain silo.

5. Which of the following property types qualifies for section 1031 like-kind exchange?

A. A personal residence.
B. Inventory property.
C. Corporation common stock.
D. An empty lot held for investment.

6. On January 10, 2014, a rental office building owned by Clovis Investments Corporation burns down. The property had an adjusted basis of $260,000, and Clovis receives an insurance reimbursement of $310,000. Clovis buys another rental office property for $290,000 in March 2014. What is Clovis's taxable gain as a result of this transaction?

A. $0.
B. $20,000.
C. $30,000.
D. $50,000.

7. Which of the following assets is not section 1231 property?

A. Office building.
B. Unharvested crops.
C. Business asset held for less than one year.
D. Patent.

8. Jennifer operates Right Hair Salon, a sole proprietorship. In 2014, she sells all of her salon chairs for $3,500 in order to buy new ones. She had purchased the chairs seven years ago for $15,000, and they were fully depreciated. Therefore, her basis in the chairs is zero. How should she report this transaction?

A. She reports a loss of $11,500 on Schedule C.
B. She reports a gain of $3,500 on Form 4797 and Schedule C. The entire $3,500 is treated as depreciation recapture, which is subject to ordinary income tax rates.
C. She reports a gain of $3,500 on Form 4797 and Schedule C. The entire $3,500 is taxed as a long-term capital gain.
D. She is not required to report this sale.

9. Barbara exchanges an apartment building with an adjusted basis of $125,000 for a business office building. The fair market value of Barbara's old property is $500,000. The fair market value of the business office building is $475,000. What is Barbara's basis in the new building?

A. $125,000.
B. $475,000.
C. $500,000.
D. $525,000.

10. Which of the following property exchanges does not qualify as a like-kind exchange?

A. Exchange of an apartment building for an office building.
B. Exchange of livestock of different sexes.
C. Exchange of improved property for unimproved property.
D. Exchange of farm machinery for factory machinery.

11. Arbordale Acres is a farming corporation. In 2014, Arbordale sells a used tractor for $25,000. The original cost of the tractor was $20,000, and it is fully depreciated. What is the tax treatment for Arbordale's sale of the tractor?

A. There is no gain or loss on the sale of the tractor.
B. Arbordale has a gain of $25,000. The first $20,000 is considered section 1245 recapture and is taxed as ordinary income. The remaining $5,000 is considered section 1231 capital gain.
C. Arbordale has a gain of $25,000. The first $15,000 is considered section 1245 recapture and is taxed as ordinary income. The remaining $10,000 is considered section 1231 capital gain.
D. The entire gain is considered section 1245 recapture and will be taxed as ordinary income.

12. Scott has a small air plane that he used in his crop dusting business for two years. Its adjusted basis is $35,000, and its trade-in value is $45,000. He trades his old plane for a new plane that costs $200,000 and pays the dealer an additional $155,000 of cash. What is Scott's basis of the new plane?

A. $35,000.
B. $155,000.
C. $190,000.
D. $200,000.

13. The Karabell Company trades a delivery truck with an adjusted basis of $11,000 and cash of $6,000 for a new truck with a fair market value of $25,000. How much gain must Karabell recognize in this exchange, and what is its basis in the new truck?

Gain	Basis of New Truck
A. $0	$17,000
B. $0	$25,000
C. $8,000	$17,000
D. $8,000	$25,000

14. Fran and Zachary are mother and son who complete a section 1031 exchange in March 2014. On January 29, 2015, Fran dies, and her property is inherited by her husband, who promptly sells it. Which of the following statements is correct?

A. Since one of the properties in the exchange has been sold before the two-year time limit for related parties, the section 1031 exchange is disallowed, and both parties must pay tax on the transaction.
B. The section 1031 exchange is still valid.
C. Since this was a related party exchange, the section 1031 exchange is still valid for Zachary, but Fran's estate must pay tax on the exchange because her husband disposed of the property before the two-year waiting period.
D. The nonrecognition treatment is lost for both parties, but Fran's husband is liable for the tax on the exchange, since he was the owner of the property when it was sold.

15. Jamal sells a duplex with an adjusted basis of $150,000. The buyer agrees to pay Jamal $300,000, with a cash down payment of $100,000 and $20,000 (plus 5% interest) in each of the next ten years. What is Jamal's gross profit and gross profit percentage on the installment sale?

A. The gross profit is $5,000, and the gross profit percentage is 50%.
B. The gross profit is $10,000, and the gross profit percentage is 100%.
C. The gross profit is $150,000, and the gross profit percentage is 50%.
D. The gross profit is $5,000, and the gross profit percentage is 100%.

16. Which of the following trades qualifies as a nontaxable like-kind exchange?

A. The exchange of a vacant lot in the city for farmland in the country.
B. The exchange of a Toyota Prius owned by one car dealer for a Ford C-Max Hybrid owned by another car dealer.
C. The exchange of shares of stock for units of bonds.
D. The exchange of an apartment building in New York City for an apartment building in Mexico City.

17. Angelina trades a laser printer used in her tax practice for a new color model. The cost of the original printer was $5,000 and she had taken $1,000 of depreciation. She exchanged her old printer as a trade-in and paid an additional $2,000 of cash to complete the exchange. What is Angelina's basis in the new printer?

A. $1,000.
B. $2,000.
C. $6,000.
D. $7,000.

18. Special rules apply to like-kind exchanges between related persons. For purposes of a section 1031 exchange, which of the following qualifies as a related person?

A. The taxpayer's spouse.
B. A corporation in which the taxpayer has a 51% ownership.
C. A partnership in which the taxpayer owns a 53% interest, and a partnership in which the taxpayer's spouse owns a 52% interest.
D. All of the above.

19. Sergio is a self-employed carpenter who owns a compressor for use in his business. He trades the compressor (adjusted basis $3,000) for a large table saw (FMV $7,500) and pays an additional $4,000 cash to the seller in a qualified exchange. What is Sergio's basis in the saw?

A. $7,000.
B. $7,500.
C. $4,000.
D. $3,000.

20. Cecil operates a sandwich shop as a sole proprietorship. During 2014, Cecil sold personal property that was used in the business for $100,000. The purchase price of the property was $120,000, and Cecil had claimed section 179 and depreciation deductions totaling $47,000. Based upon the information provided, what is the nature and amount of taxable income that will result from the sale of this property?

A. Capital gain of $27,000.
B. Ordinary income of $27,000.
C. No gain or loss.
D. Ordinary income of $47,000 and capital loss of $20,000.

21. Sadie owns a gym. She sells some used fitness equipment in 2014 for $65,000. She had purchased the equipment for $90,000. She has taken $50,000 of depreciation deductions, and a section 179 deduction of $10,000. Which of the following will Sadie report on the sale of the equipment?

A. Ordinary loss of $25,000.
B. Long-term capital gain of $35,000.
C. Ordinary income of $35,000.
D. Ordinary income of $10,000 and long-term capital gain of $25,000.

Unit 10: Partnerships in General

More Reading:
Publication 541, *Partnerships*

Partnership Basics

As described in Unit 1, an unincorporated business with two or more owners is generally classified as a partnership for federal tax purposes. A partnership is a pass-through entity that is generally not directly taxed on its income. Instead, income and loss are determined at the partnership level and are taxable to the individual partners. In this respect, a partnership is similar to a sole proprietorship.

Unlike a corporation, a partnership does not require any formal legal documents. A partnership must have at least two partners and at least one of them must be a general partner. A joint undertaking merely to share expenses is not a partnership.

Certain entities with different legal structures may be classified as partnerships for tax purposes, either based upon their election by filing Form 8832, *Entity Classification Election,* or by default (as in the case of a domestic LLC with at least two members that is classified as a partnership unless it files Form 8832 and elects to be treated as a corporation). However, the following organizations are prohibited from being classified as partnerships:

- A corporation (although a corporation can be a partner in a partnership)
- A joint-stock company or joint-stock association
- An insurance company
- Certain banks
- A government entity
- An organization required to be taxed as a corporation by the IRS
- Certain foreign organizations
- Any tax-exempt (nonprofit) organization
- Any real estate investment trust (REIT)
- Any organization classified as a trust or estate
- Any other organization that elects to be classified as a corporation by filing Form 8832

The Partnership Agreement

The term *partnership agreement* refers to any written document or oral agreement that bears on the underlying economic arrangement of the partners, including allocations of income, gain, loss, deductions, and credits. Examples of such documents include:

- Loan and credit agreements
- Assumption agreements
- Indemnification agreements
- Subordination agreements
- Correspondence with a lender concerning terms of a loan
- Loan guarantees

A partnership agreement can be modified during the tax year and even after the tax year has closed. However, the partnership agreement cannot be modified after the due date for filing the partnership return for the year, not including extensions.

Example: Terry and Dawn run a cash-basis, calendar-year partnership. They split the partnership's proceeds 50-50. In 2014, they decide to alter their partnership agreement. They have until the due date of the partnership return to change the partnership agreement. Filing for an extension does not give them additional time.

Partnership Filing Requirements

A partnership must file a tax return unless it has no activity (and no income or losses for the year). A partnership reports its income or loss on Form 1065, which is due on the fifteenth day of the fourth month following the close of the tax year. Since most partnerships are calendar-year partnerships, their tax returns are generally due on April 15, like individual returns.

Note: A partnership can request a five-month extension to file (unlike individuals and corporations that may request a six-month extension). Therefore, a calendar-year partnership can request an extension until September 15 to file its tax return.

The extension is requested on Form 7004, *Automatic Extension of Time to File Certain Business Income Tax, Information, and Other Returns.*

The partnership return must show the name and address of each partner and the partner's distributive share of taxable income (or loss) on Schedule K-1. The partnership is also required to furnish a copy of each partner's Schedule K-1 to the partner by the due date (including extensions) of the partnership tax return. The individual partner then reports his share of partnership income on Schedule E of Form 1040.

> **Example:** Lovett Partnership is a calendar-year, cash-basis partnership that is required to file Form 1065 every year. The partnership has five partners and each partner receives a Schedule K-1 for his share of partnership income and losses, which are then reportable on the partners' individual tax returns. Each partner must receive his Schedule K-1 by the due date of the partnership return (or by the extended due date, if the partnership requests an extension).

The IRS requires partnerships with more than 100 partners (Schedules K-1) to file their returns electronically. If a partnership fails to do so, it may be subject to penalty unless it was unable to file electronically (e.g., because the e-filing was rejected, the return required paper attachments, etc.) The partnership return must be signed by a general partner.

The penalty for late filing is $195 per month, per partner, for up to 12 months.

> **Example:** A partnership has four partners. It files its tax return two months late. The partnership is liable for a late filing penalty of $1,560 ($195 × two months × four partners.)

Additional penalties may apply if the partnership fails to furnish Schedules K-1 to its partners, fails to supply a tax identification number, or fails to furnish information on tax shelters. These penalties may not be imposed if the partnership can show reasonable cause for its failure.

Partners who work in the business are not employees and do not receive Forms W-2. Withholding from their distributions to pay the income and self-employment taxes that they report on their Forms 1040 is generally not required. General partners are considered to be self-employed and therefore must pay estimated payments just like other self-employed individuals. Limited partners are subject to self-employment tax only on guaranteed payments, such as salaries and professional fees for services rendered.

General Partnership vs. Limited Partnership

A partnership can either be a general partnership or a limited partnership. In a general partnership, the partners have unlimited liability for partnership debts. In a limited partnership, there must be at least one general partner and at least one limited partner. The limited partners have no obligation to contribute additional capital to the partnership and therefore do not have an economic risk of loss related to partnership liabilities. In this respect, a limited partner is like an investor in a corporation. Limited partners generally cannot participate in the management or the day-to-day administration of the partnership.

A limited partnership (LP or LLP) is formed under state limited liability law. Often, the owners of limited liability partnerships offer professional services (e.g., attorneys or doctors). This entity type protects individual partners from liability for the malpractice of other partners.

Family Partnerships

Members of a family can form a partnership together. However, family members will be recognized as partners only if one of the following requirements is met:

- If capital is a material income-producing factor, the family members must have acquired their capital interests in a bona fide transaction (even if by gift or purchase from another family member); actually own the partnership interests; and actually control the interests. This means that a family member who acquires a partnership interest from another family member needs to treat the activity as a bona fide business activity.
- If capital is not a material income-producing factor, the family members must have joined together in good faith to conduct a business. They must have agreed that contributions from each entitle them to a share in the profits and that some capital or service is provided by each partner.

Capital (investment) is a material income-producing factor if a substantial part of the gross income of the business comes from the use of capital. For example, this would apply if the operation of the business requires substantial inventories or investment in a plant, machinery, or equipment.

In general, capital is not a material income-producing factor if the income of the business consists principally of fees, commissions, or other compensation for personal services performed by members or employees of the partnership.

If a family member (or any other person) receives a gift of a capital interest in a partnership in which capital is a material income-producing factor, the donee's distributive share of partnership income is subject to both of the following restrictions:

- It must be figured by reducing the partnership income by reasonable compensation for services the donor provides the partnership.
- The share attributable to donated capital must not be proportionately greater than the donor's distributive share attributable to the donor's capital.

Example: Ronald sold 50% of his business to his daughter, Cindy. The resulting partnership had a profit of $60,000. Capital is a material income-producing factor. Ronald performed services worth $24,000, which is reasonable compensation, and Cindy performed no services. The $24,000 must be allocated to Ronald as compensation. Of the remaining $36,000 of profit due to capital, at least 50%, or $18,000 must be allocated to Ronald since he owns a 50% capital interest. Cindy's share of partnership profit cannot be more than $18,000.

For purposes of determining a partner's distributive share, an interest purchased by one family member from another family member is considered a gift from the seller. The fair market value of the purchased interest is considered donated capital. For this purpose, members of a family include only spouses, ancestors, and lineal descendants (grandchild, daughter, son, stepchild, etc.)

Costs of Organizing and Starting a Partnership

The costs to organize a partnership and to start up a business are treated much like similar costs incurred by other types of businesses. As discussed in Unit 4, $5,000 of organizational costs and $5,000 of start-up costs can be deducted in the year the partnership's active trade or business begins. Amounts not deducted can be amortized ratably over a period of 180 months. The election to either deduct these costs currently or to capitalize and amortize them is irrevocable and applies to all organizational and start-up costs related to the trade or business. The partnership must file Form 4562, *Depreciation and Amortization*, with its tax return.

Special Partnership Allocations

Unlike S corporations, which must report all income and expenses in proportion to stock ownership, partnerships have more flexibility. Partnership agreements can be written to reflect special allocations of income, gain, loss, or deductions, as long as the allocations are consistent with the economic sharing arrangement among the partners. For example, the partnership agreement may allocate all of the depreciation deductions to one partner or specify that the partners share capital, profits, and losses in different ratios.

Example: Pandora, who has design and sewing skills, forms a partnership with Jayne, who has the money to invest in developing a clothing line. Jayne contributes $100,000 of cash to the partnership. Pandora and Jayne agree to split the business profits 20/80 until Jayne recovers her entire investment; thereafter, profits will be split 50/50. These special allocations are written into their partnership agreement.

Example: Nico and Rhoda form a partnership. Nico contributes $1,000 and Rhoda contributes $99,000. Due to Nico's expertise in management and his daily participation in the partnership's business, the partnership agreement provides that he will be allocated 20% of the partnership's taxable income and 2% of the partnership's losses. Thus, although Nico owns only 1% in partnership capital, his profit sharing ratio is 20%. This tax allocation between Nico and Rhoda is allowed because it reflects their underlying economic arrangement.

Example: Alicia and Sandy form a partnership to run a cupcake bakery. The bakery is opened during the year, and the partnership has ordinary income of $10,000. The partnership agreement states they will share income and losses equally (50/50). Alicia and Sandy agree that the $10,000 of income will be distributed equally between them. However, for tax purposes, they want the income to be allocated as $7,500 to Alicia and $2,500 to Sandy. The tax allocation (75/25) is not consistent with the underlying economic arrangement in their partnership agreement (50/50). Unless the partnership agreement contains other provisions that justify this allocation, it has no economic effect and must be reallocated to the partners based on their economic sharing ratio.

Guaranteed Payments

A partnership may be required by the terms of its partnership agreement to make guaranteed payments to one or more partners without regard to whether the partnership has income or loss for the year. Guaranteed payments are not the same as partnership distributions. They may compensate the partner for services or for the use of capital, as if they were made to a person who is not a partner. Guaranteed payments are generally deducted by the partnership on Form 1065 as a business expense and reported on Schedule K-1.

The partner who receives a guaranteed payment reports the full amount of the payment as ordinary income on Schedule E (Form 1040) of his individual tax return for the tax year in which the partnership's tax year ends, and also reports his distributive share of the partnership's ordinary income or loss. Guaranteed payments are not subject to income tax withholding by the partnership.

Example: Erica is a partner in the Schultz Partnership. Under the terms of her partnership agreement, she is entitled to a guaranteed payment of $10,000 per year, regardless of how profitable the partnership is. In 2014, Erica's distributive share of partnership income is 10%. Schultz Partnership has $50,000 of ordinary income after deducting Erica's guaranteed payment. She must include ordinary income of $15,000 ($10,000 guaranteed payment + $5,000 [$50,000 × 10%] for her distributive share) on her individual income tax return.

Separately Stated Items

Many of the individual components of a partnership's income or loss are calculated similarly to those of an individual. However, some deductions are not allowed at the partnership level, and certain items of income and loss must be separately stated on the tax return.

These separately stated items flow through to the partners with a specific character. For example, a partnership that makes charitable contributions must list them as a separately stated item. Each individual partner then reports his share of the charitable contributions on his Schedule A.

Each year, a partnership provides Schedules K-1 to each of its partners, indicating their respective shares of:

- **Ordinary income or loss,** and
- **Separately stated items.**

Example: Barry is a 25% partner in a business with three other partners. The partnership makes $20,000 of charitable contributions in 2014 that are reported on the partnership tax return, Form 1065. As the partnership is a pass-through entity, it does not receive a tax benefit from deductible contributions. Instead, Barry's Schedule K-1 shows $5,000 as his share of the partnership's contributions, which he can claim on his individual tax return.

Study Note: For the EA exam, you should be able to distinguish the items that are separately stated on a partnership's tax return.

The following items must be separately stated:

- Net short-term capital gains and losses
- Net long-term capital gains and losses
- Charitable contributions
- Dividends eligible for a dividends-received deduction
- Taxes paid to a foreign country
- Taxes paid to a U.S. possession (Guam, Puerto Rico, etc.)
- Section 1231 gains and losses
- Section 179 deductions and bonus depreciation
- Any tax-exempt income and expenses related to the tax-exempt income
- Investment income and related investment expenses
- Rental income, portfolio income, and related expenses
- Any recovery items, such as bad debts

Example: The Stevenson Partnership operates as an accrual-based business. Its gross receipts for 2014 were $250,000. In addition, it had the following income and expenses:

- Liability insurance   ($5,000)
- Charitable contributions   (2,000)
- Continuing education   (9,000)
- Rental income   25,000
- Guaranteed payments to partners   (15,000)

Ordinary income for the Stevenson Partnership is figured as follows:

Gross receipts	$250,000
Liability insurance	5,000)
Continuing education	(9,000)
Guaranteed payments to partners	(15,000)
Ordinary income:	**$221,000**

The rental income and charitable contributions are not considered in determining ordinary income of the partnership. Instead, these are separately stated items that pass through to the partners and retain their character, just as they would for a sole proprietorship. Each individual partner receives a Schedule K-1 from the partnership, reporting his share of ordinary income or loss and each separately stated item. The partners report these amounts on their tax returns. Guaranteed payments are deductible by the partnership because they are treated like wages and are taxable to the partners who receive them.

Contributions to a Partnership

When a partnership is formed or new partners are added, the partners contribute property or cash in exchange for their partnership interests. Generally, neither the partner nor the partnership recognizes gain or loss in connection with contributions, whether made in connection with the partnership's formation or after it is operating. However, a partner's contribution can result in gain or loss recognition in the following situations:

- When property is contributed to a partnership that would be treated as an investment company if it were incorporated. A partnership is treated as an investment company if over 80% of the value of its assets is held for investment in cash or readily marketable items.
- When contributed property is distributed to a different partner within seven years of the original contribution date. The contributing partner would recognize gain on the

difference between the fair market value and the adjusted basis of the property as of the contribution date. The character of the gain or loss will be the same as would have resulted if the partnership had sold the property to the distributee partner.

- When a partner contributes cash or property to a partnership and then receives a distribution of different property. In this case, the transaction may be considered a disguised sale. A disguised sale is not treated as a contribution and a subsequent distribution but as a sale of property, if:
  - The distribution would not have been made if the initial contribution had not occurred; and
  - The partner's right to the distribution does not depend on the success of partnership operations.

If a contribution and distribution occur within two years of each other, the transfers are presumed to be a sale unless the facts clearly indicate they are not. If the contribution and distribution occur more than two years apart, the transfers are presumed not to be a sale unless the facts clearly indicate they are.

Example: Alberta contributes land with a fair market value of $150,000 and a basis of $100,000 to her partnership. In the same year, the partnership distributes $100,000 of cash and marketable securities worth $50,000 to Alberta. This transaction would be considered a disguised sale rather than a tax-free contribution and distribution of property.

When a partner contributes property to a partnership, the partnership's basis is generally the same as the adjusted basis of the partner, including any gain recognized by the partner in connection with the contribution. The partner's holding period for the property is also carried over. For example, if a partner contributes a building with an FMV of $100,000 and a basis of $50,000, the basis of the building in the hands of the partnership would generally be $50,000.

Contribution of Services: A partner can acquire an interest in a partnership as compensation for services performed or to be performed. The tax treatment depends upon whether the partner receives a capital interest or a profits interest.

If a partner receives a capital interest as compensation for services, the partner must recognize ordinary income equal to the fair market value of a partnership interest that is transferred in exchange for services. The amount is treated as a guaranteed payment and is included in the partner's gross income in the first tax year during which the partner can transfer the interest.

If a partner receives a profits interest as compensation for services, the receipt may not be taxable to the partner or the partnership, except in certain circumstances.

Example: Greer is an attorney who contributes her services to a partnership in exchange for a 10% partnership interest. It is deemed a capital interest, as the partnership agreement provides for distribution of assets to Greer in the event she withdraws from the partnership or the partnership liquidates. The fair market value of the partnership interest is $3,000. Greer is required to recognize $3,000 of ordinary income, and her basis in the partnership is $3,000. The payment is deducted by the partnership as a guaranteed payment and is taxable to Greer as ordinary income.

Basis of a Partner's Interest

A partner's basis in his partnership interest may be referred to as *outside basis*. This is in contrast to the partnership's basis in its assets, which is known as *inside basis*.

Study Note: Be familiar with these two terms, as the EA exam may use them in questions when test-takers are asked to determine a partner's or a partnership's basis.

Inside basis and outside basis may be equal, but certain distributions of property from the partnership or transfers of partnership interests may disrupt this equality. By means of an IRC section 754 election, the partnership may be able to make upward or downward adjustments to the basis of its assets in order to restore the equality between inside basis and outside basis.

The initial basis of a partnership interest is generally equal to the cash plus the adjusted basis of any property the partner contributed. The adjusted basis of a partner's partnership interest is ordinarily determined at the end of the partnership's tax year. However, if there is a sale or exchange of all or part of a partner's interest or a liquidation of his entire interest in a partnership, the adjusted basis must also be determined on the date of the transaction.

Example: Sam and Harriet form a partnership. Sam contributes a machine to the partnership that has an adjusted basis of $400 and an FMV of $1,000. Harriet contributes $1,000 cash. The basis of Sam's interest is $400 and the basis of Harriet's interest is $1,000.

The following items increase a partner's basis in the partnership:
- The partner's additional cash contributions to the partnership
- The partner's increased liabilities
- The partner's increased share (or assumption of) partnership liabilities
- The partner's distributive share of taxable and nontaxable partnership income
- The partner's distributive share of the excess of the deductions for depletion over the basis of the depletable property

In addition, if a partner must recognize a gain as a result of his partnership contribution, the gain is added to the basis of his partnership interest. A partner may be required to recognize a gain when he contributes an asset to the partnership that is subject to liability (such as the contribution of a building that is subject to a mortgage), as the other partners are assuming part of his liability.

Any increase in a partner's liabilities because of his assumption of partnership liabilities is treated as if it were a contribution to the partnership by the partner. If a partner's share of partnership liabilities increases, this increase is treated as if the partner contributed cash or property to the partnership.

A partner's basis in the partnership is decreased by the following items:

- The money and adjusted basis of property distributed to the partner by the partnership.
- The partner's distributive share of the partnership losses.
- The partner's distributive share of nondeductible partnership expenses (but not capital expenditures). This includes the partner's share of any section 179 expenses, even if the partner cannot deduct the entire amount on his individual income tax return.
- The partner's deduction for depletion for any partnership oil and gas wells, up to the proportionate share of the adjusted basis of the wells allocated to the partner.

If a partner's share of partnership liabilities decreases or the partnership assumes any of the partner's individual liabilities, the amounts are treated as distributions to the partner by the partnership. For example, if contributed property is subject to a debt and the debt is assumed by the partnership, the basis of the contributing partner's interest is reduced (but not below zero) by the portion of the liability assumed by the other partners. The partner must reduce his basis because the assumption of the liability is treated as a distribution to him. The other partners' assumption of the liability is treated as a contribution by them to the partnership.

Example: Stephanie acquired a 20% interest in a partnership by contributing a moving van that had an adjusted basis to her of $8,000 and a related $4,000 loan balance. The partnership assumed the loan. The basis of Stephanie's interest is:

Adjusted basis of contributed property	$8,000
Minus loan assumed by other partners (80% × $4,000)	($3,200)
Basis of Stephanie's partnership interest	**$4,800**

A partner's basis can never go below zero. To avoid this, a partner must recognize gain equal to the amount by which cash distributions or a decrease in his share of partnership liabilities exceeds his basis.

Example: Roy acquired a 20% interest in a partnership by contributing an asset that had an adjusted basis of $8,000 and a related $12,000 loan balance. Since his basis in the asset is less than the loan balance, the $1,600 difference between the portion of the loan assumed by the other partners, $9,600 (80% × $12,000), and his basis of $8,000 is treated as capital gain from the sale or exchange of a partnership interest. Roy's partnership basis is zero.

Partnership Loss Limitations

The amount of a partnership's loss that a partner is allowed to deduct on his tax return is dependent on the partner's basis in the partnership. In general, a partner cannot deduct losses that exceed his partnership basis. Losses disallowed due to insufficient basis are carried forward until the partner can deduct them in a later year.

However, debts incurred on behalf of the partnership can increase a partner's individual basis. For example, if a partner takes out a $50,000 loan to finance partnership operations and he personally guarantees the debt, the debt is considered part of his basis in the partnership for purposes of deducting partnership losses.

Example: Rebecca invests $1,000 in the Goldblatt Partnership in return for a 10% general partnership interest. The Goldblatt Partnership takes out a $500,000 loan and incurs $100,000 of losses during the first year. Rebecca's share of partnership liabilities would increase her basis to $51,000 [$1,000 cash investment + ($500,000 × 10%)]. Rebecca's share of the loss is $10,000 ($100,000 × 10%), reducing her basis to $41,000. Rebecca is allowed to deduct the entire amount because her partnership basis included her share of the partnership's debt.

This only applies if the partner is at risk for the loss. If the partner does not have any personal liability to satisfy the debt, deductible losses are limited by the at-risk rules. The at-risk rules limit the deductibility of losses to the partner's basis, not including his share of any nonrecourse debt, as described below.

This means that a partner is prohibited from taking losses based on partnership liabilities unless the partner would be forced to satisfy the debt with his personal assets. This is intended to prevent abusive deductions from real estate and other tax shelter activities.

A partner (or related person) is considered to have assumed a partnership liability when he is personally liable for it, and:

- The creditor knows that the liability was assumed by the partner or related person,
- The creditor can demand payment from the partner or related person, and
- No other partner or person related to a partner will bear the economic risk of loss on that liability immediately after the assumption.

> **Example:** Gary and Santiago form a general partnership, with cash contributions of $2,000 from each. Under the partnership agreement, they share all partnership profits and losses equally. The partnership borrows an additional $10,000 and purchases equipment. Both partners are liable for the debt. This debt is included in the partners' basis in the partnership. Each partner's basis would include his allocated share of the liability, or $5,000. Therefore, each partner's basis is $7,000 (initial $2,000 contribution + $5,000 share of the liability).

The effect of liabilities on an individual partner's basis depends mainly on two factors:

- Whether or not the liability is recourse or nonrecourse
- Whether or not the partner is a general or limited partner

A nonrecourse liability is usually secured by an asset or property, and its terms provide that the creditor has no claim against the owner of the property. At most, the creditor may have a claim against the property. An example of this would be a mortgage loan where the lender's only recourse in case of default is to repossess the property. A partnership liability is considered a nonrecourse liability if no partner has an economic risk of loss for that liability.

> **Example:** Reuben purchases a used van for his business, but he is unable to make the payments. The loan is a nonrecourse loan because the only action the lender can take is to repossess the vehicle. The lender cannot seek payment from Reuben for the balance of the loan.

A partner's share of nonrecourse liabilities is proportionate to his share of partnership profits. A partner's basis in a partnership interest includes the partner's share of a partnership liability only if, and to the extent, the liability:

- Creates or increases the partnership's basis in any of its assets,
- Gives rise to a current deduction to the partnership, or
- Is a nondeductible, noncapital expense of the partnership.

A partnership liability is a recourse liability when the individual partners have an economic risk of loss. A partner has an economic risk of loss to the extent that he or a related person would be obligated to make payments to a creditor in the event of a constructive liquidation.

Partners generally share recourse liabilities based on their ratios for sharing losses. A limited partner has no obligation to contribute additional capital to the partnership, and therefore does not have an economic risk of loss in the partnership's recourse liabilities. Thus, unless a limited partner guarantees a partnership liability or makes a loan to the partnership, his basis will generally not be affected by the partnership's recourse liabilities.

Unit 10: Study Questions

1. Todd and Charlotte form a general partnership with cash contributions of $20,000 each. Under the partnership agreement, they share all partnership profits and losses equally. They borrow $60,000 and purchase depreciable business equipment. However, Todd has poor credit, so Charlotte is the only signer on the loan. Charlotte is required to pay the creditor if the partnership defaults, so she has an economic risk of loss related to the loan. The payments on the loan are made out of the partnership bank account. What is Charlotte's basis in the partnership, and what is Todd's basis?

A. Charlotte: $80,000, Todd: $20,000.
B. Charlotte: $60,000, Todd: $20,000.
C. Charlotte: $20,000, Todd: $20,000.
D. Charlotte: $60,000, Todd: $60,000.

2. When payments are made by a partnership to partners without regard to partnership income, these payments are called:

A. Capital gains.
B. Ordinary distributions.
C. Passive income.
D. Guaranteed payments.

3. Carolyn and Jerome form a partnership in 2014. Each contributes $5,000 for an equal partnership interest. Their partnership agreement states that they will share income and losses equally. However, Carolyn will provide accounting services to the partnership and receive a guaranteed payment each year of $21,000, regardless of the partnership's income or loss. In 2014, the partnership earns $50,000 before deducting the guaranteed payment. What is Jerome's distributive share of partnership profits for 2014?

A. $0.
B. $14,500.
C. $22,500.
D. $25,000.

189

4. The G&H Partnership has two partners, Gil and Hassid, who share profits and losses equally (50/50). The partnership has the following activity during the year:

Gross income from operations:	$200,000
Business expenses:	30,000
Tax-exempt interest income:	10,000
Rental income:	120,000
Charitable contributions:	4,000

What is Hassid's share of the partnership's ordinary income?

A. $85,000.
B. $91,000.
C. $100,000.
D. $105,000.

5. Which of the following statements is correct regarding limited partners in a partnership?

A. A limited partner has an economic liability for damages and an economic risk of loss.
B. A limited partner does not have an economic risk of loss in the partnership's recourse liabilities.
C. A limited partner does not have an economic risk of loss in the partnership's recourse liabilities; however, a limited partner may be required to contribute additional capital.
D. A limited partner is treated just like a general partner when it comes to the partnership's recourse liabilities.

6. José and Carlos form a partnership. Each contributes $20,000 during the initial formation of the partnership. Their partnership agreement states that José will receive 35% of the distributive income and Carlos will receive 65%. In 2014, the partnership has income of $200,000. What is each partner's distributive share of the partnership profits?

A. José: $70,000, Carlos: $130,000.
B. José: $100,000, Carlos: $100,000.
C. José: $35,000, Carlos $65,000.
D. José: $77,000, Carlos $143,000.

7. Polly and Diane form P&D Partnership. Polly contributes $16,000 cash and Diane contributes equipment with a fair market value of $15,000 and an adjusted basis of $5,000. What amount should Diane report as a gain as a result of this transaction?

A. $0.
B. $3,000.
C. $5,000.
D. $8,000.

8. If a partnership requests additional time to file its return, how long will the filing deadline be extended?

A. Three months.
B. Five months.
C. Six months.
D. Nine months.

9. John, Robin, Shanette, and Theresa form a partnership. Each partner contributes $10,000 and receives an equal interest in the partnership (25%). Under the partnership agreement, they share partnership profits and losses equally. The partnership borrows $135,000 and purchases business equipment. All of the partners except for Theresa personally guarantee the liability. What is each partner's basis after this transaction?

A. Theresa's basis is zero, and the other partners each have a basis of $58,333.
B. Theresa's basis is $10,000, and the other partners each have a basis of $43,750.
C. Theresa's basis is $10,000, and the other partners each have a basis of $55,000.
D. Each partner has a basis of $43,750.

10. Which of the following is not a separately stated item on a partnership tax return?

A. Net long-term capital gains and losses.
B. Investment income.
C. Section 179 deductions and bonus depreciation.
D. Guaranteed payments.

11. D&D Pet Stores operates as an accrual-based partnership and files Form 1065 for 2014. In addition to receipts from pet food sales of $250,000, the partnership has the following items of income and expenses for 2014:

Salaries	$50,000
Insurance	5,000
Charitable contributions	5,000
Licenses	5,000
Rental income	25,000
Guaranteed payments	75,000

What is the ordinary income that D&D Pet Stores should report on its Form 1065?

A. $85,000.
B. $115,000.
C. $190,000.
D. $210,000.

12. Which of the following increases the basis of a partner's interest in a partnership?

A. A partner's share of tax-exempt interest from municipal bonds owned by the partnership.
B. A decrease in the partner's share of liabilities.
C. A distribution of $2,000 of cash to the partner.
D. A property distribution with an FMV of $5,000.

13. The Bissinger Partnership generated income and expenses as stated below. What is the amount of ordinary business income that Bissinger should report for 2014?
- Employee wages: $15,000
- Rental real estate income: $20,000
- Charitable contributions: $500
- Cost of goods sold: $10,000
- Income from cosmetics sales: $75,000

A. $65,000.
B. $69,500.
C. $50,000.
D. $30,000.

14. Daniel is a general partner in the Vrettos Partnership. During the year, Daniel personally assumes $100,000 of the partnership's liabilities. Which of the following statements regarding partnership liabilities is correct?

A. The assumption of partnership debt by Daniel is treated as a distribution of cash to Daniel, and it decreases Daniel's partnership basis.
B. The assumption of partnership debt by Daniel increases his basis.
C. Daniel cannot assume partnership liabilities.
D. Only limited partners are allowed to assume partnership liabilities.

15. Hatam Persian Restaurant operates as a calendar-year partnership. Hatam's two partners, Afsar and Ted, share profits and losses 60% and 40%, respectively. For tax year 2014, Hatam Restaurant had the following income and expense:
- Gross sales: $270,000
- Cost of goods sold: $80,000
- Bank interest income: $2,500
- Wages paid: $50,000
- Short-term capital loss: $5,000

Compute the partnership's ordinary income and flow-through amounts to the partners.

A. Afsar: ordinary income $85,500 and short-term capital loss $3,000; Ted: ordinary income $57,000 and short-term capital loss $2,000.
B. Afsar: ordinary income $82,500; Ted: ordinary income $55,000.
C. Afsar: ordinary income $81,000, interest income $1,500, and short-term capital loss $3,000; Ted: ordinary income $54,000, interest income $1,000, and short-term capital loss $2,000.
D. Afsar: ordinary income $84,000, interest income $1,500, and short-term capital loss $3,000. Ted: ordinary income $56,000, interest income $1,000, and short-term capital loss $2,000.

16. Monica contributes property to a partnership for a 40% interest. The property has a fair market value of $7,000, an adjusted basis of $4,000, and a related mortgage of $1,000 that the partnership assumes. What is Monica's basis in her partnership interest?

A. $4,000.
B. $3,000,
C. $6,000.
D. $3,400.

17. Derrick is a 10% partner in Hartville Roads Partnership. According to the partnership agreement, Derrick is entitled to a fixed annual guaranteed payment of $5,000. During the year, Hartville Roads has $55,000 of ordinary income before deducting the guaranteed payment. How much partnership income should Derrick report on his individual return for this year?

A. $11,500.
B. $16,000.
C. $10,000.
D. $5,000.

18. A partner is not considered at risk for which of the following amounts?

A. The money and adjusted basis of any property the partner contributed to a partnership's activity.
B. The partner's share of income retained by the partnership.
C. A partnership's nonrecourse liability.
D. Certain amounts borrowed by the partnership for use in the activity if the partner is personally liable for repayment.

19. Bea acquired a 30% interest in a partnership by contributing property in which she had an adjusted basis of $25,000. The property's fair market value was $50,000, and it had a $40,000 mortgage that was assumed by the partnership. What is Bea's gain or loss on the contribution of her property to the partnership?

A. $0.
B. $3,000 gain.
C. $12,000 gain.
D. $10,000 loss.

20. What is the latest that a partnership agreement can be modified during a taxable year?

A. Up until the close of the taxable year.
B. No later than the date for filing the partnership return (without extensions).
C. Up until the first day of the taxable year.
D. No later than the extended due date for filing the partnership return.

Unit 11: Partnership Distributions & Liquidations

More Reading:
Publication 541, *Partnerships*

Partnership Distributions

A partnership is not a taxable entity; its income and losses flow through and are reported on the partners' individual tax returns. Each partner is taxed on his distributive share of income, whether or not it is actually distributed. Therefore, when distributions are made to the partners, they are generally not taxable.

Partnership distributions may include the following:

- Distributions of the partnership's earnings for the current or prior years.
- A withdrawal by a partner in anticipation of the current year's earnings.
- A complete or partial liquidation of a partner's interest.
- A distribution to all partners in a complete liquidation of the partnership.

A partnership distribution is not taken into account in determining the partner's distributive share of the partnership's income or loss. If a gain or loss from the distribution is recognized by the partner, it must be reported on his return for the tax year in which the distribution is received. Cash or property withdrawn by a partner in anticipation of the current year's earnings is treated as a distribution received on the last day of the partnership's tax year. A partner's adjusted basis in his partnership interest is decreased (but not below zero) by the cash and adjusted basis of property distributed to the partner.

Example: The adjusted basis of Angela's partnership interest is $14,000. She receives a distribution of $8,000 cash and land that has an adjusted basis of $2,000 and a fair market value of $3,000. The distribution decreases the basis of her partnership interest to $4,000 [$14,000 − ($8,000 + $2,000)]. Because the distribution does not exceed the basis of her partnership interest, Angela does not recognize gain. Any gain related to the excess of the land's fair market value over its adjusted basis may be recognized if she later disposes of it.

Unless there is a complete liquidation of a partner's interest, the basis of property (other than cash) distributed to the partner is its adjusted basis to the partnership immediately before the distribution.

Example: The adjusted basis of Casey's partnership interest is $45,000. She receives a distribution of property that has an adjusted basis of $23,000 to the partnership plus $6,000 of cash. Her basis in the property is $23,000.

However, a partner cannot have a negative partnership basis. Therefore, the basis of property distributed to a partner cannot be more than the adjusted basis of his interest in the partnership, reduced by any cash received in the same transaction.

> **Example:** The basis of Mike's partnership interest is $10,000. He receives a distribution of $4,000 cash and a parcel of land that has an adjusted basis to the partnership of $8,000. His basis in the land is limited to $6,000 ($10,000 - $4,000, the cash he receives), since the total amount cannot exceed his partnership interest. After the distribution, his partnership basis would be zero.

A partnership generally does not recognize any gain or loss because of distributions it makes to partners. The partnership may be able to elect to adjust the basis of its undistributed property. However, when a partnership distributes the following items, the distribution may be treated as a sale or exchange of property rather than a distribution:

- Unrealized receivables or substantially appreciated inventory items distributed in exchange for any part of the partner's interest in other partnership property, including cash
- Other property, including cash, distributed in exchange for any part of a partner's interest in unrealized receivables or substantially appreciated inventory items
  This treatment does not apply to the following distributions:
- A distribution of property to the partner who contributed the same property to the partnership
- Payments made to a retiring partner or successor in interest of a deceased partner that are the partner's distributive share of partnership income or guaranteed payments

A gain or loss on a sale or exchange of unrealized receivables or inventory items a partner received in a distribution is generally treated as ordinary income or loss.

> **Example:** Marcia was a general partner in Illuminated, a retail business that sold handmade candles. In October 2014, the store closed and Marcia received, through dissolution of the partnership, inventory that had a basis of $19,000. She sold the entire inventory for $24,000 one month later. The $5,000 gain would be taxed as ordinary income.

If a partnership acquires a partner's debt and extinguishes the debt by distributing it to the partner, the partner will recognize capital gain or loss to the extent the fair market value of the debt differs from the basis of the debt. The partner is treated as having satisfied the debt for its fair market value. If the issue price of the debt exceeds its FMV when distributed, the partner may have to include the excess amount in income as canceled debt.

Sale of a Partnership Interest

A partnership interest is a capital asset. As a result, a gain or loss on the sale or exchange of a partnership interest is treated as a capital gain or loss. Gain or loss is calculated as the difference between the amount realized and the adjusted basis of the partner's interest in the partnership. If the selling partner is relieved of partnership liabilities, he must include the liability relief as part of the amount realized for his interest.

Example: Selene became a partner in the Rincon Partnership by contributing cash to the formation of the partnership. The adjusted basis of her partnership interest at the end of 2014 is $20,000, which includes her $15,000 share of partnership liabilities. Selene sells her interest in the partnership for $10,000 of cash on December 31, 2014. At the time of the sale, she had been credited for her share of the partnership's income for the tax year. Selene realizes $25,000 from the sale of her partnership interest ($10,000 cash payment + $15,000 liability relief). She must report $5,000 ($25,000 realized − $20,000 basis) as a capital gain.

An exchange of partnership interests generally does not qualify as a nontaxable exchange of like-kind property.

Liquidation of a Partnership

When a partnership dissolves or stops doing business, it is called a partnership liquidation. A partnership may dissolve when a partner dies, or when one partner drops out of the business. The basis of property received in complete liquidation of a partner's interest is the adjusted basis of the partner's interest in the partnership reduced by any cash distributed to the partner in the same transaction.

A partner's holding period for property distributed to him includes the period held by the partnership. If the property was contributed to the partnership by a partner, the holding period includes the period held by that partner also.

Example: Merle's basis in his partnership interest is $20,000. In a distribution to liquidate his entire interest, he receives a delivery truck and a utility trailer. The truck has an adjusted basis to the partnership of $15,000 and an FMV of $15,000. The trailer has an adjusted basis to the partnership of $14,000 and an FMV of $4,000. To figure his basis in each property, Merle first assigns a basis of $15,000 to the truck and $14,000 to the trailer. This leaves a $9,000 basis decrease (the $29,000 total of the assigned basis minus the $20,000 allocable partnership basis). He allocates the entire $9,000 to the trailer to reflect its unrealized depreciation. Merle's basis in the truck is $15,000, and his basis in the trailer is $5,000 ($14,000 - $9,000).

If a partnership is liquidated or dissolved with unamortized organizational or start-up expenses, the unamortized amounts can be deducted in the partnership's final tax year.

> **Example:** The Nielson Partnership is liquidating five years after it formed. It had been amortizing $36,000 of organizational and start-up costs over 180 months. After five years, the partnership had amortized $12,000 ($36,000 ÷ 60 months). Nielsen can deduct the remaining unamortized amount of $24,000 ($36,000 - $12,000) on its final tax return.

Payments made by the partnership to a retiring partner or a deceased partner's estate or in liquidation of the interest of a retiring or deceased partner in exchange for his interest in partnership property are considered a distribution, not a distributive share or guaranteed payment that could give rise to a deduction for the partnership. A retiring or deceased partner is treated as a partner until his interest in the partnership has been completely liquidated.

In a partnership liquidation, the liquidating distributions are similar to regular distributions except that the partner may recognize a loss if the total of cash and the basis of property received is less than his basis in the partnership. A partner cannot recognize a loss on a partnership distribution unless all of the following requirements are met:

- The adjusted basis of the partner's interest in the partnership exceeds the distribution.
- The partner's entire interest in the partnership is liquidated.
- The distribution is in cash, unrealized receivables, or inventory items.

> **Example:** The Webb-Bruner Partnership is liquidating. Donnie's adjusted basis in the partnership is $80,000. He receives a liquidating cash distribution of $60,000. As Donnie's adjusted basis of his partnership interest exceeds the distribution, he has a capital loss of $20,000 ($80,000 - $60,000).

Partnership Termination

A partnership generally terminates when one of the following events takes place:

- All its operations are discontinued and no part of any business, financial operation, or venture is continued by any of the partners in a partnership.
- At least 50% of the total interest in partnership capital and profits is sold or exchanged within a 12-month period, including a sale or exchange to another partner.

The partnership's tax year ends on the date of termination. If the partnership is terminated before the end of its regular tax year, Form 1065 must be filed for the short tax year from the beginning of the tax year through the date of termination. The return is due on the fifteenth day of the fourth month following the date of termination.

Example: Dyer Partnership is a calendar-year partnership. It terminates as a partnership on May 3. Its Form 1065 for the short tax year period of January 1 through May 3 is due on September 15, the fifteenth day of the fourth month following the date of termination.

If a partnership is converted into an LLC classified as a partnership, the conversion does not terminate the partnership, and there is no sale, exchange, or termination of partnership interests. The partnership's tax year does not close, and the LLC can continue to use the partnership's taxpayer identification number.

Cancellation of Debt: If a partnership terminates and one of the former partners is insolvent and cannot pay his share of the partnership's debts, the other partners may be forced to pay more than their share of the liabilities. If another partner pays any part of an insolvent partner's share of the debts, he can take a bad debt deduction.

Example: Hank and Jocelyn are 50/50 partners in a company that provides educational services. The company is struggling and Hank and Jocelyn decide to discontinue the business. The partnership is terminated and it has $50,000 of liabilities to creditors after liquidating all of its assets. However, Hank has filed for personal bankruptcy and the court has declared him insolvent. Even though Jocelyn is a 50% partner, she assumes responsibility for the entire $50,000 of partnership debt. She can claim a bad debt deduction in the amount of $25,000, equal to Hank's share that she assumed.

The cancellation of debt exclusions described in Unit 3 are applied at the partner level rather than at the partnership level. Thus, for example, an individual partner would need to be insolvent to utilize the insolvency exclusion for his share of COD income passed through from an insolvent partnership. If a partner is able to use the exclusion, he would be required to reduce specified tax attributes, including loss and credit carryforwards and the basis of assets.

Related Party Transactions

A partnership cannot deduct a loss on the sale or trade of property if the transaction is directly or indirectly between related parties. Under the related party transaction rules, an individual is considered to be the owner of a partnership interest directly or indirectly owned by his family members. Members of a family, for this purpose, include only brothers, sisters, half-brothers, half-sisters, spouses, ancestors, parents, and lineal descendants (children, grandchildren).

Losses are not allowed from a sale or exchange of property (other than an interest in the partnership) directly or indirectly between a partnership and a person whose direct or indirect interest in the capital or profits of the partnership is more than 50%.

If a sale or exchange is between two partnerships in which the same persons directly or indirectly own more than 50% of the capital or profits interests in each partnership, no loss is allowed.

> **Example:** George and Lynn are siblings. Lynn is a 60% partner in the BuildRite Machinery Partnership, and George is a 55% partner in the Schlutter Partnership. If one partnership sells property to the other at a loss, the loss will not be allowed because the partnerships are considered related parties. Losses will instead be suspended until the property is eventually disposed of in a non-related party transaction.

The basis of each partner's interest in the partnership is decreased (but not below zero) by the partner's share of a disallowed loss.

If the purchaser later sells the property, only the gain realized that is greater than the loss not allowed will be taxable. If a gain from the sale of the property is not recognized because of this rule, the basis of each partner's interest in the partnership is increased by the partner's share of that gain.

Unit 11: Study Questions

1. Davisville Partnership sold a capital asset to Winters Partnership at a loss of $50,000. Davisville had held the property for five months. Davisville is owned 30% by Marvin, 30% by LaTroy, and 40% by Geoff, Marvin's brother. Winters Partnership is owned 80% by Dixon Corporation. Marvin owns 25% of the stock of Dixon Corporation and Geoff's daughter owns 60% of Dixon Corporation. How much of the loss should Davisville Partnership recognize for tax purposes on their tax return for the year of the sale?

A. $0.
B. $3,000.
C. $35,000.
D. $50,000.

2. The adjusted basis of Allison's partnership interest is $24,000. She receives a distribution of $9,000 cash and machinery that has an adjusted basis of $1,000 and a fair market value of $7,000. How much gain should Allison recognize on this distribution?

A. $0.
B. $1,000.
C. $2,000.
D. $7,000.

3. Nina, a partner in the Maass Partnership, receives distributions of $1,000 of cash and property worth $2,000, in which Maass has a basis of $1,500. Nina's outside basis at the time of the distributions is $20,000. The partnership has assets of $40,000 and no outstanding liabilities. The distributions are made at the end of the year, after partnership income (loss) has been recorded. How much gain should Nina recognize on the distributions and what is her basis in the property received?

A. She recognizes a gain of $500 on the property received and her basis in the property is $2,000.
B. She recognizes gain of $1,500 on the property and cash received. Her basis in the property received is $3,500.
C. She recognizes no gain on the property received. Her basis in the property received is $1,500.
D. She recognizes a gain of $1,000. Her basis in the property received is $1,500.

4. The adjusted basis of Steve's partnership interest is $10,000. He receives a distribution of $4,000 cash and a van that has an adjusted basis to the partnership of $9,000 and a fair market value of $12,000. This was not a liquidating distribution. What is Steve's basis in the van?

A. $5,000.
B. $6,000.
C. $12,000.
D. $16,000.

5. Marty is retiring from Sunnyside Partnership this year. His adjusted basis in the partnership is $50,000. He receives a distribution of $65,000 of cash. How would Marty report this transaction?

A. $15,000 capital gain.
B. $50,000 capital gain.
C. $65,000 capital gain.
D. $65,000 ordinary income.

6. Bart and Ellen are equal partners in B&E Partnership. In 2014, the partnership breaks up. Bart is insolvent, and Ellen becomes responsible for paying a portion of his partnership debt. Which of the following statements is correct?

A. Ellen cannot take a bad debt deduction for any debt that the partnership incurred.
B. Bart is not responsible for paying any of his liabilities after dissolution.
C. Ellen can take a bad debt deduction for any amount that she must pay that is not her share of the partnership debt.
D. None of the above.

7. In 2014, Laney sold her partnership interest for $45,000. Her adjusted basis at the time of the sale was $29,500, which includes her $12,500 share of partnership liabilities. When she initially invested in the partnership, she contributed $10,000 worth of equipment. There was no profit or loss at the partnership level that had not been credited at the time she sold her interest. What is the amount and nature of her income or loss from the sale of her partnership interest in 2014?

A. $7,500 ordinary loss.
B. $10,000 capital gain.
C. $12,500 ordinary income.
D. $28,000 capital gain.

8. Bill owns a 75% capital interest in the Shanahan Partnership. Bill's wife, Veronica, is a 65% owner in the Underdahl Partnership. Bill and Veronica file separate tax returns and keep all their books and records separate. Shanahan Partnership sells Underdahl Partnership a factory machine for $7,600. Shanahan's basis in the machinery is $10,000. What is Shanahan Partnership's deductible loss?

A. $0.
B. $2,400.
C. $7,600.
D. $10,000.

9. The adjusted basis of Adrian's partnership interest is $17,500. He received a distribution of $9,000 cash and a piece of land with an adjusted basis of $2,500 to the partnership and a fair market value of $4,000. What is the gain to be recognized at the time of these distributions?

A. $0.
B. $1,500.
C. $4,500.
D. $6,000.

10. Alice's outside basis in Dogan Tiles Partnership on January 1, 2014 was $11,000. She is a 50% partner and shares profits and losses in the same ratio. For 2014, the partnership's ordinary business income was $40,000 and its tax-exempt interest income was $700. If the partnership were to liquidate on December 31, 2014, what would be Alice's basis for determining gain or loss?

A. $24,900.
B. $30,750.
C. $31,350.
D. $30,300.

11. The basis of Hugo's partnership interest is $150,000. He receives a nonliquidating distribution of $80,000 cash and land that has an adjusted basis to the partnership of $100,000. What is the basis of the land in Hugo's hands?

A. $70,000.
B. $100,000.
C. $120,000.
D. $150,000.

Unit 12: C Corporations in General

More Reading:
Publication 542, *Corporations*
Publication 544, *Sales and Other Dispositions of Assets*
Instructions for Form 1120, *U.S. Corporation Income Tax Return*

Most major companies are organized as C corporations, which are taxed under subchapter C of the Internal Revenue Code. A C corporation can own property in its own name and it can be sued directly. The shareholders who own stock in a corporation do not own its individual assets. Individual shareholders are protected from legal liability, except in very unusual circumstances.

The IRS requires certain businesses to be taxed as corporations. The following businesses formed after 1996 are automatically treated as corporations:

- A business formed under a federal or state law that refers to it as a corporation
- A business formed under a state law that refers to it as a joint-stock company or joint-stock association
- Insurance companies
- Certain banks
- A business owned by a state or local government
- A business specifically required to be taxed as a corporation by the IRC (for example, certain publicly-traded partnerships)
- Certain foreign businesses
- Any other business that elects to be taxed as a corporation and files Form 8832, *Entity Classification Election*

Basic Concepts of C Corporations

Basic concepts regarding C corporations include:

1. **Perpetual life and limited liability:** A C corporation enjoys perpetual life and limited liability.
2. **Double taxation:** Earnings of a C corporation may be taxed twice: first at the corporate level and again at the shareholder level if they are distributed as dividends. Shareholders of a C corporation cannot deduct corporate losses.
3. **Shareholder meetings:** A corporation must maintain a list of all its shareholders, and generally must conduct at least one shareholder meeting per year.

4. **Organization:** A C corporation must file a charter, issue stock, and be overseen by a board of directors.
5. **Number of shareholders:** A C corporation may have a single owner-shareholder or an unlimited number of shareholders.
6. **Articles of incorporation:** A corporation's existence starts when articles of incorporation are filed with the state office that handles incorporations (usually the secretary of state), along with any required filing fees.
7. **Liquidation:** If a C corporation liquidates, it will recognize gain or loss on the sale or distribution of its assets. Corporate shareholders then recognize gain or loss on the surrender of their stock to the corporation.
8. **Stock:** A C corporation may sell common and/or preferred stock with different voting rights.
9. **Tax-free fringe benefits:** A C corporation's shareholder-employees can receive tax-free employee fringe benefits that are deductible by the corporation as a business expense.

Filing Requirements

A domestic corporation in existence for any part of a tax year (including corporations in bankruptcy) must file an income tax return, regardless of its taxable income. A C corporation typically files Form 1120, *U.S. Corporation Income Tax Return*, but it may file Form 1120-A if its gross receipts, total income, and total assets are each under $500,000. Tax-exempt organizations organized as corporations file Form 990 rather than Form 1120.

A corporation must continue to file tax returns even if there is no business activity or profits. However, it does not have to file after it has formally dissolved.

A corporation must file by the fifteenth day of the third month after the end of its tax year. Thus, a calendar-year corporation must file its tax return by March 15 of the following year.

Example: Finman Design Corporation's tax year ends December 31. It must file its Form 1120 by March 15.

Example: Greenbook Inc. is a domestic corporation with a fiscal year-end of March 31. Greenbook must file Form 1120 by June 15.

Electronic filing is mandatory for C corporations with $10 million or more in assets and at least 250 or more returns of any type, including information returns such as Forms W-2 or Forms 1099.

A corporation must file Form 7004, *Automatic Extension of Time to File Certain Business Income Tax, Information, and Other Returns,* to request a six-month extension of time to file its income tax return. Form 7004 does not extend the time for paying the tax due on the return. Interest, and possibly penalties, will be charged on any part of the tax due and not paid. The interest is figured from the original due date of the return to the date of payment.

A penalty for late filing is assessed at 5% of any unpaid tax for each month the return is late, up to a maximum of 25% of the unpaid tax on the return. The late filing penalty is reduced by any late payment penalty for the same period. The minimum penalty for any return that is over 60 days late is the smaller of the tax due on the return, or $135. The penalty for late payment of corporate income tax is one half of 1% of the unpaid tax for each month that the tax is not paid, up to a maximum of 25% of the unpaid tax.

These penalties may not be imposed if the corporation shows reasonable cause for not paying or filing on time.

Estimated Tax Payments

Corporations are required to make estimated tax payments if they expect their tax due to be $500 or more during the taxable year. Penalties apply if estimated tax payments are not made on time. Most business entities, including corporations, are required to use the Electric Federal Tax Payment System, EFTPS, to make their estimated tax payments.

Installments are due on a quarterly basis, on the fifteenth day of the fourth, sixth, ninth, and twelfth months of the corporation's taxable year. Thus, a calendar-year corporation is required to make estimated payments on April 15, June 15, September 15, and December 15.

> **Example:** Longinotti Corporation's tax year ends January 31. Estimated tax payments are due on May 15, July 15, October 15, and January 15 (of the following year).

There is no penalty for underpayment of estimated tax if the tax is less than $500, or if each quarterly estimated tax payment is at least 25% of the corporation's current-year tax.

There is also no underpayment penalty if each estimated tax installment is at least 25% of the income tax on the prior year return. However, this provision will not apply in the following instances:

- If the prior tax year was a short year (less than 12 months)
- If the corporation did not file a return for the prior year
- If the prior year tax return showed zero tax liability
- If the corporation had at least $1 million of taxable income in any of the last three years

Corporate Refunds and Amended Returns

Corporations may use Form 1139, *Corporate Application for Tentative Refund,* or Form 1120X, *Amended U.S. Corporation Income Tax Return,* to apply for a refund. If a corporation does not file Form 1139, it must file Form 1120X to apply for a refund. Form 1120X must be filed within three years of the due date, including extensions, for filing the return for a year in which it sustains a loss.

If a corporation accidentally overpays its estimated tax, it may use Form 4466, *Corporation Application for Quick Refund of Overpayment of Estimated Tax,* to obtain a quick refund of its estimated tax payments. Form 4466 may be used if a corporation's overpayment is at least 10% of its anticipated tax liability and at least $500.

Corporate Taxation

Unlike a partnership or an S corporation, a C corporation is not a pass-through entity.

This means that the earnings of a C corporation may be taxed twice. Corporate income is taxed when it is earned and then may be taxed again if it is distributed to shareholders as dividends. A corporation does not receive a tax deduction for the distribution of dividends to its shareholders.

A C corporation's income does not retain its character when it is distributed to shareholders. A corporation can have revenue from many different sources, including sales of products, services, and investment income. If, for example, a C corporation has rental income, it pays tax on this and any other sources of income at the corporate level. When the corporation's after-tax income is distributed to shareholders, this portion does not retain its character as rental income. It is distributed merely as a dividend.

This also applies if the corporation earns tax-exempt income. For example, a C corporation may earn tax-exempt income from investing in municipal bonds. If this income is used to make distributions to shareholders, its tax-exempt character is lost, and the distributions will be taxable dividends to the shareholders.

Example: Riden Paper Products, a C corporation, receives tax-exempt income from bonds. Riden subsequently distributes income to its shareholders as taxable dividends. Even though a portion of the income was tax-exempt to Riden, it does not retain its tax-exempt character when distributions are made to the shareholders. In contrast, in the case of an S corporation or a partnership, the income would have retained its character when it was passed through to the partners or S corporation shareholders.

Example: Jennison, Inc. is a calendar-year C corporation with 20 shareholders. After deducting business expenses, Jennison has $150,000 of taxable net income in 2014. The corporation also earns $4,000 of interest from municipal bonds. The $4,000 of tax-exempt bond interest is excluded from the corporation's taxable income. In December 2014, Jennison distributes $120,000 to its shareholders. The company cannot take a tax deduction for the distribution. Each shareholder has an equal stake in the company, so each one receives $6,000 of dividend income ($120,000 ÷ 20 = $6,000). Each shareholder is required to recognize $6,000 of dividend income for 2014.

Accumulated Earnings Tax

A corporation is allowed to accumulate a reasonable portion of its earnings for possible expansion or other bona fide business reasons. However, a corporation may be subject to the accumulated earnings tax if it does not distribute enough of its profits to shareholders. This tax was instituted to prevent corporations from hoarding income in order to avoid income tax on distributions for its shareholders.

Note: The **accumulated earnings tax** is levied at a rate of **20%** of the excess amount accumulated. It is not automatically applied; it is assessed only after audit. A corporation would have the opportunity to try to justify the amount of its accumulated earnings during an IRS examination.

If the accumulated earnings tax applies, interest is also assessed from the date the corporate return was originally due, without extensions.

An accumulation of $250,000 or less is generally considered reasonable for most businesses. However, for personal service corporations, the limit is $150,000. Reasonable needs of the business include the following:

- Specific, definite, and feasible plans for use of the earnings accumulation in the business.
- The amount necessary to redeem the corporation's stock included in a deceased shareholder's gross estate, if the amount does not exceed the reasonably anticipated total estate and inheritance taxes and funeral and administration expenses incurred by the shareholder's estate.

The absence of a bona fide business reason for a corporation's accumulated earnings may be indicated by many different circumstances, such as a lack of regular distributions to its shareholders or withdrawals by the shareholders classified as personal loans. Actions to expand the business generally qualify as a bona fide reason for the accumulated income. Specific examples may include:

- The expansion of the company to a new area or a new facility
- Acquiring another business through the purchase of stock or assets
- Providing for reasonable estimates of product liability losses

The fact that a corporation has an unreasonable accumulation of earnings is sufficient to establish liability for the accumulated earnings tax unless the corporation can show the earnings were not accumulated to allow its shareholders to avoid income tax.

Corporate Alternative Minimum Tax

Tax laws give special treatment to some types of income and allow special deductions and credits for some types of expenses. As these laws allow some corporations with substantial economic income to significantly reduce their regular tax liabilities, the corporate alternative minimum tax (AMT) is intended to ensure that corporations pay at least a minimum amount of tax on their income.

Note: A corporation owes AMT if its tentative minimum tax is more than its regular tax.

Small corporations are exempt from corporate AMT. Most corporations will automatically qualify for the exemption in their first year of existence. After its first year, a corporation is considered a small corporation if its average annual gross receipts for the prior three years (or portion thereof) do not exceed $7.5 million ($5 million for its first three-year period). If a corporation fails the $7.5 million test for any year, it will be ineligible for the AMT exemption for that year and all subsequent years.

The starting point for the determination of income for AMT purposes is the corporation's regular taxable income. Regular taxable income is modified by a series of additional computations called adjustments and preferences. Adjustments can either increase or decrease taxable income, whereas preferences are calculated on a property-by-property basis and only apply to the extent that they are positive. Adjustments include a portion of accelerated depreciation on buildings and equipment, amortization of pollution control facilities, mining exploration and development expenses, income reported under the completed contract method of accounting, and installment sales income.

Corporations use Form 4626, *Alternative Minimum Tax-Corporations*, to calculate minimum tax for AMT purposes. This calculation includes determining the *alternative tax net operating loss deduction* (ATNOLD), which is the sum of alternative tax net operating loss (ATNOL) carrybacks and carryforwards to the tax year. The ATNOL for a loss year is the excess of the deductions allowed for figuring alternative minimum taxable income (AMTI), excluding the ATNOLD, over the income included in AMTI.

> **Note:** The amount of the ATNOL that can be deducted when calculating AMT income generally cannot exceed 90% of AMTI. If the ATNOL exceeds this limit, it can be carried back two years or forward up to 20 years.

Corporations use Form 8827, *Credit for Prior Year Minimum Tax*, to figure the minimum tax credit, if any, for alternative minimum tax incurred in prior tax years and any minimum tax credit carry forward. A minimum AMT tax credit may be carried forward indefinitely.

Accounting Methods

Like other entities, C corporations may generally use any permissible accounting method for keeping track of income and expenses, as described in Unit 2.

The nonaccrual experience method is a method of accounting for bad debts. If a corporation uses the accrual method of accounting and qualifies to use the nonaccrual experience method for bad debts, it is not required to accrue service-related income that it expects to be uncollectible.

Accrual-method corporations are not required to maintain accruals for certain amounts from the performance of services that, on the basis of their experience, will not be collected, if:

- The services are in the fields of health, law, engineering, architecture, accounting, actuarial science, performing arts, or consulting (personal service corporations); or
- The corporation's average annual gross receipts for the three prior tax years do not exceed $5 million.

This provision does not apply if the corporation charges interest on late payments, or if it charges customers any penalty for failure to pay an amount timely. Further, a corporation cannot use this method for amounts owed from activities such as lending money, selling goods, or acquiring receivables

Additional Form 1120 Schedules

Corporations may be required to submit certain additional schedules along with their Form 1120. For example, Schedule L includes balance sheets as of the beginning and end of the year, based upon the corporation's books and records. Small corporations are not required to complete Schedule L if both assets and gross receipts are below $250K for the taxable year.

Differences in accounting rules for financial reporting (book income) and tax reporting can lead to differences in the amounts of income reported to shareholders and tax authorities.

Preparation of a C corporation's income tax return includes a reconciliation of book income to taxable income.

Study Note: Be familiar with the filing requirements for Schedules L, M-1, M-2, and M-3 for the EA exam, as detailed below.

For small corporations with less than $10 million in assets, the differences in book income and taxable income are reconciled on Schedule M-1 of Form 1120. Large corporations with more than $50 million in assets use Schedule M-3, *Net Income (Loss) Reconciliation for Corporations with Total Assets of $10 million or More*.

Example: Armington Corporation had $8 million in assets in 2014. It uses Schedule M-1 to reconcile the difference between its book and taxable income. Marcus Corporation had $50 million in assets in 2014. It uses Schedule M-3 to reconcile the difference between its book and taxable income.

Starting in 2014, a new rule permits corporations that have at least $10 million but less than $50 million in total assets to file Schedule M-1 in place of Schedule M-3, Parts II and III, which reconcile net income or loss per the income statement and report expense and deduction items. However, Part 1, *Financial Information and Net Income (Loss) Reconciliation*, is still required.

Examples of items that would be included in the reconciliation on Schedule M-1 or Schedule M-3, if applicable, are:

- Excess of capital losses over capital gains (nondeductible, as discussed in Unit 13.)
- Charitable contribution carryover (the amount of charitable contributions that are disallowed for tax purposes and must be carried over to the next taxable year.)
- Travel and entertainment expenses in excess of the allowable 50% limit.
- Federal income taxes paid or accrued, which are deductible for accounting purposes but not for tax purposes.
- Other expenses recorded on the books but not deductible on the return.
- Advance rental income.
- Other income subject to tax that is not included in book income.
- Tax-exempt interest income.
- Other income included on the books but not subject to tax.
- Deductions on the return not charged against book income.

A foreign corporation that is required to file Form 1120-F generally must also complete Schedule M-2.

Note: Corporations with total receipts and total assets of $250,000 or less at the end of the year are not required to file any of these additional schedules: Schedules L, M-1, M-2, or M-3.

Contributions of Capital

A corporation is formed initially by a transfer of money, property, or services by prospective shareholders in exchange for stock in the corporation. A transfer of assets may take place when a business that previously operated as a partnership or sole proprietorship opts to become a corporation.

Contributions to the capital of a corporation are generally not taxable transactions to the corporation, whether or not they are made by the shareholders. A shareholder will not recognize gain when a cash contribution is made for stock. This is just like when a person purchases stock on the open market for cash. The shareholder's basis in the stock is the amount of cash contributed.

However, a transfer of property, rather than cash, to a corporation may have tax consequences to both the corporation and the shareholder. For example, if a shareholder contributes property to a corporation, he generally recognizes gain and the basis of the contributed property to the corporation is the same as the basis that the shareholder had in the property, after increase for any gain that the shareholder recognized in the exchange. There is an exception, however, for situations in which property is contributed and the shareholder controls the corporation immediately after the transfer. This is called a section 351 transfer, and is explained below.

The basis of property contributed to a corporation's capital by anyone other than a shareholder is zero.

Example: The city of Omaha, Nebraska gives Madera Corporation a plot of land as an enticement to locate its business operations there. Madera accounts for the property as a contribution to capital. The land has zero basis since the property was contributed by a non-shareholder.

If stock is exchanged for services, the recipient of the stock recognizes taxable income based upon fair market value of the services provided, and that amount is his basis in the stock.

Example: Justin is a web designer who provides web design services to a corporation. He agrees to accept stock as payment instead of cash. The stock is valued at $5,000. Justin must recognize ordinary income of $5,000 as payment for services he rendered to the corporation. His basis in the stock is $5,000.

Section 351: Nontaxable Corporate Transfers

If a taxpayer transfers property to a corporation in exchange for stock and immediately afterward the taxpayer controls the corporation, the exchange may not be taxable. This rule applies both to individuals and to entities that transfer property to a corporation. It also applies whether the corporation is being formed or is already in operation. The effect is to allow the investing shareholder to contribute assets to a corporation without immediate tax consequences, and to defer recognition of taxable gain until the stock received is later disposed.

This nonrecognition rule does not apply in the following situations:

- The corporation is an investment company.
- The taxpayer transfers the property in a bankruptcy proceeding in exchange for stock that is used to pay creditors.
- The stock is received in exchange for the corporation's debt (other than a security, such as a bond) or for interest on the corporation's debt (including a security) that accrued while the taxpayer held the debt.

In order to be considered in control of a corporation immediately after an exchange, the transferors must own at least 80% of the total combined voting power of all classes of stock entitled to vote and at least 80% of the outstanding shares of each class of nonvoting stock.

Example: Amanda owns an office building. Her basis in the building is $100,000. She organizes a corporation when the building has a fair market value of $300,000. Amanda transfers the building to the corporation for all its authorized capital stock. No gain is recognized by Amanda or the corporation on the transfer.

Example: Aaron and Pedro transfer property with a basis of $100,000 to a corporation in exchange for stock with a fair market value of $300,000. This represents only 75% of each class of stock of the corporation. The other 25% was already issued to someone else. Aaron and Pedro must recognize a taxable gain of $200,000 on the transaction.

This nonrecognition rule does not apply to services that are rendered in exchange for stock. The value of stock received for services is income to the recipient.

Example: Wayne is an architect. In 2014, he transfers property worth $35,000 and provides services valued at $3,000 to a corporation in exchange for stock valued at $38,000. Right after the exchange, Wayne owns 85% of the outstanding stock. No gain is recognized on the exchange of property. However, Wayne must recognize ordinary income of $3,000 as payment for services he rendered to the corporation.

If, in an otherwise nontaxable exchange of property for stock, the shareholder receives money or property in exchange for the contribution of property, he would recognize gain to the extent of the money and the fair market value of property received. If the corporation assumes the shareholder's liabilities, the assumption generally is not treated as if the shareholder received money or other property, unless:

- The liabilities the corporation assumes are more than the shareholder's adjusted basis in the property transferred, in which case gain is recognized up to the difference. However, if the liabilities assumed give rise to a deduction when paid, such as a trade account payable or interest, no gain is recognized.
- There is no good business reason for the corporation to assume the liabilities, or if the main purpose in the exchange is to avoid federal income tax.

The shareholder's basis in his stock must be reduced by the amount of the liabilities assumed by the corporation.

Example: Rasheda transfers machinery to a corporation in exchange for all of the corporation's outstanding stock. The machinery's FMV at the time of the transfer is $200,000. Rasheda's basis in the machinery is $80,000. The machinery is encumbered by an outstanding loan of $30,000, which the corporation assumes. In this example, the section 351 exchange is valid, and no gain or loss is recognized in the transaction. Rasheda's basis in the stock is $50,000 ($80,000 basis of property contributed minus the $30,000 loan that was assumed by the corporation.)

Study Note: You must understand the concepts related to section 351 transfers as you may encounter multiple questions on this topic on the EA exam.

Both the corporation and certain stockholders involved in a nontaxable exchange of property for stock must attach to their income tax returns a complete statement of all facts pertinent to the exchange. This reporting requirement applies to stockholders who own 5% or more of a public company or 1% or more of a privately held company.[15]

Exclusions from Nonrecognition Treatment

This nonrecognition rule does not apply when the property transferred is of a relatively small value when compared to the value of stock already owned, and the main purpose of the transfer is to qualify for the nonrecognition of gain or loss. Property transferred will not be considered to be of small value if its FMV is at least 10% of the FMV of the stock already owned or to be received by the transferor.

---

[15] The rules regarding section 351 exchanges also apply to S corporations.

If a group of transferors exchanges property for corporate stock, each transferor may not receive stock in proportion to his interest in the property transferred. However, if a disproportionate transfer takes place, it may be treated as if the stock were first received in proportion to the interests in the property and then portions were used to make gifts, pay compensation for services, or to satisfy the transferor's obligations.

If a corporation transfers its stock in satisfaction of indebtedness and the fair market value of its stock is less than the indebtedness, the corporation has income to the extent of the difference from the cancellation of indebtedness. For example, if stock is given to an individual to pay for a debt, the transfer does not qualify for nonrecognition treatment.

Unit 12: Study Questions

1. John transfers property worth $43,000 and renders services valued at $6,000 to a corporation in exchange for stock valued at $49,000. Right after the exchange, John owns 90% of the outstanding stock. How much income, if any, must he recognize in this transaction?

A. $0.
B. $3,000.
C. $6,000.
D. $49,000.

2. Which of these domestic business entities will be automatically taxed as a corporation?
    1. A joint stock company.
    2. An insurance company.
    3. Any business formed under a state law that refers to it as a corporation.
    4. A single member limited liability company (LLC).

A. All of the above.
B. 1, 2, and 3.
C. 3.
D. 2 and 3.

3. Ruiz Corporation has net income for books of $3 million in 2014. What is its taxable income if it also has the following?

Federal income tax expense	$1,500,000
Travel and entertainment expenses	200,000
Tax-exempt interest income	100,000
Capital losses	47,000
Capital gains	18,000

A. $4,471,000
B. $1,529,000.
C. $4,729,000.
D. $4,529,000.

4. Nell transfers property with a basis of $200,000 and an FMV of $350,000 to a corporation in exchange for stock with a fair market value of $300,000. This represents 65% of the stock of the corporation. How much gain is recognized by Nell on this transaction?

A. $0.
B. $50,000.
C. $100,000
D. $150,000.

5. The Trujillo Corporation has $1 million of total receipts and $6 million of assets at the end of the year. Which of these schedules is the corporation required to file?

A. Schedule L.
B. Schedule L and M-1.
C. Schedule M-3.
D. Schedule L and M-3.

6. The accumulated earnings tax is levied at a rate of _____ on accumulated taxable income.

A. 5%.
B. 15%.
C. 20%.
D. 50%.

7. Lori and Marcus each transfer property with a basis of $10,000 to a corporation in exchange for stock with a fair market value of $30,000. The total stock received by them represents 75% of the corporation's stock. The other 25% of the corporation's stock was issued earlier to Anne, an unrelated person. The taxable consequences are:

A. None, because it is a transfer of property for stock.
B. Lori and Marcus each recognize a gain of $20,000.
C. Lori and Marcus each recognize a gain of $30,000.
D. 80% of the transaction is recognized as a taxable gain.

8. Vihaan transferred a warehouse with an adjusted basis of $10,000 and a fair market value of $140,000 to the Data-Tech Corporation in exchange for 100% of Data-Tech stock. The building was subject to a mortgage of $25,000, which Data-Tech Corporation assumed. The fair market value of the stock was $150,000. What are the amounts of Vihaan's realized gain and his recognized gain?

A. $165,000 realized gain; $15,000 recognized gain.
B. $35,000 realized gain; $15,000 recognized gain.
C. $165,000 realized gain; $25,000 recognized gain.
D. $130,000 realized gain; $15,000 recognized gain.

9. Kersten is trying to decide whether to form an S corporation or a C corporation for her business. What are factors that may persuade her against using the C corporation structure?

A. Earnings of a C corporation are taxed twice (at the corporate level and at the shareholder level if they are distributed as dividends).
B. Shareholders of a C corporation cannot deduct corporate losses.
C. A corporation has limited liability.
D. Both A and B.

10. The amount of the alternative tax net operating loss (ATNOL) that can be deducted generally cannot exceed _____ of alternative minimum taxable income (AMTI).

A. 50%.
B. 75%.
C. 80%.
D. 90%.

11. To be eligible for section 351 treatment, immediately after the exchange, a taxpayer must own at least _____ of the total combined voting power of all classes or stock entitled to vote and at least _____ of the outstanding shares of each class of nonvoting stock.

A. 50% and 50%.
B. 70% and 80%.
C. 80% and 80%.
D. 80% and 100%.

12. Kathleen transferred a factory building with an adjusted basis of $70,000 and a fair market value of $110,000 to the Carpenteria Corporation in exchange for 100% of Carpenteria Corporation stock and $20,000 cash. The building was subject to a mortgage of $25,000, which Carpenteria Corporation assumed. The fair market value of the stock was $75,000. What are the amounts of Kathleen's realized gain and her recognized gain?

A. $25,000 realized gain; $25,000 recognized gain.
B. $50,000 realized gain; $45,000 recognized gain.
C. $50,000 realized gain; $20,000 recognized gain.
D. $35,000 realized gain; $20,000 recognized gain.

13. BRB Corporation's fiscal year ends June 30. Not counting extensions, what is the due date for its tax return?

A. September 15.
B. April 15.
C. October 15.
D. January 15.

14. The accumulated earnings tax may be imposed on C corporations that accumulate earnings beyond the reasonable needs of their businesses. Which of the following reasons would not be an example of a reasonable accumulation?

A. The expansion of the company to a new area or a new facility.
B. Acquiring another business through the purchase of stock or other assets.
C. Allowing the shareholders to take bona fide loans from the corporation.
D. Providing for reasonable estimates of product liability losses.

15. Topcare Pet Products, a cash-basis corporation that operates on the calendar year, is required to make estimated tax payments. What are the due dates for the estimated payments?

A. April 15, June 15, September 15, and December 15.
B. January 15, March 15, June 15, September 15, and December 15.
C. March 1, June 1, September 1, and December 1.
D. None of the above.

Unit 13: Corporate Transactions

More Reading:
Publication 542, *Corporations*

The tax treatment of certain items is different for C corporations, as compared with individuals and other types of entities. C corporations are subject to their own tax rate schedules.

Capital Gains and Losses

Unlike the favorable capital gains' rates available to individuals, the capital gains of a C corporation are taxed at the same rate as its ordinary income. A corporation figures its capital gains and losses much like an individual. However, in the case of a C corporation, its capital losses are only deductible to the extent of its capital gains. A C corporation is not allowed to offset capital losses against its other income the way individuals can (up to a limit).

Note: Among the drawbacks of the C corporation structure are double taxation; the inability of shareholders to deduct corporate losses; the absence of preferential capital gains tax rates; and the limitation on deductibility of capital losses, as described here.

If a corporation has an excess capital loss, it may carry the loss back or forward to other tax years and deduct it from any net capital gains that occurred in those years. The default election is for a corporation to carry back its capital losses to the earliest of the three preceding years in which it had net capital gains; any remaining losses may be carried forward a maximum of five years.

A capital loss from another year cannot create or increase a net operating loss in the year to which it is carried. Further, capital losses can be carried only to years that would otherwise have had a net capital gain.

In rare instances, longer carryback and carryforward periods may be allowed. Capital losses that are a result of foreign expropriation[16] may not be carried back, but may be carried forward for ten years. In the case of a regulated investment company (RIC), net capital losses may be carried forward eight years.

When a corporation carries back or carries forward a capital loss, the loss does not retain its character as a long-term loss. All capital loss carryforwards and carrybacks are treated

---

[16] This is when a foreign nation takes a corporation's assets for its own use.

as short-term losses. A C corporation cannot carry back capital losses to any previous year when it was an S corporation.

> **Example:** In 2014, Chambrun Corporation, a calendar-year C corporation, has a capital gain of $3,000 and a capital loss of $9,000. The capital gain offsets some of the capital loss, leaving a net capital loss of $6,000. Chambrun treats this $6,000 as a short-term loss when carried back or forward. The corporation carries the $6,000 short-term loss back to 2013. In 2013, Chambrun had a short-term capital gain of $8,000 and a long-term capital gain of $5,000 (a total of $13,000 of capital gains). It carries back the loss and subtracts the $6,000 short-term loss (carryback) first from the net short-term gain. This results in a net capital gain of $7,000 that consists of a net short-term capital gain of $2,000 ($8,000 - $6,000) and a net long-term capital gain of $5,000, which allows the corporation to receive a refund of income tax paid in 2013.

Net Operating Losses (NOLs)

A C corporation figures and deducts a net operating loss (NOL) in the same manner as an individual, an estate, or a trust, and the same carryback (two years) and carryforward (up to 20 years) periods apply. A corporation figures an NOL the same way it figures taxable income. It starts with gross income and subtracts its deductions. If its deductions are more than its gross income, the corporation has an NOL. However, the following rules apply for figuring NOLs:

- A corporation cannot increase its current year NOL by carrybacks or carryovers from other years in which it has a loss.
- A corporation cannot use the domestic production activities deduction to create or increase a current year NOL.
- A corporation can take the deduction for dividends received, without regard to the aggregate limits that normally apply.
- A corporation can figure the deduction for dividends on certain preferred stock of public utilities without limiting it to its taxable income for the year.

An NOL carryback can only be used to reduce income tax. If the corporation owes other taxes or penalties from a prior year, a carryback will not reduce the penalties.

> **Example:** Artisan Cheese Corporation had taxable income of $30,000 in 2013. Business has slowed, and Artisan Cheese has an NOL of $20,000 in 2014. The company decides to carry back its NOL to recover a portion of the income taxes it paid in 2013. Artisan Cheese also incurred a $1,200 penalty in 2013 for failing to remit estimated taxes on time. The corporation cannot recover the amount paid for the estimated tax penalty.

A C corporation with a net operating loss can file for a refund by using Form 1139 or by amending a prior year tax return using Form 1120X. If a corporation elects to waive carryback and instead carry forward its NOL, it enters the carryover on Form 1120, Schedule K. If the corporation is filing a consolidated return, it must also attach a required statement or the election will not be valid.

If a corporation reasonably expects to have a net operating loss in its current year, it may automatically extend the time for paying income tax liability for the preceding year by filing Form 1138, *Extension of Time For Payment of Taxes by a Corporation Expecting a Net Operating Loss Carryback.*

Charitable Deductions

C corporations can deduct the amount of charitable contributions made to qualified organizations, up to 10% of taxable income. A corporation figures its taxable income for this limit without regard to the following:

- The deduction for charitable contributions
- The dividends-received deduction
- The domestic production activities deduction
- Any net operating loss carryback to the tax year
- Any capital loss carryback (but not carryforward) to the tax year

The rules regarding what qualifies as a charitable organization and required supporting documentation are the same for corporations as they are for individuals. Generally, no deduction is allowed for any charitable contribution of $250 or more unless the corporation obtains a receipt from the donee organization. The written receipt or acknowledgment should show the amount of cash contributed or a description of the property contributed. The receipt or acknowledgment should also give a description and a good faith estimate of the value of any goods or services provided in return for the contribution, or state that no goods or services were provided in return for the contribution.

If a corporation (other than a closely held or personal service corporation) claims a deduction of more than $500 for contributions of property other than cash, a schedule describing the property and the method used to determine its fair market value must be attached to the corporation's return. In addition the corporation should keep a record of:

- The approximate date and manner of acquisition of the donated property.
- The cost or other basis of the donated property held by the donor for less than 12 months prior to contribution.

- Any donation of a used vehicle, boat, or similar property if it takes a deduction larger than $500 for the donated vehicle.

If the deduction claimed for donated property exceeds $5,000, the corporation must complete Form 8283, *Noncash Charitable Contributions,* and attach it to its tax return. A corporation must obtain a qualified appraisal for all deductions of property claimed in excess of $5,000. A qualified appraisal is not required for the donation of cash, publicly traded securities, or inventory.

A corporation using the cash method deducts contributions in the tax year they are paid. A corporation using the accrual method can deduct unpaid contributions if the board of directors authorized the contributions during the year, and the corporation pays the contributions within 2.5 months after the close of the year. A declaration with a statement that includes the date that the board of directors adopted the resolution must accompany the return.

Example: Ladera Corporation is a calendar-year, accrual-basis corporation. Ladera's board of directors approves a charitable contribution of $5,000 to the United Way on December 15, 2014. Ladera Corporation deducts the contribution on its 2014 corporate tax return. Ladera does not have to pay the contribution until March 15, 2015, or 2.5 months after the close of its tax year.

A corporation can carry over charitable contributions made during the current year that exceed the 10% limit to each of the subsequent five years, subject to the same 10% limitation in each year. Any excess contributions not used within that five-year period are lost. No carryback is allowed for charitable contributions. A corporation cannot deduct a carryover of excess contributions to the extent it increases a net operating loss carryover.

Example: Hernandez Sporting Goods has net income of $600,000 in 2014 before taking into account its charitable contributions. The corporation donated $80,000 to a qualified charity in 2014. It also has a net operating loss carryover of $100,000 from a prior year. Therefore, the corporation's charitable deduction is limited to $50,000. The allowable contribution deduction is figured as follows:

$$(\$600,000 - \$100,000 = \$500,000) \times 10\% = \$50,000$$

The charitable contribution that is not allowed in the current tax year can be carried forward for up to five years. If Hernandez Sporting Goods does not use the remainder at the end of five years, the deduction is lost.

Example: Gromwell Corporation, a calendar-year C corporation, makes a large charitable contribution in 2014. As a result, the corporation has a carryover of excess contributions paid in 2014 and it does not use all the excess on its return for 2015. Gromwell Corporation can carry the rest over to 2016, 2017, 2018, and 2019. After that time, it can no longer carry over the excess 2014 charitable contributions.

Dividends-Received Deduction

A corporation can deduct a percentage of certain dividends received from other corporations in which it has an ownership interest. The dividends-received deduction (DRD) is designed to reduce the consequences of double taxation. Without this deduction, corporate profits could be taxed to the corporation that earned them, then to its corporate shareholders, and then again to the individual shareholders of the parent corporation.

The DRD complements the consolidated return regulations, which allow affiliated corporations to file a single consolidated return for U.S. federal income tax purposes. It is available to C corporations but not to LLCs, S corporations, partnerships, or individuals.

Generally, if a corporation receives dividends from another corporation, it is entitled to a deduction of 70% of the dividends received, if the corporation owns less than 20% of the other corporation. If the corporation receiving the dividend owns 20% or more of the other corporation, the deduction increases to 80% of the dividends received. If the corporation receiving the dividends owns more than 80% of the distributing corporation, it is allowed to deduct 100% of the dividends it receives.

To summarize, the deduction for dividends received is based on the percentage of stock ownership in the distributing corporation:

Percentage of Ownership	Dividends-Received Deduction
Less than 20%	70%
20 - 80%	80%
Greater than 80%	100%

The percentage of stock ownership is determined without regard to preferred stock.

Example: The Quincy Corporation owns 25% of LightStar Corporation. The Quincy Corporation has taxable income of $70,000 before taking into account its dividend income. In 2014, Quincy received $100,000 of dividends from LightStar. Quincy is allowed an 80% dividends-received deduction, figured as follows: $80,000 = ($100,000 × 80%). Therefore, only $20,000 of the dividends received from LightStar Corporation are taxable. In 2014, the Quincy Corporation's taxable net income is $90,000 ($70,000 + $20,000).

Example: JRD Corporation owns 85% of the outstanding stock in Humboldt Corporation. In 2014, JRD receives $250,000 of dividends from Humboldt. Because JRD has over 80% ownership of Humboldt, it can claim the 100% dividends-received deduction and the dividends are not taxable.

If a corporation is entitled to a 100% DRD, there is no taxable income limitation, and the corporation can deduct the full amount of the dividends received. However, if a corporation is entitled to a 70% DRD, it can deduct amounts only up to 70% of its taxable income. If a corporation is entitled to an 80% DRD, it can generally deduct amounts only up to 80% of its taxable income. In each case, the corporation would determine taxable income without the following items:

- The DRD
- The net operating loss deduction
- The domestic production activities deduction
- Any adjustment due to the nontaxable part of an extraordinary dividend
- Any capital loss carryback to the tax year

If a corporation has an NOL for a tax year, the DRD must be figured differently. The limit of 80% (or 70%) of taxable income does not apply if use of the unlimited DRD by the receiving corporation would result in a net operating loss.

Example: Verde Eco-Products Corporation loses $25,000 from its own business operations in 2014. Verde Eco-Products also receives $100,000 of dividend income from a 20%-owned corporation. Therefore, Verde Eco-Product's taxable income in 2014 is $75,000 ($100,000 − $25,000 loss) before the DRD. If Verde Eco-Products claims the full DRD of $80,000 ($100,000 × 80%) and combines it with a loss from operations of $25,000, it will create an NOL of ($5,000). Therefore, the 80% of taxable income limit does not apply. The corporation can deduct the full $80,000 DRD.

Example: Redwood Patio Corporation has a loss of $15,000 from business operations in 2014. However, it also has dividends of $100,000 from a corporation in which it holds an interest of 50%. Therefore, Redwood's taxable income is $85,000 before applying the DRD. After claiming the DRD of $80,000 ($100,000 × 80%), its taxable income is $5,000. Because Redwood would not have an NOL after applying a full 80% DRD, its allowable DRD is limited to 80% of its taxable income (before the DRD), or $68,000 ($85,000 × 80%).

Corporations cannot take a deduction for dividends received from the following entities:

- A real estate investment trust (REIT)
- A tax-exempt corporation
- A corporation whose stock was held less than 46 days
- A corporation whose preferred stock was held less than 91 days
- Any corporation, if another corporation is under an obligation to make related payments for positions in substantially similar property

Dividends on deposits in domestic building and loan associations, mutual savings banks, cooperative banks, and similar organizations are taxed as interest income—not dividends. They do not qualify for the DRD. Small business investment companies can deduct 100% of the dividends received from taxable domestic corporations.

Study Note: For the EA exam, you must understand how to calculate the dividends-received deduction and how it applies to a C corporation's taxable income and net operating losses.

Related Party Transactions

Strict rules apply to related party transactions. A corporation that uses the accrual method cannot deduct business expenses and interest owed to a related person who uses the cash method until the corporation makes the related payment and the amount is included in the related person's income. These rules also deny the deduction of a loss on the sale or trade of property (other than in the complete liquidation of a corporation) between related persons.

For purposes of these rules, the following persons are considered related to a corporation:

- A corporation that is a member of the same controlled group.
- An individual who owns, directly or indirectly, more than 50% of the value of the outstanding stock of the corporation.
- A partnership, if the same persons own more than 50% of the value of the outstanding stock of the corporation and more than 50% of the partnership.

- An S corporation, if the same persons own more than 50% of the value of the outstanding stock of each corporation.
- A trust fiduciary, when the trust or its grantor owns, directly or indirectly, more than 50% of the value of the outstanding stock of the corporation.
- An employee-owner of a personal service corporation, regardless of the amount of stock owned.

In determining whether a person directly or indirectly owns any of the outstanding stock of a corporation, the following rules apply:
- Stock directly or indirectly owned by or for a corporation, partnership, estate, or trust is considered owned proportionately by or for its shareholders, partners, or beneficiaries.
- An individual is considered to own the stock that is directly or indirectly owned by or for his family. Family includes only brothers and sisters (including half-brothers and half-sisters), a spouse, ancestors, and lineal descendants.
- An individual owning any stock in a corporation is considered to own the stock that is directly or indirectly owned by his partner.

> **Example:** Robert is a 90% owner in Nampa Boots Corporation. His wife, Eileen, is a 55% owner of Terabyte Corporation. Robert is considered a related person for the purposes of ownership in Terabyte Corporation. Therefore, for the related-party transaction rules, Robert is also considered a 55% owner in Terabyte Corporation and Eileen is considered a 90% owner in Nampa Boots Corporation.

Closely Held Corporations

A closely held corporation generally has a small number of shareholders (often family members) and no public market for its stock. Corporate ownership and management often overlap. A corporation is considered to be closely held if both of the following apply:
- It is not a personal service corporation.
- At any time during the last half of the tax year, more than 50% of the value of its outstanding stock is, directly or indirectly, owned by or for five or fewer individuals. An individual in this case includes certain trusts and private foundations.

A closely held corporation is subject to additional limitations in compensation paid to corporate officers and the tax treatment of items such as passive activity losses and at-risk rules. The at-risk rules for closely held corporations are similar to those that apply to partners in a partnership. These rules dictate that a closely held corporation's losses are only deductible up to the amount at risk of financial loss in connection with an activity. The amount at risk generally equals:

- The money and the adjusted basis of property contributed by the taxpayer to the activity, and
- The money borrowed for the activity.

The at-risk amount also includes the FMV of property (adjusted for any liens or encumbered mortgages) that is pledged as security or collateral for the debts of the activity.

> **Example:** Allworth Corporation is a closely held C corporation with only two shareholders: a father and son. Allworth Corp. invests $50,000 in a business venture, and also pledges the value of a factory building as collateral for a $100,000 loan that is used in the business venture. Allworth's factory building has a fair market value of $150,000. Allworth Corp.'s amount at risk in the business venture is only $100,000 [$50,000 plus the $50,000 ($150,000 - $100,000) equity in the building].

The following items increase an entity's amount at risk:

1. A contribution of additional cash (or property) to the venture.
2. Any recourse loan for which the corporation is liable for repayment.

The amount at risk is decreased by the following items:

1. An investor's withdrawal of cash or property from the activity.
2. A nonrecourse loan where the corporation is not liable for repayment.

The amount at risk cannot be decreased below zero. If this occurs, suspended losses from prior years must be reduced.

Controlled Groups

A controlled group is a group of corporations that are related through common ownership, typically as either parent-subsidiary or brother-sister.

A **Parent-Subsidiary Controlled Group** involves a parent corporation that owns at least 80% or more of the voting power of at least one other corporation (with possible additional corporations that are at least 80% owned by either the common parent or one of the subsidiary entities).

A **Brother-Sister Controlled Group** involves situations in which five or fewer individuals, estates, or trusts own 80% or more of the combined voting power for multiple corporations, and have identical common ownership within the individual corporations of at least 50%.

Example of parent-subsidiary controlled group: Ciara Corporation owns:

- 90% of the stock of Shiffrin Corporation
- 80% of the stock of Kumagai Corporation
- 65% of the stock of Faruqi Corporation

Unrelated persons own the percentage of stock not owned by Ciara Corporation. As Ciara Corporation owns 80% or more of the stock of Shiffrin and Kumagai, it is the common parent of a parent-subsidiary group consisting of the three corporations. Faruqi Corporation is not a member of the group because Ciara Corporation's ownership is less than 80%.

Example of brother-sister controlled group: Kendrick Corporation and Leitzel Corporation are owned by four shareholders in the following percentages:

Shareholder	Kendrick Corp.	Leitzel Corp.
A	70%	30%
B	10%	50%
C	10%	10%
D	10%	10%
Total	**100%**	**100%**

The same five or fewer common owners must own more than 80% of stock or some interest in all members of the controlled group. In this example, the four shareholders together own 100% of the stock of each corporation, so the first test is met. They also meet the second test of owning more than 50% of the stock of each corporation, taking into account only the identical ownership in each corporation.

Shareholder	Identical Ownership Percentage in Both Corporations
A	30%
B	10%
C	10%
D	10%
Total	**60%**

A controlled group is allowed a single set of graduated income tax brackets, a single exemption amount for AMT purposes, and a single accumulated earnings credit of $250,000. In each case, these amounts must be allocated among the members of the group. Members of controlled groups are also subject to the rules regarding related party transactions that may require deferral of recognition for losses or expenses incurred by one party.

Unit 13: Study Questions

1. During 2014, Bernardino Jewelry, a domestic C corporation, had the following income, expenses, and deductions:

Gross receipts	$95,000
Net capital gains	10,000
Business expenses (not including charitable contributions)	65,000
Charitable contribution	20,000
NOL carryover from 2013	30,000

What is the amount of Bernardino Jewelry's allowable charitable contribution deduction for 2014?

A. $1,000.
B. $3,000.
C. $4,000.
D. $20,000.

2. Which of the following statements is correct about a controlled group of corporations?

A. Members of a controlled group are entitled to only one accumulated earnings tax credit.
B. A parent corporation and its 80% owned subsidiary would be considered members of a controlled group.
C. Members of controlled groups are subject to rules regarding related party transactions that may require deferral of recognition for losses or expenses incurred by one party.
D. All of the above.

3. James Corporation owns 50% of Nguyen Corporation's outstanding common stock. James has taxable income of $8,000, which includes dividends received of $10,000 from its investment in Nguyen Corporation. What is James Corporation's taxable income after applying the DRD?

A. $0.
B. $1,600.
C. $6,400.
D. $8,000.

4. Rosas Fine Stationery is a cash-basis C corporation. During the year, Rosas received $140,000 in dividends from a domestic corporation in which it owns less than 20% of the stock. Rosas has taxable income of $180,000 during the year, before figuring the dividends-received-deduction. Based on this information, what is the dividends-received-deduction for Rosas Fine Stationery?

A. $70,000.
B. $98,000.
C. $100,000.
D. $126,000.

5. BMD Corporation is a calendar-year corporation that uses the accrual method. What is the last day that the corporation can pay a charitable contribution and still deduct it on its 2014 tax return?

A. December 31, 2014.
B. January 15, 2015.
C. March 15, 2015.
D. April 15, 2015.

6. McClimate Corporation owns 25% of Wilson Foods Corporation. In 2014, McClimate received $10,000 of dividends from Wilson Foods. Assuming no other limitations apply, McClimate's dividends-received deduction is:

A. $7,000.
B. $8,000.
C. $2,000.
D. $0.

7. In 2014 Real Time Corporation made contributions totaling $20,000 to qualified charitable organizations. Due to income limitations, Real Time could deduct only $15,000 of the contributions on its return. Which of the following correctly states the treatment of the excess $5,000 of charitable contributions?

A. It can be carried back for two years and carried forward for 20 years.
B. It can be carried forward for 20 years.
C. It can be carried back for three years and carried forward for ten years.
D. It can be carried forward for five years. They cannot be carried back.

8. The Arbabi Plastics Corporation is a calendar-year C corporation. In 2014, it has $400,000 of taxable income before consideration of the following additional items:

- Charitable contributions: $50,000
- Dividends-received deduction: $70,000
- Domestic production activities deduction: $40,000

What portion of the charitable contributions is deductible in 2014?

A. $50,000.
B. $29,000.
C. $40,000.
D. $36,000.

9. Xena Corporation is a cash-basis C corporation. In 2014, the corporation has a net short-term capital gain of $23,000 and a net long-term capital loss of $29,000. How should these capital gains and losses be treated?

A. The corporation can deduct a $6,000 long-term capital loss on its 2014 tax return.
B. The corporation can carry back the $29,000 long-term capital loss to a prior year, where it may only be deducted against long-term capital gains.
C. The corporation can carry back the $6,000 net capital loss to a prior year, where it may be deducted against short-term capital gains.
D. The corporation must carry forward the entire capital loss to the following tax year. Carryback of capital losses is not allowed.

10. Which of the following best describes a brother-sister controlled group?

A. A brother and sister each own 50% of a corporation, or a total of 100% of the corporation combined.
B. A parent corporation that owns at least 80% or more of the voting power of at least one other corporation, with at least two brothers and one sister or two sisters and one brother as owners.
C. Five or fewer individuals, estates, or trusts own 80% or more of the combined voting power for multiple corporations, and have identical common ownership within the individual corporations of at least 50%.
D. A corporation that controls at least two other corporations where a brother and sister are chief executive officers of the different corporations and each control over 50% of their respective corporations.

11. In 2014, Mansour Corporation has a $15,000 loss from its business operations. In addition, Mansour has received $100,000 of taxable dividends from a 30%-owned corporation. Therefore, its taxable income is $85,000 before applying the dividends-received deduction. What is the corporation's dividends-received deduction?

A. $15,000.
B. $68,000.
C. $80,000.
D. $100,000.

12. The Surf's Up Corporation had an NOL of $110,000. Which of the following statements is correct?

A. The corporation can forgo the carryback period and choose to carry the entire loss forward to the next 20 years.
B. The corporation is required to carry back losses for two years and then forward for 15 years.
C. The corporation can carry back losses five years and carry them forward for 25 years.
D. A corporation cannot carry back losses. It can only carry them forward.

13. Redd Beauty Products and Helena Mountain Coffee are domestic C corporations. Redd Beauty owns 25% of Helena Mountain Coffee. Redd Beauty's income from its business operations in 2014 is $500,000. In addition to its business income, Redd Beauty received dividends from Helena Mountain Coffee of $145,000. What is Redd Beauty's dividends-received deduction?

A. $36,250.
B. $101,500.
C. $116,000.
D. $145,000.

14. Kendall Corporation has net income of $600,000 before its charitable contribution of $65,000. The company also has an NOL carryover of $200,000 from the prior year. What is Kendall Corporation's allowable charitable contribution?

A. $0.
B. $6,500.
C. $60,000.
D. $40,000.

Unit 14: Corporate Distributions & Liquidations

More Reading:
Publication 542, *Corporations*

Corporate Distributions

Corporate distributions or dividends occur when cash, stock, or other property is distributed to shareholders based on the shareholders' ownership of the corporation's stock. When a corporation earns profits, it may retain the profits in the business (as retained earnings) or pay all or a portion of the profits as dividends to shareholders. The amounts a corporation pays as dividends are not deductible expenses. Dividends are most commonly paid in cash. However, a dividend can take the form of stock or other property.

The most common kinds of corporate distributions are:

- Ordinary dividends (either in cash or in property)
- Capital gain distributions
- Nondividend distributions
- Distributions of stock or stock rights

The FMV of distributed property becomes the shareholder's basis in the property. A distribution may be reduced by the following liabilities:

- Any liability of the corporation the shareholder assumes
- Any liability applicable to distributed property, such as mortgage debt the shareholder assumes in connection with distribution of ownership in a building

The basis of distributed property can never go below zero, no matter how much liability a shareholder assumes.

Reporting Requirements: A corporation must furnish Form 1099-DIV, *Dividends and Distributions,* to each of its shareholders who receives a dividend of $10 or more during a calendar year by January 31 of the following year. The corporation must also file copies of the Forms 1099-DIV with the IRS, along with Form 1096, *Annual Summary and Transmittal of U.S. Information Returns,* by February 28 (March 31 if filing electronically) of the year following the year of the distribution.

The corporation is allowed to furnish Forms 1099-DIV to shareholders any time after April 30 of the year of the distributions if the corporation has made its final distributions for the calendar year.

Distributions from Earnings and Profits

The amount of a C corporation's earnings and profits (E&P) determines the tax treatment of corporate distributions to shareholders.

The starting point for determining corporate E&P is the corporation's taxable income. The following transactions **increase the amount of E&P**:

- Long-term contracts reported on the completed contract method
- Intangible drilling costs deducted currently
- Mine exploration and development costs deducted currently
- Dividends-received deduction

The following transactions **reduce the amount of E&P**:

- Corporate federal income taxes
- Life insurance policy premiums on a corporate officer
- Excess charitable contributions (over 10% limit)
- Expenses relating to tax-exempt income
- Excess of capital losses over capital gains
- Corporate dividends and other distributions

Accumulated Earnings and Profits

Accumulated earnings and profits are E&P that the corporation accumulated before the current year and has not distributed to its shareholders. If a corporation's current year E&P are less than the total distributions made during the year, part or all of each distribution is treated as a distribution of accumulated E&P.

Note: Any part of a distribution from current-year earnings and profits or accumulated earnings and profits is reported as dividend income to the shareholder and is generally taxable as ordinary income to the shareholder rather than as capital gains.

If accumulated earnings and profits are reduced to zero, the remaining part of a distribution reduces the adjusted basis of the shareholder's stock. This is referred to as a nondividend distribution and it is not taxable to the shareholder until his basis in the stock is fully recovered. This nontaxable portion is considered to be a *return of capital* that he had previously invested in the corporation.

Definition: Return of capital refers to the return of some or all of an investor's investment in a company or partnership. Since it represents the recoupment of investment, return of capital is not considered income, but instead decreases the net value, and tax basis, of the investment.

If the corporation makes nondividend distributions to a shareholder that exceed the adjusted basis of his stock, the excess distribution is treated as a gain from the sale or exchange of property and is taxable to the shareholder as capital gain.

Example: Tobias is the only shareholder of Seaside Corporation, a calendar-year corporation. During the year, Seaside makes four $1,000 distributions to Tobias. At the end of the year (before subtracting distributions made during the year), the corporation has $10,000 of current year earnings and profits. Since the corporation's current year E&P ($10,000) were more than the amount of the distributions it made during the year ($4,000), all of the distributions are treated as distributions of current year E&P. The corporation must issue Form 1099-DIV to Tobias by January 31 to report the $4,000 distributed to him as dividends. Seaside Corporation must use Form 1096, *Annual Summary and Transmittal of U.S. Information Returns*, to report this transaction to the IRS by February 28 (March 31 if filing electronically). The corporation does not deduct these dividends on its income tax return.

If nondividend distributions are made to shareholders, the corporation must report these distributions to the IRS on Form 5452, *Corporate Report of Nondividend Distributions*.

Distributions of Property

A sale or exchange of property by a corporation to a shareholder that is not a corporation may be treated as a distribution to the shareholder, to the extent the FMV of the property on the date of the sale or exchange exceeds the price he paid.

A distribution of property is also treated as if the corporation had sold the property to the shareholder. A corporation (either a C corporation or an S corporation) recognizes gain on a distribution of property to a shareholder if the FMV of the property is more than its adjusted basis.

Example: Wright Stuff Corporation distributes to a shareholder $65,000 of cash and an excavator with a $35,000 adjusted basis and a $50,000 FMV. Wright Stuff must recognize a $15,000 gain on the distribution of property because its FMV is more than its adjusted basis ($50,000 - $35,000 = $15,000).

For this purpose, the FMV is considered to be the greater of the property's actual FMV or the amount of liabilities the shareholder assumes in connection with the distribution. If the distributed property was depreciable or amortizable, the corporation may have to treat all or a portion of the gain as ordinary income from depreciation recapture.

These transactions may be taxable to the shareholder at FMV and are reported on Form 1099-DIV or Form 5452, *Corporate Report of Nondividend Distributions*. A corporation generally cannot recognize a loss on a distribution of property (i.e., where the property's FMV is less than the adjusted cost basis). However, a corporation is allowed to recognize losses when depreciated property is distributed to shareholders in complete liquidation (when the corporation ceases operations).

Stock Distributions

Stock distributions or stock dividends occur when a corporation issues additional shares of its own stock to shareholders, rather than paying a cash dividend or distributing property.

Stock rights, also known as stock options, may be distributed by a corporation to some or all of its shareholders to allow them to purchase additional shares at a set price.

Distributions by a corporation of its own stock or stock rights generally are tax-free to shareholders and not deductible by the corporation. However, they may be treated as taxable property distributions in certain situations, including when:

- The shareholder has the choice to receive cash or other property instead of stock or stock rights.
- The distribution gives cash or other property to some shareholders and an increase in the percentage interest in the corporation's assets or earnings and profits to other shareholders.
- The distribution is in convertible preferred stock.
- The distribution gives preferred stock to some shareholders and common stock to other shareholders.
- The distribution is paid based on ownership of preferred stock.

A corporation must capitalize, rather than deduct, the expenses of issuing a stock dividend, such as printing, postage, and any fees for listing on stock exchanges.

Constructive Distributions

A constructive distribution may occur when a corporation confers a benefit upon a shareholder. A transaction recorded by the corporation as an expense may be recategorized instead as a constructive distribution. This would make the transaction nondeductible to the corporation and in many instances taxable to the shareholder. Examples of constructive distributions include:

- **Payment of personal expenses:** If a corporation pays personal expenses on behalf of a shareholder, the amounts should be classified as a distribution rather than expenses of the corporation.
- **Unreasonable compensation:** If a corporation pays an employee-shareholder an unreasonably high salary considering the services actually performed, the excessive part of the salary may be treated as a distribution.
- **Unreasonable rents:** If a corporation rents property from a shareholder and the rent is unreasonably higher than the shareholder would charge an unrelated party for use of the property, the excessive part of the rent may be treated as a distribution.
- **Cancellation of a shareholder's debt:** If a corporation cancels a shareholder's debt without repayment by the shareholder, the amount canceled may be treated as a distribution.
- **Property transfers for less than FMV:** If a corporation transfers or sells property to a shareholder for less than its FMV, the excess may be treated as a distribution.
- **Below market or interest-free loans**: If a corporation gives a loan to a shareholder on an interest-free basis or at a rate below the applicable federal rate, the uncharged interest may be treated as a distribution.

Example: Arevalo Corporation rents office space from a 75% shareholder, Otto, who is the sole owner of the office building. The corporation pays Otto $15,000 a month for its space. He charges other tenants $5,000 a month for offices with the same square footage. The excessive rent of $120,000 ($15,000 - $5,000 = $10,000 × 12 months) in 2014 would likely be disallowed as an expense for Arevalo Corporation and recharacterized as a constructive distribution to Otto.

Stock Redemptions

A stock redemption occurs when a corporation buys back its own stock from a shareholder in exchange for cash or property. The stock acquired may be canceled, retired, or held as Treasury stock.

A shareholder is required to treat the amount realized on a stock redemption as either a dividend or a sale of stock. Stock redemptions are generally treated as dividends unless certain conditions are met, as follows:

- The redemption is not equivalent to a dividend, meaning that the shareholder's proportionate interest and voting power in the corporation has been substantially reduced.

- There was a substantially disproportionate redemption of stock, meaning that the amount received by the shareholder is not in proportion to his stock ownership.
- The redemption was due to a complete termination of a shareholder's interest in the corporation.
- The redemption is of stock held by a non-corporate shareholder and was part of a partial liquidation.
- The distribution is received by an estate and does not exceed the sum of death taxes plus funeral and administration expenses to be paid by the estate.

The corporation may realize a gain from the redemption, as if property were sold at its fair market value to the shareholder. The corporation must recognize income on the distribution of depreciated property to the extent of depreciation or the amount realized, whichever is less. The corporation may not recognize a loss on a stock redemption unless:

- The redemption occurs in a complete liquidation of the corporation, or
- The redemption occurs on stock held by an estate.

Corporate Liquidations and Dissolutions

Liquidating distributions are distributions received by a shareholder during a complete or partial dissolution of a corporation. When a corporation dissolves, it redeems all of its stock in a series of distributions.

Complete liquidation occurs when the corporation ceases to be a going concern and its activities are merely for the purpose of winding up its affairs, paying its debts, and distributing any remaining balance to its shareholders. In certain cases in which the buyer is a corporation in control of the distributing corporation, the distribution may not be taxable. A corporate dissolution or liquidation must be reported on Form 966, *Corporate Dissolution or Liquidation*, within 30 days after the resolution or plan is adopted to dissolve the corporation or liquidate any of its stock. Exempt entities are not required to file Form 966, even if they are organized as corporations.

When property is distributed in a complete liquidation, the transaction is treated as if the corporation sold the assets to a buyer at fair market value. The corporation recognizes gain or loss on the liquidation in an amount equal to the difference between the FMV and the adjusted basis of the assets distributed. A corporation is allowed to recognize losses during the liquidation, except for losses resulting from transactions with related parties.

Example: Blair Corporation distributes a building to one of its shareholders as part of a complete liquidation. The adjusted basis of the building is $750,000 and its fair market price is $400,000. Blair Corporation can recognize a loss of $350,000.

Amounts received by the shareholder in complete liquidation of a corporation are treated as full payment in exchange for the shareholder's stock. A liquidating distribution is considered a return of capital and is not taxable to the shareholder until the shareholder recovers all of his basis in the stock. After the basis of the stock has been reduced to zero, shareholders must report any additional amounts as a capital gain.

If a dissolving corporation distributes property that is subject to a liability, the gain or loss is adjusted to reflect assumption of the liability. If the liability is greater than the FMV of the property, the amount of the liability is treated as the FMV of the property. A corporation is required to provide each shareholder a Form 1099-DIV showing the amount of the liquidating distribution.

Example: Maurer Farm Equipment Corporation is going through a complete liquidation. Saul, a shareholder, receives a liquidating distribution of property (a tractor). Maurer Corporation's basis in the tractor is $3,000. The fair market value of the tractor is $13,000. However, the tractor is encumbered by a liability of $15,000 (an unpaid loan), which Saul assumes. Because the remaining loan amount is more than the FMV of the tractor, the amount of the liability is treated as the FMV. The corporation must recognize a $12,000 gain on the distribution ($15,000 loan - $3,000 basis), and Saul is treated as having received a liquidating distribution of $15,000.

A corporation must file an income tax return for the year it goes out of business, even if it has no income or business activity in that year. If the dissolution is effective on any day other than the last day of the corporation's tax year, the final tax return is due on the fifteenth day of the third month following the close of its short tax year.

Unit 14: Study Questions

1. Ryan is a shareholder in PRK Corporation with a basis of $20,000 in his stock. He also has an outstanding $10,000 loan that he owes to the corporation. In 2010, Ryan files for bankruptcy and defaults on the loan. PRK Corporation cancels Ryan's debt in 2014. How should this cancellation of debt be reported?

A. The debt cancellation is treated as a $10,000 distribution to Ryan.
B. The debt cancellation is considered a return of capital to Ryan.
C. The debt cancellation is a charitable contribution to Ryan.
D. The debt cancellation is a $10,000 capital gain to Ryan.

2. Pasqual Corporation has operated on a fiscal year runs from July 1 through June 30. However, the corporation is dissolved on February 10. When is its final tax return due?

A. April 15.
B. May 15.
C. June 30.
D. September 15.

3. Trotter Corporation distributes to a shareholder $75,000 of cash and a delivery truck with a $40,000 adjusted basis and a $60,000 FMV. What gain or loss, if any, must Trotter Corporation recognize?

A. No gain or loss is recognized in this transaction.
B. $20,000 gain.
C. $40,000 gain.
D. $20,000 loss.

4. Three years ago, Mark purchased 100 shares of Rock Star, Inc. for $10 per share. In 2014 Rock Star completely liquidated and distributed $20,000 to Mark in exchange for all of his stock. Mark must report this distribution as:

A. $20,000 of long-term capital loss.
B. $19,000 of short-term capital gain.
C. $19,000 of long-term capital gain.
D. $19,000 of ordinary income.

5. All of the examples below are considered corporate distributions except:

A. Ordinary dividends to a shareholder.
B. Capital gain distributions to a shareholder.
C. Constructive distributions to an employee-shareholder.
D. Wage compensation to an employee-shareholder.

6. Geraldine owns 1,000 shares of Kimball Software Corporation. Her shares were all acquired three years ago, and her basis in the stock is $20,000. Kimball Software completely liquidated in 2014 and distributed $56,000 in two payments to Geraldine. She received $16,000 in December 2014 and $40,000 in January 2015. How much gain or loss does Geraldine recognize in 2014 and 2015?

A. $4,000 loss in 2014 and $40,000 gain in 2015.
B. $4,000 loss in 2014 and $44,000 gain in 2015.
C. No gain or loss in 2014 and $40,000 gain in 2015.
D. No gain or loss in 2014 and $36,000 gain in 2015.

7. Distributions of stock rights are generally tax-free to shareholders. Which of the following statements is not correct?

A. Even if a shareholder has a choice to receive cash instead of stock rights, so long as the shareholder chooses to receive stock rights, the distribution will be tax-free.
B. Stock rights are distributions by a corporation of rights to acquire its own stock.
C. Stock rights are sometimes called stock options.
D. Stock rights can be taxable in some circumstances.

8. The Midwestern Grain Corporation distributes property with an adjusted basis of $1,000 and a fair market value of $4,000 subject to a liability of $6,000 to Joseph, a shareholder. What is the gain or loss, if any, Midwestern Grain must recognize as a result of the distribution?

A. $1,000 loss.
B. $3,000 gain.
C. $5,000 gain.
D. $0.

9. April bought corporate stock five years ago for $1,000. In 2012, she received a return of capital distribution of $800. April did not include this amount in her income, but correctly reduced the basis of her stock to $200. She received another return of capital distribution of $300 in 2014. The first $200 of this amount reduced April's stock basis to zero. How should she report the remaining $100 distribution?

A. April must report $100 of long-term capital gain in 2014.
B. April does not have to report the additional return of capital.
C. April must report the $100 as ordinary income.
D. April must report any additional return of capital as a capital loss.

10. Which of the following statements about stock distributions is correct?

A. A stock distribution must be treated like a cash distribution that is taxable to the shareholder.
B. Stock distributions are usually taxable to the corporation when distributed to shareholders.
C. Stock distributions are deductible by a corporation as an expense.
D. Stock distributions are generally not taxable to shareholders and not deductible by the corporation.

11. Buffalo Corporation displays a collection of fine artwork in its main office. When the 75% shareholder retires, he is presented with his choice from the art collection. He selects a painting with a fair market value of $250,000. Buffalo Corporation's basis in the painting is $100,000. How should the transaction be reported on the Buffalo Corporation's tax return?

A. $150,000 loss.
B. $150,000 distribution.
C. $150,000 taxable gain.
D. $250,000 taxable gain.

12. When using taxable income as a starting point, which of the following transactions increases the amount of a C corporation's earnings and profits?

A. Excess of capital losses over capital gains.
B. Dividends-received deduction.
C. Life insurance premiums on a corporate officer.
D. Excess charitable contributions.

13. Millerton Software is a C corporation that was formed in 2004. At the beginning of 2014, Millerton Software had accumulated earnings and profits of $100,000. The company makes a $5,000 distribution to its 100% shareholder in the first month of each quarter. In 2014, Millerton Software had $150,000 of gross income and $140,000 of expenses from ordinary business operations. Millerton also received $5,000 in fully tax-exempt interest from state bonds. What part of the second quarter distribution is treated as a distribution of accumulated earnings and profits?

A. $1,250.
B. $2,500.
C. $3,750.
D. $5,000.

14. Six years ago, Sabine purchased 100 shares of Vitality Nature Corporation stock for $50 per share. In 2014, the corporation liquidated. After paying its outstanding liabilities, Vitality Nature distributed $10,000 of cash and appreciated property worth $90,000 to its shareholders. Sabine's portion of the distributed assets and cash was $12,000. What must she report from this liquidating distribution in 2014?

A. $0 gain.
B. $3,000 capital gain.
C. $7,000 capital gain.
D. $10,000 capital gain.

Unit 15: S Corporations

More Reading:
Form 1120S and Instructions

The rules governing S corporations are found in subchapter S of the Internal Revenue Code. An S corporation has similarities to both a C corporation and a partnership. Like a partnership, an S corporation is a pass-through entity and is generally not taxed on its earnings. Instead, income and losses pass through to shareholders. Like a C corporation, an S corporation enjoys liability protection that a partnership does not.

S corporations do have some drawbacks. They are less flexible than partnerships. There are instances in which an S corporation is forced to pay tax on its earnings. There are also restrictions on the number and types of shareholders an S corporation can have.

Electing S Corporation Status

To become an S corporation, a business must file an election on Form 2553, *Election by a Small Business Corporation.* The filing must be made within 2.5 months after the start of its tax year for the election to be effective at the beginning of the year. An election made after the first 2.5 months of the tax year becomes effective on the first day of the following tax year, unless the corporation receives IRS approval to make the election retroactive to the beginning of the tax year.

Based on updated guidelines, the IRS will generally accept a late S election if the following requirements are met:

- The entity intended to be classified as an S corporation, is an eligible entity, and failed to qualify as an S corporation solely because the election was not timely;
- The entity has reasonable cause for its failure to make the election timely;
- The entity and all shareholders reported their income consistent with an S corporation election in effect for the year the election should have been made and all subsequent years; and
- Less than three years and 75 days have passed since the effective date of the election (unless certain additional conditions are met).

If an entity does not qualify for relief under these guidelines, it may request relief through a private letter ruling.

An S corporation generally may choose to use either the cash or the accrual method of accounting, subject to the requirements outlined in Unit 2.

S Corporation Requirements

The main requirements for S corporation status are:

- It must be a domestic corporation.
- It cannot have more than 100 shareholders.
- Shareholders generally must be U.S. citizens or residents, if individuals, or certain kinds of trusts, banks, estates, or certain tax-exempt corporations. Corporate shareholders and partnerships are generally excluded. However, certain tax-exempt corporations, including 501(c)(3) corporations, may be S corporation shareholders. In contrast, an S corporation is allowed to own a partnership interest or own stock in a C corporation. Nonresident aliens cannot be shareholders.
- A business must meet the definition of a small business corporation, per IRC section 1361.
- An S corporation can only have one class of stock, but that stock can be voting or nonvoting. The difference in voting rights allows one group of shareholders to retain voting control, while allowing other shareholders to benefit from corporate earnings. However, all the stock of an S corporation must possess identical rights to distribution and liquidation proceeds.
- Profits and losses must be allocated to shareholders in proportion to each one's interest in the business.
- All shareholders of an S corporation must give written consent for the S election.

If the S election is made during the corporation's tax year for which it first takes effect, each individual shareholder who holds stock at any time during the part of that year before the election is made must also consent to the election. This is true even if the person may have sold or transferred his stock before the election is made.

Example: Ron, Tara, and William are all equal shareholders in a C corporation. In January 2014, William decides to retire and sells all his shares in the C corporation to Sandra, an unrelated person. In February, Ron, Tara, and Sandra vote to elect S corporation status. All the current shareholders must agree to the election. William must also agree, even though he sold all his stock before the election was made.

Example: A husband and wife own 90% of an S corporation and their son owns the remaining 10% of the stock. The son announces his marriage to a nonresident alien and he gives her one-half of his stock. The S corporation's status is revoked, because a nonresident alien cannot hold stock ownership in an S corporation.

For the 100-shareholder limit, related persons are considered one shareholder. Spouses are automatically treated as a single shareholder. A family, defined as a group of individuals descended from a common ancestor, plus spouses and former spouses of either the common ancestor or anyone lineally descended from that person, is considered a single shareholder as long as any family member elects such treatment.

When a shareholder dies, the deceased shareholder's spouse and the estate are still considered one shareholder for the shareholder limit. However, a husband and wife cannot be considered a single shareholder if they divorce, or if the marriage is dissolved for any other reason than death. Therefore, a shareholder's divorce can potentially increase the number of shareholders to a number in excess of the 100-shareholder limit. If an S corporation fails to meet this restriction, the S election is considered terminated, and the S corporation ceases to be an S corporation and is instead taxed as a C corporation.

The following entities cannot elect S corporation status:

- A bank or thrift institution that uses the reserve method of accounting for bad debts
- An insurance company
- A domestic international sales corporation (DISC)
- Any foreign entity

Filing Requirements for S Corporations

An S corporation files its tax return on Form 1120S, and allocated amounts of income, deductions, and credits pass through to individual shareholders and are reported on Schedule K-1. The return must be signed and dated by an authorized corporate officer or, in certain instances, by a fiduciary such as a receiver, trustee, or assignee, on behalf of the corporation.

An S corporation is always required to file a tax return, regardless of income or loss. The filing requirement ends only when the corporation is dissolved. The IRS mandates electronic filing for S corporations with $10 million or more in assets that file 250 or more returns of any type (W-2, 1099, K-1) per year. The tax return is due on the fifteenth day of the third month following the tax year end. For a calendar-year corporation, the tax return is due March 15. A corporation that has dissolved must generally file by the fifteenth day of the third month after the date it dissolved.

A six-month extension of time to file can be requested using Form 7004, *Automatic Extension of Time to File Certain Business Income Tax, Information, and Other Returns.*

Shareholders of an S corporation are required to pay estimated taxes in connection with their own returns. S corporations are only required to pay estimated taxes if $500 or more of certain corporate-level taxes apply.

Required Tax Year

As discussed in Unit 2, an S corporation must use one of the following as its tax year:

- A calendar year
- A natural business year
- An ownership tax year (the tax year that coincides with greater than 50% ownership of the corporation)
- A fiscal year duly elected and approved by the IRS under section 444
- A 52-53 week year that ends with reference to a year listed above

An S corporation may always use a calendar year, or any other tax year for which it establishes a bona fide business purpose.

A new S corporation must use Form 2553, *Election by a Small Business Corporation*, to elect a tax year. An existing S corporation that wishes to change its existing tax year may use Form 1128, *Application to Adopt, Change, or Retain a Tax Year*. However, Form 8716, *Election to Have a Tax Year Other Than a Required Tax Year*, is used to apply for a tax year change under section 444.

Termination of an S Election

Once the S election is made, it stays in effect until terminated. In addition to the ways already discussed, the election will terminate automatically in any of the following cases:

- The corporation no longer qualifies as a small business corporation.[17]
- For each of three consecutive tax years, the corporation
  - Has accumulated earnings and profits,[18] and
  - Derives more than 25% of its gross receipts from passive investment income.
- The corporation creates a second class of stock.
- The shareholders willingly revoke the S election.

Absent an automatic termination due to failure to meet the requirements of S election status, an S election can be revoked only with the consent of the majority shareholders (those holding more than 50% of the corporation's stock, including nonvoting stock). The corporation

---

[17] This termination of an election is effective as of the day the corporation no longer meets the definition of a small business corporation. A statement notifying the IRS of the termination and the date it occurred is attached to Form 1120S for the final year of the S corporation.

[18] This applies only to S corporations that were previously C corporations. An S corporation cannot accumulate earnings and profits as a C corporation can. However, it is possible for a C corporation to elect S corporation status and still have accumulated earnings and profits at the time of the election.

must file a statement of revocation with the IRS that is signed by each shareholder who consents.

A shareholder revocation may specify an effective revocation date that is on or after the day the revocation is filed. If no date is specified and the revocation is made on or before the fifteenth day of the third month of that tax year, the revocation is effective at the start of a tax year. If no date is specified and the revocation is made after the fifteenth day of the third month of the tax year, the revocation is effective at the start of the next tax year. A revocation may be rescinded before it takes effect.

When an S election is terminated, two short tax years are created for the corporation. Income and loss must be allocated on a pro rata basis between the period the corporation operated as an S corporation and the period as a C corporation that was created when the S election was terminated. The entity must file Form 1120S for the S corporation's short year by the due date (including extensions) of the C corporation's short year return.

> **Example:** On May 1, 2014, Zander Corporation, a calendar-year S corporation, exceeded 100 shareholders. This will create two short tax years—one for the S corporation and one for the C corporation. Zander must file a Form 1120S and a Form 1120; the due date for each return will be March 15, 2015.

If the IRS deems that a revocation was inadvertent (that the shareholders did not mean to revoke their S election or that the revocation was accidental), the corporation may be allowed to correct the error and retain its S election status.

> **Example:** In 2014, Morrison Window Blinds, a calendar-year S corporation, inadvertently terminates its S status. The S corporation shareholders immediately correct the problem. Therefore, the S corporation status is considered to have been continuously in effect, and no termination is deemed to have occurred. Only a single S corporation tax return will need to be filed for tax year 2014.

A terminating event will be considered inadvertent if the event was not within the control of the corporation, and the shareholders did not plan to terminate the election. Further, all of the following must occur:

- The S election must have involuntarily terminated either because:
  - The corporation no longer qualified as a small business corporation, or
  - It had accumulated earnings and profits from past C corporation activities.
- The IRS must agree that the termination was inadvertent.
- The corporation must take reasonable and immediate steps to correct the issue.
- The shareholders and the corporation must agree to any adjustments proposed by the IRS.

- The corporation must request a private letter ruling from the IRS for any inadvertent termination relief.

Note: If the status of an S corporation is terminated, either because the shareholders elect to become a C corporation or because a terminating event has occurred, the S corporation cannot elect to become an S corporation within the next five years. However, the IRS may choose to waive the five-year restriction.

S Corporation Income and Expenses

As with a partnership, all the income of an S corporation must be allocated to the shareholders, even if it is not distributed. Income, gains, losses, deductions, and credits are allocated to each shareholder on a pro-rata basis, according to the number of shares of stock held by the shareholder on each day of the corporation's tax year, and retain their character when they are passed through. The shareholder then reports the items on his tax return.

Some of the items that pass through to shareholders on a pro rata basis and retain their character must be separately stated on an S corporation's tax return. These include:

- Net income or loss from rental real estate activity (rental income)
- Portfolio income or loss that include:
  - Interest income
  - Dividend income
  - Royalty income
- Capital gains or losses
- Section 1231 gain or loss
- Charitable contributions
- Section 179 expense deduction
- Foreign taxes paid or accrued
- Expenses related to portfolio income or loss
- Credits, including:
  - Low-income housing credit
  - Qualified rehabilitation expenses
- Investment interest expense
- Tax preference and adjustment items needed to figure a shareholder's AMT
- Nonbusiness bad debts

Unlike a C corporation, an S corporation is not eligible for a dividends-received deduction.

> **Example:** The Oliveira Company is an S corporation with a single shareholder. In 2014, it has $100,000 of gross receipts; $40,000 wage expense to its shareholder; $15,000 of charitable contributions; $10,000 of rental losses; and $8,000 of capital gains. Its ordinary income is $60,000 ($100,000 gross receipts minus $40,000 wages). The other items are all separately stated on Form 1120S but are not used to determine ordinary income or loss.

Limited Taxation of S Corporations

S corporations generally are not subject to taxation since they are primarily pass-through entities. However, in certain cases, S corporations are subject to taxes. A subchapter S corporation may have to pay income tax due to:

1. Excess net passive investment income
2. Built-in gains
3. Investment credit recapture
4. LIFO recapture

None of these taxes are deductible as business expenses by the S corporation.

An S corporation may also be responsible for other taxes, such as payroll taxes if it has employees, and penalties, such as late filing penalties.

Excess Net Passive Income Tax

An S corporation that had been a C corporation previously and had accumulated E&P during that period may have to pay tax at the corporate level on excess net passive income (ENPI) if its passive investment income exceeds 25% of its gross receipts. The purpose of this requirement is to discourage a corporation with accumulated earnings and profits (E&P) from functioning as a holding company and gaining favorable tax treatment as an S corporation.

For this purpose, passive investment income includes interest, dividends, rents, and royalties. If income is generated in the ordinary course of business, it is non-passive, or active, income.

The tax rate on excess net passive income is 35% and is applied against the lesser of:

- Excess net passive income, or
- Taxable income figured as though the corporation were a C corporation.

> **Example:** Trailblazer Inc. is an S corporation with accumulated E&P from earlier years when it was a C corporation. In 2014, Trailblazer has gross receipts of $80,000, comprised as follows:
> - Rental income: $25,000
> - Interest income: $10,000
> - Additional gross receipts from business operations: $45,000
>
> Trailblazer's passive investment income for the year is $35,000, or 44% of its gross receipts. As this exceeds the 25% threshold, Trailblazer will be subject to the 35% excess net passive income tax on the lesser of its excess net passive income or its taxable income (calculated as if it were a C corporation).

If the corporation has always been an S corporation, it would not have accumulated E&P and the ENPI tax would not apply.

If the corporation has accumulated E&P at the end of the tax year and has ENPI in excess of 25% of its gross receipts for three consecutive taxable years, the S election is terminated as of the beginning of the fourth year.

> **Example:** For 2012, 2013, and 2014, Herzing Corporation, a calendar-year S corporation, earned passive investment income in excess of 25% of its gross receipts. If Herzing Corporation has accumulated E&P from earlier years in which it was a C corporation, its S election would be terminated as of January 1, 2015, and the corporation would be taxed as a C corporation as of January 1, 2015.

Built-in Gains (BIG) Tax

The built-in gains (BIG) tax may apply to the following S corporations:
- An S corporation that was a C corporation before it elected to be an S corporation.
- An S corporation that acquired an asset with a basis determined by reference to its basis (or the basis of any other property) in the hands of a C corporation (a transferred-basis acquisition).

An S corporation must measure for each asset the amount of unrecognized appreciation that existed at the time an S election was made or an asset was acquired. The net amount of unrecognized built-in gains and built-in losses is subject to tax when those assets are sold, unless the assets are held for at least five years after conversion from a C corporation to an S corporation.

The S corporation pays tax on the recognized built-in gain at the highest corporate rate. The tax is reported on Form 1120S and is a deduction for the shareholders.

The built-in gains tax applies only to corporations that elected S status after 1986, and it only affects property dispositions during the five-year period beginning:

- On the first day of the first tax year for which the corporation is an S corporation, for an asset held when the S corporation was a C corporation, or
- On the date the asset was acquired by the S corporation, for an asset with a basis determined by reference to its basis in the hands of a C corporation.

Investment Credit Recapture

Business credit recapture is generally the responsibility of the entity that claims the credit. If a company is an S corporation when the credit originates, the credit passes through to the shareholders and they must report any subsequent recapture on Form 4255, *Recapture of Investment Credit*. However, if a C corporation claims the general business credit and then converts to S status, the S corporation itself may be responsible for the recapture.

LIFO Recapture Tax

A corporation that accounts for inventory using the last in, first out (LIFO) method is subject to a LIFO recapture tax in its final year as a C corporation after making an S corporation election. This tax is intended to address built-in gains in inventory that might not otherwise be recognized. The taxable LIFO recapture amount is the amount by which the amount of inventory assets calculated under the first in, first out (FIFO) method exceeds the amount under the LIFO method. If the LIFO value is higher than the FIFO value, no negative adjustment is allowed.

Inventory assets include stock in trade of the corporation, or other property of a kind that would properly be included in the inventory of the corporation if on hand at the close of the taxable year.

The LIFO recapture tax is paid in four equal installments, beginning on the due date of the final C corporation return. The three subsequent installments are payable on the due dates of the first three S corporation returns.

S Corporation Basis

To compute basis in the stock of an S corporation, a shareholder starts, just as for a C corporation, with his initial capital contribution or the initial cost of the stock purchased.

However, his basis may vary based on how the stock was acquired (by purchase, gift, or inheritance). In general, a shareholder's basis in S corporation stock is determined as follows:

Stock Acquired	How Stock Basis is Determined
Stock purchase	If the S corporation shares were purchased outright, initial basis is the cost of the shares.
S corporation capitalized	If the shares were received when the S corporation was formed under IRC §351,[19] the basis in the stock is equal to cash invested and/or the basis of property transferred to the corporation, increased by any gain recognized on the transfer, and decreased by any boot received from the corporation (IRC §358).
Prior C corporation	Initial basis in S corporation stock is the basis in the C corporation stock at the time of conversion.
Gift	The recipient's basis in shares received by gift is generally the donor's basis (IRC §1015). Suspended passive activity losses can increase the basis of a gift (IRC §469).
Inheritance	The basis of inherited stock is its fair market value at the date of death or, if elected, the alternate valuation date (IRC §1014).
Services rendered to the S corporation	Basis in stock received in exchange for services is measured by the stock's fair market value, rather than by the value of the services (Treas. Reg. §1.61-2).

Both the taxability of a distribution and the deductibility of a loss are dependent on a shareholder's stock basis, and basis is adjusted annually, on the last day of the S corporation year, in the following order:
- Increased for income items and excess depletion
- Decreased for distributions
- Decreased for nondeductible, noncapital expenses and depletion
- Decreased for items of loss and deductions

S corporation shareholders must pay taxes on their share of the corporation's current year income, regardless of whether the amounts are distributed. The shareholder's Schedule K-1 reflects the income, loss, and deductions that are allocated to him but does not state the

---

[19] The provisions of section 351 described in Unit 12 that allow for nontaxable transfers apply to S corporations as well as to C corporations.

taxable amount of a distribution. The taxable amount of each distribution is contingent upon a shareholder's stock basis, and it is the shareholder's responsibility to track his individual basis.

Distributions from an S corporation must be paid to all shareholders on the same date, as a pro rata distributions based on the shareholders' individual ownership percentages.

S corporation distributions are generally not treated as dividends and not subject to income tax, except in cases where a corporation has accumulated E&P from years before it elected to become an S corporation. Distributions from an S corporation with no accumulated earnings and profits are considered a return of capital and reduce the shareholder's basis in the stock of the corporation. Distributions that exceed the shareholder's adjusted stock basis are treated as capital gains and must be reported by the shareholder on Schedule D.

Example: Lucinda is the sole shareholder of an S corporation. Her basis as of January 1, 2014 is $25,000. She receives a distribution of $28,000 in December 2014, which reduces her basis to zero. She must report the excess $3,000 as a capital gain.

The amount of an S corporation distribution is equal to the sum of cash and the fair market value of the property received by a shareholder. If an S corporation distributes appreciated property, the distribution is treated as a sale to the shareholder. To the extent the FMV of the property exceeds the corporation's adjusted basis, the corporation would recognize gain. The gain passes through to the shareholders and increases the basis of their stock. No loss is recognized if the FMV of the distributed property is less than the corporation's basis.

S corporation shareholders are required to compute both stock basis and debt basis. A shareholder's basis in S corporation stock can never be reduced below zero.

The amount of loss that is deductible on a shareholder's tax return is limited to the shareholder's at-risk basis, and is applied in the following order:

- Cash and the adjusted basis of property that the shareholder contributed to the S corporation, subject to annual adjustments as described above (adjusted stock basis), and
- Any loans the shareholder makes to the corporation or any amounts that are borrowed for use by the S corporation for which the shareholder is directly liable (debt basis).

If a shareholder has S corporation losses and deductions in excess of his adjusted stock basis and those losses and deductions are claimed based on debt basis, the debt basis of the shareholder will be reduced by the claimed losses and deductions. If an S corporation repays reduced basis debt to the shareholder, part or all of the repayment is taxable to the shareholder.

Note: These concepts are complex and can be hard to visualize without specific details. The following example shows how S corporation stock and debt basis are calculated.

Example: Samuel, the sole shareholder of an S corporation, has $15,000 of stock basis on January 1, 2014. Samuel received a 2014 K-1 reflecting the following:

- ($20,000) of ordinary business income (loss)
- $4,000 of net section 1231 gain
- $5,000 of cash contributions (50%)
- $1,000 of nondeductible expenses
- $12,000 of distributions

Assume Samuel does not have any debt basis. Using the ordering rule, stock basis is first increased by items of income, so his initial stock basis of $15,000 is increased by the $4,000 net section 1231 gain. His stock basis before distributions is $19,000. Then he reduces stock basis by distributions of $12,000. Since Samuel has adequate stock basis before the distributions, the distributions reduce his stock basis to $7,000 and do not result in any taxable gain for him. Next, his stock basis is reduced by the $1,000 of nondeductible expenses. His stock basis before loss and deduction items is $6,000. Samuel has $25,000 of loss and deduction items:

- $20,000 of ordinary loss
- $5,000 of charitable contributions

The loss and deduction items exceed his stock basis. Since there is no debt basis, the loss and deduction items are pro-rated to determine the amounts currently allowable:

- 20,000/25,000 * 6,000 = $4,800 ordinary loss
- 5,000/25,000 * 6,000 = $1,200 charitable contribution

January 1, 2014 stock basis:	**$15,000**
Plus: Net section 1231 gain	4,000
Stock basis before distributions	19,000
Less: Nondividend distributions	(12,000)
Stock basis before nondeductible expenses	7,000
Less: Nondeductible expenses	(1,000)
Stock basis before loss and deductions	6,000
Less: Ordinary business loss	(4,800)
Less: Cash contributions	(1,200)
December 31, 2014 Stock basis:	**$0**

The basis adjustment rules under IRC §1367 are similar to the partnership rules. However, while a partner has a unitary basis in his partnership interest, the adjustments to the basis of stock of an S corporation are applied on a separate share basis.

The following additional rules apply:

- Losses and deductions not allowable in the current year due to basis limitations are suspended. However, if nondeductible expenses exceed basis, they do not get carried forward.
- Suspended losses and deductions retain their character in subsequent years. They are carried forward indefinitely until basis is increased in subsequent years or until the shareholder permanently disposes of the stock.
- If stock is sold, suspended losses are lost. The sales price does not have an impact on the stock basis. A stock basis computation should be reviewed in the year stock is sold or disposed.
- If the current year has different types of losses and deductions that exceed the shareholder's basis, the allowable losses and deductions must be allocated pro rata based on the size of the particular loss and deduction items.
- In determining current year allowable losses, current year loss and deduction items are combined with the suspended losses and deductions carried over from the prior year, though the current year and suspended items should be separately stated.
- A shareholder only has debt basis to the extent he has personally lent money to the S corporation. A loan guarantee does not create debt basis.
- Part or all of the repayment of a reduced basis debt is taxable to the shareholder.

If an S corporation engages in rental activity or has a shareholder who does not materially participate in S corporation activities, the passive activity loss rules described in Unit 3 apply to the individual shareholders. If the passive activity loss rules apply, the shareholders' at-risk amounts must be reduced by the full amounts allowable as current deductions.

In contrast to the treatment applicable for a partnership, cancellation of debt income is applied at the entity level for corporations, including S corporations. The debtor is required to reduce specified tax attributes, including loss and credit carryforwards and the basis of assets.

The Accumulated Adjustments Account (AAA)

If a C corporation elects to become an S corporation, it may have an accumulated adjustments account (AAA). The AAA is a corporate account that does not relate to individual shareholders. The S corporation maintains the account to track undistributed income that has been taxed during the period its S election is in effect.

S corporations with accumulated E&P must maintain the AAA to determine the tax effect of distributions during S years and, if applicable, during the period after termination of an S election. It is not mandatory to track AAA if the S corporation does not have prior year C corporation E&P (IRC section 1368). Nevertheless, if an S corporation without accumulated E&P engages in certain transactions where an AAA account is required, such as a merger into an S corporation with accumulated E&P, the S corporation must be able to calculate its AAA at the time of the merger. Therefore, it is recommended that the AAA be maintained by all S corporations. The AAA may have a negative balance at year end.

The ordering rules for distributions from an S corporation with accumulated E&P are as follows:

- First, from the AAA, tax-free to the shareholders and a reduction of each shareholder's basis.
- Second, from E&P, and taxable as dividends.
- Third, if applicable, from the corporation's Other Adjustments Account (OAA), which includes accumulated tax-exempt interest income that has not been distributed previously, and reduce basis.
- Additional distributions are considered return of capital, up to the amount of each shareholder's basis in his stock.
- Distributions in excess of a shareholder's basis in his stock are considered capital gains from the sale of property.

Termination of a Shareholder's Interest

If a shareholder sells or disposes of his stock interest in an S corporation, it is treated in the same manner as the sale of stock in a C corporation. The shareholder reports the sale of the stock on Schedule D. The gain or loss that is recognized by the shareholder is the difference between the shareholder's basis and the sale price of the stock.

If a shareholder in an S corporation terminates his interest in a corporation during the tax year, the corporation, with the consent of all affected shareholders (including those whose interest is terminated), may elect to allocate income and expenses as if the corporation's tax year consisted of two separate short tax years, the first of which ends on the date of the shareholder's termination.

To make this election, the corporation must attach a statement to a timely filed original or amended Form 1120S for the tax year for which the election is made and state that it is electing to treat the tax year as if it consisted of two separate tax years.

The statement must also explain how the shareholder's entire interest was terminated (e.g., sale or gift), and state that the corporation and each affected shareholder consented to the election. A single statement may be filed for all terminating elections made for the tax year.

If this election is made, "Section 1377(a)(2) Election Made" should be written at the top of each affected shareholder's Schedule K-1.

Reasonable Compensation

An S corporation may wish to pay little or no salary or wages to employees or officers who are also shareholders, as these amounts are subject to employment taxes while distributions to shareholders are not.

However, if an S corporation is not paying a reasonable compensation to a shareholder-employee, distributions to him may be reclassified as wages subject to employment taxes. Therefore, an S corporation will be at risk if it attempts to avoid paying employment taxes by having its officers treat their compensation as cash distributions, payments of personal expenses, or loans rather than as wages.

Example: Leonard was the sole shareholder and employee of a professional corporation that he elected to be taxed as an S corporation. He was an experienced accountant with a master's degree in business administration. His firm had annual revenues of $1.5 million. In 2014, Leonard paid himself an annual salary of $24,000 and received distributions from the firm of $200,000. The IRS concluded Leonard was deliberately paying himself a low salary to avoid employment taxes and required that $125,000 of the dividends be reclassified as salary. Additional employment taxes, penalties, and interest were assessed on the reclassified payments.

There are no specific guidelines in the IRC or in IRS regulations for what is considered reasonable compensation. Factors considered by the courts in determining reasonable compensation for employees or officers of an S corporation include:

- Training and experience
- Duties and responsibilities
- Time and effort devoted to the business
- Dividend history
- Payments to non-shareholder employees
- Timing and manner of paying bonuses to key people
- Amounts that comparable businesses pay for similar services
- Compensation agreements
- The use of a formula to determine compensation

The regulations provide an exception for an officer of a corporation who does not perform any services or performs only minor services and receives no compensation. Such an officer would not be considered an employee for tax purposes.

Health Insurance Premiums for Shareholders

Fringe benefits paid to employees who are not shareholders or who have ownership of less than 2% are generally deductible by the S corporation and tax-free to the employees.

However, for shareholder-employees who have at least 2% ownership, health and accident insurance premiums paid on their behalf are deductible by the S corporation as fringe benefits and are reportable as wages for income tax withholding purposes on the shareholder-employees' Forms W-2. The S corporation can exclude these health benefits from the wages subject to Social Security, Medicare, and FUTA taxes.

A 2% shareholder-employee is eligible for an AGI deduction for amounts paid during the year for health insurance premiums if the health insurance coverage is established by the S corporation. If the coverage plan is in the name of the shareholder rather than the name of the S corporation, the coverage can still be considered to be established by the S corporation if:

- The S corporation either paid or reimbursed the shareholder for the premiums, and
- It reported the premium payment as wages on the shareholder's Form W-2.

Neither Schedule K-1 (Form 1120S) nor Form 1099 can be used as an alternative to Form W-2 to report this additional compensation.

> **Example:** Victory Energy Bars, an S corporation, provides health insurance coverage to its two owner-shareholders. Victory paid $5,000 of insurance premiums. The corporation treats the shareholders as having received the health insurance as additional compensation and reports the insurance premiums as W-2 wages.

An S corporation cannot take a deduction for amounts incurred during periods in which the shareholder-employee is eligible to participate in any subsidized health plan maintained by another employer (or the spouse's employer).

> **Example:** Edward is the sole owner-shareholder in an S corporation. He pays the health insurance premiums for himself and his wife. His wife works full-time for an employer who has offered to provide family health coverage. Edward and his wife declined the coverage because they did not want to switch doctors. Because Edward had the option to participate in an employer plan (through his wife), the health insurance premiums paid on his behalf by his S corporation are not deductible.

Unit 15: Study Questions

1. Lydia transferred a residential rental building to an S corporation for stock and immediately after the transfer she owned 90% of the corporation. She received stock with a fair market value of $155,000 plus cash of $60,000. The corporation also assumed a $30,000 mortgage on the property for which Lydia was personally liable. Her basis in the transferred property was $175,000. What amount of gain must Lydia recognize, if any?

A. $70,000.
B. $60,000.
C. $30,000.
D. $0.

2. Greenhouse Gardens is an S corporation with four shareholders. The corporation has 10,000 shares outstanding. The shareholders have the following ownership:

Shareholder	Ownership
Jordan	4,500 shares
Mai	2,000 shares
Simon	2,000 shares
Nora	1,500 shares
Total	10,000 shares

Nora and Jordan wish to terminate the S election, but Mai and Simon do not. Which of the following statements is correct?

A. Jordan can elect to terminate the corporation's S status on his own.
B. All of the shareholders must agree to terminate the election.
C. Nora and Jordan have enough stock ownership to terminate the election.
D. At least 75% of the shareholders with active ownership must agree to the termination.

3. How much is the tax on excess net passive income?

A. 10%.
B. 15%.
C. 25%
D. 35%.

4. What is the total amount of the separately stated income items of this S corporation?

Gross Receipts	$700,000
Rental real estate income	300,000
Interest income	25,000
Royalty income	10,000
Section 1231 gain	20,000

A. $355,000.
B. $345,000
C. $700,000.
D. $720,000.

5. Francisco is the sole employee-shareholder of an S corporation that has no accumulated earnings and profits. At the beginning of the year, his stock basis was $50,000. The corporation had no income in 2014. The corporation distributed property to Francisco with an FMV of $75,000 and an adjusted basis of $62,000. What is the treatment of the distribution?

A. $63,000 as a return of capital and $25,000 taxable capital gain.
B. $50,000 as a return of capital and $12,000 taxable capital gain.
C. $60,000 as a return of capital and $15,000 taxable capital gain.
D. $62,000 as a return of capital and $0 taxable gain.

6. Close family members can be treated as a single shareholder for S corporation purposes. A family member in this instance includes:

A. A nonresident alien spouse.
B. A first cousin.
C. The estate of a shareholder's deceased spouse.
D. A divorced spouse.

7. Which of the following events would cause the termination of an S corporation's status?

A. An S corporation that has an estate as a shareholder.
B. An S corporation that has a nonprofit corporation 501(c)(3) shareholder.
C. An S corporation that issues one share of stock to a C corporation.
D. An S corporation that owns one share of stock in a C corporation.

8. On January 1, 2014, Seth purchased 50% of the stock of Rancho Sendero, an S corporation, for $100,000, and also loaned the corporation $20,000. At the end of 2014, Rancho Sendero incurred an ordinary loss of $180,000. How much of the loss can Seth deduct on his personal income tax return for 2014?

A. $90,000.
B. $180,000.
C. $0.
D. $120,000.

9. On December 31, 2013, Adrienne had a $2,000 basis in Liaison Corporation, an S corporation. She owns 50% of Liaison's outstanding stock. At the beginning of 2014, Adrienne contributed a patent that she had acquired for $1,000 to Liaison. During 2014 Liaison received $5,000 of royalty income from that patent. Liaison also had $2,500 of ordinary income and $500 of section 179 deductions. At the end of 2014, Liaison returned ownership of the patent, which now had a fair market value of $5,000, to Adrienne. What is Adrienne's basis in Liaison Corporation at the end of 2014?

A. $1,000.
B. $3,500.
C. $2,500.
D. $5,000.

10. In which circumstance is a C corporation unable to elect to become an S corporation?

A. The C corporation has 50 shareholders.
B. The C corporation is incorporated in Canada.
C. The C corporation has common stock with voting and nonvoting rights.
D. The C corporation is on a fiscal year with a legitimate business purpose.

11. Bettendorf River Company is a calendar-year C corporation that wishes to elect S corporation status in 2014. What is the latest date that Bettendorf River Company can elect S status for tax year 2014?

A. March 15, 2014.
B. March 15, 2015.
C. January 1, 2014.
D. December 31, 2014.

12. A calendar-year S corporation operating on the accrual basis has the following income items and expenses. What is the ordinary income of this S corporation, not counting the separately stated items?

Gross receipts	$300,000
Interest income	25,000
Royalty income	10,000
Salary paid to shareholder	20,000

A. $55,000.
B. $280,000.
C. $320,000.
D. $345,000.

13. Danielle is a 50% owner in Duo Software Corporation, an S corporation. Danielle's basis in her stock at the end of 2013 is $5,000. At the end of 2014, Duo Software reports $10,000 of ordinary income. In December 2014, the corporation makes a distribution to Danielle of appreciated property. It is a rare motorcycle originally purchased for $1,000 but now worth $8,000. How much income must Danielle report on her individual tax return in connection with the distribution?

A. $3,500.
B. $1,000.
C. $0.
D. $8,000.

14. An S corporation, regardless of when it became an S corporation, must use a permitted tax year. A permitted tax year is any of the following except:

A. The calendar year.
B. A tax year elected under section 444.
C. A fiscal tax year with a legitimate business purpose.
D. A short tax year.

15. S corporations are generally not subject to taxation and are primarily pass-through entities. But in certain cases, S corporations are subject to taxes. Which of the following taxes do not apply to S corporations?

A. Excess net passive investment income.
B. Built-in gains tax.
C. Self-employment tax.
D. LIFO recapture.

16. On January 1, 2014, Gloria, Kristin, and Nancy are all equal shareholders in Fairview Heights Corporation, a calendar-year C corporation that has been in existence for four years. On March 1, 2014, Gloria sells her entire stock interest in the corporation to an unrelated party, Irving. Irving immediately wants to convert the corporation to an S corporation effective January 1, 2014. Whose consent is required for Fairview to convert to S status?

A. Irving may convert the corporation into an S corporation so long as Kristin and Nancy consent.
B. Gloria must also consent to the election, along with Kristin and Nancy.
C. Irving may convert the corporation to an S corporation on his own.
D. The corporation cannot convert to S status until it has been in existence for five years.

17. In January 2014, Christopher and Eva are shareholders in Garabedian Company, a C corporation. Christopher owns 65% of the corporate stock and Eva owns the remainder. Christopher decides that he wants to convert to an S corporation. Which of the following statements is correct regarding the conversion?

A. They must both consent to the conversion to the S corporation.
B. The election to become an S corporation is taken on Form 1120S.
C. Christopher may choose to convert the C corporation to an S corporation because he owns more than 50% of the stock.
D. They cannot elect S corporation status, because a C corporation cannot elect to become an S corporation.

18. A C corporation may not elect to become an S corporation if:

A. It is a domestic corporation.
B. It has voting and nonvoting stock.
C. It has two classes of stock.
D. It has common stock.

19. Sydney owns 50% of the Vega Company, a calendar-year S corporation. As of January 1, 2014, Sydney's stock basis was $13,000. Vega has $2,000 of income in 2014 and distributes a machine with an FMV of $7,000 and a basis of $3,000 to Sydney. How much income must Sydney report on her individual tax return in connection with the distribution?

A. $0.
B. $3,000.
C. $2,000.
D. $7,000.

20. Which of the following will not terminate an S corporation's status?

A. The S corporation no longer qualifies as a small business corporation.
B. The S corporation, for each of three consecutive tax years, has accumulated earnings and profits, and derives more than 25% of its gross receipts from passive investment income.
C. The S corporation creates a second class of stock.
D. The S corporation earns the majority of its revenue from passive activities.

21. Which of the following items is not a separately stated item on an S corporation return?

A. Charitable contributions.
B. Net short-term capital gains or losses.
C. Interest income.
D. Interest expense on a business loan.

22. On January 15, 2014, Elliott decides to voluntarily terminate his corporation's S status and convert to a C corporation. The termination was approved by the IRS. He later changes his mind and wishes to elect S corporation status again. How long does Elliott have to wait to elect S corporation status again?

A. 18 months.
B. Two years.
C. Four years.
D. Five years.

Unit 16: Farming Businesses

More Reading:
Publication 225, *Farmer's Tax Guide*

Farming businesses may be engaged in activities such as crop production, animal production, or forestry and logging. They may include stock, dairy, poultry, fish, fruit, and tree farms, as well as plantations, ranches, timber farms, and orchards. The entity type does not matter; a business will be classified as a "farming business" as long as the business cultivates, operates, or manages a farm (or fishery) for profit.

A farming or fishing business operating as a sole proprietorship reports income and loss on Schedule F, *Profit or Loss from Farming*. A farmer is usually self-employed if he operates his own farm or rents farmland from others to engage in the business of farming. Self-employed farmers and fishermen must also complete Schedule SE.

Alternatively, a farming business may be organized as a partnership or a corporation.

Not Classified as Farming Businesses: Certain associated businesses are not considered farming businesses and instead must file on Schedule C (if a sole proprietorship). Examples include:

- Veterinary businesses
- Businesses that only supply farm labor
- Businesses that only sell farm supplies, such as pesticides or herbicides
- Businesses that are only in the business of breeding, including those that raise or breed dogs, cats, or other household pets
- Businesses that provide agricultural services such as soil preparation and fertilization

Not Classified as Farm Income: Certain types of income associated with farming businesses are not classified as farm income. Farm income does not include any of the following:

- Wages received as a farm employee
- Income received under a contract for grain harvesting with workers and machines furnished by the taxpayer
- Gains received from the sale of farm land and depreciable farm equipment
- Gains from the sale of securities, regardless of who owns the securities

Rents

If a farmer rents his farmland for someone else to use, the related revenue is generally rent income, not farm income. This also applies to crop shares, when a tenant farmer pays a proportion of crop harvest proceeds to the land owner for use of his farmland. This passive activity income is reported on Form 4835, *Farm Rental Income and Expenses.* However, if a farmer materially participates in farming operations on the land he owns, the rent is considered farm income and is reported on Schedule F.

Estimated Taxes

Special rules apply to the payment of estimated tax by qualified farmers and fishermen.

If at least two-thirds of the individual's or business's gross income comes from farming or fishing activities, the following rules apply:

- The taxpayer does not have to pay estimated tax if he files his return and pays all the tax owed by the first day of the third month after the end of his tax year (usually this date is March 1).
- If the taxpayer must pay estimated tax, he is required to make only one estimated tax payment (called the "required annual payment") by the fifteenth day after the end of his tax year (usually this date is January 15).

Accounting Methods for Farming

Farmers can use the following accounting methods:

- **Cash Method** (subject to the limitations described in Unit 2)
- **Accrual Method**
- **Combination (Hybrid) Method** (using two or more of the methods listed)
- **Special Methods, including the Crop Method:** The IRS allows a number of different special methods of accounting that apply to items such as depreciation or farm business expenses or income. Among these is the crop method, which requires IRS approval and is allowed only for farming businesses. If crops are not harvested and disposed of in the same tax year they are planted, the farmer can deduct the entire cost of producing the crop, including the expense of seed or young plants, in the year income is realized.

Example: Will is a self-employed farmer who uses the accrual method. He keeps his books on a calendar-year basis. Will sells grain in December 2014, but he is not paid until January 2015. He must include the sale on his 2014 tax return. He can also deduct the costs incurred in producing the grain on his 2014 return.

Example: Miguel is also a self-employed farmer, but he uses the cash method. Miguel sells livestock in December 2014, but he is not paid until January 2015. Since Miguel uses the cash method and there was no constructive receipt of the sale proceeds in 2014, Miguel includes the sale proceeds in income in 2015, the year he receives payment.

Although the accrual method of accounting generally must be used when there is inventory, farmers are exempt from the usual requirements to maintain an inventory, and as a result most farmers use the cash method. Inventory requirements do not apply to most crops.[20] Consequently, few farming operations are required to adopt the accrual method of accounting.

However, the following farming businesses must use the accrual method:

- A corporation (other than a family farming corporation) that had gross receipts of more than $1 million for any tax year
- A family farming corporation that had gross receipts of more than $25 million for any tax year
- A partnership with a corporate partner
- A tax shelter (of any size or income)

To qualify as a family farming corporation, the business must meet at least one of the following requirements:

- Members of the same family own at least 50% of the corporation's stock
- Members of two families have owned since October 1976, either directly or indirectly, at least 65% of the corporation's stock
- Members of three families have owned since October 1976, either directly or indirectly, at least 50% of the corporation's stock

Example: Dave and Raymond are brothers. They are also the only shareholders of Da-Ray Farms Corporation, which is a qualified family farming corporation. Da-Ray Farms raises cattle, and in 2014 it has $20 million of gross receipts. Since Da-Ray is a qualified family farm, the entity is allowed to use the cash method of accounting.

---

[20] Generally, growing crops are not required to be included in inventory unless they have a pre-productive period of more than two years. Plants with a pre-productive period of less than two years include many common crops such as corn and wheat. Plants with a pre-productive period of more than two years include many kinds of fruit and nut trees, grapes, and avocados, among others.

Farm Inventory

Farm inventory includes all items that are held for sale, purchased for resale, and for use as feed or seed, such as the following:

- Eggs in the process of hatching.
- Harvested farm products that are held for sale, such as grain, cotton, hay, or tobacco.
- Supplies that become a physical part of an item held for sale, such as containers, wrappers, or other packaging. A business may expense the cost of supplies consumed in operations during the year.
- Any livestock that is held primarily for sale or purchased for resale.
- Fur-bearing animals (such as mink, fox, or chinchilla) that are being held for breeding.
- Purchased farm products that are being held for seed or feed.

If livestock was purchased primarily for draft, breeding, sport, or dairy purposes, the farmer can choose to depreciate it, or include the livestock in inventory. Regardless of the method chosen, it must be consistent from year to year.

Note: Farm inventory does not include real property, such as land or buildings, or depreciable equipment, such as tractors.

Farmers may use the same inventory methods that are available to other businesses, such as cost and lower of cost or market, which were covered in Unit 2 under inventory methods. However, there are two other inventory methods that are unique to farming businesses:

Farm-Price Method: Under the farm-price method each item, whether raised or purchased, is valued at its market price less the costs of disposition. The costs of disposition include broker's commissions, freight, hauling to market, and other marketing costs. If a farming business chooses to use the farm-price method, it must use it for the entire inventory, except that livestock can be inventoried under the unit-livestock-price method.

Unit-Livestock-Price Method: The unit-livestock-price method is an easier inventory method that allows farmers to group livestock together rather than track the costs of each animal. A farmer may classify livestock according to type and age and use a unit price for each animal within a class. The unit price must reasonably approximate the costs incurred in producing the animal.

If a farming business uses the unit-livestock-price method, it must include all raised livestock in inventory, regardless of whether they are held for sale or for draft, breeding, sport, or dairy purposes. This method accounts only for the costs incurred while raising an animal to maturity. It does not provide for any decrease in the animal's market value after it reaches maturity.

UNICAP: Except for corporations, partnerships, and tax shelters that are required to use the accrual method, farming businesses are not required to apply the UNICAP rules to the costs of:

- Raising plants for which the pre-productive period is two years or less
- Animals
- Replanting certain plants lost or damaged due to casualty

If a farmer's crop has a pre-productive period of more than two years, the farmer can generally elect not to have the UNICAP rules apply, unless he is required to use the accrual method.

Example: Jane owns a peach orchard that produces an annual crop. The trees have a pre-productive period of more than two years. Jane must capitalize the direct costs of the orchard and an allocable part of indirect costs incurred due to the production of the trees. However, she is not required to capitalize the costs of producing the annual peach crop because its pre-productive period is two years or less.

For crops, pre-productive period costs include the costs of irrigation, pruning, spraying, and harvesting. For livestock, pre-productive costs include the costs of feed, maintaining pasture or pen areas, breeding, veterinary services, and bedding.

Sales of Farm Products and Farm Assets

When a self-employed farmer sells products raised on a farm, his entire proceeds are reported on Schedule F, in a manner similar to any other taxpayer who sells inventory and reports the sales proceeds on Schedule C. Gain on the sale of livestock raised on a farm is generally the gross sales price reduced by any expenses of the sale, such as commissions or freight charges. The basis of the animal sold is zero if the costs of raising it were deducted during the years the animal was being raised.

Example: In 2013, five goats were born on Lisa's farm. She deducted the cost of feed and other expenses of raising the goats on her 2013 tax return. In 2014, the goats were hauled to a nearby town for auction, where they sold for a total of $900, with $75 of sales expenses. Lisa will report a gain of $825 on her 2014 tax return ($900 - $75 = $825).

When a farmer sells farm products bought for resale, his profit or loss is the difference between his basis in the item (usually cost) and any payment received for it.

Example: In 2013, Oscar bought 20 feeder calves for $6,000 for resale. He sold them in 2014 for $11,000. Oscar reports the $11,000 sales price, subtracts his $6,000 basis, and reports the resulting $5,000 gain on his 2014 Schedule F.

However, income reported on Schedule F does not include gains or losses from sales or other dispositions of the following farm assets:

- Land
- Depreciable farm equipment
- Buildings and structures
- Livestock held for draft, breeding, sport, or dairy purposes (unless held as inventory or held primarily for sale)

The sale of these assets is reported on Form 4797, *Sales of Business Property*, and may result in ordinary or capital gains or losses.

Like other businesses, when a farming business disposes of depreciable property (section 1245 property or section 1250 property) at a gain, the taxpayer may have to recognize ordinary income under the depreciation recapture rules. Any gain remaining after applying the depreciation recapture rules may be section 1231 gain, which may be taxed as capital gain.

Section 1245: Part or all of the gain of the sale of section 1245 property is treated as ordinary income under the rules of depreciation recapture. Buildings and structural components are excluded under section 1245. However, "single purpose agricultural (livestock) or horticultural structures" are section 1245 property. So, for example, a barn that houses different animals and is used to store supplies would not be section 1245 property because it is not a single purpose facility.

Example: A greenhouse that is used only to grow plants would be single purpose and thus section 1245 property. If a cash register is installed in the greenhouse so that a farmer can sell plants in addition to growing them there, the greenhouse would no longer be section 1245 property because it is no longer single purpose.

Other examples of farming-related section 1245 property include a grain silo, fencing for the confinement of livestock, and wells for providing water to livestock.

Section 1231: Section 1231 assets include certain business (noncapital) assets that have been held for more than one year, as well as certain business and investment property disposed of in involuntary conversions.

Note: As discussed in Unit 9, section 1231 assets receive special tax treatment. If a taxpayer has a net loss from all section 1231 transactions, the loss is treated as ordinary loss. If the section 1231 transactions result in a net gain, the gain is generally treated as capital gain, with the exception of depreciation recapture, which is taxed as ordinary income.

Gain or loss on the following farm-related transactions is subject to section 1231 treatment:

1. Sale or exchange of cattle or horses held for draft, breeding, dairy, or sporting purposes and held for 24 months or longer.
2. Sale or exchange of other livestock held for draft, breeding, dairy, or sporting purposes and held for 12 months or longer. Other livestock includes hogs, mules, sheep, and goats, but does not include poultry.
3. Sale or exchange of depreciable property used in the farming business and held for longer than one year. Examples include farm machinery and trucks.
4. Sale or exchange of real estate used in the farming business and held for longer than one year. Examples are a farm or ranch, including barns and sheds.
5. Sale or exchange of unharvested crops.
6. Sale from cut timber.
7. The condemnation of business property held longer than one year. Condemnations of business property usually qualify for nonrecognition treatment if replacement property is purchased within a certain time period, under the involuntary conversion rules.

Postponing Gain Due to Weather Conditions

There are special rules for farmers regarding the postponement of gain due to weather conditions. If a farmer sells or exchanges more livestock (including poultry), than he normally would in a year because of a drought, flood, or other weather-related conditions, he may postpone reporting the income from the additional animals until the following year.

The taxpayer must meet all the following conditions to qualify:

- The principal trade or business must be farming.
- The farmer must use the cash method of accounting.
- The farmer must be able to show that he would not have sold or exchanged the additional animals in that year except for the weather-related condition.
- The area must be designated as eligible for federal disaster assistance.

The livestock does not have to be raised or sold in the affected area. However, the sale must occur solely because the weather-related condition affected the water, grazing, or other requirements of the livestock. The farmer must figure the amount to be postponed separately for each generic class of animals, such as hogs, sheep, and cattle.

Example: Yolanda is a calendar-year farmer, and she normally sells 100 head of beef cattle a year. As a result of drought, she sells 135 head during 2014 and realizes $70,200 from the sale. On November 9, 2014, because of drought, the affected area is declared a disaster area eligible for federal assistance. The income Yolanda can postpone until 2015 is $18,200 [($70,200 ÷ 135) × 35], which is the portion of the income attributed to the additional animals that she sold over her normal amount.

To postpone gain, the farmer must attach a statement to his tax return for the year of the sale providing specific information about the weather conditions and circumstances that led to the postponement of gain for each class of livestock. For a sale that qualifies as an involuntary conversion, the farmer can file this statement at any time during the replacement period. The replacement period for the sale of livestock due to weather-related conditions is four years, and up to five years if the property is subject to an involuntary conversion in a federally declared disaster area.

A weather-related sale or exchange of livestock held for draft, breeding, or dairy purposes (but in this case, not including poultry) may also qualify as an involuntary conversion.

Livestock that is sold or exchanged because of disease may not trigger taxable gain if the proceeds of the transaction are reinvested in replacement animals within two years of the close of the tax year in which the diseased animals were sold or exchanged.

Example: Paulo is a farmer who owns 3,000 head of cattle. In 2014, his herd is struck by virus, and he is forced to send 1,500 to slaughter. His insurance company reimburses his losses, and he promptly reinvests all the insurance proceeds into new livestock. This is treated as an involuntary conversion.

Crop Insurance and Government Payments

Insurance proceeds, including government disaster payments, may be received as a result of destruction or damage to crops or the inability to plant crops because of drought, flood, or other natural disaster. These payments are generally taxable in the year they are received.

However, a farmer can elect to postpone reporting the income until the following year if he meets all of these conditions:

- The farming business must use the cash method of accounting.
- Crop insurance proceeds were received in the same tax year the crops were damaged.
- Under normal business practices, the farming business would have reported income from the damaged crops in any tax year following the year the damage occurred.

A statement must be attached to the tax return indicating the specific crops that were damaged and the total insurance payment received. To make this election to postpone income, the farmer must be able to prove that the crops would have been harvested or otherwise sold in the following year.

If a farmer forgoes the planting of crops altogether and receives agricultural program payments from the government, payments are reported on Schedule F, and the full amount of the payment is subject to self-employment tax.

Other Unique Tax Rules for Farmers

Other examples of tax rules that are unique to farming businesses include the following:

Car and Truck Expenses: Farmers can claim 75% of the use of a car or light truck as business use without any records (such as a mileage log) if the vehicle is used in a farming business.

Soil Conservation: Farmers can choose to deduct as a business expense land-related expenses for soil or water conservation or for the prevention of erosion. Examples include leveling, eradication of brush, removal of trees, or planting of windbreaks. For most businesses, these would be considered capital expenses and would be added to the basis of the land.

Net Operating Losses: Farming losses qualify for longer carryback periods. The carryback period for farming losses is five years rather than the two-year carryback period that applies to other businesses.

Excise Tax Credits: Farmers may be eligible to claim a credit or a refund of federal excise taxes on fuel used on a farm.

Farm Income Averaging: Certain farmers that operate as sole proprietorships or partnerships may use Schedule J, *Income Averaging for Farmers and Fishermen,* to average all or some of their current year's farm income by allocating it to the three prior years. This may lower a farmer's current year tax liability if the current year is high and his taxable income from one or more of the three prior years was low. Income from the three previous years does not have to originate from farming or fishing activity.

Example: Jed is a citrus farmer in Florida. In 2014, he has a record crop, with gross income nearly double that of 2012 and 2013 when frost had damaged a large percentage of his fruit. Jed elects to average his income by filing Schedule J. His taxable income for 2014 is averaged with the corresponding amounts for 2011 through 2013, which significantly reduces his tax liability in the current year.

Unit 16: Study Questions

1. Luke is a qualified farmer. A bull calf was born on his farm in 2013. Luke raised the calf for breeding purposes. Luke spent $750 in feed for the calf, and it was sold for $5,000 for breeding use in 2014. How much is Luke's gain from the sale of the bull calf?

A. $0.
B. $4,250.
C. $4,750.
D. $5,000.

2. Becky is a calendar-year, self-employed farmer who files on the cash basis. For purposes of the estimated tax for qualified farmers, all of the following statements are correct except:

A. Becky does not have to make any estimated payments if she files by April 15 and pays all her taxes with her return.
B. Becky is a qualified farmer if at least two-thirds of her previous year's gross income is from farming.
C. The required annual estimated tax payment for farmers is due on the fifteenth day after the close of their tax year.
D. The required annual payment is two-thirds of the current year's tax or 100% of the previous year's tax.

3. All of the following should be included in farming inventory except:

A. Farming equipment and machinery.
B. Livestock held primarily for sale.
C. Farm products held for feed or seed.
D. Supplies that become a physical part of items held for sale.

4. Joel is a qualified farmer who usually sells 500 beef cattle every year. However, because of a severe drought, he was forced to sell 800 beef cattle. Which of the following statements is correct?

A. Joel may choose to postpone all of the gain in this transaction.
B. Joel may choose to postpone a portion of his gain in this transaction.
C. Joel must use the accrual method in order to postpone gain.
D. Postponement of gain is not allowed.

276

5. Jon owns a dairy business and has income from the following sources:

Income from milk production	$50,000
Sale of old dairy cows	20,000
Sale of feed	15,000
Sale of used machinery	4,000

What amount of income should be reported on Jon's Schedule F, *Profit or Loss from Farming?*

A. $50,000.
B. $65,000.
C. $74,000.
D. $85,000.

6. Which of the following statements about farmers is correct?

A. Gross income from farming includes capital gains from the sale of equipment.
B. A farmer who is a sole proprietor may use income averaging to reduce his tax liability.
C. A farmer does not have to report income from crop insurance payments.
D. An individual who owns livestock as a hobby and grows a large garden can be considered a farmer for tax purposes.

7. All of the following would be considered section 1245 property except:

A. A greenhouse.
B. A grain silo.
C. A wire chicken coop.
D. A barn that houses cows and horses.

8. Oliver is a farmer who receives agricultural program payments after refraining from growing any crops in 2014. How should these payments be reported?

A. As "other income" on Oliver's individual Form 1040.
B. On Schedule E, *Supplemental Income and Loss.*
C. As farm income on Schedule F, not subject to self-employment tax.
D. As farm income on Schedule F, subject to self-employment tax.

9. Holly is an accrual-basis farmer who has the following income in the current year:

Rental of farmland in which the taxpayer does not materially participate	$30,000
Sale of harvested oats	145,000
Gain from sale of cattle held primarily for breeding	85,000
Crop insurance payments	115,000

What amount of income must Holly report on Schedule F?

A. $145,000.
B. $260,000.
C. $290,000.
D. $345,000.

10. All of the following are acceptable methods for valuation of farm inventory except:

A. Cost.
B. Harvest discount.
C. Farm-price method.
D. Unit-livestock-price method.

11. Andy owns 150 acres of farmland that he rents to other farmers. He does not actively participate in any of the farming activity. How should the income from this activity be reported?

A. As rental income on Form 4835.
B. As farming income on Schedule F.
C. As ordinary income on Schedule C.
D. As passive income on Schedule 4797.

12. The carryback period for farming losses is:

A. Two years.
B. Four years.
C. Five years.
D. Farmers are not allowed to carry back their losses.

13. Hope is a qualified farmer who grows soybeans. In 2014, her soybean crop was destroyed by flood. If the crop had not been destroyed, she would have harvested it in 2015. Hope receives federal disaster payments in 2014. Which of the following statements is correct?

A. Hope can choose to postpone the income from this disaster payment until 2015.
B. Disaster payments are not taxable income.
C. Hope must report the income on her 2014 return.
D. Hope may delay recognition of the gain for two years.

14. Farm income averaging is computed on Schedule J, which may be filed:

A. For the current year when a taxpayer files Schedule F showing a farm loss.
B. For the current year when a taxpayer files Schedule F showing net income from farming.
C. For the current year, along with Schedule C.
D. As an amended return showing the past three years of farming income.

15. Frank is a rancher in California who lives in an area that was declared a federal disaster area due to drought. The drought forced him to sell 50 head of cattle in 2014 that he would not have otherwise sold. Frank has _____ to replace his livestock.

A. Two years.
B. Three years.
C. Four years.
D. Five years.

16. To be eligible as a qualified farmer and not have to pay quarterly estimated taxes during the year, at least _____ of a farmer's gross income must be from farming.

A. Half.
B. Two-thirds.
C. Three-quarters.
D. 80%.

Unit 17: Exempt Organizations

More Reading:
Publication 4220, *Applying for 501(c)(3) Tax-Exempt Status*
Publication 557, *Tax-Exempt Status for Your Organization*
Publication 4221-PC, *Compliance Guide for 501(c)(3) Public Charities*
Publication 598, *Tax on Unrelated Business Income of Exempt Organizations*

Nonprofit organizations may qualify for exemption from the requirement to pay income taxes, but they are still subject to certain filing and recordkeeping requirements under federal tax law.

IRC Section 501(c)(3)

The majority of nonprofit organizations qualify for tax-exempt status under section 501(c)(3) of the IRC. They are exempt from paying income tax in connection with their charitable activities, and they are eligible to receive tax-deductible charitable contributions. To qualify for these benefits, an organization must file an application with the IRS and must meet the following requirements:

- **Organization:** It must be organized as a corporation, a trust, or an unincorporated association, and its purpose must be limited to those described in section 501(c)(3). A nonprofit entity may not be organized as a partnership or sole proprietorship.
- **Exempt Purpose:** It must have one or more exempt purposes as listed under section 501(c)(3): charitable, educational, religious, scientific, literary, fostering national or international sports competition, preventing cruelty to children or animals, and testing for public safety.
- **Operation:** A substantial portion of its activities must be related to its exempt purpose(s). Further, a 501(c)(3) organization must:
  - Refrain from participating in political campaigns of candidates
  - Restrict its lobbying activities to an "insubstantial" part of its total activities
  - Ensure that its earnings do not benefit any private shareholder or individual
  - Not operate for the benefit of private interests such as those of its founder, the founder's family, or its shareholders
  - Not operate for the primary purpose of conducting a trade or business that is not related to its exempt purpose

Applying for 501(c)(3) Status

Before applying for tax-exempt status, an organization must be created by preparing an organizing document. This document must limit the organization's purposes to those set forth in section 501(c)(3) and must specify that the entity's assets will be permanently dedicated to the specified exempt purpose(s). The organizing document should also contain a provision for distributing funds if it dissolves.

To request exempt status under section 501(c)(3), an entity uses Form 1023, *Application for Recognition of Exemption*. An organization with annual gross receipts of no more than $5,000 is not required to file Form 1023. However, it must file Form 1023 to request formal exemption within 90 days of the end of the year in which it exceeds this threshold.

> **Example:** An animal rescue organization that was created five years ago did not exceed the $5,000 gross receipts threshold until its fiscal year ended September 30, 2014. The organization must file Form 1023 to request formal tax exemption by December 30, 2014, 90 days after reaching that threshold.

In 2014, a new streamlined Form 1023-EZ was introduced for small tax-exempt organizations. The application is three pages long, compared to 26 pages for the traditional Form 1023. To qualify for the shorter form, an organization must have:

- Gross receipts of $50,000 or less, and
- Assets of $250,000 or less.

> **Note:** A private foundation is always required to request exemption, regardless of the amount of its gross receipts.

An organization must generally request exemption from the IRS by the end of the fifteenth month after it is created, with a 12-month extension available.

The IRS will review an organization's application and determine if it meets the requirements for exemption. If approved, the IRS will issue a letter recognizing the organization's exempt status and providing its public charity classification.

An organization that files its application before the deadline may be recognized as tax-exempt from the date of its creation. An organization that files an application after the deadline also may be recognized as tax-exempt from the date of the application by requesting exemption retroactive to the date of creation.

While an organization's Form 1023 is pending approval, the organization may operate as if it were tax-exempt. Donor contributions made while an application is pending would qualify, assuming the IRS later approves its 501(c)(3) status. If the application is not approved, these contributions would not qualify. The organization would also be liable for filing federal income tax returns unless its income is otherwise excluded from federal taxation.

Other Section 501(c) Organizations

Organizations that do not qualify for exemption under section 501(c)(3) may qualify for tax-exempt status by filing Form 1024, *Application for Recognition of Exemption Under 501(a).* However, they may or may not qualify to receive contributions that are deductible by the donor.

Examples include the following:

- 501(c)(4) Civic leagues and social welfare organizations
- 501(c)(5) Labor unions, agricultural, and horticultural organizations
- 501(c)(6) Business leagues
- 501(c)(7) Social and recreation clubs
- 501(c)(8) and 501(c)(10) Fraternal beneficiary societies
- 501(c)(4), 501(c)(9), and 501(c)(17) Employees' associations
- 501(c)(12) Local benevolent life insurance associations
- 501(c)(13) Nonprofit cemetery companies
- 501(c)(14) Credit unions and other mutual financial organizations
- 501(c)(19) Veterans' organizations

Note: 501(c)(4) social welfare organizations were the subject of Congressional hearings in 2013 to investigate whether certain groups were unfairly targeted with heightened scrutiny during the application process. After extensive public comment, the IRS withdrew proposed new regulations governing how much political activity tax-exempt 501(c)(4) organizations may legitimately conduct. It is unclear when new proposed regulations will be introduced. For the EA exam, test-takers should focus primarily on the tax requirements affecting 501(c)(3) organizations.

Public Charity or Private Foundation

Every organization that qualifies for tax-exempt status under section 501(c)(3) is further classified as either a public charity or a private foundation. Tax-exempt entities are presumed to be private foundations, unless they fall into certain categories of organizations that are specifically excluded. Even if an organization falls into one of these excluded categories, it is presumed to be a private foundation unless it files a timely Form 1023 showing that it is not a private foundation.

The primary distinction between classification as a public charity or a private foundation is the organization's source of financial support. A public charity tends to have a broad base of support while a private foundation has more limited sources of support. Generally, an exempt organization will not be considered a private foundation if it receives more than one-third of its annual support from governmental units and/or the general public.

> **Example:** Friedreich's Ataxia Research Alliance (FARA) is dedicated to finding a cure for a rare and disabling genetic disorder. Its funding comes from individual donations from the public and various fundraising events that it sponsors, so FARA is classified as a public charity. Willette Educational Ventures supports charter schools and 90% of its funding comes from members of the Willette family, so it is classified as a private foundation.

The classification of public charity vs. private foundation is important because different tax rules apply: deductibility of contributions to a private foundation is more limited than deductibility of contributions to a public charity. Further, there is an excise tax on the net investment income of domestic private foundations. This excise tax must be paid annually or, if the total tax for the year is $500 or more, in quarterly estimated tax payments.

All private foundations must file Form 990-PF, *Return of Private Foundation*, every year regardless of their income.

Filing Requirements

Every exempt organization must file an annual information return with the IRS, generally on Form 990, *Return of Organization Exempt from Income Tax*, unless it is specifically exempt from the filing requirement. The following organizations are not required to file:

- Churches and their affiliated organizations
- Government agencies

If an organization has gross receipts of less than $200,000 and total assets at the end of the year of less than $500,000, it can file Form 990-EZ. Tax-exempt organizations with gross receipts of $50,000 or less may file Form 990-N, *Electronic Notice for Tax Exempt Organizations Not Required to File Form 990*. This form is also called an "e-postcard" because it is filed electronically and is short. A small tax-exempt organization may voluntarily choose to file a long form (Form 990) instead.

An exempt entity may choose to file on a fiscal-year or a calendar-year basis. The applicable annual information return is due by the fifteenth day of the fifth month after the year ends. For a calendar-year entity, the due date is May 15.

> **Example:** Friends of the Oak Knoll Library is a 501(c)(3) organization that operates on the calendar year. It had gross receipts of $20,000 in 2014. The organization files Form 990-N, the e-postcard, by May 15, 2015.

If the organization has been dissolved, the return is due by the fifteenth day of the fifth month after the dissolution.

An exempt entity may request a three-month extension of time to file by filing Form 8868, *Application for Extension of Time to File an Exempt Organization Return*. An additional three-month extension can be requested, if needed, using the same form. When filing a request for the first three-month extension, neither a signature nor an explanation is required. However, when requesting an additional three-month extension, both a signature and an explanation are required.

An organization must file Form 990 electronically if it files at least 250 returns during the calendar year and has total assets of $10 million or more at the end of the tax year. A private foundation is required to file Form 990-PF electronically if it files at least 250 returns during the calendar year.

A section 501(c)(3) organization must make its application (Form 1023) and its three most recent annual returns (Form 990) available to the public. The IRS also makes these documents available for public inspection and copying.

Every tax-exempt entity must have an EIN, regardless of whether it has employees.

Penalties

An exempt organization that fails to file a required return must pay a penalty of $20 a day for each day the return is late. The same penalty may apply if the organization provides incorrect information on the return. Generally, the maximum penalty is the smaller of:

- $10,000, or
- 5% of the organization's gross receipts for the year.

However, for an organization that has gross receipts of more than $1 million for the year, the late filing penalty is $100 a day, up to a maximum of $50,000.

An organization's exempt status may be revoked for failure to file. Failure to file an annual information return for three years in a row will result in the automatic revocation of exempt status. In this case, the organization would be required to reapply for exemption. However, no penalty will be imposed if reasonable cause for failure to timely file can be shown.

If an organization's tax-exempt status was automatically revoked for failing to file a return or notice for three consecutive years, it must apply to have its tax-exempt status reinstated by filing either Form 1023 or Form 1024 and paying the appropriate fee.

Note: In 2014, the IRS introduced new streamlined procedures for organizations that have had their tax exemptions revoked. The retroactive reinstatement procedures apply to organizations eligible to file either Form 990-EZ or Form 990-N. To apply using the streamlined procedures, an organization must act within 15 months after the later of the date of the revocation letter or the date on which the IRS posted the organization's name on a revocation list.

Employment Tax Returns: Just like other businesses, exempt organizations are subject to the basic requirements for tax and wage reporting compliance, calculating withholding, making deposits, and keeping tax and reporting records.

Even though some organizations (such as a church or other religious organization) are not required to file Forms 990, any entity with employees must withhold and remit income and Social Security and Medicare taxes on its employees' wages, and some exempt organizations are also responsible for Federal Unemployment Tax (FUTA).

Example: Trinity Methodist Church is not required to file an application for exemption in order to be recognized as tax-exempt by the IRS. Trinity applies for an EIN as an exempt entity and begins regular worship. In the same year, Trinity Church hires three employees: a part-time pastor, a Sunday child care worker, and a music leader. Although Trinity does not have to file Form 990, the church is still required to file employment tax returns and remit and collect employment taxes from its employees. In this way, an exempt organization is treated like every other employer.

Unrelated Business Income Tax (UBIT)

Although an exempt organization must be operated primarily for tax-exempt purposes, it may engage in income-producing activities that are unrelated to those purposes, so long as these activities are not a substantial part of the organization's regular activities. Income from unrelated business activities is subject to a federal tax called the *unrelated business income tax* (UBIT). For most organizations, an activity is considered an unrelated business and subject to UBIT if:

- It is a trade or business,
- It is regularly carried on, and
- It is not substantially related to furthering the exempt purpose(s) of the organization.

An exempt organization that has $1,000 or more of gross income from an unrelated business must file Form 990–T by the fifteenth day of the fifth month after the tax year ends. An exempt organization must make quarterly payments of estimated tax on unrelated business income if it expects its tax for the year to be $500 or more.

Example: A university enters into a multi-year contract with a company to be its exclusive provider of sports drinks for the athletic department and concessions. As part of the contract, the university agrees to perform various services for the company, such as guaranteeing that coaches make promotional appearances on behalf of the company. The university itself is a qualified nonprofit organization, but the income received from the exclusive contract is subject to UBIT. The university is therefore required to file Form 990-T.
Example: A college negotiates discounted rates for the soft drinks it purchases for its cafeterias in return for an exclusive provider arrangement. Generally, discounts are considered an adjustment to the purchase price and do not constitute gross income to the purchaser. Thus, the amount of the negotiated discount is not includable in UBIT. The college is not required to file Form 990-T.

Summary of Exempt Entity Requirements

Exempt Entities: Financial Activity	Annual Information Return Required
Gross receipts less than $50,000	Form 990-N (e-postcard)
Gross receipts less than $200,000 and total assets less than $500,000	Form 990-EZ or Form 990
Gross receipts more than $200,000, or total assets more than $500,000	Form 990
Unrelated business income of $1,000 or more	Form 990-T
Private foundation (must file every year, regardless of financial activity)	Form 990-PF
Churches and similar religious organizations	No annual information return filing requirement, but may be required to file payroll returns if the entity has employees

Unit 17: Study Questions

1. Under streamlined application procedures, an exempt organization may use Form 1023-EZ if it has up to _____ of gross receipts for the year.

A. $5,000.
B. $25,000.
C. $50,000.
D. $250,000.

2. Which of the following exempt organizations is not required to file an annual information return?

A. A church with gross receipts exceeding $250,000.
B. An exempt literary organization with $6,000 of gross receipts.
C. A Chamber of Commerce with $26,000 of gross receipts.
D. A private foundation with income of less than $5,000.

3. An organization will have its tax-exempt status revoked if it fails to file information returns for _____ years in a row.

A. Two.
B. Three.
C. Five.
D. Never. Once tax-exempt, an organization cannot have its status revoked.

4. The local Catholic church has two employees: Martha, who works as a secretary in the church rectory, and Jack, who is the church custodian. Which return(s) must the church file in order to fulfill its IRS reporting obligations?

A. Form 990.
B. Form 8300.
C. Employment tax returns.
D. Form 990-PF.

5. Child Rescue Inc. is a calendar-year nonprofit organization that helps prevent child abuse. It is required to file Form 990 in 2014. What is the due date of its tax return, not including extensions?

A. April 15.
B. March 15.
C. May 15.
D. October 15.

6. Most organizations seeking recognition of exemption from federal income tax must use specific application forms prescribed by the IRS. Which form must be filed in order to request recognition as a 501(c)(3) nonprofit organization by the IRS?

A. Form 1023.
B. Form 1024.
C. Form 1040.
C. Form 990.

7. What action does the IRS take if a nonprofit with $500,000 of gross receipts fails to file its required information returns or notices?

A. Nothing. Information returns are voluntary.
B. A maximum penalty of up to $10,000 or 5% of the organization's gross receipts for the year.
C. Automatic revocation of tax-exempt status if the organization fails to file returns or notices for three consecutive years.
D. Both B and C are correct.

8. Which of the following statements is correct?

A. If an exempt organization qualifies for tax-exempt status with the IRS, any contributions it receives are fully deductible by the donors.
B. A church is not required to file an annual information return (Form 990).
C. A religious entity does not have to file payroll tax returns if it has employees.
D. A church may be organized as a sole proprietorship.

9. Which of the following organizations does not qualify for tax-exempt status?

A. A charitable organization.
B. A religious organization.
C. A private foundation.
D. An educational partnership.

10. What does an organization that wishes to be recognized as a 501(c)(3) charity need to file with the IRS?

A. Form 990.
B. Form 990 and its organizing document.
C. Form 1023 and its organizing document.
D. Form 1023, its organizing document, a listing of its board of directors, and its bylaws.

11. All of the organizations listed below would qualify for tax-exempt status under the Internal Revenue Code except:

A. A Christian church with only eight members.
B. A political action committee.
C. A trust for a college alumni association.
D. A local boys club.

12. A charitable organization has $2,000 in unrelated business income in the current year. How is this income reported?

A. The organization must file a business tax return for the unrelated business income.
B. The organization is required to file Form 990-T.
C. The organization will have its exempt status revoked.
D. The organization must file Schedule C to correctly report the business income.

13. Which kind of organization is allowed to file an e-postcard?

A. A private foundation.
B. A nonprofit with gross receipts of $25,000 or less.
C. A nonprofit with gross receipts of $50,000 or less.
D. A nonprofit with gross receipts of $100,000 or less.

Unit 18: Retirement Plans for Businesses

> **More Reading:**
> **Publication 560, *Retirement Plans for Small Business***

Employers may establish retirement plans as fringe benefits for their employees. Self-employed taxpayers are also allowed to set up retirement plans for themselves.

There are numerous forms of retirement plans: they include Simplified Employee Pension (SEP) plans, Savings Incentive Match Plan for Employees (SIMPLE) plans, and qualified plans.

Note: The term **qualified** refers to certain IRS requirements that the plan and the employer must adhere to in order to obtain tax-favored status. SEP and SIMPLE plans must also meet certain requirements, but they are much less complex than those that apply to qualified plans.

If retirement plans are structured and operated properly, businesses can deduct retirement contributions they make on behalf of their employees or, if self-employed, themselves. Both the contributions and the earnings are generally tax-free until distribution.

The rules vary depending on the type of business. Any business, including a sole proprietorship or a partnership, can deduct retirement plan contributions made on behalf of employees, even if the business has a net operating loss for the year.

Example: Gemma is self-employed and reports her income and losses from her catering business on Schedule C. She has a retirement account set up for herself and her five employees. In 2014, Gemma's catering business showed a loss from operations on her Schedule C, and Gemma has no other source of taxable income. She made regular contributions to her employees' retirement accounts in 2014, and she can deduct these contributions as a regular business expense. However, Gemma cannot make a retirement contribution for herself in 2014 because she has no self-employment income. Since her business showed a loss, she has no qualifying income for purposes of her own retirement plan contribution.

In the case of a sole proprietorship or partnership, if the owners of the business contribute to their own retirement accounts, they must take the deduction on Form 1040, and only if they have self-employment income. Self-employment income for the purpose of this deduction means net profits from Schedule C or Schedule F, or self-employment income from a partnership.

Since an S corporation is a pass-through entity, certain shareholder-employees in an S corporation are also required to report these deductions on their individual returns.[21]

However, as a C corporation is not a pass-through entity, the corporation deducts the expense on Form 1120, *U.S. Corporation Income Tax Return,* whether the contributions are made for employee-shareholders, officers, or other employees.

Retirement plans generally must adhere to certain nondiscrimination requirements intended to ensure they do not favor owners or executives of the sponsoring employer over other employees. Depending upon the type of plan, these requirements may include:

- Minimum coverage tests that limit elective deferral and employer contributions to highly compensated employees (HCEs) as percentages compared to the corresponding percentages for non-highly compensated employees.
- Prohibition of terms that favor HCEs' dollar amounts of contributions or benefits, or other rights.

Simplified Employee Pension (SEP) Plans

A SEP plan provides the simplest and least expensive method for employers to make contributions to a retirement plan for themselves and their employees.

An employer may establish a SEP as late as the due date (including extensions) of its income tax return and have it be effective for that year. The employer must also make its contribution to the plan by the due date (including extensions).

Example: Julie is a sole proprietor with two employees. She files her 2014 tax return on the extended due date of October 15, 2015. On that same date, Julie establishes a SEP plan and makes contributions for herself and her two employees for 2014.

There is no requirement for a plan document such as those needed for qualified retirement plans. However, the employer must execute a formal written agreement to provide benefits to all eligible employees under the SEP. Except in certain circumstances, including when the employer also maintains a qualified plan, this can be done using Form 5305-SEP. Using this form will typically eliminate the need to file annual information returns with the IRS and the Department of Labor.

Contributions to a SEP can vary from year to year, so it is a very flexible option for small employers. A SEP can be set up for an individual person's business even if he participates in another employer's retirement plan.

---

[21] This rule applies to employee-shareholders who own more than 2% of the S corporation stock.

Example: Mitch works full-time for the post office as a mail carrier, and also runs a profitable photo booth business with his wife on the weekends. They have self-employment income from the business. Mitch may set up a SEP for himself and his wife, even though he is already covered by the post office retirement plan.

Under a SEP, employers make contributions to an individual retirement arrangement (called a SEP-IRA) which must be set up for each eligible employee. The SEP-IRA is owned and controlled by the employee, and the employer makes contributions to the financial institution where the SEP-IRA is maintained. SEP-IRAs are funded exclusively by contributions from the employer. A SEP does not require employer contributions every year, but it cannot discriminate in favor of HCEs.

Example: Vazquez Company decides to establish a SEP for its employees. Vazquez has chosen a SEP because its industry is cyclical in nature. In good years, Vazquez can make larger contributions for its employees, and in down years it can reduce or eliminate contributions. Vazquez knows that under a SEP, the contribution rate (whether large or small) must be uniform for all employees. The financial institution that Vazquez identifies to be the trustee for its SEP has several investment funds for employees to choose from. Individual employees have the opportunity to divide their employer's contributions to their SEP-IRAs among these fund options.

An eligible employee is one who meets all the following requirements:
- Is at least 21 years old
- Has worked for the employer in at least three of the last five years
- Has received at least $550 of compensation in 2014

Note: If an employer sets up a SEP, all employees who are eligible employees must be allowed to participate.

An employer can use less restrictive participation requirements than those listed, but cannot use more restrictive ones. For example, an employer could choose to include all employees who are at least 18 years old rather than at least 21 years old.

The following employees can be excluded from coverage under a SEP:
- Employees covered by a union agreement
- Nonresident alien employees who have received no U.S. source income from the employer

Contributions to a SEP must be made in cash; an employer cannot contribute property to a SEP. However, plan participants may be able to transfer or roll over certain property from another retirement plan account to a SEP-IRA. Each year that an employer contributes to a SEP, it must contribute to the SEP-IRAs of all participants who had qualified compensation, including employees who die or terminate employment before the contributions are made. A SEP-IRA cannot be a Roth IRA. Employer contributions to a SEP-IRA do not affect the amount an individual can contribute to a Roth or traditional IRA.

SEP Contribution Limits: The following SEP limits apply in 2014:

- For an employee: Contributions cannot exceed the lesser of 25% of the employee's compensation or $52,000.

- For a self-employed individual: Contributions cannot exceed the lesser of 20% of net self-employment income, after considering both the deduction for self-employment tax and the deduction for the SEP-IRA contribution, or $52,000.

Employers cannot make contributions conditional, or require that any part of the contribution be kept in the employee's account after the business has made its contributions.

SEP Distributions: Employees have control over their own SEP-IRAs, so employers cannot prohibit distributions from a SEP-IRA. As with traditional IRAs, money withdrawn from a SEP-IRA (and not rolled over to another qualified retirement plan or account) is subject to income tax for the year in which a distribution is received.

If an employee withdraws money from a SEP-IRA before age 59½, a 10% additional tax generally applies. Further, a participant in a SEP-IRA must begin receiving required minimum distributions (RMDs) by April 1 of the year following the year the participant reaches age 70½. However, unlike a traditional IRA, contributions can be made for participants over age 70½.

SEP Snapshot

	Rules for Employers	Rules for Employees
Eligibility	Any business or self-employed individual may set up a SEP.	Employees aged 21 or older who have worked for the business for three of the last five years and earned at least $550 in the current year are eligible.
Contributions	Vesting is immediate.	Only employers and self-employed individuals can contribute to a SEP. Employees cannot contribute to a SEP.
Pros	Contributions can vary from year to year. Inexpensive to set up and administer.	Employers cannot prohibit distributions from a SEP, because vesting is immediate.
Drawbacks	A SEP must cover all qualifying employees. Employers cannot discriminate in favor of HCEs. Only employers can contribute.	Employees cannot contribute.

SIMPLE Plans

A SIMPLE (Savings Incentive Match Plan for Employees) plan provides another simplified way for a business and its employees to contribute toward retirement. Like SEPs, SIMPLE plans have lower start-up and annual costs than most other types of retirement plans.

If a business has 100 or fewer employees who received $5,000 or more of compensation during the preceding year, it can establish a SIMPLE plan.[22] The business cannot maintain another retirement plan unless the other plan is for a union workforce.

The business must continue to meet the 100-employee limit each year. However, if a business maintains a SIMPLE plan for at least one year and subsequently fails to meet the 100-employee limit, the business is allowed a two-year grace period to establish another retirement plan. Another exception may apply if the business fails to meet the 100-employee limit as a result of an acquisition, disposition, or similar transaction.

Employees can choose to make retirement plan contributions by allocating a portion of their salaries, and businesses can contribute matching or nonelective contributions. SIMPLE plans can only be maintained on a calendar-year basis. A SIMPLE plan can be structured in one of two ways: using SIMPLE IRAs or as a SIMPLE 401(k) plan, covered below.

SIMPLE IRAs

Unlike a SEP, SIMPLE IRAs allow employee contributions and require employer contributions.

A SIMPLE IRA must be set up for each eligible employee. An eligible employee is generally one who received at least $5,000 of compensation during any two years preceding the current calendar year and is reasonably expected to receive at least $5,000 in the current calendar year, except for:

- Employees covered by a union agreement
- Nonresident alien employees who have received no U.S. source income from the employer

Prior to an election period (generally 60 days) preceding the start of the calendar year, employees must receive formal notice of their rights to participate and make salary reduction contributions, and information regarding the employer's planned contributions.

---

[22] For purposes of the 100-employee limitation, all employees employed at any time during the year are taken into account, regardless of whether all of them are eligible to participate in the SIMPLE plan.

Contributions to a SIMPLE IRA

During the election period, an employee may execute or modify a salary reduction agreement to defer a portion of his salary (up to $12,000 for 2014.) Employees age 50 or over can also make a catch-up contribution of up to $2,500 (for a total of up to $14,500 for 2014). The salary reduction contributions under a SIMPLE IRA plan are elective deferrals that count toward an overall annual limit on elective deferrals an employee may make to this and other plans permitting elective deferrals.

Each year, the employer must choose to make either matching contributions or nonelective contributions. Employer matching of the employee's salary reduction contributions is generally required on a dollar-for-dollar basis up to 3% of the participant's compensation. The employer may elect to make matching contributions at less than 3%, but not lower than 1% for more than two years within a five-year period.

Instead of matching contributions, the employer may choose to make nonelective contributions of 2% of each eligible employee's compensation. An individual employee's compensation used for this contribution is limited to $260,000 in 2014.

If the employer chooses to make nonelective contributions, it must make them for all eligible employees, regardless of whether they make salary reduction contributions. The employer must notify employees of its choice to make nonelective contributions within a specified period prior to the employees' annual period for making their own salary reduction contribution elections.

An eligible employee may choose not to make salary reduction contributions for a given year. In this case the employee would accrue no employer matching contributions but would receive an employer nonelective contribution if the employer elects to make this type of contribution for the year.

Example: Riley works for the Skidmore Tire Company, a small business with 75 employees. Skidmore Tire has decided to establish a SIMPLE IRA plan and will make a 2% nonelective contribution for each of its employees. Under this option, even if Riley does not contribute to her own SIMPLE IRA, she would still receive an employer nonelective contribution to her SIMPLE IRA equal to 2% of her salary. Riley has a yearly salary of $40,000 and has decided not to make a contribution to her SIMPLE IRA this year. Even though she does not make a contribution, Skidmore must make a nonelective contribution of $800 (2% of $40,000). The financial institution that Skidmore uses for the SIMPLE IRA has several investment options from which Riley and the other plan participants can choose.

Example: Rockland Quarry Company is a small business with 50 employees. Rockland has decided to establish a SIMPLE IRA plan for all of its employees and will match its employees' contributions dollar-for-dollar up to 3% of each employee's salary. Under this option, if a Rockland employee does not contribute to his SIMPLE IRA, the employee does not receive any matching employer contributions. Elizabeth is an employee of Rockland Company. She has a yearly salary of $50,000 and decides to contribute 5% of her salary to her SIMPLE IRA. Elizabeth's yearly contribution is $2,500 (5% of $50,000). The Rockland matching contribution is $1,500 (3% of $50,000). Therefore, the total contribution to Elizabeth's SIMPLE IRA that year is $4,000 (her $2,500 contribution plus the $1,500 contribution from Rockland).

Employee and employer contributions are 100% vested.

Definition: Vesting refers to a person's rights to receive some type of benefit, such as retirement benefits as discussed in this unit, or other employee benefits such as stock options. Vesting may occur on a gradual schedule, such as a certain percentage per year of employee service, or at a set time, such as five years after an employee has begun work for a company.

The money an employee has put aside plus employer contributions and net earnings from investments cannot be forfeited. The employee has the right to withdraw funds at any time, but those withdrawals may be subject to tax.

Salary reduction contributions must be deposited with the applicable financial institution within 30 days after the end of the month in which they would otherwise have been paid to the employee. Matching or nonelective contributions must be made by the due date (including extensions) for filing the company's income tax return for the year.

An employer can set up a SIMPLE IRA plan effective on any date from January 1 through October 1 of a year, provided the employer did not previously maintain another SIMPLE IRA plan. A new employer may set up a SIMPLE IRA plan as soon as administratively feasible after the business comes into existence.

A business cannot suspend its employer matching contributions mid-year or terminate its SIMPLE IRA plan mid-year. The business must maintain the plan for a full calendar year (except in the year the business first establishes the plan). The employer is required to make the contributions that were promised to the employees.

A SIMPLE IRA plan may not require a participant to be employed on a specific date to receive an employer contribution. If a participant terminates employment during the year after making a salary reduction contribution, he would still be entitled to an employer contribution.

SIMPLE IRA contributions are not included in the "Wages, tips, other compensation" box of Form W-2, *Wage and Tax Statement*. However, salary reduction contributions must be included in the boxes for Social Security and Medicare wages.

Distributions from a SIMPLE IRA

Distributions are subject to income tax in the year they are received. If a participant takes a withdrawal from a SIMPLE IRA before age 59½, an additional tax of 10% generally applies. If the withdrawal occurs within two years of beginning participation in the SIMPLE IRA plan, the additional tax is increased to 25%.

SIMPLE IRA contributions and earnings may be rolled over tax-free from one SIMPLE IRA to another. A rollover may also be made from a SIMPLE IRA to another type of IRA, or to another employer's qualified plan, but it will be tax-free only if it is made after two years of participation in the SIMPLE IRA plan.

A participant in a SIMPLE IRA plan must begin receiving required minimum distributions by April 1 of the year following the year the participant reaches age 70½.

SIMPLE IRA Snapshot

	Rules for Employers	Rules for Employees
Eligibility	Any employer with 100 or fewer employees who received at least $5,000 in the preceding year. The employer cannot maintain another retirement plan in addition to the SIMPLE IRA.	Any employee who has earned at least $5,000 in any two prior years and who is expected to earn at least $5,000 in the current year.
Contribution Thresholds	Employers may choose to make either matching contributions at 1% to 3% of compensation for employees that make salary deferral contributions, or nonelective contributions at 2% of compensation for all eligible employees.	An employee can contribute up to $12,000 of his salary (or self-employment earnings, for a self-employed owner), plus an additional $2,500 if 50 or older for a total of $14,500.
Pros	Employees can make contributions. Vesting is immediate.	Employees can make contributions. Vesting is immediate.
Drawbacks	Employer matching is mandatory.	Employees with higher salaries may prefer a retirement plan option that allows them to contribute more.

SIMPLE 401(k) Plans

A SIMPLE 401(k) plan can be adopted as part of a traditional 401(k) plan (see below) if the business meets the 100-employee limit discussed above for SIMPLE IRA plans and does not maintain another qualified retirement plan.

An employee can elect to make salary reduction contributions as a percentage of his compensation, but not more than $12,000 for 2014. An employee age 50 or over can also make a catch-up contribution of up to $2,500 (for a total of up to $14,500 for 2014).

Unlike a regular 401(k) plan, the employer must make either:

- A matching contribution up to 3% of compensation for each employee who makes a salary reduction contribution, or
- A nonelective contribution of 2% of compensation for each eligible employee who receives at least $5,000 of compensation from the employer that year.

Participants are fully vested in all contributions. SIMPLE 401(k) plans must file Form 5500, *Annual Return/Report of Employee Benefit Plan*, annually.

Pros and Cons of a SIMPLE 401(k)

- The plan is not subject to the discrimination rules that apply to traditional 401(k) plans.
- The plan may offer optional participant loans and hardship withdrawals to add flexibility for employees.
- No other retirement plans can be maintained if a business has a SIMPLE.
- Withdrawal and loan flexibility adds an administrative burden for the employer.

Qualified Plans

There are two basic kinds of qualified retirement plans, defined contribution plans and defined benefit plans, and different rules apply to each. An employer is allowed to have more than one type of qualified plan, but maximum contributions cannot exceed annual limits.

All qualified plans are subject to federal regulation under the Employee Retirement Income Security Act (ERISA). The federal government does not require an employer to establish a retirement plan, but it provides minimum federal standards for qualified plans.

ERISA covers qualified retirement plans, as well as health and welfare benefit plans. Among other requirements, ERISA specifies that individuals who manage plans (and other fiduciaries) meet certain standards of conduct. The law also contains detailed provisions for reporting to the government and for disclosure to participants. Further, there are provisions aimed at assuring plan funds are protected and participants receive their benefits. ERISA mandates minimum funding requirements to ensure that benefits will be available to employees when they retire. For defined benefit plans, it requires that plan funding be certified by an actuary.

ERISA also mandates that qualified plans meet specific requirements regarding eligibility, vesting, and communications with participants. The administrator of an employee benefit plan subject to ERISA must file an information return for the plan each year. Form 5500, *Annual Return/Report of Employee Benefit Plan*, must be filed by the last day of the seventh month after the plan year ends.

Defined Benefit Plans

A defined benefit plan (often called a traditional pension plan) promises a specified benefit amount or annuity after retirement. Most federal and state governments offer defined benefit plans to their employees. However, fewer companies now offer defined benefit plans because they are costly to administer and inflexible. The benefits in many defined benefit plans are protected by federal insurance.

Contributions to a defined benefit plan are not optional. They are typically based on actuarial calculations. Contributions for self-employed taxpayers are limited to 100% of compensation. If the business does not have any income for the year, no contribution can be made.

Defined Contribution Plans

A defined contribution plan provides an individual account for each participant in the plan. It provides benefits to the participant based on the amounts contributed to the participant's account, along with subsequent income, expenses, gains, losses, and, in some instances, allocations of forfeitures among participant accounts.

The participant, the employer, or sometimes both may contribute to the individual participant accounts. The value of the account will fluctuate due to the changes in the value of investments that have been made with the amounts contributed. A participant's retirement benefits depend primarily on the amount of contributions made on his behalf, rather than upon his years of service with the employer or his earnings history.

Examples of defined contribution plans include 401(k) plans, 403(b) plans, and 457 plans.

Traditional 401(k) Plans

A 401(k) plan is a defined contribution plan that allows each eligible employee to defer receiving a portion of his salary, which is instead contributed on his behalf to the 401(k) plan. Deferrals generally are made on a pretax basis, although some plans allow employees the option to make them on an after-tax basis.

Pretax deferrals are not subject to income tax withholding, and they are not included in taxable wages on the employee's Form W-2. However, they are subject to Social Security, Medicare, and federal unemployment taxes.

Sometimes the employer will make matching contributions. Employee deferrals and any employer matching contributions are accounted separately for each employee. Earnings on the retirement account grow tax-free until distribution.

401(k) plans can vary significantly in their complexity. However, many financial institutions administer 401(k) plans, which can lessen the administrative burden on individual employers of establishing and maintaining these plans.

Distributions from Qualified Plans

Generally, distributions cannot be made from a qualified plan until one of the following occurs:

- The employee retires, dies, becomes disabled, or otherwise terminates employment.
- The plan terminates.
- The employee reaches age 59½ or suffers financial hardship.

Unless a distribution is properly rolled over into another retirement plan or individual retirement account, it will be subject to income tax upon receipt.

If a distribution is made to an employee before he reaches age 59½, the employee may have to pay a 10% additional tax on the distribution.

However, the additional tax may not apply in the following situations:

- Distributions are for the taxpayer's medical care, up to the amount allowed as a medical deduction.
- Disability or death.
- Distributions in the form of an annuity.
- Distributions are made because of an IRS levy on the plan.
- Distributions are made to a qualified reservist (an individual called up to active duty).

Even if these distributions are not subject to the additional 10% tax, they would be subject to tax at the taxpayer's applicable rate.

> **Example:** Lauren, age 43, takes a $5,000 distribution from her traditional IRA account. She does not meet any of the exceptions to the 10% additional tax, so the $5,000 is an early distribution. Lauren must include the $5,000 in her gross income for the year the distribution is received and pay income tax on it. She must also pay an additional tax of $500 (10% × $5,000).

Required Minimum Distributions: A participant in a qualified retirement plan must begin receiving distributions by April 1 of the first year following the later of:

- The calendar year in which he reaches age 70½
- The calendar year in which he retires from employment with the employer maintaining the plan

However, the plan may require distributions by April 1 of the year after the participant reaches age 70½ even if he has not retired. Further, if the participant is a 5% owner of the employer, he must begin receiving distributions by April 1 of the year after the year he reaches age 70½.

Penalties for not taking required minimum distributions (RMDs) can be severe. Penalties are assessed if an account owner fails to withdraw an RMD, fails to withdraw the full amount of the RMD, or fails to withdraw the RMD by the applicable deadline. The penalty is 50% of the amount that is not withdrawn from the account when required.

Limits on Benefits and Contributions

For 2014, the following overall limits apply:

The annual benefit for a participant in a defined benefit plan cannot exceed the lesser of $210,000 or 100% of the participant's average compensation for his highest three consecutive calendar years.

A combined limit of $17,500 applies to each employee's elective deferrals and salary reduction contributions, other than catch-up contributions, to all defined contribution retirement plans and any SIMPLE IRA plan under which he is covered. If the limit is exceeded, the amount that would otherwise have been nontaxable must be included in the employee's gross income. Catch-up contributions are limited to $2,500 for each participant in a SIMPLE plan and $5,500 for each participant in other defined contribution plans.

Annual contributions to the account of a participant in a defined contribution plan cannot exceed the lesser of $52,000 or 100% of the participant's compensation.

An employer's deduction for contributions to a defined contribution plan cannot be more than 25% of the compensation paid or accrued during the year for the eligible employees. The maximum compensation that can be considered for each employee is $260,000.

Penalties apply to excess contributions. An excise tax of 6% applies to excess amounts contributed by employees and self-employed individuals if these amounts and related earnings are not withdrawn by the due date of their returns (with or without extensions, depending upon the type of plan). An excise tax of 10% applies to excess employer contributions.

Comparison of Defined Benefit and Defined Contribution Plans		
Rule	**Defined Benefit Plan**	**Defined Contribution Plan**
Employer Contributions	Employer contributions are required based upon actuarial calculation of amounts needed to fund specified plan benefits.	The employer may choose to match a portion of employee contributions or to contribute without employee contributions.
Employee Contributions	Employees often do not contribute.	For many plans, employees are the primary contributors.
Managing the Investments	The employer must ensure that contributions to the plan plus investment earnings will be enough to pay the promised benefits.	The employee often is responsible for managing the investment of his account, choosing from investment options offered by the plan. For some plans, the plan administrator is responsible for investing the plan's assets.
Benefits Paid Upon Retirement	A promised benefit is based on a formula, often using a combination of the employee's age, years worked, and salary history.	The benefit depends on contributions made by the employee and/or the employer and investment earnings on the contributions.
Type of Retirement Benefit Payments	Traditionally, these plans pay the retiree monthly annuity payments that continue for life.	The retiree may transfer the account balance into an Individual Retirement Account (IRA) from which he may withdraw money. Some plans also offer monthly payments through an annuity.
Guarantee of Benefits	The government, through the Pension Benefit Guaranty Corporation (PBGC), may partially guarantee benefits.	No federal guarantee of benefits.

Prohibited Transactions

A prohibited transaction is a transaction between a retirement plan and a disqualified person that is prohibited by law. A disqualified person may include the following:

- A fiduciary of the plan
- A person providing services to the plan
- An employer, any of whose employees are covered by the plan
- An employee organization, any of whose members are covered by the plan
- An indirect or direct owner of 50% or more of the applicable employer or employee organization
- A member of the family of anyone described in the bullet points above
- A corporation, partnership, trust, or estate of which any direct or indirect owner described in the bullet points above holds a 50% or more interest
- An officer, director, 10% or more shareholder, or highly compensated employee of the entity administering the plan

An initial 15% tax is applied on the amount involved in a prohibited transaction for each year (or part of a year) in a taxable period. If the transaction is not corrected within the taxable period, an additional tax of 100% of the amount involved is imposed. These taxes are payable by any disqualified person who takes part in a prohibited transaction. If more than one person takes part, each can be jointly and severally liable for the entire amount of tax. Prohibited transactions include the following:

- A transfer of plan income or assets to, or use for the benefit of, a disqualified person
- Any act of a fiduciary by which plan income or assets are used for his own benefit
- The receipt of money or property by a fiduciary for his own account from any party dealing with the plan in a transaction that involves plan income or assets
- The sale, exchange, or lease of property between a plan and a disqualified person
- Lending money between a plan and a disqualified person
- Furnishing goods or services between a plan and a disqualified person

Example: A plan fiduciary had a prohibited transaction by investing in a life insurance company's group annuity contract, resulting in a 10% commission paid to his company on the investment. This is a prohibited transaction between a plan fiduciary and a retirement plan.

If a prohibited transaction is not corrected during the taxable period, the taxpayer usually has an additional 90 days after the day the IRS mails a notice of deficiency for the 100% tax to correct the transaction.

Unit 18: Study Questions

1. Sarah is a small employer with a defined contribution plan for her employees. Her highest paid employee has total compensation of $50,000. In 2014, what is the maximum she can contribute to an employee/participant's plan?

A. $17,500.
B. $50,000.
C. $52,000.
D. $210,000.

2. Jensen Biomedical Corporation maintains a SIMPLE IRA for its employees and has elected to make 3% matching contributions. A former employee, Grace, quit her job on January 27, 2014 after the business had already deducted $75 from her wages based upon her election to contribute to its SIMPLE IRA plan. Grace had earned $2,000 of wages before she quit. How must Jensen Biomedical treat this $75 deduction from Grace's wages?

A. Jensen must return Grace's $75 salary reduction contribution.
B. Jensen must deposit Grace's salary reduction contribution in her SIMPLE IRA account. The company must also match Grace's salary reduction contributions up to 3% of her $2,000 compensation ($60).
C. Jensen must deposit Grace's salary reduction contribution in her SIMPLE IRA account. However, the company is not required to make a matching contribution for an employee who has terminated employment.
D. Jensen is required to remit the $75 to the U.S. Treasury.

3. "Prohibited transactions" are transactions between a retirement plan and a disqualified person. Which of the following is exempt from the prohibited transaction rules?

A. A fiduciary of the plan.
B. A person providing services to the plan.
C. An employer whose employees are covered by the plan.
D. A disqualified person who receives a benefit to which he is entitled as a plan participant.

4. What types of employers cannot establish a SEP?

A. A self-employed taxpayer without any employees.
B. A corporation with 90 employees.
C. A nonprofit entity with five employees.
D. All of the above can establish a SEP.

5. Ram is a sole proprietor whose tax year is the calendar year. He made a contribution to his SIMPLE IRA on May 15, 2015. What is the earliest year for which he can deduct this contribution?

A. His 2014 tax return.
B. His 2015 tax return.
C. The contribution is not deductible on his tax return because it was made late.
D. None of the above.

6. Huang Software, Inc. decides to establish a SEP for its employees. All of the following statements about Huang's retirement plan are correct except:

A. In good years, Huang can make larger contributions for its employees, and in down years it can reduce the amount.
B. Individual employees have the opportunity to divide the employer's contributions to their SEP-IRAs among the funds made available to Huang employees.
C. Under a SEP, the contribution rate can be different for each employee, based on length of service and sales performance.
D. Only employers and self-employed individuals can make contributions to SEPs.

7. Maura, age 26, began participating in a SIMPLE IRA retirement account on March 10, 2013. She took an early distribution from the account on December 26, 2014. She does not qualify for any of the exceptions to the early withdrawal penalty. The distribution amount was $10,000. What is the amount of additional tax that Maura must pay on the early distribution?

A. $1,000.
B. $1,500.
C. $2,500.
D. $3,000.

8. Brenda owns the Fresh Berry Company, a sole proprietorship with 150 employees. All of the following plans are available for Brenda's company except:

A. A qualified plan.
B. A defined benefit plan.
C. A SIMPLE IRA.
D. None of the above.

9. Can a SIMPLE IRA plan be maintained on a fiscal-year basis?

A. Yes, if the business is on a fiscal year.
B. Yes, even if the business uses a calendar year.
C. Yes, but only if the business requests a 444 election.
D. No, a calendar year must be used.

10. The Azalea City Partnership has 15 employees and contributes to their retirement accounts. How is this transaction reported?

A. The business can take the deduction for its contributions to its employees' retirement accounts on Form 1065, *Partnership Income Tax Return*.
B. The business cannot take a deduction for its contributions to its employees' retirement accounts. Instead, the amounts contributed are added to the partnership basis.
C. The individual partners are allowed to deduct contributions to the employee retirement accounts on their individual returns.
D. None of the above.

11. Leah is a sole proprietor who establishes a SEP. She has two employees. Leah has a net loss in 2014 on her Schedule C. Which of the following statements is correct?

A. Because the business shows a loss, she is prohibited from contributing to her retirement account, as well as the retirement accounts of her employees.
B. Because the business shows a loss, she is prohibited from contributing to her retirement account, but she can contribute to the retirement accounts of her employees.
C. Leah can make a retirement contribution to her own retirement account as well as the accounts of her employees.
D. None of the above.

12. All of the following are requirements of ERISA (the Employee Retirement Income Security Act) except:

A. ERISA requires that employers file an annual report on Form 5500 for their sponsored retirement plans.
B. ERISA requires employers to set up retirement plans for their employees.
C. ERISA requires minimum funding standards for retirement plans.
D. ERISA requires certain communications with plan participants.

13. Under the rules for prohibited transactions, all of the following would be considered disqualified persons except:

A. A 5% shareholder of the entity administering the plan.
B. A fiduciary of the plan.
C. An employer whose employees are covered by the plan.
D. A person providing services to the plan.

14. Theresa is a small business owner who maintains a SEP plan for her employees. Which of the following employees can be excluded from the plan, if Theresa chooses?

A. Stan, a 32-year-old part-time employee who has worked for Theresa for five years.
B. Aldo, a 42-year-old seasonal employee and U.S. resident alien who has worked for Theresa for three years.
C. Noel, a 21-year-old part-time employee who is also a union member.
D. Millie, a 55-year-old full-time employee who has worked for Theresa for four years.

15. Josie works full-time and participates in her employer's retirement plan. She also has her own graphic design business. She does not have any employees. Can Josie set up a SEP for self-employment income, even though she is already participating in her employer's plan?

A. Yes, Josie can still set up a SEP for her business.
B. No, Josie cannot set up a SEP because she is covered by an employer plan.
C. No, Josie cannot set up a SEP because she is a prohibited individual.
D. Josie can set up a SEP only if she hires employees.

16. Which of the following statements regarding a SEP-IRA is correct?

A. Money can be withdrawn from a SEP-IRA by the employee at any time without tax or penalty.

B. Money can be withdrawn from a SEP-IRA by the employee at any time, but taxes may apply.

C. An employee must wait at least two years to withdraw money from a SEP-IRA.

D. An employee must wait at least three years to withdraw money from a SEP-IRA.

17. What are the penalties imposed on a disqualified person who takes part in a prohibited transaction?

A. 25% tax of the amount involved.

B. 50% tax of the amount involved.

C. An initial tax of 15% of the amount involved, and an additional tax of 100% if the transaction is not corrected within the taxable period.

D. An initial tax of 25% of the amount involved, and an additional tax of 100% if the transaction is not corrected within the taxable period.

18. What happens if an eligible employee entitled to a contribution is unwilling to set up a SIMPLE IRA?

A. Eligible employees may decline to participate in an employer's SIMPLE IRA.

B. Eligible employees may not opt out of a SIMPLE IRA.

C. Eligible employees may choose to set up a ROTH IRA in lieu of a SIMPLE IRA.

D. None of the above.

19. The Esslinger Company has started a SEP plan for its employees. The company currently has four employees. Which of the following employees is the company not required to cover under the SEP plan?

A. Faye, age 45, a full-time employee for the last five years.

B. Larry, age 25, a part-time employee for the last three years.

C. Randolph, age 20, a full-time employee for the last three years.

D. Mack, age 42, a seasonal employee for the last six years.

20. If an employer makes an excess contribution to a defined contribution plan, an excess tax of _____ will apply:

A. 6%
B. 10%.
C. 25%.
D. 50%.

21. A 401(k) is a type of:

A. SEP-IRA.
B. Government pension plan.
C. Defined contribution plan.
D. Defined benefit plan.

22. Marcelo owns Perez Auto and sets up a SEP-IRA for all of his employees. In his benefits handbook, he makes the following statements regarding the shop's SEP-IRA plan. All are correct except:

A. Only employees age 21 and older are eligible.
B. An employee cannot withdraw from his SEP-IRA while he is employed by Perez Auto.
C. A SEP-IRA will be set up for all eligible employees.
D. An employee must have worked for Perez Auto for at least three of the last five years to be eligible.

Unit 19: Trusts and Estates

More Reading:
Publication 559, *Survivors, Executors, and Administrators*
Publication 950, *Introduction to Estate and Gift Taxes*
Publication 536, *Net Operating Losses (NOLs) for Individuals, Estates, and Trusts*

Estates and trusts are separate legal entities that are defined by the assets they hold. An estate is created when a taxpayer dies and the estate tax may be imposed on the assets held by the estate.

A trust is created while the taxpayer is alive or by a taxpayer's last will, and can determine how property will be distributed during his lifetime or at death. A trust can hold title to property for the benefit of one or more persons or entities. An estate or trust is generally required to obtain an employer identification number (EIN), like other legal entities.

Estates and trusts generally terminate when all of their assets and income have been distributed and all of their liabilities have been paid. If a trust or estate's existence is unnecessarily prolonged, the IRS can step in and terminate it after a reasonable period for completing the final administration. If an estate or trust has a loss in its final year, the loss can be passed through to the beneficiaries, allowing them deductions on their returns. Losses cannot be passed through to beneficiaries in a non-termination year.

Estates in General

For federal tax purposes, an estate is a separate legal entity that is created when a taxpayer dies. A person who inherits property from an estate is generally not taxed on the transfer. Instead, the estate itself is responsible for paying any applicable taxes before the property is distributed. However, if the estate's assets are distributed to beneficiaries before the taxes are paid, the beneficiaries can be held liable for the tax debt, up to the value of the assets distributed.

After a person dies, a personal representative, such as an executor named in his will or an administrator appointed by a court, will typically manage the estate and settle the decedent's financial affairs. If there is no executor or administrator, another person with possession of the decedent's property may act as the personal representative. The personal representative is responsible for filing the final income tax return and the estate tax return, if required. The personal representative is also responsible for determining any estate tax liability before the estate's assets are distributed to beneficiaries.

Either the personal representative or a paid preparer must sign the appropriate line of each of the following tax returns that may need to be filed:

- The final income tax return (Form 1040) for the decedent (for income received before death);
- Fiduciary income tax returns (Form 1041) for the estate for the period of its administration; and
- The estate tax return (Form 706).

Example: James was unmarried when he died on April 20, 2014. His only daughter, Lillian, was named as the executor of his estate. James earned wages in 2014 before his death, so a final tax return is required for 2014. Lillian asks her accountant to help prepare her father's final Form 1040, which will include all the taxable income that James received in 2014 before his death. The accountant also helps Lillian with the valuation of her father's estate. After determining the fair market value of all her father's assets, they conclude that James's gross estate is valued at approximately $7 million. As this exceeds the threshold of $5.34 million for 2014, an estate tax return (Form 706) is also required to be filed. Lillian is the executor, so she is responsible for filing and signing both returns.

Final Income Tax Return (Form 1040)

The taxpayer's final income tax return is filed on the same form that would have been used if the taxpayer were still alive, but "deceased" is written after the taxpayer's name. The filing deadline is April 15 of the year following the taxpayer's death, the same deadline that applies for individual income tax returns.

The personal representative must file the final individual income tax return of the decedent for the year of death and any returns not filed for preceding years. If an individual died after the close of a tax year but before the return for that year was filed, the return for that year will not be the final return. The return for that year will be a regular return and the personal representative must file it.

Example: Milly dies on March 2, 2014. At the time of her death, she had not yet filed her 2013 tax return. She earned $51,000 of wages in 2013. She also earned $18,000 of wages between January 1, 2014 and her death. Therefore, Milly's 2013 and 2014 tax returns must be filed by her representative. The 2014 return would be her final individual tax return.

On a decedent's final tax return, the rules for personal exemptions and deductions are the same as those that apply for any individual taxpayer. The full amount of the applicable personal exemption may be claimed on the final tax return, regardless of how long the taxpayer was alive during the year.

On a decedent's final tax return, the rules for personal exemptions and deductions are the same as those that apply for any individual taxpayer. The full amount of the applicable personal exemption (subject to any phaseout limitations based on income) may be claimed on the final tax return, regardless of how long the taxpayer was alive during the year.

Income in Respect of a Decedent

Income in respect of a decedent (IRD) is any taxable income that was earned but not received by the decedent by the time of death. IRD is not taxed on the final return of the deceased taxpayer. IRD is reported on the tax return of the person (or entity) that receives the income. This could be the estate, in which case it would be reported on Form 1041, as described below. Otherwise it could be the surviving spouse or another beneficiary, such as a child.

IRD retains the same tax nature that would have applied if the deceased taxpayer were still alive. For example, if the income would have been short-term capital gain, it is taxed the same way to the beneficiary. IRD can come from various sources, including:

- Unpaid salary, wages, or bonuses
- Distributions from traditional IRAs and employer-provided retirement plans
- Deferred compensation benefits
- Accrued but unpaid interest, dividends, and rent
- Accounts receivable of a sole proprietor

Example: Carlos was owed $15,000 of wages when he died. The check for these wages was not remitted by his employer until three weeks later and was received by his daughter and sole beneficiary, Rosalie. The wages are considered IRD, and Rosalie must recognize the $15,000 as ordinary income, the same tax treatment that would have applied for Carlos.

Example: Beverly died on April 30. At the time of her death, she was owed (but had not yet received) $1,500 of interest on bonds and $2,000 of rental income. Beverly's beneficiary will include $3,500 of IRD in gross income when the interest and rent are received. The income retains its character as interest income and passive activity rental income.

IRD is included in the decedent's estate and may be subject to estate tax. If it is received by a beneficiary and subject to income tax on the beneficiary's return, the beneficiary can claim a deduction for estate tax paid on the IRD. This deduction is taken as a miscellaneous itemized deduction on Schedule A and is not subject to the 2% floor.

Fiduciary Income Tax Return (Form 1041)

Form 1041 is a fiduciary return used to report the following items for a domestic decedent's estate, a trust, or a bankruptcy estate:

- Current income and deductions, including gains and losses from disposition of the entity's property and excluding certain items such as tax-exempt interest (collectively, *distributable net income* or DNI);
- A deduction for income that is either held for future distribution or distributed currently to the beneficiaries (income distribution deduction) that is limited to DNI; and
- Any income tax liability.

An estate or trust may exist as a taxable legal entity until all of its assets have been distributed. Current income of an estate may include IRD, if it was received by the estate rather than specific beneficiaries. As investment assets will usually continue to earn income after a taxpayer has died, this income, such as rents, dividends and interest, must be reported. The expenses of administering an estate can be deducted either from the estate's income on Form 1041, in determining its income tax, or from the gross estate on Form 706, in determining the estate tax liability, but cannot be claimed for both purposes. Schedule K-1 is used to report any income that is distributed or distributable to each beneficiary and is filed with Form 1041, with a copy also given to the beneficiary.

The due date for Form 1041 is the fifteenth day of the fourth month following the end of the entity's tax year, but is subject to an automatic extension of five months if Form 7004 is filed. The tax year of an estate may be either a calendar or a fiscal year, subject to the election made at the time the first return is filed. An election will also be made on the first return as to method (cash, accrual, or other) to report an estate's income. Form 1041 must be filed for any domestic estate that has gross income for the tax year of $600 or more, or a beneficiary who is a nonresident alien (with any amount of income).

Distributable Net Income: Taxable income earned by an estate or trust is taxable to either the entity or the beneficiaries, but not to both. Distributable net income (DNI) is income that is currently available for distribution. If the beneficiary receives a distribution in excess of DNI, only the DNI is taxed.

The income distribution deduction (IDD) is allowed to trusts and estates for amounts that are paid, credited, or required to be distributed to beneficiaries. The income distribution deduction is calculated on Schedule B (Form 1041) and is limited to the lesser of distributions less tax-exempt income or DNI less tax-exempt income.

313

> **Example:** The Camden Family Trust has the following income in 2014: $25,000 of taxable interest and dividends; $35,000 of capital gains; and $10,000 of tax-exempt interest. The trust also incurred fiduciary and investment fees of $5,000. The trust document provides that capital gains are allocated to income, rather than the trust's corpus. The trust has DNI of $65,000 ($25,000 + $35,000 + $10,000 - $5,000). The trust makes distributions of $45,000 and an IDD of $35,000 may be claimed for the year. This amount represents the lesser of its DNI ($65,000) and its distributions ($45,000), minus its tax-exempt income.

Net Investment Income Tax: Estates and certain trusts are subject to the additional tax of 3.8% on net investment income. The provisions for this tax are generally similar to those for individuals, and it must be reported on Form 8960, *Net Investment Tax: Individuals, Estates, and Trusts.* For trusts and estates, the tax applies to the lesser of undistributed net investment income or the excess of adjusted gross income over the threshold amount ($11,950 for 2013) at which the highest tax bracket begins. The tax does not apply to tax-exempt trusts or to grantor trusts.

Net investment income that is subject to the tax includes:

- Interest
- Dividends
- Capital gains
- Rental and royalty income
- Non-qualified annuities
- Income from businesses involved in trading of financial instruments or commodities
- Income from businesses that are passive activities for the taxpayer

Form 706: The Estate Tax Return

An estate tax return is filed using Form 706, *United States Estate (and Generation-Skipping Transfer) Tax Return.* The estate tax applies to an individual's taxable estate, which is the gross estate less certain deductions. After the taxable estate is computed, it is added to the value of taxable gifts made during the decedent's lifetime. The applicable estate tax rate is applied to derive a tentative tax, from which any gift taxes paid or payable are subtracted to determine the gross estate tax. The maximum estate tax rate is 40% in 2014.

However, all or a portion of the gross estate tax may be eliminated after consideration of the estate's available:

- **Basic Exclusion Amount:** This amount is adjusted for inflation each year and may be used to reduce or eliminate gift and/or estate taxes. For 2014, the basic estate tax exclusion amount is $5.34 million.

- **Deceased Spousal Unused Exclusion (DSUE):** This is the unused portion of the decedent's predeceased spouse's basic exclusion (the amount that was not used to offset gift or estate tax liabilities). The predeceased spouse must have died on or after January 1, 2011 and a portability election must be made to claim the DSUE on behalf of the surviving spouse's estate. This election can be made automatically by timely completion and filing of Form 706 for the estate of the predeceased spouse.

Only estates valued in excess of the sum of these amounts need to file a return and pay estate tax. Essentially, this means that a surviving spouse's estate with value up to $10.68 million of estate value could be excluded from taxation if both spouses died during 2014, neither spouse had used any of his basic exclusion amount to offset gift tax liabilities, and the portability election for DSUE was properly made on Form 706 for the first spouse's estate.

Example: Marlene dies in 2014 and leaves an estate valued at $3 million. She had not previously used any of her basic exclusion amount to avoid paying gift taxes, so the entire exclusion amount of $5.34 million is available to her estate. As this amount exceeds the estate's value, no estate tax is owed and an estate tax return does not need to be filed.

Example: Matt dies in early 2014 and leaves a gross estate valued at $9 million. His assets transfer to his wife, Leslie, and none are taxed because of the unlimited marital deduction. Thus, none of the $5.34 million basic exclusion amount available to Matt's estate is used (and none had been used to offset gift tax liabilities during his lifetime). Leslie dies later in the year. Assuming Form 706 was timely filed for Matt's estate and Leslie had not used any of her basic exclusion amount, Matt's unused basic exclusion is added to Leslie's basic exclusion, for a total exclusion amount of $10.68 million ($5.34 million × 2). If Leslie's estate is valued at less than $10.68 million, the full amount can be excluded and no estate tax will be owed.

Applicable Credit: The gross estate tax described above is reduced by the *applicable credit*, also referred to as the *unified credit*, which is a tax credit amount that corresponds with the basic exclusion amount and, if applicable, the DSUE available to a surviving spouse. An applicable credit amount of $2,081,800 in 2014 corresponds with the basic exclusion amount of $5.34 million.

Just as with the basic exclusion amount, any portion of the applicable credit amount used to avoid payment of gift taxes reduces the amount of credit available in later years that can be used to offset gift or estate taxes. For example, if someone had used the full $2,081,800 applicable credit to avoid payment of gift taxes during his lifetime, he would have exhausted his entire $5.34 million basic exclusion. If he then died in 2014, his estate would be liable for tax on the taxable estate without further offset.

> **Example:** June, who is single, dies in 2014 and leaves an estate valued at $20 million. During her lifetime, she had used $1 million of her basic exclusion to offset payments of gift tax. That reduces the amount her estate may exclude to $4.34 million, which is then subtracted from her $20 million taxable estate. That leaves a total of $15.66 million to be taxed at a 40% rate, resulting in an estate tax liability of $6.26 million.

If required to be filed, the due date for Form 706 is nine months after the decedent's date of death. An automatic six-month extension may be requested by filing Form 4768. However, the tax is due by the due date and interest is accrued on any amounts owed that are not paid at that time. The assessment period for estate tax is three years after the due date for a timely filed estate tax return. The assessment period is four years for transfers from an estate.

The Gross Estate

The gross estate is based upon the fair market value of the decedent's property, which is not necessarily equal to his cost, and includes:

- The FMV of all tangible and intangible property owned by the decedent at the time of death.
- The full value of property held as joint tenants with the right of survivorship (unless the decedent and spouse were the only joint tenants)
- Life insurance proceeds payable to the estate, or payable to the heirs, for policies owned by the decedent.
- The value of certain annuities or survivor benefits payable to the heirs.
- The value of certain property that was transferred within three years before the decedent's death.

The gross estate does not include property owned solely by the decedent's spouse or other individuals. Lifetime gifts that are complete (so that no control over the gifts was retained) are not included in the gross estate.

Deductions from the Gross Estate: Once the gross estate has been calculated, certain deductions (and in special circumstances, reductions to value) are allowed to determine the taxable estate. Deductions from the gross estate may include:

- Funeral expenses paid out of the estate.
- Administration expenses for the estate (if not deducted on Form 1041).

- Debts owed at the time of death.
- The marital deduction (generally, the value of the property that passes from the estate to a surviving spouse).
- The charitable deduction (generally, the value of the property that passes from the estate to qualifying charities).
- The state death tax deduction (generally, any inheritance or estate taxes paid to any state).

The following items are not deductible from the gross estate:

- Federal estate taxes paid.
- Alimony paid after the taxpayer's death. These payments would be treated as distributions to a beneficiary.

Property taxes are deductible only if they accrue under state law prior to the decedent's death.

Study Note: For both Parts 1 and 2 of the EA exam, you should be familiar with what is included in the gross estate and the taxable estate.

The Marital Deduction: Transfers from one spouse to the other are typically tax-free. The marital deduction allows spouses to transfer an unlimited amount of property to one another during their lifetimes or at death without being subject to estate or gift taxes.

Decedent's Medical Expenses: Debts that were not paid before death, including medical expenses subsequently paid on behalf of the decedent, are liabilities of the estate and can be deducted from the gross estate on the estate tax return. However, if medical expenses for the decedent are paid out of the estate during the one-year period beginning with the day after death, the personal representative can alternatively elect to treat all or part of the expenses as paid by the decedent at the time they were incurred, and deduct them on the final tax return (1040) for the decedent.

Basis of Estate Property

The basis of property inherited from a decedent is generally one of the following:

- The FMV of the property on the date of death.
- The FMV on an alternate valuation date, if elected by the personal representative.
- The value under a special-use valuation method for real property used in farming or another closely-held business, if elected by the personal representative.
- The decedent's adjusted basis in land to the extent of the value excluded from the taxable estate as a qualified conservation easement.

Property that is jointly owned by a decedent and another person will be included in full in the decedent's gross estate unless it can be shown that the other person originally owned or otherwise contributed to the purchase price. The surviving owner's new basis in property that was jointly owned is calculated by adding his original basis in the property to the value of the part of the property included in the decedent's estate. Any deductions for depreciation of the property allowed to the surviving owner are subtracted from the sum.

If property is jointly held between husband and wife as tenants by the entirety or as joint tenants with the right of survivorship (if they were the only joint tenants), one-half of the property's value is included in the gross estate, and there is a step-up in basis for that one-half. If the decedent holds property in a community property state, half of the value of the community property will be included in the gross estate of the decedent, but the entire value of the community property will receive a step-up in basis.

Trusts in General

A trust is an entity created under the laws of the state in which it is formed. A trust may be created during an individual's life (an inter-vivos trust) or at the time of death under a will (a testamentary trust). A trust can be created to hold property for the benefit of other persons. It may be created for the benefit of a disabled individual, or it can be used to legally avoid certain taxes. The establishment of a trust creates a fiduciary relationship between three parties:

- **The Grantor:** The person who contributes property to the trust.
- **The Trustee (or Fiduciary):** The person or entity charged with the fiduciary duties associated with the trust.
- **The Beneficiary:** The person who is designated to receive the trust income or assets.

Example: AJ is having medical problems and decides to put her assets in a trust. She asks her attorney to create the trust and to manage the assets. The trust is structured so that it will pay AJ's living expenses, with the remainder of the assets going to her grandson after she dies. In this scenario, AJ is the **grantor**, the lawyer is the **trustee**, and AJ and her grandson are the **beneficiaries**.

Sometimes, a trust is used to transfer property in a controlled manner. For example, a parent may wish to transfer ownership of assets to his child, but does not want the child to waste the assets or spend them unwisely. The assets could be transferred to a trust, with the parent as both the grantor and the trustee. The child would be the beneficiary. The parent still has control over the assets, and the child is prevented from using them all up.

The accounting period for a trust is generally the calendar year. The filing due date for a calendar-year trust is April 15. A trust must file Form 1041, *U.S. Income Tax Return for Estates and Trusts* if it has:

- Any taxable income for the year (after subtracting the allowable exemption amount),
- Gross income of $600 or more (regardless of whether the income is taxable), or
- Any beneficiary who is a nonresident alien.

Example: The Russick Family Trust has $400 of tax-exempt interest from municipal bonds during the year. There is no other income. Normally, the trust would not be required to file a tax return because the income earned by the trust is tax-exempt. However, the Russick Family Trust has a beneficiary who is a nonresident alien. Therefore, the trust is required to file Form 1041.

A trust calculates its gross income in a manner similar to an individual taxpayer. Trusts are allowed an exemption, but the amount varies based on the type of trust. A trust that must distribute all of its income currently (a simple trust) is allowed an exemption of $300. Any other trust is allowed an exemption of $100 per year.

Most deductions and credits allowed to individuals are also allowed to trusts. However, there is one major distinction: a trust is a pass-through entity that is allowed a deduction for its distributions to beneficiaries. The beneficiaries (and not the trust) pay income tax on their distributive share of income. Schedule K-1 (Form 1041) is used to report income that a trust distributes to beneficiaries. The income must then be reported on the beneficiaries' income tax returns.

Simple and Complex Trusts

With regard to income distribution, there are two types of trusts: a simple trust and a complex trust. The IRC defines a simple trust as a trust that:

- Distributes all of its income currently;
- Makes no distributions of principal; and
- Makes no distributions to charity.

Any trust that is not a simple trust is automatically a complex trust. A complex trust:

- Is allowed to accumulate income;
- Can make discretionary distributions of income;
- Can make mandatory (or discretionary) distributions of principal; and
- Can make distributions to charity.

A trust may be a simple trust one year, and a complex trust in another year. For example, if a simple trust fails to distribute all its income in the current year, it becomes a complex trust. Unlike an estate or a simple trust, a complex trust reports its accounting income, which may differ from its taxable income and its DNI and may be more or less than distributions for the year, on Form 1041.

Study Note: For Part 2 of the EA exam, you should understand the differences between a simple trust and a complex trust and know the rules for how each distributes income.

Grantor Trusts

A grantor trust is a valid legal entity under state law, but it is not recognized as a separate entity for income tax purposes.

The grantor (also known as trustor, settlor, or creator) creates the trust relationship and retains control over the trust. In the eyes of the IRS, the grantor is the owner of the trust for income tax purposes. The grantor establishes the terms and provisions of the trust relationship between the grantor, the trustee, and the beneficiary. These will usually include the following:

- The rights, duties, and powers of the trustee;
- Distribution provisions;
- Ability of the grantor to amend, modify, revoke, or terminate the trust agreement;
- The designation of a trustee or successor trustees; and
- The designation of the state under which the trust agreement is to be governed.

Example: The Kenneth Chiang Trust is a grantor trust. Kenneth is the grantor. During the year, the trust sold 100 shares of ABC stock for $1,010 in which it had a basis of $10 and 200 shares of XYZ stock for $10 in which it had a $1,020 basis. The trust does not report these transactions on Form 1041 or issue Kenneth a Schedule K-1. Instead, a schedule is attached to Form 1041 showing each stock transaction separately and in the same detail as Kenneth (grantor and owner) will need to report these transactions on his Schedule D (Form 1040). The trust does not net the capital gains and losses to show a $10 long-term capital loss.

Revocable Trusts: Revocable trusts, including revocable living trusts, are grantor trusts in which the grantor retains the right to make changes or end the trust during his lifetime. The trust assets are subject to estate tax upon the grantor's death. The trust is generally created to manage and distribute property. Many taxpayers use this type of trust instead of, or in addition to, a will.

Non-Grantor Trusts

A non-grantor trust is any trust that is not a grantor trust. A non-grantor trust is considered a separate legal entity from the individual or organization that created it. The trust's income and deductions are reported on Form 1041.

If a non-grantor trust makes distributions to a beneficiary, in general those distributions carry any taxable income to the beneficiary. Examples include:

1. **Irrevocable Trusts**: An irrevocable trust is a trust that cannot be revoked after it is created. The transfer of assets into this type of trust is generally considered a "completed gift" subject to gift tax.

2. **Disability Trusts:** A qualified disability trust is a non-grantor trust created solely for the benefit of a disabled individual under age 65. In 2014, a qualified disability trust can claim an exemption of up to $3,950; the exemption is subject to phaseout if modified AGI exceeds $250,000. This is a specific exception to the regular exemption of $600 that applies to most trusts.

3. **Charitable Trusts:** A charitable trust is a trust devoted to qualified charitable contribution purposes. Charitable trusts are irrevocable.

> **Example:** Pamela creates a charitable trust. Its governing instrument provides that the Presbyterian Church (a qualified religious organization), and the SPCA (a 501(c)(3) charity) are each to receive 50% of the trust income for 10 years. At the end of the 10-year period, the corpus will be distributed to the American Red Cross, also a 501(c)(3) organization. Pamela is allowed an income tax deduction for the value of the assets placed in trust.

Abusive Trust Arrangements

Certain trust arrangements purport to reduce or eliminate federal taxes in ways that are not permitted under the law. These abusive or fraudulent trust arrangements may be used to hide the true ownership of assets and income or to disguise the substance of transactions. They frequently involve more than one trust, each holding different assets of the taxpayer (for example, the taxpayer's business, business equipment, home, automobile, etc.)

Some trusts may hold interests in other trusts, purport to involve charities, or be foreign trusts. Participants and promoters of abusive trust schemes may be subject to civil or criminal penalties.

Abusive or fraudulent trust arrangements may promise such benefits as:

- Deductions for personal expenses paid by the trust

- Depreciation deductions for an owner's personal residence
- A stepped-up basis for property transferred to the trust
- The reduction or elimination of self-employment taxes
- The reduction or elimination of gift and estate taxes

Although these schemes give the appearance of separating responsibility and control from the benefits of ownership, as would be the case with legitimate trusts, the taxpayer in fact controls them. When trusts are used for legitimate business, family, or estate planning purposes, either the trust, the beneficiary, or the grantor will pay the tax on the income generated by the trust.

Trusts cannot be used to transform a taxpayer's personal, living, or educational expenses into deductible items. A taxpayer cannot use a trust to avoid tax liability by ignoring either the true ownership of income and assets or the true substance of transactions.

> **Example:** Hugo Edwards transfers his family residence and its furnishings to a trust, which rents the residence back to Hugo and his children. He deducts depreciation and the expenses of maintaining and operating the home, including landscaping, pool service, and utilities. Hugo's second trust transfers assets to the Edwards Charity Fund, which claims to be a charitable organization but is not an IRS-qualified exempt organization. The trust pays for personal, education, and recreational expenses on behalf of Hugo and his family. The trust then claims the deductions on its tax returns. Both the trusts Hugo created are fraudulent, and he would be subject to civil and criminal penalties.

Foreign Trusts

Foreign trusts are not always created to evade taxation. However, the IRS gives increased scrutiny to foreign trusts because of their growing popularity in foreign countries that provide financial secrecy and impose little or no tax on trusts. These are often in "tax haven" countries that are supposedly outside the jurisdiction of the U.S.

Typically, abusive foreign trust arrangements enable taxable funds to flow through several trusts or entities until the funds ultimately are distributed or made available to the original owner tax-free. Legally, however, the income from these arrangements is fully taxable.

Example: Shauna is a U.S. citizen with substantial business income. She forms an asset management company as a domestic trust, listing herself as the director and another individual as the trustee. She then forms a business trust, very similar to the domestic trust, with both intended to show she is not managing her own business. Next, Shauna forms a foreign trust in Bermuda, with the income from the business trust distributed to this foreign trust. Because the source of income is U.S.-based and there is a U.S. trustee, this foreign trust has filing requirements (discussed below). Her next step is to form a second foreign trust. The first foreign trust funnels all of its income to this second foreign trust, which has a foreigner as a trustee. Since the trustee and sources of income are now foreign, Shauna claims there are no U.S. filing requirements. In actuality, she retains control of the income in this second foreign trust and has set up an elaborate scheme to evade U.S. tax laws.

Since 1996, a trust is considered foreign unless a U.S. court supervises it and a U.S. fiduciary controls all substantial decisions. U.S. taxpayers are required to file Form 3520, *Creation of or Transfer to Certain Foreign Trusts*, Form 3520-A, *Annual Return of Foreign Trust with U.S. Beneficiaries*, and Form 926, *Return by a Transferor of Property to a Foreign Estate or Trust*, when contributing property to a foreign trust. These trusts are usually U.S. tax neutral and are treated as grantor trusts with income taxable to the grantor that should be included on Form 1040.

Foreign Accounts: Both individuals and entities including trusts may be required to report their foreign accounts to the IRS by filing an electronic Financial Crimes Enforcement Network (FinCEN), Form 114, *Report of Foreign Bank and Financial Accounts* (FBAR). The report must be e-filed by June 30, 2014 if:

- The taxpayer had a financial interest in or signature authority over at least one financial account located outside of the United States, and
- The aggregate value of all foreign financial accounts exceeded $10,000 at any time during the calendar year to be reported.

Certain exceptions apply to the filing requirement. For example, if the foreign financial accounts are owned by a governmental entity, international financial institution, participants or beneficiaries of a qualified retirement plan, or IRA owners and beneficiaries, they are exempt from the FBAR filing requirements.

1. Mulhern Trust had the following in 2014:
   - Taxable interest: $4,000
   - Capital gains: $12,000
   - Fiduciary fee: $2,000

At the end of 2014, the fiduciary distributes $4,000. The trust instrument allocates capital gains to income. What is the distributable net income (DNI) of Mulhern Trust for 2014?

A. $12,000.
B. $14,000.
C. $16,000.
D. $18,000.

2. All of the following are characteristics of a simple trust except:

A. The trust may distribute assets to charity.
B. The trust distributes all its income currently.
C. The trust makes no distributions of principal.
D. The trust makes no distributions to charity.

3. The calculation of the gross estate includes all of the following except:

A. Life insurance proceeds payable to the decedent's heirs.
B. The value of certain annuities payable to the estate.
C. Property owned solely by the decedent's spouse.
D. The value of certain property transferred within three years before the taxpayer's death.

4. Dominique, an American citizen, has a trust in Panama where she regularly deposits funds. Which of the following statements is correct regarding the trust?

A. Income deposited in the Panama trust is shielded from all U.S. taxes.
B. Dominique is not subject to any filing requirements in connection with her foreign trust.
C. Dominique may have to pay gift taxes on funds distributed from the trust, but will not owe income tax.
D. All income in Dominique's foreign trust is fully taxable.

5. The Chessmore estate is required to distribute all of its income currently and has distributable net income (DNI) of $20,000 on its 2014 return. The only distribution the executor made during the year was $5,000, paid to the decedent's son, Carlton. Accordingly to the terms of the will, Carlton is entitled to 50% of the estate's DNI. Which of the following statements is correct?

A. Carlton must pay tax on $10,000 in 2014.
B. Carlton must pay tax on $20,000 in 2014.
C. Carlton is not required to pay tax on the distribution.
D. Carlton must pay tax on $5,000 in 2014.

6. All of the following are examples of potentially abusive trusts except:

A. A taxpayer who claims charitable deductions from a charity trust he has created, without receiving an IRS exemption letter.
B. A taxpayer who forms a grantor trust and retains the power to control or direct the trust's income or assets.
C. A taxpayer who forms a foreign trust in a "tax haven" country so funds distributed will be outside the jurisdiction of the United States.
D. A taxpayer who transfers an ongoing business to a series of trusts to avoid taxation but continues to run the day-to-day activities of the business and control its income stream.

7. Roberto died on May 3, 2014. The estate's tax year ends on December 31, 2014. The estate had the following items of income during the year:
- Interest: $250
- Dividends: $150
- Stock-sale proceeds, net of brother's commission: $10,000. Basis of the stock was $9,900

The estate made no distributions during 2014. Based upon the information provided, which of the following statements is correct?

A. The estate is not required to file an income tax return.
B. The estate is required to file an income tax return.
C. The estate is required to file a return on Form 706.
D. Both B and C.

8. The terms of Regina's will required annual payments of $30,000 and $10,000 to her husband (the surviving spouse) and her son, respectively, out of her estate's income during each year of the administration. The estate's distributable net income (DNI) for 2014 was $20,000. What are the amounts of income that will be reported by the estate to each beneficiary on their 2014 Forms K-1?

A. Husband: $10,000; Son: $10,000.
B. Husband: $15,000; Son: $5,000.
C. Husband: $20,000; Son: $0.
D. Husband: $0; Son: $0.

9. Parker, a single taxpayer, died on June 6, 2014. Based on the following information, determine the value of his gross estate:

FMV on date of death	
Life insurance on Parker's life (payable to his estate)	$250,000
Parker's revocable grantor trust	700,000
Liabilities owed by Parker when he died	150,000

A. $250,000.
B. $800,000.
C. $950,000.
D. $1.1 million.

10. In 2014, an estate has distributable net income of $12,000, consisting of $6,000 of rents, $4,000 of dividends, and $2,000 of taxable interest. Connie and her three brothers are equal beneficiaries of the estate. The executor distributes the income under the provisions of the will, which includes a stipulation that allocates dividend income to Connie. How is the distribution to Connie characterized for tax purposes?

A. $0 rents; $3,000 dividends; $0 taxable interest.
B. $0 rents; $4,000 dividends; $0 taxable interest.
C. $2,000 rents; $1,333 dividends; $667 taxable interest.
D. $1,500 rents; $1,000 dividends, and $1,000 taxable interest.

11. Who pays income tax on a trust's distributive share of income?

A. The trust.

B. The beneficiaries.

C. Income tax is split equally between the trust and its beneficiaries.

D. Income tax is not assessed on a trust's distributive share of income.

12. What is included in the gross estate?

A. The gross estate of the decedent includes everything the taxpayer owns at the date of death.

B. The gross estate of the decedent includes everything the taxpayer owns six months after the date of death.

C. The gross estate of the decedent includes everything the taxpayer owns at the date of death, including income that the taxpayer was owed but had not yet received.

D. The gross estate includes everything the decedent earned in the prior year, as well as income estimates for future years.

13. Georgiana died on March 1, 2014. The executor of her estate has elected to file the estate's income tax return on a calendar-year basis. No distributions have been made by the estate. Based on the following, what is the taxable income (Form 1041) of the estate for the December 31, 2014 year-end before consideration of the estate's exemption amount?

Taxable interest	$2,000
Tax-exempt interest	1,000
Capital gain	3,000
Executor's fees	300

A. $5,700.

B. $4,700.

C. $5,100.

D. $6,000.

Answers to Practice Questions

Unit 1: Answers

1. The answer is B. A domestic LLC with at least two members that does not file Form 8832 is classified as a partnership for federal income tax purposes.

2. The answer is A. They may choose to report their qualified joint venture as a sole proprietorship on two separate Schedules C, as long as they file jointly.

3. The answer is D. A partnership is not required to obtain a new EIN simply to add business locations. In all of the other circumstances, the entity would need to obtain a new EIN.

4. The answer is C. C corporations are subject to double taxation. The other statements are facts about C corporations but are not considered drawbacks.

5. The answer is A. If a taxpayer's net earnings from self-employment are less than $400, he should enter the net profit on line 12 of Form 1040 and attach Schedule C to the return. A taxpayer is not required to file Schedule SE unless he has net earnings from self-employment of $400 or more.

6. The answer is D. Mandy and Tammy are working as a partnership and should report their income and expenses on Form 1065, *U.S. Return of Partnership Income.* Each partner should receive a Schedule K-1 to report her individual share of the partnership's income on her Form 1040.

7. The answer is B. Julian must complete Schedule C to report his business income and expenses.

8. The answer is A. Only a C corporation may have an unlimited number of shareholders. An S corporation is limited to no more than 100 shareholders.

9. The answer is A. A sole proprietor who is required to file excise tax returns (or employment tax returns) must obtain an EIN. A sole proprietorship is not required to obtain a new EIN when it changes location or its business name. An individual may operate multiple businesses using the same EIN, so long as the businesses are sole proprietorships.

10. The answer is C. A personal service corporation (that is a C corporation) pays a 35% flat rate on its taxable income. The principal activity of a PSC is providing personal services to individuals or groups. PSCs are not eligible for graduated tax rates.

11. The answer is C. Federal law requires businesses to provide a Form 1099-MISC for each independent contractor paid at least $600 for services during a year. If a business makes payments to a corporation (rather than an individual), it is generally not required to issue a Form 1099-MISC.

12. The answer is B. Statutory employees are unique because they report their wages, income, and allowable expenses on Schedule C, like self-employed taxpayers. However, statutory employees are not required to pay self-employment tax because their employers treat them as employees for Social Security tax purposes.

13. The answer is C. Income level is not a factor in determining a worker's status. The main issue involves whether the employer or the worker has the right to direct or control how the work is done and to control the financial and business aspects of the job. This helps determine whether a worker should be classified as an employee or an independent contractor.

14. The answer is A. Family members who work for other family members are subject to different tax requirements. Only income tax is withheld from the paycheck of a child under age 18 who is working for a parent who is a sole proprietor.

15. The answer is C. A business must file Form 8300, *Report of Cash Payments Over $10,000 Received in a Trade or Business,* when it receives a cash payment of more than $10,000 from one transaction or from two or more related transactions.

16. The answer is D. A sole proprietorship without employees does not require an employer identification number. The other choices listed all require an EIN.

17. The answer is B. The trust fund recovery penalty applies to any person who is responsible for collecting or paying income and employment taxes, or for paying excise taxes collected, and who willfully fails to collect or pay these taxes. The amount of the penalty is equal to the unpaid balance of the trust fund taxes.

Unit 2: Answers

1. The answer is C. A fiscal tax year is any tax year that is 12 consecutive months and ends on the last day of any month except December. Answer A is incorrect because this is a calendar year, not a fiscal year. Answer B is incorrect because a fiscal year, other than a 52-53 week year or a short tax year, must end on the last day of the month. Answer D is incorrect because it is more than 12 consecutive months.

2. The answer is B. Shipping finished products to customers is not an expense that should be included in inventory. This cost is a current expense and would be deductible when incurred, rather than capitalized as a cost of the inventory.

3. The answer is D. The correction of a math error does not require prior approval from the IRS. Consent from the IRS is not required for the following changes:

- Correction of a math error for computing tax liability or other mathematical error
- A correction in depreciable life or correction of a depreciation error
- An adjustment to an asset's useful life

4. The answer is A. A family farming corporation may use the cash method of accounting if its average annual gross receipts are $25 million or less. A C corporation with gross receipts exceeding $5 million is required to use the accrual method. A tax shelter must always use the accrual method, regardless of its gross receipts. A corporation with long-term contracts must always use the accrual method.

5. The answer is B. April 15 is the IRS due date for individual tax returns but would not be the end of a tax year, except in a rare instance in which an entity's existence terminates or an individual dies on that date. Answer A is incorrect because January 31 is the last day of the month, which qualifies as a fiscal tax year-end. Answer C is incorrect because December 31 is a calendar year-end. Answer D is incorrect because a tax year that ends on the same day of the week every year is a 52/53-week tax year, which is a legitimate type of fiscal year.

6. The answer is A. Generally, an entity cannot use the cash method if it has average annual gross receipts exceeding $5 million. However, if a company has inventory, the threshold for gross receipts is generally $1 million. A qualified family farming corporation can use the cash method if its average gross receipts do not exceed $25 million.

7. The answer is D. To value inventory using the lower of cost or market method, compare the cost and the fair market value of each of the items in inventory, and choose the lower of the two to obtain the inventory's value. The answer is calculated as follows:
($200 for shirts + $200 for shoes + $150 for shorts) = $550 inventory valuation.

8. The answer is A. The income would be included on Banner's 2014 tax return, because Banner is using the accrual method of accounting for income and expenses. Under the accrual method, income is reported in the year earned and expenses are deducted in the year incurred. Since Banner sold the sofas in 2014, the income would be reported in 2014, regardless of when payment is received.

9. The answer is C. Since the corporation chose a calendar year, its first tax return is due March 15, 2015. This short period return will cover the period from April 1, 2014 through December 31, 2014. Corporate tax returns are due on the fifteenth day of the third month after the end of the corporation's tax year.

10. The answer is B. A taxpayer is subject to the uniform capitalization rules if he produces real or personal property for use in a trade or business. Producing items for personal use or as a hobby would not be subject to the UNICAP rules. Independent (self-employed) authors, writers, and artists are exempt from the rules.

11. The answer is B. A taxpayer may use different methods of accounting for two distinct and separate businesses. Separate accounting books must be kept for each business.

12. The answer is C. According to the doctrine of constructive receipt, income is included in gross income when a person has an unqualified right to the funds. Constructive receipt must be more than just a billing, an offer, or a mere promise to pay. The amount promised to Ben as an IOU, therefore, does not have to be included in income for 2014.

13. The answer is A. Chris should include the consigned goods in his inventory, since he retains title to the goods on consignment until they are sold by the retailer. Merchandise sent COD is included in inventory until it reaches the buyer; at that time, title passes to the buyer when the item is delivered and paid for. Machinery and other fixed assets used by a business are not included in its inventory.

14. The answer is D. A corporation that produces audio recordings or films would be subject to UNICAP. Generally, the uniform capitalization rules apply to a taxpayer that produces property for use or resale in a business. A company that provides only services would not carry an inventory, so it is not subject to UNICAP. Independent (self-employed) authors, writers, and artists are exempt from the rules.

15. The answer is B. The shipping cost related to a purchase increases an asset's cost basis. If the property is merchandise bought for resale (such as inventory), the shipping cost is part of the cost of the merchandise and must be capitalized and later recovered as cost of goods sold when the watches are resold.

16. The answer is B. A business must adopt its first tax year by the due date (not including extensions) for filing a return for that year. A business adopts a tax year when it files its first income tax return.

17. The answer is A. Taxpayers must include direct and indirect costs in inventory. Taxpayers can claim a casualty or theft loss of inventory by increasing the cost of goods sold to properly report beginning and ending inventories. Taxpayers may choose to use different accounting methods for different businesses, so long as the businesses are kept separate and distinct accounting records are maintained for each.

18. The answer is A. Resellers of property with annual gross receipts of $10 million or less are exempt from UNICAP. A reseller with average annual gross receipts of $25 million would be subject to UNICAP.

19. The answer is B. The cost of goods sold is calculated as follows:

Beginning inventory	$80,000
Raw materials purchased	12,000
Freight-in	$550
Manufacturing costs	80,000
Ending inventory	(52,500)
COGS	$120,050

The cost of freight-out to customers is not included in the calculation of inventory or capitalized as COGS. It is instead deductible as a business expense.

Unit 3: Answers

1. The answer is D. Trade or business activities in which the taxpayer does not materially participate during the year are generally considered passive activities. Rental activities, even if the taxpayer does materially participate, are generally considered passive activities. However, there is an exception for real estate professionals. Portfolio income, such as interest, dividends, annuities, and royalties not derived in the ordinary course of a trade or business, or gain or loss from the disposition of property that produces these types of income or that is held for investment, is not passive activity income.

2. The answer is B. Canceled debt is not taxable income for a business to the extent that payment of the debt would have led to a business deduction.

3. The answer is B. The refundable security deposits are not taxable income, because those amounts are returned to the customer if the items rented are returned in good condition. The amounts included in gross income would be the rental income and the nonrefundable cleaning deposits ($50,000 + $1,500 = $51,500).

4. The answer is B. Certain items of income are excluded from gross income. Gross income does not include most types of compensation for physical injuries.

5. The answer is C. Under the rules of advance payment for services, Camille must recognize income from the eight lessons she gives in 2014 and the rest in 2015, regardless of whether she actually has given all of the lessons by the end of 2015.

6. The answer is A. Camille must include the entire payment in income in 2014 since some of the services may be performed after 2015.

7. The answer is D. In general, a rental activity cannot be grouped with a trade or business activity. However, they can be grouped together if the activities form an appropriate economic unit and:
- The rental activity is insubstantial to the trade or business activity,
- The trade or business activity is insubstantial in relation to the rental activity, or
- Each owner of the trade or business activity has the same ownership interest in the rental activity, in which case the part of the rental activity that involves the rental of items of property for use in the trade or business activity may be grouped with the trade or business activity.

8. The answer is B. Normally, rental income is not subject to employment taxes, and it is reported on Schedule E, *Supplemental Income and Loss*. However, as he is a real estate professional, Harley's income is subject to employment taxes and must be reported on Schedule SE as well as on Schedule C, *Profit or Loss for Business*.

9. The answer is D. Losses from passive activities that exceed the income from passive activities in a given year are generally disallowed. The losses may be carried forward to the next year. Generally, only when a taxpayer materially participates in a trade or business activity are his losses not limited.

10. The answer is A. Advance rental payments received under a lease must be recognized in the year received, regardless of which accounting method is used. This means that a taxpayer who owns rental properties and receives rent in advance cannot delay recognizing the income, even if the taxpayer is on the accrual basis.

11. The answer is C. Under the passive activity limitation rules, Sean would not be able to deduct the full amount of his losses in 2014. Since he had passive activity income of $31,000 in 2014, he can offset losses up to that amount. He can carry over the remaining losses of $6,500 to 2015.

12. The answer is D. As a cash-basis taxpayer, Allen's Exotic Pets would have been able to deduct the cost of the legal services as a business expense. It is therefore not required to recognize the canceled debt income.

13. The answer is C. Personal property has a similar name but should not be confused with "personal-use" property that a taxpayer uses for personal purposes rather than for business purposes. In a broad definition, personal property includes any asset other than real estate. Personal property is movable, unlike land and buildings that generally remain in one location.

14. The answer is D. A barter exchange of services between two sole proprietors would be business income. The fair market value of goods and services received in a barter exchange must be included in income by each party in the year received. If the two parties agree in advance to the fair market value of the goods or services being exchanged, the IRS will generally accept that amount as the FMV.

15. The answer is D. A taxpayer can treat one or more trade or business or rental activities as a single activity if the activities form an appropriate economic unit for measuring gain or loss under the passive activity rules. If two activities are grouped together, he needs only to show material participation in the activity as a whole. If the two activities are separate, he must show material participation in each one. Grouping cannot be done simply to avoid the passive activity rules, and activities generally cannot be regrouped in a later year if they were grouped into appropriate economic units.

Unit 4: Answers

1. The answer is B. Many businesses, including self-employed individuals but not C corporations, can choose to use either the standard mileage rate or actual vehicle expenses in order to claim deductions for the cost of vehicles used in the business. However, a business is prohibited from using the standard mileage rate if it operates five or more vehicles at the same time.

2. The answer is C. The answer is $458 ($400 + $35 + $10 + [26 × 50%]). Her deductible meal expenses are subject to a 50% limit, but the taxi fare, the train ticket, and the seminar are fully deductible.

3. The answer is A. The partnership is on the cash basis; therefore, it can only deduct interest actually paid during the year. Since the partnership did not actually pay any interest, it does not have a deductible expense. The fact that the loan was refinanced has no bearing on the deductibility of the interest.

4. The answer is C. A taxpayer who is subject to the Department of Transportation's hours of service can deduct a larger percentage of his meal expenses when traveling away from his tax home. He would multiply his meal expenses incurred while away from home on business by the DOT hours of service limit of 80% ($3,064 × .80 = $2,451).

5. The answer is A. Self-employed taxpayers can deduct these contributions on Schedule A, subject to applicable AGI limits. The contributions cannot be deducted as a business expense on Schedule C. Only C corporations can deduct charitable contributions as a business expense, subject to a limit of 10% of taxable income.

6. The answer is D. The taxpayer is not required to prove that the entertainment event actually produced a profit. The taxpayer must meet either the directly-related test or the associated test in order to deduct an entertainment expense. The directly-related test requires that business was engaged in during the entertainment event; the main purpose was the conduct of business; and there was more than just the general expectation of business benefit.

7. The answer is C. There is a $25 limit per person per tax year for business gifts; however, the cost of packaging, insuring, and mailing are not included in determining the cost of a gift for purposes of the $25 limit. Promotional items such as the display rack are also not included in the cost. Therefore, the business can deduct $580 ($500 + $25 + $35 + $20) = $580:

- Glass display: $500
- Coffee and tea basket: $25 (only $25 is deductible as a gift expense)
- 20 imprinted pens: $35
- Postage for the gift basket: $20

8. The answer is B. Delia can deduct the cost of her hotel room, one-half of her meal expense, and her train ticket to attend the convention ($100 + $90 + (80 × 50%) = $230). The cost of the computer game is a personal expense and not deductible.

9. The answer is C. A loan to a client, customer, employee, or distributor for a business reason can be deducted as a business bad debt if it becomes worthless. The amount of the loan, minus what was repaid, is the deduction on Mountain Supplier's tax return: $10,000 - $2,000 = $8,000.

10. The answer is A. The repairs, property tax, and utilities are all deductible as business expenses. The property tax is deductible as a business expense on Schedule C (rather than on Schedule A) because it is assessed on business property. Assessments for streets, sidewalks, sewer lines, and other public services generally add value to the property and must be added to the basis of the property rather than deducted currently.

11. The answer is D. Since the advance payment covers more than 12 months (36 months), the $3,600 must be deducted ratably over the three-year period. To figure the monthly premium amount, the policy cost is divided by the coverage period: ($3,600 ÷ 36 = $100). The number of months of coverage in each tax year is then multiplied by the monthly premium:

- 2014: Deduction of $300 ($3,600 ÷ 36 × 3)
- 2015: Deduction of $1,200: ($3,600 ÷ 36 × 12)
- 2016: Deduction of $1,200 ($3,600 ÷ 36 × 12)
- 2017: Deduction of $900 ($3,600 ÷ 36 × 9)

12. The answer is C. Only the loan to the client would be deductible as a business bad debt expense. A loss related to a loan to a client, customer, employee, or distributor for a business reason can be deducted as a business bad debt. Since Keith is a related person and not a regular employee and the loan was for personal reasons, Bob cannot deduct his loss on the loan to his brother as a business bad debt.

13. The answer is B. Lily is not required to amend her prior year return to report the recovery of the bad debt. Since Lily recovered a bad debt that was deducted properly in a prior year, she must include the recovered portion as income in her current year tax return.

14. The answer is A. If a taxpayer pays rent in advance, only the amount that applies to the current year is deductible. The balance must be deducted over the period to which it applies.
> Deductible lease expense for 2014:
> $1,620/36 (months) = $45 per month
> $45 × 11 months (February to December 2014) = $495

15. The answer is C. Generally, interest on a business loan is fully deductible. However, debt incurred for personal reasons is not deductible as a business expense. The amount of interest attributable to the portion of loan proceeds used to purchase the business machine is deductible, but not the amount for the jet ski, which is a personal expense.

16. The answer is B. A taxpayer cannot deduct the costs of driving a car between his home and his main workplace. These costs are personal commuting expenses. The costs of driving to meet with clients or do other business-related errands are deductible.

17. The answer is D. Penalties paid for the late performance or non-performance of a contract are deductible. Penalties or fines paid to any government entity because of a violation of laws or regulations are not deductible.

18. The answer is D. As a retailer, Only-a-Dollar acts as a collection agent for the taxing authorities. The amounts of taxes it collects and remits to them should be excluded from its taxable gross income and deductible expenses.

19. The answer is C. A business can deduct up to $5,000 of start-up costs. Start-up costs are costs incurred in creating an active trade or business or investigating the creation or acquisition of an active trade or business.

20. The answer is C. A self-employed individual with a net profit for the year can deduct premiums paid for medical and dental insurance for herself, her spouse (if married), and her dependents. The deduction is not available for any month the individual (or spouse) was eligible to participate in an employer-sponsored health plan, even if she did not participate.

21. The answer is C. Business start-up and organizational costs are generally capitalized and amortized over a period of 180 months, but a business can elect to deduct up to $5,000 of business start-up costs and $5,000 of organizational costs in the year incurred.

Unit 5: Answers

1. The answer is D. Under the rules for cafeteria plans, a key employee may include a 5% owner of the business, an officer with annual pay of more than $170,000, or a 1% owner of the business with annual pay of more than $150,000. Both A and B are correct in describing key employees.

2. The answer is B. The value of an employer-provided cell phone is only excludable from an employee's wages if it is given for a noncompensatory business purpose or is considered a de minimis benefit. A cell phone used to boost morale or in this case as a type of financial bonus would be taxable to the employee.

3. The answer is C. Employer-paid memberships at athletic facilities are generally taxable benefits. A workout area on the employer's premises is the exception.

4. The answer is A. Employers may exclude the value of meals and on-site lodging from an employee's wages if they are provided for the convenience of the employer. Meals provided to employees for the convenience of the employer are 100% deductible by the employer.

5. The answer is C. The value of a vehicle for personal use by an employee is a taxable benefit. If an employer provides a car for an employee's use, the amount that can be excluded as a working condition benefit is the amount that would be allowed as a deductible business expense if the employee paid for its use. There are exceptions for emergency personnel such as police officers who are required to use their emergency vehicles. Employee achievement awards may be exempt up to $1,600. Meals are exempt if either furnished for the employer's convenience or if considered de minimis, such as occasional snacks.

6. The answer is B. Travel reimbursements made under a nonaccountable plan are taxable to the employee as wages.

7. The answer is B. Although all of the expenses are qualified educational expenses, only the first $5,250 is excluded from Renee's wages as a qualified fringe benefit, and the remaining amount is taxable as wage income to her. If an employer pays more than $5,250 for educational benefits for an employee during the year, the excess is taxed as wages.

8. The answer is C. Gifts of cash or cash equivalents such as gift cards must be included in income. Fringe benefits that may be excluded from income include employee discounts, amounts reimbursed through a qualified flexible spending plan, and de minimis holiday gifts.

Unit 6: Answers

1. The answer is B. Based on the information provided, Lorelei may qualify for a credit of up to 50% of the premiums she paid for her employees. The actual percentage credit is determined by the number of full-time equivalent employees and their average annual wages. Small tax-exempt employers can qualify for a credit of up to 35% of the health insurance premiums paid for their employees. The Small Business Health Care Tax Credit is refundable; is designed for small business employers with fewer than 25 low to moderate income workers; and may be claimed for two consecutive years.

2. The answer is C. Selling food or beverages prepared at restaurants in the United States is specifically disallowed for purposes of the DPAD. Most U.S.-based manufacturing qualifies for the DPAD.

3. The answer is B. The amount of the Disabled Access Credit is 50% of the qualified expenses, but the maximum credit per year is $5,000.

4. The answer is D. Normally, businesses can carry back unused business credits one year and carry them forward for 20 years.

5. The answer is D. The WOTC offers credits to businesses who hire out-of-work veterans, as well as other individuals in eight different targeted groups.

6. The answer is B. In general, a net operating loss may be carried back to the two previous years, and the remaining loss may be carried forward to the subsequent 20 years.

7. The answer is B. The Investment Credit is the sum of five credits that are designed to spur investment in activity that reduces greenhouse emissions and rehabilitates historic property. In 2014, the Investment Credit consists of the Rehabilitation and Energy Credits and the Advanced Coal, Advanced Energy, and Gasification Projects. There is no credit for hydroelectric power.

8. The answer is C. Only the casualty loss is potentially deductible for purposes of the net operating loss. Losses from the sale of stock are capital losses and cannot be used to create an NOL. Losses from the sale of personal-use property or a primary residence are not deductible.

9. The answer is A. The DPAD cannot be more than 50%, not 25%, of the wages a business pays its employees. All of the other statements are correct about this business deduction designed to stimulate manufacturing and other production activities in the United States.

10. The answer is D. The losses due to the theft of business property would be allowed in figuring a net operating loss.

11. The answer is C. The Disabled Access Credit is a nonrefundable tax credit for an eligible small business that pays expenses to provide access to disabled persons. The taxpayer must pay or incur the expenses to enable the business to comply with the Americans with Disabilities Act.

12. The answer is D. Angela is entitled to a DPAD deduction based upon the *lower* of:

- 9% of her net business income or
- 50% of her qualified wages.

Therefore, her DPAD deduction is $27,000 (9% X $300,000) since the 50% of wages equals $59,000 ($118,000 X 50%).

13. The answer is B. NOLs can generally be carried back two years. Any remaining amount of an NOL must be carried forward for up to 20 years.

Unit 7: Answers

1. The answer is D. The tangible property regulations include rules regarding "materials and supplies" that allow a unit of property with a cost of $200 or less to be deducted in the year it is used or consumed in the business. Each printer would be treated as a separate unit of property, so the entire amount could be deducted currently rather than capitalized.

2. The answer is A. Demolition costs or other losses related to the demolition of any building are added to the basis of the land.

3. The answer is D. Interest charges are not added to an asset's basis. Interest is a currently deductible expense.

4. The answer is C. Ian's basis is $196,000. The title fees, mortgage amount, and the down payment are added to figure the cost basis of the building. The points are not included in the basis.

5. The answer is A. Cheryl cannot deduct the taxes as a current expense, since they are delinquent real estate taxes and the person who is legally liable for the debt is Alex. However, the taxes may be added to the property's basis and depreciated as part of her purchase price.

6. The answer is B. The cost of defending title to a property increases its basis.

7. The answer is B. Under the materials and supplies rules of the tangible property regulations, a unit of property with a useful life of a year or less may be deducted rather than capitalized. Although Anya's business may be subject to the Form 3115 filing requirement as a result of the new regulations related to capitalization and repairs expense, this requirement would not affect the deductibility of other types of business expenses.

8. The answer is C. Irina expects to be fully reimbursed for her loss, so reporting it on her 2014 return is not necessary. However, if Irina's insurance company reimbursement is ultimately either more or less than her loss, she may realize an additional gain or loss. Whether a gain would be taxable will depend on how she uses the insurance proceeds.

9. The answer is D. A stock split increases the number of outstanding shares, which decreases the basis per share, but it does not change the basis of the stock as a whole.

10. The answer is A. Under the new regulations, an improvement is redefined as a cost involving a betterment of the unit of property, a restoration of the unit of property, or an adaptation of the unit of property to a new or different use.

11. The answer is C. The basis is the stock's purchase price plus the broker's fee ($3,500 + $100 = $3,600). After the stock split, Franco has 180 shares of stock [(50 shares + 40 shares) × 2 = 180]. The stock split reduces his per share basis by half to $20 ($3,600 ÷ 180 shares of stock = $20).

12. The answer is C. The basis is $307,500 ($250,000 + $13,000 + $35,000 + $9,500). The settlement fees, the mortgage assumed by the buyer, and the legal fees for defending the title are all included in the basis of the property. The property taxes are not included in the basis of the building because they were incurred when Priscilla was already the legal owner. Instead, the property taxes may be deducted as a current expense.

13. The answer is B. If a business does not have qualifying financial statements, it may be permitted to deduct items that cost up to $500 per invoice or per item. A business that has a written capitalization policy or procedure for expensing items can deduct amounts expensed in its financial statements that cost up to $5,000.

14. The answer is B. All items are added to the property's basis except for the points on the loan (an expense that is deducted over the life of the loan) and the construction loan ($125,000 + $20,000 + $10,000 + $50,000 + $300,000 = $505,000).

15. The answer is A. Marjorie must reduce the basis of her van by the portion of any insurance proceeds that are not used for repairs. Since she uses $500 of the proceeds to repair the windshield, the adjusted basis is $21,500 ($25,000 - $4,000 + $500 = $21,500.)

16. The answer is D. When property is transferred in lieu of wages, the employer is entitled to deduct its fair market value at the time of the transfer. A gain or loss is realized if there is a difference between the fair market value and the adjusted basis of the property. The transfer is treated as a sale, so Chan Delivery would have to report a gain. Chan Delivery should deduct $7,000 as wage expense and report the gain on the sale of the truck, figured as follows: ($7,000 - $5,500) = $1,500.

17. The answer is A. Vaughn Partnership must include the FMV of the coins ($5,000) and the FMV of the scooter ($2,000) as income. Property exchanged for services must be included as income at its fair market value.

Unit 8: Answers

1. The answer is A. If the entire cost of business property cannot immediately be deducted as a section 179 expense, a business may elect to take bonus depreciation for certain types of new property. This provision allows a business to write off 50% of certain property costs in the first year, with the remaining cost depreciated over the asset's useful life. Applicable section 179 deductions are generally used first, followed by bonus depreciation, unless the business has an insufficient level of taxable income.

2. The answer is C. Goodwill and a covenant not to compete are both section 197 intangible assets. A business must amortize over 15 years (180 months) the capitalized costs of section 197 intangibles.

3. The answer is D. A gasoline refinery would not qualify since its activity involves refining a product rather than the depletion of a natural resource. Depletion is the exhaustion of natural resources, such as mines, wells, and timber, as a result of production.

4. The answer is B. The computers do not qualify as section 179 property because Levi and his grandfather are related persons, meaning Levi cannot claim a section 179 deduction. However, Levi may still depreciate the computers using the MACRS depreciation schedule.

5. The answer is A. Tangible personal property generally qualifies for the section 179 deduction. With the exception of certain qualified real property (QRP), most real property generally does not qualify for section 179 treatment. Intangible assets do not qualify for section 179 treatment.

6. The answer is C. The business part of the cost of the property is $825 (75% × $1,100).

7. The answer is A. When a taxpayer uses property for both business and nonbusiness purposes, he can elect the section 179 deduction only if he uses the property more than 50% for business in the year the asset is placed into service. Lou may nevertheless claim depreciation deductions for the business portion of the phone.

8. The answer is B. Kerman may consider the truck to have been placed in service when it is ready for its intended purpose, which was on January 10, 2015. Kerman does not actually need to use it for that purpose in order to begin depreciation.

9. The answer is A. Property placed in service and disposed of in the same year is not depreciated.

10. The answer is B. Regular passenger automobiles weighing 6,000 pounds or less are listed property.

11. The answer is B. The corporation must reduce its section 179 dollar limit by $25,000, the amount of its qualifying purchases that exceeds the $2 million limit ($2,025,000 - $2,000,000). Its maximum section 179 deduction is $475,000 ($500,000 - $25,000). The corporation's taxable income from the active conduct of all its trades or businesses for the year was $600,000, so it can deduct the full $475,000.

12. The answer is B. The section 179 deduction applies only to the amount actually paid in cash and not to the value of his trade-in allowance, and further applies only to the portion used for business purposes. Thus, the deduction is limited to 90% of $15,000, or $13,500.

13. The answer is B. Taxpayers can deduct up to $250,000 of qualified real property (QRP) under section 179. This special allowance for QRP is included within the maximum $500,000 section 179 limit. For example, a taxpayer can claim $250,000 for QRP and $250,000 for other business property to use the $500,000 section 179 deduction allowance.

14. The answer is C. The partnership's section 179 deduction for the $30,000 oven is limited to the partnership's income of $25,000. The deduction is split between the two partners ($25,000 × 50%) = $12,500. Section 179 is a separately stated item on a partnership tax return. Assuming she has no section 179 deductions from other sources, Lucy's deduction would be $12,500.

15. The answer is D. Commercial real property is depreciated over a 39-year recovery period.

Unit 9: Answers

1. The answer is B. The total gain on the sale is $17,000 ($25,000 - $8,000). Because the machine is section 1245 property, the partnership must recognize ordinary income of $12,000 (to recapture depreciation deductions taken on the machine) and the remaining $5,000 ($17,000 - $12,000) is treated as a capital gain.

2. The answer is A. An installment sale can trigger recapture. If a business reports the sale of previously depreciated property using the installment method, any applicable depreciation recapture under section 1245 or 1250 is taxable as ordinary income in the year of sale.

3. The answer is D. Because the business asset was held for less than one year, the business has an ordinary loss.

4. The answer is B. Section 1245 property does not include real estate such as buildings and structural components. Storage structures such as oil and gas storage tanks, grain storage bins, and silos are not treated as buildings but as section 1245 property.

5. The answer is D. Real property held for investment qualifies for like-kind exchange treatment. A personal residence, inventory, and common stock do not qualify under section 1031.

6. The answer is B. This transaction is treated as an involuntary conversion. Clovis recognizes a taxable gain of $20,000 ($310,000 - $290,000), equal to the portion of the insurance reimbursement that was not reinvested in replacement property. Clovis's unrecognized gain is $30,000, the difference between the $50,000 realized gain and the $20,000 recognized gain. The basis of the new property is as follows:

Cost of replacement property	$290,000
Minus gain not recognized	(30,000)
Basis of replacement property	**$260,000**

If Clovis had reinvested all the insurance proceeds in a new property, the entire gain would have been deferred.

7. The answer is C. In order to qualify as section 1231 property, the property must have been held by the business for over one year.

8. The answer is B. Since the amount realized from the sale is less than Jennifer's original cost for the chairs, the entire gain of $3,500 is treated as depreciation recapture, which is subject to ordinary income tax rates. She reports the sale on Form 4797 and Schedule C.

9. The answer is A. Generally, an exchange of real property qualifies as a nontaxable exchange under section 1031. In a nontaxable exchange situation, the FMV of the properties exchanged may have no bearing on the basis of the property received. In this case, the basis of the new property is the same as the basis of the old property ($125,000).

348

10. The answer is B. The exchange of livestock of different sexes does not qualify. The exchange of real estate for real estate and the exchange of business property for similar business property are exchanges of like-kind property.

11. The answer is B. The first $20,000 is considered section 1245 recapture and is taxed as ordinary income. The remaining $5,000 is considered section 1231 capital gain.

12. The answer is C. Scott's basis is $190,000 ($155,000 of cash paid plus the $35,000 adjusted basis of the old plane).

13. The answer is A. This exchange qualifies as a nontaxable exchange for Karabell. Any gain on the exchange is deferred until the new asset is later disposed. The $6,000 of cash is added to the basis of the old truck to determine the basis of the new truck ($11,000 + $6,000 = $17,000).

14. The answer is B. In a related-party exchange, the nonrecognition treatment will generally be lost if either property in the exchange is disposed of within two years. However, the section 1031 exchange will still be valid if either party in the transaction dies, or if the property is subject to an involuntary conversion.

15. The answer is C. Jamal's gross profit is $150,000 ($300,000 selling price - $150,000 adjusted basis), and the gross profit percentage is 50% ($150,000 ÷ $300,000). Jamal must report half of each payment received as gain from the sale. He must also report all interest received as ordinary income

16. The answer is A. The exchange of a vacant lot for a tract of farmland qualifies for like-kind exchange treatment. Section 1031 specifically excludes exchanges of inventory; stocks, bonds, notes, or other securities; partnership interests; livestock of different sexes; and property used predominantly in the United States for property used predominantly outside the United States. Properties are like-kind if they are of the same nature or character, even if they differ in grade or quality.

17. The answer is C. The adjusted basis of the old printer was $4,000 ($5,000 - $1,000 depreciation). She paid an additional $2,000 to acquire the new printer. Therefore, the basis of the new model is $6,000 ($4,000 adjusted basis + $2,000 cash paid).

18. The answer is D. A taxpayer and a member of his immediate family are related persons for purposes of like-kind exchanges. Any business in which the taxpayer has ownership of over 50% is also considered a related person.

19. The answer is A. The basis of the saw is $7,000 (the $3,000 basis of the old asset plus the $4,000 paid).

20. The answer is B. The disposition of the property results in a gain of $27,000, equal to the proceeds of $100,000 less adjusted basis of $73,000 (purchase price of $120,000 less depreciation and section 179 deductions of $47,000). Because this was section 1245 property, the gain is characterized as ordinary income to the lesser of the actual gain or the amount of depreciation and section 179 expenses recaptured ($47,000).

Purchase price	$120,000
Less depreciation and section 179 deductions	(47,000)
Adjusted basis at date of sale	73,000

Proceeds	100,000
Gain on sale	**27,000**
Potential depreciation recapture (as ordinary income)	$47,000

21. The answer is C. Sadie has a gain of $35,000, equal to the difference between her sales proceeds of $65,000 and her adjusted basis of $30,000 (cost of $90,000 less accumulated depreciation of $60,000). Although she has had the property for more than one year, it is personal property classified as section 1245 property and therefore is subject to depreciation recapture to the extent of the entire amount of depreciation (and section 179 deductions) taken. Since this amount exceeds her gain, the entire amount of the gain is treated as ordinary income.

Unit 10: Answers

1. The answer is A. This loan amount is included in Charlotte's basis in the partnership because she has an economic risk of loss related to this liability. An additional $60,000 of basis in the partnership's depreciable property was created as a result of incurring this debt. Her basis in the partnership would be $80,000 ($20,000 + $60,000), while Todd's basis would be only $20,000.

2. The answer is D. Guaranteed payments are made by a partnership to a partner and determined without regard to the partnership's income. A partnership treats guaranteed payments for services, or for the use of capital, as a business expense, just as if they were made to a person who is not a partner.

3. The answer is B. The guaranteed payment must be deducted before figuring each partner's distributive share. The answer is figured as follows:

$50,000 - $21,000 = $29,000

$29,000 × 50% = $14,500

Guaranteed payments are deducted from partnership income before determining the distributive share of income or loss for each partner.

4. The answer is A. The rental income, tax exempt income, and charitable contributions are all separately stated items that do not affect the calculation of ordinary income. Instead, each partner's share of the separately stated items is passed through to him. The partnership's ordinary income is split evenly, so Hassid's portion is as follows:

($200,000 - $30,000) = $170,000 of ordinary income

$170,000 × 50% = **$85,000**

5. The answer is B. A limited partner generally has no obligation to contribute additional capital to the partnership. Therefore, absent some other factor such as the guarantee of a partnership liability by the limited partner or the limited partner making a loan to the partnership, a limited partner generally does not have an economic risk of loss in connection with the partnership's recourse liabilities.

6. The answer is A. The profits are allocated according to the partnership agreement. Jose's distributive share is calculated as follows: 35% × $200,000 = $70,000. Carlos's share is calculated as follows: 65% × $200,000 = $130,000.

7. The answer is A. Usually, neither the partner nor the partnership recognizes a gain or loss when property is contributed to the partnership in exchange for a partnership interest. This applies whether a partnership is being formed or is already operating. However, if an asset is encumbered by a liability, such as a mortgage, there is a possibility that the partner will recognize a gain in connection with the contribution.

8. The answer is B. Form 7004, *Automatic Extension of Time to File Certain Business Income Tax, Information, and Other Returns*, is used by partnerships to extend their filing deadline for five months.

9. The answer is C. If a partner's share of partnership liabilities increases, this increase is treated as a contribution of money by the partner to the partnership. The debt is included in the bases of the three partners who signed the personal guarantees. Since Theresa does not have an economic risk of loss for this liability, the liability does not increase her basis. The basis for each of the other partners would include his or her share of the liability ([$135,000 ÷ 3 partners] = $45,000 + $10,000 cash investment).

10. The answer is D. Guaranteed payments are deductible by the partnership because they are treated like wages and are taxable to the partners who receive them. The other items are separately stated on the partnership's Form 1065. Each individual partner receives a Schedule K-1 from the partnership, reporting his share of ordinary income or loss and each separately stated item. Separately stated items pass through to the partners and retain their character as the partners report these amounts on their individual tax returns.

11. The answer is B. All of the items listed are included in the calculation of ordinary income except the charitable contributions and the rental income, both of which must be separately stated on Form 1065. Thus, ordinary income will be $115,000 ($250,000 - $50,000 - $5,000 - $5,000 - $75,000). Like the other deductions listed, guaranteed payments to partners are treated as a deduction in determining ordinary income or loss.

12. The answer is A. Partnership income, including tax-exempt interest, increases a partner's basis in his partnership interest.

13. The answer is C. Bissinger's ordinary income for 2014 is equal to its sales income less cost of goods sold and wages ($75,000 - $10,000 - $15,000 = $50,000). The income from rental real estate and the charitable contributions must be separately stated on the partnership's tax return.

14. The answer is B. The assumption of partnership debt by Daniel increases his basis. If a partner's share of partnership liabilities increases, or a partner's individual liabilities increase because he assumes partnership liabilities, it is treated as if the partner made a contribution to the partnership.

15. The answer is D. Interest income and short-term capital losses are separately stated items that flow through to each partner and retain their character. The other items listed are components of ordinary income, determined as follows: gross sales of $270,000, less cost of goods sold of $80,000 and wages of $50,000 = ordinary income of $140,000. Absent any provisions in the partnership agreement to the contrary, both ordinary income and the separately stated items would be allocated according to the 60%/40% profit-sharing arrangement.

16. The answer is D. The basis of Monica's partnership interest is the adjusted basis of the property she contributes ($4,000) less the portion of the related mortgage liability assumed by the other partners (60% × $1,000 = $600), or $3,400.

17. The answer is C. Derrick must include $10,000 of ordinary income from the partnership on his tax return. The answer is figured as follows:

1. $55,000 - $5,000 guaranteed payment = $50,000 of ordinary income
2. $50,000 × 10% = $5,000 Derrick's share of the partnership's ordinary income
3. ($5,000 guaranteed payment + $5,000 ($50,000 × 10%) distributive share) = **$10,000**

Guaranteed payments are determined without regard to the partnership's income. They are deducted as a business expense when figuring the partnership's ordinary income. The individual partner who receives the guaranteed payments reports the payments on Schedule E (Form 1040) as ordinary income, along with his distributive share of the partnership's ordinary income.

18. The answer is C. The at-risk rules limit the deductibility of losses to the partner's basis, not including his share of any of the partnership's nonrecourse debt.

19. The answer is B. The basis of Bea's partnership interest should be the adjusted basis of the property contributed ($25,000) less the portion of the mortgage liability assumed by the other partners (70% × $40,000 = $28,000). However, this would result in a basis of negative $3,000, and a partner's basis in a partnership can never go below zero. In order to avoid creating a negative basis, Bea must recognize a gain of $3,000.

20. The answer is B. Partners can modify their partnership agreement after the close of the tax year but no later than the due date (without extensions) for filing the partnership return.

Unit 11: Answers

1. The answer is A. A loss is not allowed from a sale or exchange of property directly or indirectly between a partnership and a person whose direct or indirect interest in the capital or profits of the partnership is more than 50%. In this case, Marvin and Geoff own a combined interest of 70% in the Davisville Partnership, and they indirectly own over 50% in Winters Partnership. (Since Marvin and Geoff's daughter own a combined interest of 85% in Dixon Corporation, their indirect interest in Winters Partnership is 85% × 80%, or 68%.)

2. The answer is A. Because the sum of cash and the adjusted basis of the property does not exceed the basis of her partnership interest, Allison does not recognize any gain on the distribution. Any gain on the machinery will be recognized when she sells it.

3. The answer is C. Nina recognizes no gain because the total of cash and the basis of property received does not exceed her basis in the partnership. She assumes the partnership's basis of $1,500 in the property received, and may recognize gain or loss if she later sells the property.

4. The answer is B. Steve's basis for the van is limited to $6,000 ($10,000 basis - $4,000, the cash he receives), equal to the remaining basis in his partnership interest after subtracting the cash received. After the distributions, his basis in the partnership interest is zero.

5. The answer is A. A retiring partner or the successor in interest of a deceased partner recognizes gain to the extent that any cash (and marketable securities treated as cash) distributed is more than the partner's adjusted basis in the partnership. Marty must recognize $15,000 of capital gain. This is the difference between his adjusted basis in the partnership and the amount of his distribution ($65,000 - $50,000).

6. The answer is C. If a business partnership dissolves and one of the former partners is insolvent and cannot pay his share of the partnership's debts, other partners may have to pay more than their respective shares. If a partner pays any part of the insolvent partner's share of the debts, she can take a bad debt deduction for the amount paid. Ellen is allowed to take a bad debt deduction for the liabilities she must pay that are in excess of her share of partnership liabilities.

7. The answer is D. When Laney sold her partnership interest, she was relieved of her $12,500 share of the partnership's liabilities, so her adjusted basis for purposes of calculating her gain on sale of the interest is $17,000 ($29,500 - $12,500). Thus, her gain is $28,000 (proceeds of $45,000 less adjusted basis of $17,000). Approached differently, the amount of liability relieved from Laney upon sale of her interest might be viewed as additional proceeds, but her gain would still be $28,000 ($45,000 + $12,500 - $29,500). As a partnership interest is a capital asset, any gain or loss recognized on the sale of the interest is typically treated as a capital gain or loss.

8. The answer is A. Shanahan Partnership's loss of $2,400 is not deductible. A loss on the sale or exchange of property between related persons is not deductible. This applies to both direct and indirect transactions. The fact that Bill and Veronica file separate tax returns does not prevent them from being related parties for purposes of this transaction.

9. The answer is A. Because the total of cash and the basis of property distributed ($9,000 + $2,500 = $11,500) does not exceed Adrian's adjusted basis of $17,500 in his partnership interest, he will recognize no gain as a result of the distribution. He assumes the partnership's adjusted basis of $2,500 in the property received, and will recognize gain or loss if he later sells this property.

10. The answer is C. Alice's basis on December 31, 2014 would be determined as follows: ($11,000 + $20,000 + $350 = $31,350).

Basis on January 1, 2014	$11,000
50% share of ordinary business income	20,000
50% share of tax-exempt interest income	350
Basis on December 31, 2014	**$31,350**

11. The answer is A. Hugo's basis for the distributed property is limited to $70,000 ($150,000 - $80,000, the cash received). In a nonliquidating distribution, the basis of property (other than cash) distributed to the partner by a partnership is the adjusted basis to the partnership immediately before the distribution. However, the basis of the property distributed to the partner cannot be more than the adjusted basis of his interest in the partnership.

Unit 12: Answers

1. The answer is C. John recognizes ordinary income of $6,000 as payment for services he rendered to the corporation. Normally, the exchange of money or property for a controlling interest in a corporation is treated as a nontaxable exchange. However, the exchange of services for stock does not qualify for this treatment. The value of stock received in exchange for services is taxed as income to the recipient.

2. The answer is B. A single member LLC will be taxed as a sole proprietorship unless an election is made by filing Form 8832, *Entity Classification Election*. The rest of the choices are automatically required to be taxed as corporations.

3. The answer is D. Based upon the information provided, Ruiz Corporation's taxable income would be calculated as follows:

Net income for books	$3,000,000
Plus federal income tax expense	1,500,000
Plus 50% of travel and entertainment expenses	100,000
Plus excess of capital losses over capital gains	29,000
Less tax-exempt interest income	(100,000)
Taxable income	**$4,529,000**

A corporation must generally report on either Schedule M-1 or Schedule M-3 the items that reconcile from net income (loss) on their books to taxable income reported on the return. Specific examples may include:

- Excess of capital losses over capital gains.
- Charitable contribution carryover (the amount of charitable contributions that are disallowed and must be carried over to the next taxable year.)
- Travel and entertainment in excess of the allowable 50% limit.
- Federal income taxes paid or accrued, which are deductible for accounting purposes but not for tax purposes.
- Advance rental income.
- Differences in book and tax depreciation.

4. The answer is C. Nell must recognize a taxable gain of $100,000 ($300,000 FMV of stock minus $200,000 basis) on the transaction. IRC section 351 provides that no gain or loss will be recognized if property is transferred to a corporation solely in exchange for stock, if immediately after the exchange the shareholder is in control of the corporation. However, Nell did not control the corporation after the transfer. In order to be in control of a corporation, the transferor must own, immediately after the exchange, at least 80% of the total combined voting power of all classes of stock entitled to vote and at least 80% of the outstanding shares of each class of nonvoting stock. Since Nell owns only 65% of the shares, the exchange is taxable.

5. The answer is B. The Trujillo Corporation is required to file both Schedule L, *Balance Sheets Per Books*, and Schedule M-1, *Reconciliation of Income (Loss) per Books with Income per Return,* along with its Form 1120. For small corporations with less than $10 million in assets, the differences in book and taxable income are reconciled in Schedule M-1 of Form 1120. Corporations with less than $250,000 of total receipts and total assets at the end of the year are not required to complete Schedules L, M-1, M-2, or M-3.

6. The answer is C. The accumulated earnings tax is levied at a rate of 20% of the excess amount accumulated.

7. The answer is B. If a shareholder contributes property to a corporation, he generally recognizes gain. The basis of the contributed property to the corporation is the same as the basis that the shareholder had in the property, after increase for any gain that the shareholder recognized in the exchange. There is an exception for situations in which property is contributed and the shareholder controls the corporation immediately after the transfer. In order to be considered in control of a corporation immediately after the exchange, the transferors must own at least 80% of the total combined voting power of all classes of stock entitled to vote and at least 80% of the outstanding shares of each class of nonvoting stock. In this case, Lori and Marcus do not own at least 80% of the corporation immediately afterward, so the exception does not apply. They each recognize a gain of $20,000 ($30,000 FMV of stock - $20,000 basis.)

8. The answer is A. In situations where a shareholder contributes property for stock in a corporation and controls the corporation immediately after the transfer, he typically would not recognize gain. However, if the shareholder receives money or property in addition to the corporation's stock in exchange for his contribution of property, he would recognize gain to the extent of any money received plus the fair market value of property received. If the corporation assumes the shareholder's liabilities, the assumption generally is not treated as if the shareholder received money for this property. However, if the liabilities the corporation assumes are more than the shareholder's adjusted basis in the property transferred, gain is recognized up to the difference. In this case, Vihaan's realized gain is calculated as follows:

Fair market value of stock received	$150,000
Mortgage assumed by corporation	25,000
Total fair market value received	175,000
Adjusted basis of property	(10,000)
Realized gain	**$165,000**

Vihaan recognizes gain to the extent the mortgage assumed ($25,000) exceeds his basis in the property contributed ($10,000), or $15,000.

9. The answer is D. Earnings of a C corporation may be taxed twice: first at the corporate level and again at the shareholder level if they are distributed as dividends. Further, shareholders of a C corporation cannot deduct corporate losses. Both are drawbacks of structuring a business as a C corporation, as opposed to an S corporation or a partnership, both of which are pass-through entities. One of the main benefits of a corporation structure, including C corporations, is the limited liability it affords directors, officers, shareholders, and employees.

10. The answer is D. When calculating the alternative minimum tax, a corporation can substitute the net operating loss with the alternative tax net operating loss (ATNOL). The ATNOL for a loss year is the excess of the deductions allowed for figuring alternative minimum taxable income (AMTI), excluding the ATNOL deduction, over the income included in AMTI. The amount of the ATNOL that can be deducted when calculating AMT income generally cannot exceed 90% of AMTI. If the ATNOL exceeds this limit, it can be carried back two years or forward up to 20 years.

11. The answer is C. When a taxpayer transfers property to a corporation in exchange for stock and immediately afterward controls the corporation, the exchange may qualify for section 351 treatment. The exchange generally would not be taxable until the stock received is later disposed. To be eligible as a section 351 nontaxable exchange, the taxpayer must own, immediately after the exchange, at least 80% of the total combined voting power of all classes of stock entitled to vote and at least 80% of the outstanding shares of each class of nonvoting stock.

12. The answer is C. In situations where a shareholder contributes property for stock in a corporation and controls the corporation immediately after the transfer, she typically would not recognize gain. However, if the shareholder receives money or property in addition to the corporation's stock in exchange for her contribution of property, she would recognize gain to the extent of any money received plus the FMV of property received. In this case, Kathleen's realized gain is calculated as follows:

Fair market value of stock received	$75,000
Cash received	20,000
Mortgage assumed by corporation	25,000
Total fair market value received	120,000
Adjusted basis of property	(70,000)
Realized gain	**$50,000**

Kathleen recognizes gain only to the extent of the cash received ($20,000).

13. The answer is A. The due date for BRB Corporation's income tax return is September 15. Generally, a corporation must file its income tax return by the fifteenth day of the third month after the end of its tax year.

14. The answer is C. Allowing shareholders to draw personal loans from a corporation is not a valid reason for a corporation to accumulate earnings. In fact, this is one of the items the IRS looks for that may lead to imposing the accumulated earnings tax upon a corporation. Making loans to shareholders would allow them to access the corporation's earnings without taking taxable distributions.

15. The answer is A. Installments for corporations are due by the fifteenth day of the fourth, sixth, ninth, and twelfth months of the year. For example, a calendar-year corporation would have estimated tax due dates of April 15, June 15, September 15, and December 15.

Unit 13: Answers

1. The answer is A. A C corporation can deduct charitable contributions made to qualified organizations, up to 10% of taxable income. Taxable income for this purpose is determined without regard to certain items, including the charitable contribution deduction itself and any net operating loss carryback (but not carryforward) to the tax year. Therefore, Bernardino Jewelry's charitable contribution deduction would be determined as follows:

Gross receipts	$95,000
Expenses	(65,000)
Net capital gains	10,000
NOL from 2012	(30,000)
Taxable income before contribution deduction	10,000
Deduction limit at 10%	**$1,000**

2. The answer is D. A parent-subsidiary controlled group involves a parent corporation that owns at least 80% or more of the voting power of at least one other corporation. A controlled group is allowed a single set of graduated income tax brackets, a single exemption amount for AMT purposes, and a single accumulated earnings credit of $250,000. Members of controlled groups are also subject to rules regarding related party transactions that may require deferral of recognition for losses or expenses incurred by one party.

3. The answer is B. James Corporation cannot deduct the full $8,000 (80% × $10,000) dividends-received deduction that would normally apply based upon its 50% ownership because doing so would not result in a net operating loss. The deduction is instead limited to 80% of taxable income (before applying the DRD), which is $6,400 (80% × $8,000). Taxable income after applying the IRD is $1,600 ($8,000 - $6,400).

4. The answer is B. The DRD deduction for a corporation that owns less 20% of the stock is 70% of the dividends received ($140,000 × 70% = $98,000). The DRD is limited to taxable income unless the corporation has an NOL after considering the deduction.

5. The answer is C. The corporation can have until March 15 of the following year to pay the contribution. A corporation using the accrual method can choose to deduct unpaid contributions for the tax year if the board of directors authorizes the contribution during the tax year, and the corporation pays the contribution within 2.5 months after the close of the year.

6. The answer is B. If a corporation receiving dividends owns 20% or more of the corporation issuing the dividends, it generally qualifies for a dividends-received deduction equal to 80% of the dividends received. It can deduct amounts up to 80% of its taxable income, calculated without regard to the DRD itself and certain other items ($10,000 × .80 = $8,000).

7. The answer is D. The corporation can carry over excess charitable contributions made during the year that result from the 10% limit on deductibility to each of the subsequent five years. Any excess charitable contributions that are not used in this five-year period are lost. A corporation cannot carry back excess charitable contributions.

8. The answer is C. The corporation's deductible charitable contributions are limited to 10% of its taxable income, before consideration of the following items:
- The deduction for charitable contributions
- The dividends-received deduction
- The domestic production activities deduction
- Any net operating loss carryback to the tax year
- Any capital loss carryback to the tax year

Qualifying contributions in excess of this limitation can be carried over for five years. In this case, $40,000 ($400,000 × 10%) would be deductible, and $10,000 would be carried over to the next year.

9. The answer is C. The corporation may carry back the $6,000 capital loss ($29,000 - $23,000) to the earliest of the three preceding years, where it may be deducted against short-term capital gains. Any remaining losses can be carried forward for up to five years. The corporation treats this $6,000 as a short-term loss when carried back or forward, because capital loss carrybacks and carryforwards do not retain their original character.

10. The answer is C. A brother-sister controlled group is when five or fewer individuals, estates, or trusts own 80% or more of the combined voting power for multiple corporations, and have identical common owner ship within the individual corporations of at least 50%. Despite the name, the owners do not have to be related as siblings.

11. The answer is B. The corporation would not have an NOL after applying the full dividends-received deduction, so its allowable dividends-received deduction is limited to 80% of its taxable income (before applying the DRD), or $68,000 ($85,000 × 80%).

12. The answer is A. A corporation is not required to carry back losses. It may elect to forgo the carryback period. Net operating losses can be carried back to the two years before the loss year and forward for up to 20 years following the loss year.

13. The answer is C. Generally, if a corporation receives dividends from another corporation in which it owns an interest of 20% to 80%, it is entitled to a deduction of 80% of the dividends received, subject to limitation based upon its taxable income without regard to the DRD and certain other items. Since Redd owns 25% of Helena, its DRD is $116,000 ($145,000 × 80%).

14. The answer is D. The corporation's charitable contribution is limited to $40,000 and is calculated as follows: ($600,000 - $200,000) × 10% = $40,000. A C corporation can claim a limited deduction for charitable contributions. The deduction is limited to 10% of taxable income, calculated before the charitable contribution, dividends-received deduction, and net operating loss or capital loss carrybacks (but not carryforwards).

Unit 14: Answers

1. The answer is A. If a corporation cancels a shareholder's debt without repayment by the shareholder, the amount canceled is treated as a distribution to the shareholder.

2. The answer is B. A corporation must file an income tax return for the year it goes out of business, even if it has no income or business activity in that year. If the dissolution is effective on any day other than the last day of the corporation's tax year, the final tax return is due on the fifteenth day of the third month following the close of its short tax year. In Pasqual Corporation's case, that date is May 15.

3. The answer is B. A corporation will recognize a gain on the distribution of property to a shareholder if the FMV of the property is more than its adjusted basis ($60,000 FMV - $40,000 adjusted basis = $20,000 gain). This is the same treatment that would apply if the property were sold for its FMV.

4. The answer is C. Mark has a $19,000 long-term capital gain. His basis in the stock was $1,000 [100 shares stock × $10], so his gain is figured as follows: ($20,000 distribution - $1,000 basis). Gain or loss recognized by shareholders on distributions in a corporate liquidation is generally determined by the difference between the total of the cash and property received by the shareholders and the basis of the stock they surrendered. The gain or loss will be long-term or short-term depending on the length of time the stock was held. Since Mark purchased the shares several years ago, his holding period exceeds one year and is therefore recognized as long-term capital gain on his return.

5. The answer is D. Salaries or wages paid to an employee-shareholder are not considered a distribution. Instead, the wages would be treated as a business expense just like wages for the corporation's other employees. The wages are deductible by the corporation and taxable to the employee-shareholder.

6. The answer is D. The liquidating distribution is not taxable until the shareholder's stock basis ($20,000) has been recovered. Geraldine recovered $16,000 of her basis in 2014 and the remaining balance of $4,000 in 2015. Her recognized gain is $36,000 ($56,000 total distribution - $20,000 basis). She will recognize no gain or loss in 2014, but must recognize $36,000 of capital gain in 2015.

7. The answer is A. If the shareholder has an option to receive cash instead of stock rights, the distributions of stock and stock rights are taxable.

8. The answer is C. A distribution of property to a shareholder is treated as if the corporation had sold the property to the shareholder. The corporation recognizes gain on the distribution if the FMV of the property is more than its adjusted basis. The FMV is considered to be the greater of the property's actual FMV or the amount of liability the shareholder assumes in connection with the distribution. In this case, the FMV is considered to be the liability of $6,000 assumed by Joseph, so Midwestern Grain must recognize a gain of $5,000 ($6,000 – adjusted basis of $1,000).

9. The answer is A. When the basis of a shareholder's stock has been reduced to zero, the shareholder must report any additional return of capital received as a capital gain. Since April has held the stock for more than one year, the gain is reported as a long-term capital gain.

10. The answer is D. Generally, distributions of stock and stock rights are not taxable to shareholders and not deductible by the corporation.

11. The answer is C. The corporation must recognize a gain for any property distributed that has an FMV higher than its adjusted basis. This is the same treatment the corporation would receive if the property were sold for its FMV. The answer is figured as follows:

FMV of distribution	$250,000
Subtract adjusted basis	$100,000
Recognized gain	**$150,000**

It should be noted that the FMV of $250,000 is also reported as a distribution to the shareholder, and will be his basis in the painting.

12. The answer is B. The amount of a C corporation's earnings and profits determines the tax treatment of corporate distributions to shareholders. The starting point for determining corporate E&P is the corporation's taxable income. The following transactions increase the amount of E&P:
- Long-term contracts reported on the completed contract method
- Intangible drilling costs deducted currently
- Mine exploration and development costs deducted currently
- Dividends-received deduction

The following transactions reduce the amount of E&P:
- Corporate federal income taxes
- Life insurance policy premiums on a corporate officer
- Excess charitable contributions (over 10% limit)
- Expenses relating to tax-exempt income
- Excess of capital losses over capital gains
- Corporate dividends and other distributions

13. The answer is A. Distributions from a C corporation are deducted first from current E&P, and then from any accumulated E&P. Any part of a distribution from current-year E&P or accumulated E&P is reported as dividend income to the shareholder. If a corporation's current E&P are less than the total distributions made during the year, part or all of each distribution is treated as a distribution of accumulated E&P. Since Millerton's distributions during the year ($20,000) were more than its current year E&P of $15,000 ($150,000 - $140,000 + $5,000), the amount of each distribution is treated as having been paid partially from current year E&P [in the ratio of current E&P for the year to total distributions for the year ($15,000/$20,000) × $5,000 = $3,750].The remainder of each distribution ($5,000 - $3,750 = $1,250) is treated as having been paid from accumulated E&P.

14. The answer is C. The capital gain is calculated as follows: Her basis is $5,000 ($50 × 100 shares). The excess of her portion of the distribution over her basis ($12,000 distribution - $5,000 basis) results in a $7,000 capital gain.

Unit 15: Answers

1. The answer is B. In an otherwise nontaxable section 351 exchange, a shareholder might have to recognize gain if she receives money or property other than the corporation's stock. The gain is limited to the total of money and the FMV of the other property received. If the corporation assumes the shareholder's liabilities, the assumption generally is not treated as if the shareholder received money or other property, unless:

- The liabilities the corporation assumes are more than the shareholder's adjusted basis in the property transferred, in which case gain is recognized up to the difference. However, if the liabilities assumed give rise to a deduction when paid, such as a trade account payable or interest, no gain is recognized.
- There is no good business reason for the corporation to assume the liabilities, or if the main purpose in the exchange is to avoid federal income tax.

The shareholder's basis in her stock must be reduced by the amount of the liabilities assumed by the corporation. Lydia receives a total of $245,000 ($155,000 stock + $60,000 cash + $30,000 debt relief) and has a $70,000 gain ($245,000 - $175,000 adjusted basis.) As the liability assumed was less than Lydia's adjusted basis in the property, and absent any indication the exchange was undertaken with the main purpose of avoiding federal income tax, the debt relief would not be considered in determining her recognized gain. Therefore, the gain is limited to the $60,000 of cash received.

2. The answer is C. An S election may be revoked if shareholders holding more than 50% of the stock consent. Since Nora and Jordan together own more than 50% of the outstanding stock, they can elect to revoke the S election.

3. The answer is D. Excess net passive income earned by S corporations is taxed at a rate of 35%.

4. The answer is A. All of the items, except for the gross receipts, must be separately stated on the S corporation's tax return.

5. The answer is A. Distributions from an S corporation with no accumulated E&P are generally treated as a nontaxable return of capital, up to the amount of the shareholder's adjusted stock basis. However, if an S corporation distributes appreciated property, the distribution is treated as a sale to the shareholder. To the extent the FMV of the property exceeds the corporation's basis, the corporation would recognize gain. The gain passes through to the shareholders and increases the basis of their stock.

Adjusted basis 1/1/2014:	$50,000
S corporation net income	$0
Gain related to distribution	**$13,000**
Adjusted basis 12/31/14:	$63,000
Distribution	
FMV of property:	$75,000
Less shareholder's basis:	$63,000
Additional capital gain:	**$12,000**

Francisco must report $25,000 of capital gain income on his tax return. This includes the gain of $13,000 recognized by the corporation and passed through to him. In addition, since the distribution reduces the basis of his stock to zero, the amount exceeding his basis ($12,000) is also treated as capital gain.

6. The answer is C. Spouses are automatically treated as a single shareholder, and when a shareholder dies, the deceased shareholder's spouse and the estate are still considered one shareholder for the purpose of the shareholder limit. A husband and wife cannot be considered a single shareholder if they divorce, or if the marriage is dissolved for any reason other than death. An S corporation cannot have a nonresident alien member, so a nonresident alien spouse would not qualify.

7. The answer is C. An S corporation may own stock in a C corporation but it cannot have a C corporation as a shareholder. S corporation shareholders must generally be U.S. citizens or U.S. residents, and must be physical entities (persons), so corporate shareholders and partnerships are excluded. Certain estates, trusts, and tax-exempt corporations, including 501(c)(3) corporations, are also permitted to be shareholders.

8. The answer is A. An S corporation shareholder can deduct his share of the corporation's losses only to the extent of his stock and debt basis. Before consideration of Rancho Sendero's 2014 loss, Seth's stock basis and debt basis were $100,000 and $20,000, respectively. Therefore, he can deduct his entire 50% share of the company's ordinary loss ($180,000 ÷ 2 = $90,000).

9. The answer is B. Adrienne's basis is calculated as follows:

Basis at December 31, 2013	$2,000
Contribution of patent	1,000
50% share of 2014 income:	
• Royalty income	2,500
• Ordinary income	1,250
Basis prior to consideration of distribution	6,750
50% share of gain related to patent	2,000
Distribution of patent, at FMV	(5,000)
Subtotal	**$3,750**
50% share of section 179 deduction	(250)
Basis at December 31, 2014	**$3,500**

10. The answer is B. A C corporation can elect to become an S corporation if it otherwise qualifies. Only domestic U.S. corporations are allowed to elect S status. An S corporation can only have one class of stock, but differences in voting rights are allowed. An S corporation can have a fiscal year if it has a legitimate business purpose for doing so.

11. The answer is A. An eligible corporation must make an S election within two months and 15 days from the start of its tax year (or within 2.5 months of its inception). Since Bettendorf is a calendar-year corporation, its tax year begins January 1. It must make the election on or before March 15, in order to be effective for that year.

12. The answer is B. Ordinary income would reflect the gross receipts of $300,000 less salary expense to the shareholder of $20,000, or $280,000. Interest income and royalty income would be separately stated items on Form 1120S, but would not be considered in determining ordinary income or loss. The amount is figured as follows: ($300,000 - $20,000 = $280,000).

13. The answer is A. If an S corporation distributes appreciated property, the distribution is treated as if the property had been sold to the shareholder. To the extent the FMV of the property exceeds the corporation's basis, the corporation would recognize gain. The gain passes through to the shareholders and increases the basis of their stock. In this case, the amount of the distribution ($8,000) is less than Danielle's adjusted stock basis after recognition of her share of the corporation's gain ($3,500). Therefore, she would reduce her basis by the distribution but would recognize no additional income from the transaction:

Danielle's basis as of 1/1/2014:	$5,000
S corp. ordinary income × 50%:	$5,000
Adjusted basis before distribution	$10,000
Distribution	
Gain on sale of $7,000 × 50%	$3,500
Less FMV of property distributed:	(8,000)
Adjusted basis as of 12/31/2014:	$5,500

14. The answer is D. A short tax year is only applicable when an S corporation is in its first year or its S status is terminated.

15. The answer is C. S corporations are not subject to self-employment tax. Self-employment tax applies only to individuals. The S corporation may have to pay tax due to:

- Excess net passive investment income
- Built-in gains
- Investment credit recapture
- LIFO recapture

16. The answer is B. In order for the election to be made, Gloria must also consent to the election, even though she has sold all of her shares to Irving. All the shareholders must consent to the election. If the S election is made during the corporation's tax year for which it first takes effect, any individual shareholder who holds stock at any time during the part of that year before the election is made must also consent to the election, even though the person may have sold or transferred his stock before the election is made.

17. The answer is A. All the shareholders must consent to an S election.

18. The answer is C. A corporation may not elect S corporation status if it has two classes of stock. A corporation may have both voting and nonvoting stock because they are not considered different classes of stock. A corporation must be a domestic corporation to qualify for S corporation status.

19. The answer is C. After recognizing her 50% share of Vega's income for the year, the basis of Sydney's stock is $14,000. In connection with the distribution, Vega recognizes a gain of $4,000, of which 50% ($2,000) is passed through to Sydney and reportable by her as a gain. Since her basis exceeds the FMV of the property distributed, the distribution itself is treated entirely as a return of capital, and she recognizes no income in addition to her share of the corporation's gain on the distribution.

Adjusted basis 1/1/2014	$13,000
S corp income × 50%	1,000
Adjusted basis before distribution	14,000
Gain from distribution	**2,000**
Subtotal	16,000
FMV of machine	(7,000)
Remaining basis	**$9,000**

20. The answer is D. All of the following actions will terminate an S election:
- When the corporation no longer qualifies as a small business corporation.
- For each of three consecutive tax years, the corporation
  - Has accumulated earnings and profits, and
  - Derives more than 25% of its gross receipts from passive investment income.
- The S election may be willingly revoked by the shareholders.
- If the corporation creates a second class of stock (such as common and preferred stock).

21. The answer is D. Charitable contributions, interest income, and short-term capital gains and losses are all separately stated items. The interest on a business loan is not a pass-through item; it is a business expense, as it would be for any other entity.

22. The answer is D. A corporation must generally wait five years to make another S election.

Unit 16: Answers

1. The answer is D. The basis of livestock is generally its cost. However, since the bull calf was born on the farm, its basis is zero. The cost of the feed is deductible and is listed on the return as a regular business expense and as a deduction from gross income. The cost of the feed is not added to the basis of the calf. The sale of livestock held for breeding is not included in regular farming income and is not reported on Schedule F. Special rules apply to the sale of livestock held for draft, breeding, sport, or dairy purposes. In this case, the sale resulted in a gain of $5,000 that Luke must report on Form 4797, *Sales of Business Property*.

2. The answer is A. If a farmer waits until April 15 to file her return, she must pay estimated taxes just like any other business. If the taxpayer is a qualified farmer, she can either:
- Pay all her estimated tax by the fifteenth day after the end of her tax year (this date is usually January 15)
- File her return and pay all the tax owed by the first day of the third month after the end of her tax year (usually March 1).

3. The answer is A. Farming equipment is a depreciable asset and therefore not included in inventory.

4. The answer is B. Joel may postpone a portion of his gain to the following year. If a farmer sells or exchanges more livestock, including poultry, than he normally would in a year because of a drought, flood, or other weather-related condition, he may postpone reporting the gain from the additional animals until the next year. The farmer must use the cash method of accounting in order to postpone gain in this manner.

5. The answer is B. The farming income reported is from milk production and sale of feed ($50,000 + $15,000 = $65,000). Gross income from farming activity is reported on Schedule F, and includes farm income, farm rental income, and gains from livestock that were raised specifically for sale on the farm, or purchased specifically for resale. The sale of old dairy cows and the sale of used machinery do not qualify. The sale of depreciable machinery and the sale of livestock used for dairy purposes are not reported on Schedule F. Instead, these amounts should be reported on Form 4797, *Sales of Business Property*.

6. The answer is B. Certain farmers may average all or some of their current year's farm income by allocating it to the three prior years. This may lower a farmer's current year tax if the current year is high and his taxable income from one or more of the three prior years was low. Income averaging is only available to farmers and fishermen who operate as sole proprietors or partnerships. It is reported on Schedule J, *Income Averaging for Farmers and Fishermen*.

7. The answer is D. Section 1245 typically excludes buildings and other structural components. However, there is an exception for single purpose agricultural or horticultural structures. A barn for cows and horses is not a single purpose structure so it would not be considered section 1245 property.

8. The answer is D. An agricultural program payment is reported on Schedule F, and the full amount of the payment is subject to self-employment tax.

9. The answer is B. The answer is calculated as follows: $145,000 sale of harvested oats + $115,000 of crop insurance payments = $260,000. If a farmer rents his farmland for someone else to use, the related revenue is generally considered rental income, rather than farm income. This passive activity income is reported on Form 4835, *Farm Rental Income and Expenses. (*If a farmer materially participates in farming operations on the land he owns, the rent is considered farm income and is reported on Schedule F.) Insurance proceeds, including government disaster payments, are generally taxable in the year they are received. A cash-basis farming business may elect to postpone reporting the income until the following year under certain conditions, but an accrual-basis business cannot. Income reported on Schedule F does not include gains or losses from sales or other dispositions of the following farm assets:
- Land
- Depreciable farm equipment
- Buildings and structures
- Livestock held for draft, breeding, sport, or dairy purposes (unless held as inventory or held primarily for sale)

The sale of these assets is reported on Form 4797, *Sales of Business Property*, and may result in ordinary income or capital gains or losses.

10. The answer is B. The harvest discount method does not exist. All of the other inventory valuation methods listed are allowed for farming businesses.

11. The answer is A. The rent received for the use or rental of farmland is generally rental income, not farm income. If the farmer does not materially participate in operating the farm, the income is reported on Form 4835, *Farm Rental Income and Expenses*, and the income is not subject to self-employment tax.

12. The answer is C. The carryback period for farming losses is five years. Other businesses are allowed to carry back their losses only two years.

13. The answer is A. She can delay recognizing income on the payment until 2015. Payments for disaster relief may be included in income in the tax year following the year in which they were awarded. In order to make this election, the farmer must be able to prove that the crops would have been harvested or otherwise sold in the following year.

14. The answer is B. If a farmer or fisherman elects income averaging, he must file Schedule J along with a Schedule F showing his net farming income.

15. The answer is D. Farmers generally have a four-year period to replace livestock sold due to weather conditions. However, in a federally-declared disaster area, a farmer can have up to five years to replace livestock.

16. The answer is B. An individual is a qualified farmer if at least two-thirds of his gross income from all sources was from farming.

Unit 17: Answers

1. The answer is C. The new streamlined Form 1023-EZ is designed for small tax-exempt organizations that have gross receipts of $50,000 or less and assets of $250,000 or less.

2. The answer is A. Only the church would not be required to file a tax return. Tax-exempt organizations must file a Form 990 or Form 990-N (e-postcard) unless specifically exempt. Private foundations must file a Form 990-PF, regardless of income.

3. The answer is B. An organization's failure to file an annual information return for three years in a row will result in the automatic revocation of its exempt status. The organization would be required to reapply for exemption. The IRS has introduced new streamlined procedures for retroactive reinstatement of organizations eligible to file either Form 990-EZ or Form 990-N.

4. The answer is C. Exempt churches, their integrated auxiliaries, and conventions or associations of churches are not required to file information returns. However, every employer is responsible for filing employment tax returns.

5. The answer is C. Since Child Rescue is on a calendar year, its tax return is due May 15. Each tax-exempt organization is required to file by the fifteenth day of the fifth month after its fiscal year ends.

6. The answer is A. The form required by the IRS to apply for 501(c)(3) status is Form 1023, *Application for Recognition of Exemption Under Section 501(c)(3) of the Internal Revenue Code.* Form 1023-EZ may also be used by some small tax-exempt organizations.

7. The answer is D. Exempt organizations are subject to failure-to-file penalties and to automatic revocation if returns are not filed for three consecutive years. For exempt organizations with gross receipts of less than $1 million for the year, the maximum penalty is up to $10,000 or 5% of the organization's gross receipts for the year. For exempt organizations with gross receipts of more than $1 million a year, the maximum penalty is increased to $50,000.

8. The answer is B. A religious organization is not required to file an annual information return.

9. The answer is D. A partnership does not qualify for exemption from income tax. A tax-exempt organization cannot be organized as a partnership or a sole proprietorship.

10. The answer is C. Form 1023, *Application for Recognition of Exemption Under Section 501(c)(3 of the Internal Revenue Code,* must be filed with the IRS, along with the entity's organizing document. This document should contain the required information as to purposes and powers of the organization and disposition of its assets upon dissolution. Form 1023-EZ is available for smaller tax-exempt organizations.

11. The answer is B. A political action committee would not qualify. In general, if a substantial part of an organization's activities includes attempting to influence legislation, the organization's exemption from federal income tax will be denied.

12. The answer is B. An exempt organization that has $1,000 or more of gross income from unrelated business activity must file Form 990–T.

13. The answer is C. A tax-exempt organization, other than a private foundation, with gross receipts of $50,000 or less may file the short "e-postcard" Form 990-N, *Electronic Notice for Tax Exempt Organizations Not Required to File Form 990*, instead of the longer information return, Form 990, if it so chooses.

Unit 18: Answers

1. The answer is C. In 2014, annual contributions by an employer to the account of a participant in a defined contribution plan cannot exceed the lesser of $52,000 or 100% of the participant's compensation. In contrast, the maximum amount for contribution to a SEP plan is the lesser of $52,000 or 25% of the participant's compensation.

2. The answer is B. Jensen Biomedical Corporation must deposit Grace's salary reduction contribution in her SIMPLE IRA account. The company must also match Grace's salary reduction contributions at 3% of her $2,000 compensation ($60). An employer cannot return a salary reduction contribution after it has already deducted it from wages as a SIMPLE IRA plan contribution. A SIMPLE IRA plan may not require a participant to be employed on a specific date to receive an employer contribution. If a participant terminates service during the year after making a salary reduction contribution, she would still be entitled to an employer contribution, regardless of whether it is matching or nonelective.

3. The answer is D. It is not a prohibited transaction if a disqualified person receives a benefit to which he is entitled as a plan participant or beneficiary.

4. The answer is D. Any employer or self-employed individual can establish a SEP.

5. The answer is A. Taxpayers can deduct contributions for a particular tax year if they are made by the due date (including extensions) of the federal income tax return for that year. Assuming the contributions made in May 2015 were within the applicable limits based upon his compensation for 2014, he could make deductible contributions until his extended due date of October 15, 2015 for his 2014 tax return.

6. The answer is C. Under a SEP, the contribution rate must be uniform for all employees. Employers may contribute less when they have less income, but the plan cannot discriminate among employees.

7. The answer is C. Early withdrawals generally are subject to an additional tax of 10%. However, the additional tax is increased to 25% if funds are withdrawn within two years of beginning participation in a SIMPLE IRA. The answer is $10,000 × .25 = $2,500.

8. The answer is C. Brenda cannot set up a SIMPLE IRA for her employees, because her company exceeds the 100-employee threshold, unless at least 50 of the employees earned less than $5,000 in the prior year.

9. The answer is D. A SIMPLE IRA plan may only be maintained on a calendar-year basis.

10. The answer is A. A partnership can deduct contributions to an employee's retirement plan, just as it would deduct any other ordinary business expense. However, the rules are different for contributions to the retirement accounts of the partners. Contributions made on behalf of the partners are passed through to each of them on Schedule K-1.

11. The answer is B. Leah is self-employed, so she must have compensation in order to contribute to her own retirement plan. However, she is not prohibited from contributing to her employees' retirement plan, even if the business has a loss.

12. The answer is B. ERISA does not require that employers set up retirement plans for their employees.

13. The answer is A. A 10% or more shareholder of the entity administering the plan would be a disqualified person under the rules for prohibited transactions. A 5% shareholder would not be a disqualified person.

14. The answer is C. Employers may choose to exclude employees covered by a union agreement. Since Aldo is a resident alien, he still qualifies to participate. Only nonresident aliens who do not have any U.S.-source income may be excluded.

15. The answer is A. Josie can set up a SEP. A SEP can be established for a person's independent business activity even if she participates in an employer's retirement plan.

16. The answer is B. Although income tax may apply, including an additional 10% tax for withdrawals prior to age 59½, participants are allowed to withdraw money from a SEP-IRA at any time. Withdrawals can be rolled over tax-free to another SEP-IRA, to another traditional IRA, or to another employer's qualified retirement plan.

17. The answer is C. An initial 15% tax is applied on the amount involved in a prohibited transaction for each year in a taxable period. If the transaction is not corrected within the taxable period, an additional tax of 100% of the amount involved is imposed. These taxes are payable by any disqualified person who takes part in a prohibited transaction.

18. The answer is B. An eligible employee may not opt out of participation. However, any eligible employee may choose not to make salary reduction contributions for a year. In that case the employee would accrue no employer matching contributions for the year, but would still receive an employer nonelective contribution (if the plan provides for such contributions for the year.)

19. The answer is C. Randolph is not automatically eligible because he is younger than 21 years old. For purposes of a SEP, an eligible employee is an individual who meets all the following requirements:

- Has reached age 21
- Has worked for the employer in at least three of the last five years
- Has received at least $550 of compensation

An employer can use less restrictive participation requirements than those listed (such as choosing to allow an employee younger than 21 to participate), but an employer cannot use more restrictive participation requirements.

20. The answer is B. An excise tax of 10% applies to excess employer contributions to a defined contribution plan. For employees and self-employed individuals, a penalty of 6% applies if excess contribution amounts and related earnings are not withdrawn by the due date of their returns (with or without extensions, depending upon the type of plan.)

21. The answer is C. A 401(k) is a very common type of defined contribution plan in which employees contribute to their own accounts, generally on a pretax basis. Earnings grow tax-free until distribution. Employers often supplement or match employee contributions.

22. The answer is B. Employers cannot prohibit distributions from a SEP-IRA. Employers also cannot make their contributions contingent on the condition that any part of them must be kept in the account. All of the other statements are correct regarding SEP-IRA plans.

Unit 19: Answers

1. The answer is B. Distributable net income is income that is currently available for distribution. In this case, it is $14,000 ($4,000 taxable interest + $12,000 capital gains = $16,000 - $2,000 fiduciary fee.)

2. The answer is A. The IRC defines a simple trust as one that distributes all its income currently, makes no distributions of principal, and makes no distributions to charity. Any trust that is not a simple trust is automatically a complex trust.

3. The answer is C. The gross estate does not include property owned solely by the decedent's spouse or other individuals.

4. The answer is D. Although foreign trusts are often established in certain countries in an effort to evade taxation, the income from such arrangements is fully taxable under U.S. law. Dominique would also be subject to an annual filing requirement, Form 3520-A, *Annual Return of Foreign Trust with U.S. Beneficiaries.*

5. The answer is A. The beneficiary of an estate that is required to distribute all its income currently must report his entire share of DNI, whether or not he actually received distributions for the full amount during his tax year. Thus, Carlton must report and pay tax related to his entire share of DNI, $10,000, rather than the portion he received in distributions during the year.

6. The answer is B. A grantor trust is a legitimate form of trust. All of the other trusts described are potentially abusive. Trusts cannot be used to transform a taxpayer's personal, living, or educational expenses into deductible items. A taxpayer cannot use a trust to avoid tax liability by ignoring either the true ownership of income and assets or the true substance of transactions.

7. The answer is A. An income tax return (Form 1041) must be filed for any domestic estate that has gross income of more than $600 for the tax year, or a beneficiary who is a nonresident alien, regardless of the estate's gross income. Roberto's estate has gross income of $500 ($250 + $150 + $100 gain from stock sale). Since the gross income is below the $600 exemption amount, an income tax return is not required to be filed for 2014.

8. The answer is B. The beneficiaries of an estate that is not required to distribute all its income currently must report all income that is required to be distributed to them currently (whether or not actually distributed), plus all other amounts paid, credited, or required to be distributed to them, up to their share of distributable net income. In this case, since DNI is higher than the total amounts required to be distributed, it forms the limit on the amounts that must be reported as income to each beneficiary. DNI is allocated to each beneficiary in proportion to the required annual payments he received, thus 75% ($30,000/$40,000) or $15,000 to Regina's husband and 25% ($10,000/$40,000) or $5,000 to her son.

9. The answer is C. Life insurance payable to a trust and assets held in a grantor trust are included in a decedent's gross estate. Liabilities of the decedent are not included in the gross estate. However, they are an allowable deduction from the gross estate in determining the taxable estate.

10. The answer is B. Based upon the stipulation that allocates dividend income to Connie, the full amount of dividends included in distributable net income ($4,000) is taxable to Connie.

11. The answer is B. A trust is a pass-through entity that is allowed a deduction for its distributions to beneficiaries. The beneficiaries pay income tax on their distributive share of income. Schedule K-1 (From 1041) is used to report income that a trust distributes to beneficiaries. The income must then be reported on the beneficiaries' income tax returns.

12. The answer is A. The gross estate of the decedent includes everything the taxpayer owns at the date of death.

13. The answer is B. Taxable income of $4,700 can be reported for the estate, determined as follows: Taxable interest of $2,000 plus capital gain of $3,000, less executor's fees of $300. The expenses of administering an estate can be deducted either from the estate's income on Form 1041 in determining its income tax or from the gross estate on Form 706 in determining the estate tax liability, but cannot be claimed for both purposes. The tax-exempt interest retains the character that would have applied if it had been reported by the decedent. The estate would be eligible for an exemption amount of $600 in determining its actual taxable income.

Index

A

accountable plan
    employee guidelines, 110
    moving expense reimbursements, 113
    reimbursement of mileage, 93
accounting methods, 47
    accrual method, 51
    cash method, 48
    farmers, 267
    hybrid method, 51
    switching methods, 52
accounting periods, 42
    for an estate, 43
    short tax year, 42
    trusts, 318
accrual method, 51, 67, 80
accumulated earnings and profits
    distributions from E&P, 234
    of an S corporation, 248
    termination of S election, 247
accumulated earnings tax, 207
additional Medicare tax, 32
adoption assistance, 107, 111
advance payments, 67
Affordable Care Act, 114
    Small Business Health Care Credit, 121
alternative minimum tax, 208
alternative tax net operating loss deduction, 208
amortization
    of intangible business assets, 150
    of start-up costs, 82
assessments, 84
assets
    capital assets, 156
    depreciation of assets, 142
    disposition of business assets, 156
at-risk limits, 69
average cost method, 55

B

backup withholding, 32
bad debt, 209
    business bad debt, 85
    deduction upon partnership dissolution, 198
    nonaccrual experience method, 209
balance sheet, 29
bartering income, 74
basis
    business assets, 128
    construction costs, 130
    demolition costs, 130
    estate property, 316
    improvements to property, 130
    insurance reimbursements, 135
    property exchanged for services, 136
    real property, 129
    repairs to property, 130
    S corporations, 252
bonus depreciation, 149
built-in gains tax, 252
business credits, 119
business expenses, 80
business gifts, 95
business meals, 90
business travel, 90

C

C corporations
    accumulated earnings and profits, 234
    accumulated earnings tax, 207
    book income, 209
    capital gains and losses, 219
    charitable deductions, 221
    closely held corporations, 226
    constructive distributions, 236
    controlled groups, 228

distributions, 233, 235, 239
dividends received deduction, 223
estimated tax payments, 205
filing requirements, 204
liabilities, 239
liquidation, 238
net operating loss, 220
related party transactions, 225
Schedule L, 209
Schedule M-1, 209
Schedule M-3, 209
section 351 transfers, 212
stock distributions, 236
stock redemptions, 237
cafeteria plans, 106
capital assets, 156
cash method, 48
casualty losses
    carryback period, 118
    effect of insurance reimbursement, 135
    theft losses, 135
charitable contributions
    corporate carryovers, 222
    exempt organizations, 279
    Schedule M-1 differences, 354
closely held corporations, 226
COGS. *See* cost of goods sold
complex trusts, 318
constructive distributions, 236
constructive receipt, 50
controlled groups, 228
cost method, 58
cost of goods sold, 59

D

de minimis benefits, 111
depletion, 151
depreciation, 142
    bonus, 149
    changes in accounting method, 52
    double-declining balance method, 145
    listed property, 149
    MACRS, 145

recapture, 159, 271
    straight-line, 144
Disabled Access Credit, 120
dispositions
    installment sales, 161
    like-kind exchanges, 163
    of business assets, 156
    of farm assets, 270
    of inventory, 60
    recordkeeping requirements, 29
    section 1245 property, 159
disregarded entity, 26
distributable net income, 312
dividends-received deduction, 223
DNI. *See* distributable net income
domestic production activities deduction, 118, 122, 151
DRD. *See* dividends-received deduction

E

E&P. *See* earnings and profits
EA exam
    application, 14
    pass rates, 13
    question format, 12
    scheduling, 16
    scoring, 13
earnings and profits
    accumulated earnings tax, 207
    distributions from E&P, 234
EFTPS, 31
employee classification, 34
employee compensation, 104
employer identification number, 27
employment taxes, 31, 105, 284
entertainment expenses, 92
    accountable plans, 110
    recordkeeping requirement, 94
ERISA, 297
estates, 309
    accounting period, 43
    deductions, 315
    distributable net income, 312

filing requirements, 314
Form 706, 314
gross estate, 315
income in respect of a decedent, 311
estimated tax payments
C corporations, 205, 206
farmers, 267
on unrelated business income, 285
S corporations, 246
excise taxes, 85
health savings accounts, 108
trust fund recovery penalty, 33
exempt organizations, 26, 279
501(c)(3), 279
filing requirements, 282
organizing document, 280
penalties, 283
private foundation, 282
public charity, 280
revocation of status, 283
unrelated business income, 284

F

family businesses, 36
family partnerships, 178
farmers, 25, 266
crop insurance proceeds, 273
depreciation, 271
disaster area provisions, 273
farm income averaging, 274
inventory, 269
net operating losses, 274
rental income, 267
sale of livestock, 270, 273
FBAR, 322
financial statements, 29
foreign accounts, 322
foreign trusts, 320
Form 1023, 280
Form 1024, 281
Form 1041, 43
Form 1065, 176, 180
Form 1099-DIV, 233

Form 1099-MISC, 105
Form 114, 322
Form 3115, 52
Form 8300, 29
Form 990, 282
Form W-2, 30
Form W-4, 31
fringe benefits, 105
adoption assistance, 107, 111
dependent care assistance, 107
educational assistance, 111
retirement plans, 289
S corporations, 259

G

group-term life insurance, 107

H

health insurance premiums, 121
health savings account, 108
highly compensated employees
cafeteria plans, 106
HSA rules, 108
rules for employee awards, 106
home office deduction, 89
HSA. *See* heath savings account

I

incentive stock options, 112
income distribution deduction, 312
income in respect of a decedent, 311
income statement, 29
independent contractor, 35
installment sales, 161
insurance reimbursements, 135
inventory, 49
average cost method, 55
cash method, 49
cost of goods sold, 59
first-in, first-out (FIFO), 56
last-in, first-out (LIFO), 57

shipping terms, 54
tracking inventory costs, 53
valuation, 58
investment credit, 119
involuntary conversions, 167, 273

L

like-kind exchanges, 163
limited liability company (LLC), 24
limited liability partnership (LLP), 23
limited partner, 22
listed property, 149
LLC. *See* limited liability company
lower of cost or market, 59

M

MACRS, 145
moving expense reimbursements, 113

N

net investment income tax, 313
net operating losses, 117
    C corporation, 220
    dividends-received deduction, 224
nonaccountable plans, 110
nondiscrimination rules
    for HSAs, 112
nonqualified stock options, 112

O

ordinary income, 70

P

partnerships, 21
    agreement, 176
    basis, 185, 195
    cancellation of debt, 187
    contribution of services, 183
    debt, 195, 198

distributions, 194
due dates, 176
family partnerships, 178
filing requirements, 176
formation, 175
guaranteed payments, 180
inside basis, 185
liabilities, 186, 196
limited liability partnership, 23, 178
limited partners, 22, 177
liquidation, 196
loss limitations, 186
outside basis, 185
partner contributions, 182
related party transactions, 199
separately stated items, 181
termination, 197
passive activity limits, 69, 256
    grouping of businesses, 71
    loss limitations, 70
payroll taxes. *See* employment taxes
per diem expenses, 92
personal service corporations, 25
    calendar year, 44
    related party transactions, 226
    use of the cash method, 49
placed-in-service date, 143
private foundations, 282

Q

qualified joint venture, 21
qualified plans, 297

R

reasonable compensation, 258
recordkeeping
    automobile expenses, 93
    for asset dispositions, 29
    for business entities, 28
    per diem rates, 92
related party transactions
    C corporations, 225

like-kind exchanges, 166
rent expenses, 88
rental income, 72
    farmers, 267
    security deposit, 73
replacement period, 168
reportable cash transactions, 30
required minimum distributions, 300
retirement plans, 289
    401(k), 299
    contributions, 290, 294, 297, 300
    defined benefit, 298
    defined contribution, 298
    distributions, 292, 296, 299
    nondiscrimination rules, 290
    penalties, 292, 300
    prohibited transactions, 302
    qualified plans, 297
    SEP, 289, 290
    SIMPLE plan, 293

S

S corporations, 24, 244
    accumulated adjustments account, 256
    basis, 252
    built-in gains tax, 251
    cancellation of debt, 256
    distributions, 254
    election, 244
    excess net passive income tax, 250
    fringe benefits, 259
    passive activity loss rules, 256
    reasonable compensation, 258
    requirements, 245
    separately stated items, 249
    tax year, 247
    termination, 247, 257
sales taxes, 85
salvage value, 144
Schedule F, 25, 266, 270
Schedule J, 274
Schedule K-1, 246
Schedule L, 209

Schedule M-1, 210, 354
Schedule M-2, 210
Schedule SE, 21
section 1031 exchange, 163
section 1033, 167
section 1231 property, 271
section 1245 property, 271
section 1250 property, 160
section 1377 election, 258
section 179 deduction
    for business entities, 146
    limits for 2014, 147
section 197 intangibles, 150
section 199 deduction, 122
section 351 transfers, 212
section 444 election, 45
self-employed health insurance, 87
self-employment tax, 118
    imposed on partners, 32
SEP-IRAs, 291
SIMPLE 401(k) plan, 297
SIMPLE IRA, 293
simple trusts, 318
simplified home office deduction, 89
Small Business Health Care Tax Credit, 121
sole proprietorship, 19
    disregarded entity, 26
    farmers, 25, 266
    real estate professional, 72
    retirement plans, 289
    self-employed health insurance, 87
standard mileage rate, 93, 336
start-up costs
    of a business entity, 82
    partnerships, 179
    qualifying costs, 83
statutory employees, 35
statutory nonemployees, 35
stock distributions, 236
stock options, 112
stock redemption, 237
straight-line depreciation, 144
supplemental wages, 104

T

tangible property regulations, 131
    Form 3115, 132
    materials and supplies, 132
    safe harbor rules, 132
tax year
    calendar year, 42
    exempt organizations, 283
    fiscal year, 42
    required tax year, 44
    section 444 election, 45
taxes
    as a business expense, 84
    backup withholding, 32
    employment taxes, 31, 105
    FUTA, 33
    real estate taxes, 129
TFRP. *See* trust fund recovery penalty
theft losses, 134
transportation expenses
    as an employee fringe benefit, 114
    for businesses, 90
    standard mileage rate, 93
trust fund recovery penalty, 32

trusts, 309, 317
    abusive, 320
    accounting period, 318
    complex, 318
    distributable net income, 312
    grantor, 319
    irrevocable, 320
    non-grantor, 320
    revocable, 319
    simple, 318
twelve-month rule, 49

U

uniform capitalization rules, 60
    cost method, 58
    exemptions, 61
    farmers, 269
unit-livestock-price method, 269
unrelated business income tax, 284

W

work opportunity tax credit, 120
worker classification, 34

About the Authors

David V. Sherwood, CPA, EA

David V. Sherwood is a Certified Public Accountant and Enrolled Agent with more than thirty-five years of professional experience. He received his BBA in Accounting from the College of William and Mary, and later was a partner with a predecessor firm of PricewaterHouseCoopers. He has provided accounting, auditing, and consulting services to a diverse group of private and publicly traded clients.

Christy Pinheiro, EA, ABA®

Christy Pinheiro is an Enrolled Agent and an Accredited Business Accountant. Christy was an accountant for two private CPA firms and for the State of California before going into private practice. She is a member of the California Society of Enrolled Agents and CalCPA.

Richard Gramkow, EA, MST

Richard Gramkow is an Enrolled Agent with more than eighteen years of experience in various areas of taxation. He holds a master's degree in taxation from Rutgers University and is currently a tax manager for a publicly held Fortune 500 company in the New York metropolitan area.

Kolleen Wells, EA

Kolleen Wells is an Enrolled Agent and a Certified Bookkeeper who specializes in tax preparation for individuals and small businesses. She has worked in the accounting field for many years, including positions at a CPA office and at the county assessor's office.

22925262R00219

Made in the USA
San Bernardino, CA
27 July 2015